D1279710

JOHN DEWEY'S
PHILOSOPHY OF VALUE

JOHN DEWEY'S PHILOSOPHY OF VALUE

JAMES GOUINLOCK

HUMANITIES PRESS
New York
1972

121.8
D51zg

"copyright © 1972 by Humanities Press, Inc."
Library of Congress Catalog No. 78-190119

SBN 391 00229 5

m.R.

Printed in the United States of America

Dedicated to my parents:

Ruth S. Gouinlock
Edward V. Gouinlock

UNIVERSITY LIBRARIES
CARNEGIE-MELLON UNIVERSITY
PITTSBURGH, PENNSYLVANIA 15213

Table of Contents

Acknowledgments

The articulation of several of the ideas in this book was greatly clarified by suggestions made to me by Justus Buchler. Professor Buchler also aided me in acquiring a better understanding of certain of Dewey's views. I am grateful to him for his kind help, and I am happy to have this opportunity to express my thanks.

My greatest debt and deepest gratitude are owing to John Herman Randall, Jr. He provided me with the best advice in formulating the concept of this study; and his criticisms of the manuscript aided me greatly in maintaining whatever unity and coherence I have been able to put into it. More fundamentally, it was Randall's teaching that provided me with the insights requisite to understanding the philosophic enterprise. I hope I have used these effectively in my attempt to capture some of the main lessons in the work of Dewey. In any case, I am pleased to add my name to the long list of students who acknowledge their profound debt to this great and kind teacher.

Grateful acknowledgment is made to the following for permission to quote from the works and authors indicated:

Beacon Press, for John Dewey, *Reconstruction in Philosophy,* enlarged edition. Copyright 1948 by the Beacon Press.

Estate of Roberta L. Dewey, for John Dewey, *The Public and Its Problems.* Copyright 1927 by Henry Holt & Co. Copyright renewed 1954 by Mrs. John Dewey.

Holt, Rinehart and Winston, Inc., for John Dewey, *Human Nature and Conduct.* Copyright 1922 by Holt, Rinehart and Winston, Inc. Copyright 1950 by John Dewey. For John Dewey, *Logic: The Theory of Inquiry.* Copyright 1938 by Holt, Rinehart and Winston, Inc. Copyright © 1966 by Roberta L. Dewey. And for John Dewey and James H. Tufts, *Ethics,* revised edition. Copyright 1908, 1932 by Holt, Rinehart and Winston, Inc. Copyright 1936 by John Dewey and James H. Tufts. Copyright ©1960 by Roberta L. Dewey.

The Macmillan Company, for George P. Adams and William Pepperell Montague (eds.), *Contemporary American Philosophy,* Vol. II. Copyright 1930 by The Macmillan Company. And for John Dewey, *Democracy and Education.* Copyright 1916 by The Macmillan Company. Copyright renewed 1944 by John Dewey.

Open Court Publishing Company, for John Dewey, *Experience and Nature* (1925) and 2nd edition, revised (1929). Copyright 1925, 1929 by Open Court Publishing Company.

G.P. Putnam's Sons, for John Dewey, *Art as Experience.* Copyright 1934 by John Dewey. Copyright renewed 1962 by Roberta Dewey. For John Dewey, *Freedom and Culture.* Copyright 1939 by John Dewey. Copyright renewed 1967 by Roberta Dewey. For John Dewey, *Individualism Old and New.* Copyright 1929, 1930 by John Dewey. For John Dewey, *Liberalism and Social Action.* Copyright 1935 by John Dewey. Copyright renewed 1962 by Roberta Dewey. For John Dewey, *Philosophy and Civilization.* Copyright 1931 by John Dewey. Copyright renewed 1958 by Roberta Dewey. For John Dewey, *The Quest for Certainty.* Copyright 1929 by John Dewey. Copyright renewed 1957 by Frederick A. Dewey. And for S. Ratner (ed.), *The Philosopher of the Common Man.* Copyright 1940 by the Conference on Methods in Philosophy.

Joseph Ratner, for J. Ratner (ed.), *Intelligence in the Modern World: John Dewey's Philosophy.* Copyright 1939 by Random House, Inc.

The University of Chicago Press, for John Dewey, *Theory of Valuation.* Copyright 1939 by The University of Chicago. And for Paul Tillich, *The Protestant Era,* abridged edition. Copyright 1948 and 1957 by The University of Chicago.

Yale University Press, for John Dewey, *A Common Faith.* Copyright 1934 by Yale University Press, Inc.

Preface

This book attempts to exhibit John Dewey's philosophy of value in its continuities with his most fundamental philosophic assumptions. That is, it will show how Dewey's main conclusions about value are integral with an explicitly elaborated theory concerning the nature of nature. Inasmuch as Dewey's philosophy is inseparable from certain considerations regarding philosophic method, his guiding assumptions concerning the latter will also be set forth.

It is hoped that a number of different purposes will be accomplished – at least in part – by this undertaking. First of all, the very fact that Dewey's moral philosophy possesses its distinctive character precisely because it is an integral part of a far more inclusive philosophy needs both to be asserted and to be elaborated in some detail. (I will bring up this point again in a moment.) Secondly, this sort of examination will impart a good deal of clarity to Dewey's explicitly moral views. These have been interpreted with an inaccuracy ranging from mild to outrageous; and the chief remedy for such misunderstanding, as we shall see, is reference to the primary subject matter in nature that Dewey is attempting to characterize. (It might be noted as well that this approach also proves to be the chief remedy for overcoming the obstacles of Dewey's frequently tortuous style and unsystematic arrangement of topics.) Third: This is, I contend, the best way of bringing the most important features of Dewey's moral philosophy into sharp focus. Much is to be gained by doing so. The majority of his critics have simply failed to understand what were the problems with which Dewey was principally occupied. Hence they have failed to discern the principal resources and potentialities of his thought. Fourth, it will be seen that Dewey's approach to his subject matter resolves – and frequently obviates –

many philosophical problems about value which have plagued modern philosophy.

There is a fifth purpose which this study might fulfill, but it is perhaps more implied than deliberately developed. This is to suggest the notable differences between Dewey's way of approaching the subject matter of moral philosophy and the ways exemplified in current philosophizing of various schools. Some of these contrasts are made explicit and their implications examined in some degree. Two considerations, however, militate against developing these themes in detail: My central concern is to provide an exposition of Dewey's treatment of value insofar as it is intimately linked with his theory of nature. Hence I could not consistently develop comparisons with work going on at present. Moreover, Dewey's creative work and criticism in philosophy came to an end at least a generation ago; so, much of contemporary preoccupation in moral philosophy is cast in a way which never explicitly received his attention. It is to be hoped, nevertheless, that it will be impressed on some readers familiar with the field that Dewey's guiding assumptions are remarkably more fecund than those implied by most current work. I would hope that all readers discern that there is a continuing and vital pertinence in his thought to both philosophy and problems of men. I have presented an elaborate example of a certain mode of philosophizing – one which is scarcely found today. What I am referring to is not only Dewey's customary procedure of examining experience in all its natural continuities and of utilizing the results of other intellectual disciplines to clarify and enlarge his analyses. I refer also – and most significantly – to his practice of carrying on his inquiries specifically in reference to fundamental problems of life experience, such as knowing and valuing. That is, Dewey does not concern himself with philosophers' problems as such; but he uses philosophy to deal with human problems. Unlike many thinkers, however, he does this by commanding – rather than ignoring – a host of logical and scientific resources.

Setting forth the assumptions of Dewey's thinking about value involves these additional and noteworthy consequences: It is shown that this is an exceptionally rich moral philosophy; and the all-important functions of intelligence in the moral life are clarified and explicated in detail. Hence there is a final purpose which this work might fulfill: In the present day, when various forms of irrationalism are so much in vogue, a systematic exposition of the organic relation of intelligence and the richest human experience is especially pertinent.

I suggested above that there is a decisively important vein of thought in Dewey's philosophy which has received astonishingly little attention; and it is this vein that I draw upon throughout the chapters to follow. I am referring to the remarkably unified and inclusive character of his thought. The various parts of his philosophy are integrated to a degree rarely equaled in the history of philosophy. This is neither accident nor contrivance. Rather, the unity in Dewey's thought is a consequence of the fact that his philosophy is primarily concerned with analyzing all phases and constituents of human experience as functions of nature. Whether the subject be ethics, inquiry, language, mind, art, aesthetic experience, religion – in any case it is treated as an affair of nature. Art, science, religion, morality, are all affairs of nature: they are nature functioning in various ways; and in every case it is the same inclusive thing called nature that is functioning, not independent and separate realms of being. Hence to understand these affairs in all their natural continuities is, at least implicitly, to presuppose a theory of what nature inclusively is. That is, there are certain implied conceptions of nature as that which functions in diverse and distinctive ways and as that which presents characteristic traits throughout this diversity. Dewey makes such presuppositions explicit and provides a detailed account of them; and he deliberately undertakes his particular inquiries with them in mind. Any elaborated philosophical position has implications for a theory of nature, and Dewey's way of determining the validity of many important concepts (his own as well as those of others) is to consider whether they are consistent with an intelligible and scientifically warranted philosophy of nature. If different philosophical concepts imply differing theories about the nature of nature, a basic inconsistency is thereby disclosed.

We shall investigate Dewey's examination of the moral life in all its implications with nature. The same could be done with his examination of art and science and religion; and in every case the same theory of nature is implied. Hence the central theme of this volume will be to explicate the main characteristics of this theory and to show how his principal considerations about value are organic to it. As I have already suggested, this approach to Dewey's thought will provide the best understanding of both the nature and import of his specifically moral views. His constant reference to the interaction between particular philosophic inquiries and an inclusive theory of nature distinguishes Dewey's work from that of almost all contemporary writers. Remarkably, however, almost none of the extensive literature devoted to examination of his philosophy reflects any insight into the nature and uses of this philosophic orientation; and in no case has a full-length study been undertaken of its embodiment in a specific subject matter.

I have asserted that Dewey's philosophy is unusually comprehensive and unified. He did not, however, articulate it in anything like a unified way. Within a single book, he usually leaps from topic to topic with inordinate haste, only to take up the same topics again in further books and in different contexts, where his ideas continue in development. Thus one can find his thorough and considered views on most subjects only by persistent research throughout a massive corpus of writings. I venture to say that if Dewey had possessed the patience to present his views more systematically, the scope and integrity of his analyses would be more widely appreciated. In addition, he might well be considered deserving of inclusion in the company of history's greatest moral philosophers. The present study will by no means be uncritical, but perhaps it will display some of Dewey's accomplishments sufficiently well to substantiate these claims.

It is not at all uncommon today for Dewey to be regarded as a nice old man who hadn't the vaguest conception of real philosophical rigor or the nature of a real philosophical problem. On the contrary, Dewey is far more implicated with reality and truth than many of those who today enjoy the best reputations in philosophy. His moral philosophy is not by any means, of course, the last word; but work in value theory and ethics today could proceed far more constructively and creatively by taking up critically the works of Dewey than by engaging in the busy-work that passes for ethics and metaethics, or by soul-searching with the existentialists.

There is some difficulty in determining just what criteria should be employed in determining the confines of the present study. I have focused on issues concerning value that depend for their treatment on specifiable assumptions concerning the nature of nature. Accordingly, not all problems in Dewey's moral philosophy are introduced. Nevertheless, it is not possible to delimit the subject matter with precision. This is so because virtually everything Dewey has to say about the moral life can be traced in significant respects to certain assumptions about nature. Thus it is that decisions have to be made about the limits of inquiries into the connections of value theory and more basic and comprehensive theories. For the most part, my discussions deal with analyses in which Dewey gave explicit treatment to these connections; yet in some cases, primarily for the sake of completing and clarifying certain crucial theses, I have presented Dewey's arguments beyond the point simply of explicating the continuities of value theory and theory of nature.

Dewey's mode of philosophizing is sufficiently distinctive to warrant an important note of caution prior to beginning the basic inquiry: His moral philosophy must be read as a body of thought directed essentially to the understanding of the actual world in which we daily strive and suffer, find bafflement and knowledge, exult and despair. He tries to provide men with the assumptions and methods most crucial for reflecting upon and inquiring into that world – and to the end, ultimately, of acting in it. Dewey tries to discriminate the fundamental instrumentalities requisite to our achieving and sharing the most intrinsically satisfying life. Hence his work must be primarily read and judged relative to that end, and not relative to whatever problems happen to be vexing professional philosophers in a particular academic environment.

JOHN DEWEY'S PHILOSOPHY OF VALUE

Introduction

Dewey was frequently careless in formulating and preserving certain distinctions. In order to structure some of the following materials and to make them easier to understand, I will introduce here a distinction which is only implicit in Dewey's work. This is the distinction between philosophy of nature and naturalistic metaphysics.[1] A philosophy of nature is an account of what nature is such that it (nature) is inclusive of all the events and constituents of experience of all kinds. For Dewey this means that nature must not be regarded as something radically juxtaposed to man, or mind, or experience. We cannot resort to the highly dubious intellectual shortcut of merely postulating separate realms or layers of being (such as the natural, the transcendent, and the subjective), presuming that each is independently responsible for different kinds of phenomena. (Why Dewey demands this inclusive concept will receive attention in these chapters.)

Naturalistic metaphysics is the formulation of the traits which belong to nature in this inclusive sense. That is, it is what Aristotle called the science of existence as existence.

These two inquiries cannot be carried on in complete independence of each other. A philosophy of nature need not include a specific description of the generic traits of nature; but to be intelligible it must – at least implicitly – acknowledge the fact that nature does indeed possess certain pervasive characteristics: e.g., qualities, histories, structures. The metaphysical inquiry proceeds by way of attempting to generalize concepts which have

---

[1] In my prefatory remarks, this distinction was not used, for it was not yet needed. What I wrote there pertained to philosophy of nature and naturalistic metaphysics collectively. Henceforth, on whatever occasion it is convenient to refer to them both together, I will use the expression "theory of nature."

been found to be applicable to particular subject matters. This formulation and generalization of concepts is predicated upon investigations of how specifiable phenomena function in nature: e.g., science, language; and these are typical topics in philosophy of nature. It is clear that the pursuit of both these disciplines requires careful attention to all areas of human experience; and each of the two can profit greatly from attentive investigation of the other. This will be made clear in subsequent discussions. (Of course, in any thoroughly developed naturalistic philosophy, both the metaphysics and the philosophy of nature would have to be articulated.)

Dewey sometimes used "naturalistic metaphysics" to denote both enterprises, and sometimes "philosophy of nature" or "philosophical theory of nature." His principal work, *Experience and Nature,* is his most thorough and systematic treatment of both. However, he apparently never explicitly recognizes the distinction I have outlined, although the distinction itself is evident in his work. The important point to be made here in reference to the present study is that Dewey's treatment of value and valuing in all their facets is related organically to both his philosophy of nature and his naturalistic metaphysics.

The distinction between metaphysics and philosophy of nature determines the subject matter of my first two chapters. Chapter I will be concerned to characterize Dewey's metaphysics as a philosophic discipline. Chapter II will deal with fundamental topics in philosophy of nature which are inseparable from certain problems of value.

As we shall see in Chapter I, Dewey's metaphysics consists primarily in the discrimination of traits common to all contexts, or situations, of experience. The existence of these traits is a function of the interaction of man and nature. They are discriminated by analyzing the characteristics of particular kinds of experience (such as moral, scientific, aesthetic) and determining what traits of nature are implied by all these experiences in common. This chapter also includes an elaboration of Dewey's basic methodological assumption. Briefly, it is that the characterization of nature must be such that it clarifies and enlightens experience as we actually find it, rather than making it obscure and unintelligible.

Chapter II elaborates the general nature of three principal interactions of man and nature: experience and nature, body and mind, and individual and society. Their connections with metaphysics and value theory are indicated throughout. Chapter III deals specifically with value as a function of the inclusive relation of man and nature. It indicates what are the traits of nature implied by moral experience. These traits (the precarious, the stable, quality, ends, and histories) must be acknowledged in some form in order to make the actual experience of the moral life intelligible. Their nature is explicated with special reference to their occurrence in moral experience. Value is distinguished from mere likings or approvals, it is the consummatory phase of intentional conduct. This chapter also characterizes conduct as art, that kind of activity in which man and nature work in fullest concert.

The fourth chapter indicates what Dewey regarded as the main deficiencies of some principal theories of value. These consist in erroneous metaphysical and/or methodological assumptions. Certain evident traits of moral experience are either denied to nature or misunderstood; and philosophical concepts are developed which obscure rather than enlighten such experience.

The following chapter explicates the continuities of experience and science and hence also of value and science. Chapter VI provides a detailed analysis of Dewey's concept of growth and its values. This analysis is elaborated in terms of conduct as art.

The final chapter considers the function of intelligence in the moral life. For Dewey, the focus of attention is the process of value *formation,* for whatever functions as value in experience is the crucial determinant of voluntary conduct; and this determinant is subject to reconstruction by methods of intelligence. Hence also, moral reflection is not devoted to producing imperatives or prescriptions of duty, but to inquiring into all the conditions which are relevant to the formation of what actually functions as value in experience. It is clear, then, that all propositions which fulfill the functions of moral deliberation are cognitive; for these functions are neither to prescribe obligations nor to prove that certain actions possess inherent moral properties. Their function is, rather, to enlighten the formation of values. The chapter details the instrumentalities of moral reflection, including those of science and of democracy.

By making reference to the connections between value theory and theory of nature, Dewey's treatment of crucial issues in moral philosophy will be clarified throughout the book. At the same time, typical misinterpretations of his views are indicated.

CHAPTER I

Naturalistic Metaphysics

This chapter will provide a general characterization of Dewey's naturalistic metaphysics. It will also elucidate the methodological assumptions which are organic to his thought both in metaphysics and all other fields of philosophic inquiry. The subject may be conveniently divided into three principal topics: 1) What is naturalistic metaphysics, 2) philosophic method, and 3) abuses and uses of the method of experience. The discussion of the third of these topics will provide an opportunity both to elaborate the themes introduced in the first two sections and to illustrate the particular relation between Dewey's assumptions about method and his metaphysical analyses.[1]

1. What Is Naturalistic Metaphysics?

In an article of 1915, "The Subject Matter of Metaphysical Inquiry," Dewey argues that the legitimate form of metaphysics is that which discriminates the "ultimate and irreducible" traits of nature. This inquiry is to be distinguished from the investigations of specific subject matters by the various sciences, and also from inquiries into the temporally original traits of any subject matter. The metaphysical problem is not to look for the first causes (or ultimate ends) of events, but to specify what *kind* of

[1] It will sometimes happen in this chapter and subsequent ones that at a given stage in the analysis a particular issue seems to receive insufficient attention. I am sensitive to this problem, which appears to be in some measure unavoidable when dealing with complex philosophical positions. In order to maintain continuity of theme in a section or chapter, I have had to avoid prolonged digressions which would otherwise serve to elaborate certain phases of the argument. The overall study remedies these omissions somewhat; for at progressive stages of development I have returned to certain important issues for further clarification of them.

world it is in which such events take place. That is, it undertakes the most general and irreducible description of the world in which such events are a constituent part. In this article, he is concerned to indicate what traits of the world are implied by the fact of evolution and to distinguish this inquiry from science:

> We may also mark off the metaphysical subject matter by reference to certain irreducible traits found in any and every subject of scientific inquiry. With reference to the theme of evolution of living things, the distinctive trait of metaphysical reflection would not then be its attempt to discover some temporally original feature which caused the development, but the irreducible traits of a world in which at least some changes take on evolutionary form. A world where some changes proceed in the direction of the appearance of living and thinking creatures is a striking sort of a world. While science would trace the conditions of their occurrence in detail, connecting them in their variety with their antecedents, metaphysics would raise the question of the sort of world which *has* such an evolution, not the question of the sort of world which causes it. . . . [2]

Note that here Dewey might seem to suggest that metaphysics is concerned only with the subject matter of any *scientific* inquiry. In his subsequent works as he developed his notion of metaphysics, he persisted in the endeavor of "detection and description of the generic traits of existence," [3] while rejecting any suggestion that this mode of inquiry was confined only to the examination of man's cognitive transactions with nature or only to those subject matters with which scientists are concerned. Indeed, what is emphasized with unrelieved urgency is that any and every mode of experience is evidential of the traits of nature. Not only knowing, but valuing, loving, worshiping, desiring, and dreaming also go on in nature; and the metaphysical inquiry concerns what are the irreducible traits of that nature in which such diversity of events occur.

> That esthetic and moral experience reveal traits of real things as truly as does intellectual experience, that poetry may have a metaphysical import as well as science, is rarely affirmed, and when it is asserted the statement is likely to be meant in some mystical or esoteric sense rather than in a straightforward sense.

---

[2] *The Journal of Philosophy,* XII (1915), pp. 337-45. This article has been reprinted in Richard J. Bernstein (ed.), *John Dewey on Experience, Nature, and Freedom* (New York: Liberal Arts Press, 1960). Reference is to p. 213 in the Bernstein volume. Dewey acknowledges in this article (p. 215) that this conception of metaphysics is also that of Aristotle's science of existence as existence.

[3] *Experience and Nature* (New York: Dover Publications, 1958), p. 54.

> Suppose, however, that we start with no presuppostions save that what is experienced, since it is a manifestation of nature, may, and indeed, must be used as testimony of the characteristics of natural events. Upon this basis, reverie and desire are pertinent for a philosophic theory of the true nature of things; the possibilities present in imagination that are not found in observation, are something to be taken into account.[4]
>
> There are traits, qualities, and relations found in things experienced, in the things that are typically and emphatically matters of human experience, which do not appear in the objects of physical science; namely, such things as immediate qualities, values, ends. Are such things inherently relevant and important for a philosophical theory of nature? I have held that a philosophical empiricism must take the position that they are intrinsically pertinent.[5]

Dewey, as metaphysician, is not looking for the causes of the generic traits (as he usually refers to them in *Experience and Nature)*; their antecedent conditions are a matter of scientific inquiry. Rather, they are a description of the world in which there are such things as science, value, and the experiences celebrated by artists. The perplexities of decision, the furies of a storm, and the bloom on the cheek of a maid are equally natural events. As the previous quotations put it, such things as poetry and revery are "manifestations of nature" and are therefore "testimony of the characteristics of natural events." The problem for metaphysical inquiry, then, is not to challenge the reality of such things. It is to determine what are the traits of existence which are implied by all the various events of human experience. Such inquiry aims at finding the traits common to all occasions of experience. It seeks fullest generality: the generic traits of nature. That the traits are generic means, as Dewey puts it, that they are "sure to turn up in every universe of discourse," "manifested by existences of all kinds."[6] A naturalistic metaphysics attempts to discriminate those traits of nature which are present in any encountered subject matter or situation.

Nature, it is plain, functions in a variety of different ways; it eventuates in qualitatively distinctive events: it is an "affair *of* affairs, wherein each one, no matter how linked up it may be

---

[4] *Ibid.*, pp. 19-20.

5 "Nature in Experience," *The Philosophical Review,* XLIX (1940), pp. 244-58. Reprinted in Bernstein (ed.), *op. cit.*, pp. 244-60. Reference is to Bernstein, p. 248.

[6] *Experience and Nature,* pp. 412, 413.

with others, has its *own* quality."[7] These "affairs" Dewey also calls situations or contexts. The notion of situation and its relation to metaphysics requires further elaboration. It must be recognized that "situation"always implies for Dewey conscious human participation. If there were no human beings (or comparably sentient creatures) there would be no situations in nature.

There are various combinations of circumstances in which human beings function. These can be characterized in a general way: there are aesthetic situations, cognitive, moral, indeterminate, religious situations, and so on; a number of distinctions could be made. These are situations of nature – various ways in which nature functions. The adjectives which describe situations (e.g., moral, aesthetic) mark the general, pervasive qualities which distinguish one kind of situation from another and which provide the context for the various phases of human experience. The quality of the situation, or context, brings about the kind of behavior which will effect a transition to a particular determination in which objects and relations are discriminated, and discriminated in a way which is stimulated by the original quality. Thus situations move by means of their own instrumentalities from indeterminate and problematic stages to settled and determinate fulfillments. This is true of the man facing a moral choice, a practical problem, or a scientific puzzle in the laboratory.[8]

That there are distinguishable kinds of situations does not mean, however, that there is only one kind of transaction within the entire set of relations qualified as moral, aesthetic, cognitive, etc. The situation presents a complex of interacting processes and possesses a variety of different elements. Presumably, however, any such situation possesses certain traits in common with all other situations and can be characterized by reference to such traits. The moral situation, for example, contains a variety of features, and these are subject to metaphysical description:

---

[7] *Ibid.*, p. 97.

[8] In reference to the situation, see especially "Context and Thought," "Qualitative Thought," and Dewey's letter defending his theory of inquiry ("In Defense of the Theory of Inquiry"), all of which have been reprinted in Bernstein (ed.), *op. cit.* See also *Logic: The Theory of Inquiry* (New York: Holt, Rinehart and Winston, 1938), pp. 66-9.

> Qualitative individuality and constant relations, contingency and need, movement and arrest are common traits of all existence. This fact is source both of values and their precariousness; both of immediate possession which is casual and of reflection which is a precondition of secure attainment and appropriation.[9]

And the aesthetic situation:

> . . . art is solvent union of the generic, recurrent, ordered, established phase of nature with its phase that is incomplete, going on, and hence still uncertain, contingent, novel, particular;. . . .[10]

Any situation displays the generic traits in various ways. The stable elements, the precarious, and the qualitatively immediate will be manifested in different ways and will bear different relations to each other; and the individual implicated in these situations must somehow interact with the features so characterized. It is the particular way in which these features are present that distinguishes the quality and aims of a situation.

> If the general traits of nature existed in watertight compartments, it might be enough to sort out the objects and interests of experience among them. But they are actually so intimately intermixed that all important issues are concerned with their degrees and the ratios they sustain to one another. Barely to note and register that contingency is a trait of natural events has nothing to do with wisdom. To note, however, contingency in connection with a concrete situation of life is that fear of the Lord which is a least the beginning of wisdom.[11]

It should be clear that one does not encounter quality as such, value as such, contingency as such; but quality, contingency, etc., qualify the specific elements of the situation in their peculiar intermixtures.

In the following section Dewey's distinction between primary and refined experience will be introduced; and it will be remarked in that connection that the traits of situations and the traits of primary experience are the same thing.

Dewey's remarks suggest that for him metaphysics is not a mere intellectual entertainment; for metaphysical inquiry has a significant application to other forms of inquiry and activity. No philosophy could be of positive practical consequence if it denied to reality what is in fact most vital to human endeavor. Dewey says,

---

[9] *Experience and Nature,* p. 413.

[10] *Ibid.,* p. 359.

[11] *Ibid.,* p. 413.

> We have selected only a few of the variety of the illustrations that might be used in support of the idea that the significant problems and issues of life and philosophy concern the rate and mode of the conjunction of the precarious and the assured, the incomplete and the finished, the repetitious and the varying, the safe and sane and the hazardous. If we trust to the evidence of experienced things, these traits, and the modes and tempos of their interaction with each other, are fundamental features of natural existence. The experience of their various consequences, according as they are relatively isolated, unhappily or happily combined, is evidence that wisdom, and hence the love of wisdom which is philosophy, is concerned with choice and administration of their proportioned union. . . . It is not egotism that leads man from contemplative registration of these traits to interest in managing them, to intelligence and purposive art. Interest, thinking, planning, striving, consummation and frustration are a drama enacted by these forces.[12]

(The principal illustrations referred to in the first sentence in this quotation are inquiry and the discrimination of value.) Dewey discusses in detail the almost universal propensity of philosophers to presume a radical separation between what he calls the stable and the precarious traits of existence. Without analyzing these concepts here, it can be said that they correspond, roughly, to such traditional notions as being and becoming, essence and flux, reality and appearance. These have been conceived as separate realms of some sort, the former term in each case denoting in some sense a "higher" ontological status, the latter an inferior status. Dewey's complaint concerns not only the separations, but also the analysis of these kinds of being. The dualism of the stable and the precarious entails a dualism of science and knowledge on the one hand and the problems of life experience on the other. If value is assigned to the superior realm, experience has no connection with it; if value is assigned to the inferior realm, then science and knowledge are irrelevant to it. If the stable and the precarious are consigned to separate ontological orders, then, in fact, science and evaluation become unintelligible; and philosophical theory stands aloof from problems of men. An adequate metaphysics dissolves this false and pernicious dualism and points the way to an understanding of man's actual predicament in nature and the resources for dealing with it.

The character of inquiry, knowledge, evaluation, and value is a consequence of peculiar interminglings of the actual traits of

---

[12] *Ibid.*, pp. 75-6.

nature; and so are all events of experience. Thus, for example, if precariousness is a trait of nature, it behooves the philosopher not only to recognize and analyze this trait, but to consider its relations to other traits and its actual functions in human experience of all kinds. (Chapter Two of *Experience and Nature* deals with the stable and the precarious. It is a brilliant analysis — and a brilliant critique of the gross mishandling of these ideas in a number of philosophies.)

This stage of the exposition can be readily brought to a conclusion: Dewey's naturalistic metaphysics is an attempt to determine those traits which are present in every situation. The conceptual characterization and analysis of these traits constitutes the explicit formulation of a metaphysical position. A naturalistic metaphysics is then a basic and inclusive set of concepts which are applicable to all instances of experienced reality. These generic traits of nature must be acknowledged in some form in any attempt to characterize any such reality thoroughly and accurately. As we shall see further on in this chapter, a great many formulations of philosophical problems are precisely a consequence of leaving out of account some of these generic characteristics. A philosophy thus begun is henceforth burdened with impossible problems by any test of experience.

Dewey develops and articulates an inclusive philosophy by characterizing such things as art, science, and value with a common set of concepts denoting the generic traits of experience; and his analysis of these traits shows them to be inextricably interrelated in nature. A characterization of all the distinctive situations which together constitute man's experience in nature by reference to these interrelated traits is precisely to show that nature itself is the inclusive reality. That is, from the hypothesis that all situations manifest a common set of existentially inseparable traits there follows at once a fundamentally important implication: All of the distinctive things that human beings do and suffer are shown to be situated in a common matrix. Aesthetic, moral, religious, and cognitive experience are not concerned with separate realms of being, but are eventuations of situations in which conditions subject to a common metaphysical analysis stand in different relations to each other. The division of reality into "watertight compartments," as we shall see, is the consequence of inadequate metaphysical analysis.

There are important ways in which Dewey neglected to carry out his program in metaphysics; and one might well wish that his specific metaphysical analyses had been elaborated a good deal further than we find them.[13] He did not, for example, undertake rigorous tests to indicate whether his concepts were genuinely inclusive. That is, there is not a sufficiently thorough inquiry to determine whether all the particular traits encountered in various subject matters can be regarded as instances of those generic traits which he specifcally introduces. Similarly, he did not make a systematic effort to determine just how many generic traits he might discern. Dewey appears to hold that any distinguishable trait of a situation will in some form manifest itself in any other situation. Thus all particular traits are indicative of a common set of generic traits. This is a plausible hypothesis, but it would require more deliberate and painstaking attention than Dewey gives it; and even if it is a true hypothesis, it is by no means clear that Dewey's accounting of the generic traits is sufficiently exhaustive. In addition, the analysis of what is meant by such terms as "history," "precarious," and others is rarely carried out in adequate detail. (The stable, however, is treated at great length in the *Logic.)* To compound this difficulty, he does not adhere to a consistent terminology. (This is obvious simply from the few quotations I have made.)

Still further reservations could be made, but to do so would not contribute to an understanding of the central themes of this book. Regardless of the difficulties I have indicated, there are two fundamentally important facts to be borne in mind. First: The generic traits that Dewey does distinguish are essential ingredients of any intelligible naturalistic metaphysics. Second: The analysis of these traits shows them to be indissolubly interrelated in the existential context of nature. In light of the typical theories of the nature of reality to be found in modern philosophy,

[13] It seems to be entirely within the spirit of Dewey's enterprise to say that metaphysical inquiry can be concerned with developing from particular subject matters concepts of the widest possible applicability, even though such applicability may not turn out to be generic. That is, metaphysical analysis can be concerned with the extension of originally limited ideas to further areas where they find fruitful application. Dewey himself was extremely successful in thus utilizing such concepts as interaction, evolution, and continuity of process.

these two facts possess a farreaching and decisive significance.

As I have suggested, there are ways in which Dewey was rather careless and slack as a metaphysician. But such a judgment is very far from furnishing a just appraisal of his achievements, for Dewey's naturalistic metaphysics even as it stands is clearly one of the signal accomplishments of modern philosophy. It is so not only because Dewey progressed rather far in characterizing the diversity of experience with common concepts, but also because he developed a metaphysics which restored to nature all the traits and qualities of which it had been divested by the dualisms of modern thought, and he thereby made all of human experience subject matter for experimental intelligence. For much of modern philosophy, all the color and richness and value of existence had been placed – either explicitly or by implication – in something called mind, which in turn was something wholly other than nature. The locus of all that is important to human beings was placed in either the so-called subject or – at the opposite extreme – in some transcendent supernatural realm inaccessible to experience. And nature – at least to the philosopher – remained coldly indifferent to and without implication in human good. Such conclusions, however, directly involve a denial of what in fact human experience is found to be. That is, the genuine and thorough assessment of experience discloses that our goods and evils, delights and agonies, aspirations and terrors are experienced to be in nature. That is, there is an experienced reality of the qualitative world – "The world in which we immediately live, that in which we strive, succeed, and are defeated. . . ." [14]

It is not my problem here to hazard an analysis of modern philosophy with all the contrived difficulties and bizarre conclusions which were forced upon it by the absolute separation of subject and object, of experience and nature. My point is to indicate that Dewey made nature whole again in a way which philosophers had not known since Aristotle. Beauty and value, triumph and defeat, knowing and doubting – the entire spectrum of qualitative and cognitive experience – were once again characteristic of nature, and were discriminated in such a way that the

[14] "Qualitative Thought," in Bernstein (ed.), *op. cit.*, p. 176.

philosopher could indicate the methods by which such things could be subject to human reckoning. According to this metaphysics, nature really possesses those traits which it is experienced to have; the deliverances of experience are not sacrificed to some theory of ultimate reality. As I have pointed out, Dewey did not provide a carefully articulated list of generic and irreducible traits. What he was first of all concerned with was to indicate the fundamentally important traits and to show that these traits – however they might ultimately be described – properly find their place in nature. (What these traits are and their importance will be studied in subsequent chapters.)

The key to this achievement is in the recognition that experience is organic with nature.[15] Experience and nature are not discontinuous orders of being. Rather, what we experience is the outcome of inclusive natural processes, including the biological. Experience is both in and of nature; and it is as characteristic of nature as the outcome of any other process. The result is that at once quality is restored to nature; so are contingency, values, ends. Thus our experience is made intelligible; i.e., the organic connection of experience and nature is essentially understandable, and nature is affirmed to be what it is experienced to be. Accordingly, the generic traits are traits *of* nature; there is not one set of traits for experience and another for nature. The fact that Dewey was insufficiently thorough as a metaphysician seems a relatively small matter. His work constitutes both a very important and fecund beginning to further metaphysical inquiry and a brilliant example of the uses of metaphysics in treating philosophic problems.

What is central in the present work, moreover, is not to analyze his metaphysics as metaphysics. Rather, it is to examine the way in which Dewey's fundamental conclusions about nature inform his ethical thought. As further preliminary to specific treatment of this subject, and as preliminary to further elucidation of the nature and function of metaphysical analysis, it is necessary to examine some fundamental methodological presuppositions.

---

[15] The way in which the continuity of experience and nature is established will be stated in the section immediately following and further elaborated in Chapter II.

2. Philosophic Method

Dewey calls his procedure "the method of experience"[16] or "denotative empirical method,"[17] which, stated in at least a preliminary way, is disarmingly simple. The method requires that inquiries generated by any sort of human experience lead to concepts and distinctions which in turn are validated by the measure in which they make intelligible the sort of experience which prompted their formulation:

> What empirical method exacts of philosophy is two things: First, that refined methods and products be traced back to their origin in primary experience, in all its heterogeneity and fullness; so that the needs and problems out of which they arise and which they have to satisfy be acknowledged. Secondly, that the secondary methods and conclusions be brought back to the things of ordinary experience, in all their coarseness and crudity, for verification.[18]

Contrary to first impressions, this is not simply a plea for the employment of the methods of experimental science. It is this, of course, but it is significantly more. It is a plea that philosophy not be an intellectual diversion, consisting in puzzling over problems largely of the creation of philosophers themselves. Rather, philosophy has the indispensable function of enlightening human experience and conduct in a way not accomplished by any of the special sciences.

> Thus there is here supplied, I think, a first-rate test of the value of any philosophy which is offered us: Does it end in conclusions which, when they are referred back to ordinary life-experiences and their predicaments, render them more significant, more luminous to us, and make our dealings with them more fruitful?[19]
>
> There is a special service which the study of philosophy may render. Empirically pursued it will not be a study of philosophy but a study, by means of philosophy, of life experience.[20]

In brief, Dewey urges not only that experience is the essential test of all philosophic ideas, but also that to clarify and enlighten experience is the aim of philosophy. In respect to this aim,

---

[16] *Experience and Nature*, p. 2a.

[17] *Ibid.*, p. 6.

[18] *Ibid.*, p. 36.

[19] *Ibid.*, p. 7.

[20] *Ibid.*, p. 37.

Dewey regards most philosophies as failures.

There are many problems in giving concrete meaning to the notion of the method of experience and in understanding what resources it possesses to fulfill the function Dewey assigns to it. The test of experience is, indeed, widely demanded in various philosophies. Yet in these philosophies there are widely differing assumptions about what are the elements of which experience is composed, what is its subject matter, what is its relation to nature, and what are its inherent limitations. We often find, moreover, that the demand for the test of experience is not met by reference to experience itself, but by taking recourse to a presupposed *theory* of experience. Philosophers have not only disagreed about what experience is, but they have for the most part lacked a sensitive capacity for learning from it and explicating its lessons. "Too often, indeed, the professed empiricist only substitutes a dialectical development of some notion about experience for an analysis of experience as it is humanly lived."[21]

As Dewey repeatedly pointed out, the various modern concepts of experience have actually served to make our experience unintelligible: They have been wholly inadequate to explain how experience could possibly be what it is experienced to be and hence, also, have been of very little service in controlling the constituents of experience for human good. ". . . problems can be made to emerge which exercise the ingenuity of the theorizer, and which convince many a student that he gets nearer to the reality of experience the further away he gets from all the experience he has ever had."[22] Dewey's convictions on this issue found

---

[21] *Experience and Nature,* first edition (Chicago: The Open Court, 1925), p. 4. The significant difference between the first and subsequent editions of *Experience and Nature* is in the extensive revision of Chapter One. Although that chapter was revised, it seems altogether suitable to use it as representing Dewey's thought, for he rewrote the chapter to make it clearer and simpler, not to repudiate it. He said of the original first chapter that it ". . . was intended as an introduction. It failed of its purpose; it was upon the whole more technical and harder reading than the chapters which it was supposed to introduce. It was also rather confused in mode of presentation, ... It is hoped that its new form is both simpler and possessed of greater continuity" (introduction to the second edition, p. viii). Henceforth, references to the first edition will be so indicated; references to the revised edition will make no special indication of the edition. All quotations I have used from *Experience and Nature* up to the present point have been from the revised edition.

[22] *Ibid.,* p.5.

rather poignant expression in a letter to William James. Complaining of the burdens imposed on experience by existing philosophical theories, and praising James for the liberating ideas in *The Principles of Psychology,* Dewey said, "Many of my students, I find, are fairly hungering. They almost jump at any opportunity to get out from under the load and to believe in their own lives."[23]

Perhaps the most blatant example of a concept which is manifestly irreconcilable with experience is that of mind as immaterial, unextended substance. (The entire sensationalistic psychology is an equally good example.) The mind-substance theory, with its correlative concept of material substance, renders wholly mysterious the familiar experiences of knowing, valuing, and acting. This concept of mind is evidently derivative of the widely held view that experience experiences only itself. Thus is created the so-called egocentric predicament, which cannot be surmounted in any but an arbitrary way. These related views, according to Dewey, are an example of a theory that is tested only by a theory; and they leave unexplored the resources of experience for guiding thought and action. In general, traditional philosophies of experience have been of such nature that they are incapable of realizing the potentialities of experience for knowledge and control of human concerns.

It will be explained later in this chapter how Dewey's method of experience forbids an impasse, such as the general problem of knowledge, or of mind and body, to arise at all. It will also be obvious that Dewey's method does not involve any such paradox as having to test a theory of experience by presupposing what experience is.

What will be offered in the balance of this section is a summary account of certain of Dewey's basic conclusions about experience. These conclusions must be presented to make fully intelligible subsequent discussions about the nature and significance of Dewey's method. We shall begin by explaining two crucial features of his general concept of experience. These are, 1) There is an organic unity of subject and object in experience; and

---

[23] Quoted in Ralph Barton Perry, *The Thought and Character of William James,* Vol. II (Boston: Little, Brown and Company, 1935), p. 517.

(what follows from the first point) 2) The traits of experience are the traits of nature.

First, the organic unity of subject and object is such that the distinction between them is perceived by deliberate analysis and is not found in immediate experience itself. This unity implies that in experience there is not an antecedently given and independent subject and an antecedently given and independent object. That is, neither subject nor object is wholly determinate antecedent to the situation in which they come into relation. Rather, the nature of each is in a crucial way determined by virtue of the relations which each – and other features of the environment – sustain to each other in the situation. A red object is red, for example, because certain of its properties interact with certain of those of a subject; and the subject experiences red because certain properties of the subject interact with certain of those of the object. The red is neither "in the subject" nor "in the object," nor even in an exclusive relation between antecedently determinate subject and object. Rather, it is a feature of the situation itself, which is inclusive of subject and object; what are called subject and object are two functional constituents of that entire set of relations constituting the situation. To fill in this example more amply, it should be noted that such further constituents are all those conditions of the situation which are necessary for the event "seeing red" to take place – such as the existence of light, various biological organs, the immediate conditions of support for these organs, and other physical processes constituting the object. The experience of a red object is an outcome of all the various functional constituents of the inclusive situation. In this situation – that is, in this set of relations – the object is really red, and it is this object which is experienced. Thus the quality red has as "objective" or "real" a status as any other event in nature. For, if physical theory is correct, there are no independent substances or events in nature, but all are constituted of interacting processes. Just as certain biological conditions are necessary to the existence of red, so also are certain specifiable conditions necessary to the existence of the Rock of Gibraltar or the Andromeda nebula. Dewey makes a point of insisting that *no* qualities ("primary," "secondary," or "tertiary") can be said to exist in an object in an unqualified or absolute sense.[24] To suppose that qualities are "in the subject" or "in the object" is to presuppose intrinsically discrete substances or processes. It is essential to be reminded that the situation contains no such subject-object dualism.

It follows – which is of the first importance – that there is no problem *überhaupt* of either the ontological status of qualities or of correspondence between qualities in an object and images in a subject – whether these qualities be colors, sounds, values, etc. Qualities are the consequence of organically conjoint processes of organism and environment. Thus it is crucially misleading to say, for example, that precariousness, indeterminateness, value, or beauty are found only in subjects or are relations between antecedently given subjects and objects. They are traits of the situation, of nature; it is the inclusive situation which determines the nature of the subject as experiencer and the object as experienced. Thus Dewey argues the immediate unity of experience and nature and disposes of the assumption that experience is the Veil of Maya. It is always crucially important to bear in mind that when Dewey speaks of experience he is not talking of something going on inside a subject:

> We begin by noting that 'experience' is what James called a double-barrelled word. Like its congeners, life and history, it includes *what* men do and suffer, *what* they strive for, love, believe and endure, and also *how* men act and are acted upon, the ways in which they do suffer, desire and enjoy, see, believe, imagine – in short, processes of *experiencing*. . . . It is 'double-barrelled' in that it recognizes in its primary integrity no division between act and material, subject and object, but contains them both in an unanalyzed totality.[25]

This point cannot be stressed enought, for "experience" is used

---

[24] "When one searches through philosophical commentary and discussion (based mainly on Locke's version of Newton's results), one finds a great deal of discussion about the fact that the so-called secondary qualities, color, sound, odor, taste, were eliminated from 'reality.' But not a word as far as I can discover is said about the fact that *other* sensible qualities under the name of primary were retained in defining the object of science. And yet this retention is the *fons et origo malorum.* The actual fact was that science by means of its operational conceptions was instituting as its objects of thought things in a dimension different from *any* of the direct *qualities* of objects. It was not a question of getting rid of some immediate sense qualities; but of a treatment indifferent to any and all qualities." *(The Quest for Certainty* [New York: G.P. Putnam's Sons, 1960], p. 120.)

[25] *Experience and Nature,* p. 8.

repeatedly by Dewey, and it must be understood that he is talking about this "unanalyzed totality." There seems to be an ineradicable compulsion on the part of modern philosophers to think of experience as something subjective. In irritation, Dewey says, "When the notion of experiences in introduced, who is not familiar with the query, '*Whose* experience?' The implication is that experience is not only always somebody's, but that the peculiar nature of 'somebody' infects experience so pervasively that experience is *merely* somebody's and hence of nobody and nothing else."[26] Dewey recognized this integral unity of experience as fundamental to all his work:

> For *denial* of the primacy and ultimacy of this relation [dualism of subject and object] (supposed to be the inherent epistemological-metaphysical basis and background from which philosophical theory must proceed) is the basic feature of my general theory of knowledge, of judgment and verification, my theory of value-judgments being but a special case of this general theory.[27]

How does Dewey know that there really is such organic unity? His position is established in two different ways: First, experience as experience is found to be that way, and, second, the developments of modern natural science wholly support such a conclusion. In respect to the first point, it is clear that when we have a perception of something – say, for example, a red rose – a single inclusive event takes place. That is, we perceive the red, scented rose directly and as such. There are not two distinct experiences – on the one hand the perception of the object and on the other the perception of the perception. There is not a merger of two distinct events or experiences: we *perceive* the rose and the perception is *of* the rose. This is plainly a matter of experience being an existentially indissoluble unity of subject and object. Yet philosophers can hardly be considered sensitive to this fact, for they *describe* experience as something different than it is found to be. Dewey complains, "We get the absurdity of an experiencing which experiences only itself, states and processes of consciousness, instead of the things of nature. . . .

---

[26] *Experience and Nature,* (first edition), p. 4.

[27] "Valuation Judgments and Immediate Quality," *The Journal of Philosophy,* XL, (1943); reprinted in *Problems of Men* (New York: Philosophical Library, 1946). Quotation is from *Problems of Men,* p. 258.

This conception of experience . . . has wrought havoc in philosophy."[28]

The second reason Dewey has for supposing this organic unity of subject and object is that the biological-environmental relations as disclosed and explained scientifically warrant that conclusion. This position involves the abandonment of the mentalistic psychology initiated by Descartes and also of that Newtonian view which understands events in nature as the mechanical relation of intrinsically discrete, self-subsistent, unchanging substances. Dewey here finds support in modern physics, of course, and especially in biology.[29] It is by an extension of the assumption that the nature and behavior of biological organisms are a consequence of the functioning of inclusive situations that Dewey develops his notion that all phases of experience are also transactions of the live creature and its environment. Experience consists of various kinds of "doing and undergoing" with the environment:

> That the physiological organism with its structures, whether in man or in the lower animals, is concerned with making adaptations and uses of material in the interest of maintenance of the life-process, cannot be denied. The brain and nervous system are primarily organs of action-undergoing; biologically, it can be asserted without contravention that primary experience is of a corresponding type. Hence, unless there is a breach of historic and natural continuity, cognitive experience must originate within that of a non-cognitive sort.[30]

It is clear why Dewey usually uses the terms "organism" and "environment" instead of "subject" and "object": the two sets of complementary terms have very different connotations, one set implying interaction, the other dualism. Dualisms of any sort imply a radical separation of the live creature from its surroundings.

It is essential to note that both approaches to understanding

---

[28] *Experience and Nature,* p. 11.

[29] This biological approach is reflected in a fundamental way in such works as *Essays in Experimental Logic, Reconstruction in Philosophy, Human Nature and Conduct, Experience and Nature, Art as Experience, Logic: The Theory of Inquiry,* and most of the works pertaining to ethics and value theory. The initial (and profound) influence leading in this direction was James's *The Principles of Psychology* (1890). The implications of the theories of Darwin evidently were impressed on Dewey through the latter work.

[30] *Experience and Nature,* p. 23.

experience reach coincident results: We *experience* organic unity with objects in an inclusive functional situation, and science indicates that conclusion as well. In subsequent discussion of the method of experience I shall have occasion to indicate the fuller significance of that fact and to point out how both kinds of approach are indispensable.

I have been providing the main outlines of Dewey's argument that there is an inclusive unity of the subject as experiencer and the object as experienced. The second point to be studied is that the traits of experience are the traits of nature. If Dewey's position as indicated thus far is valid, then it follows that this second assumption is also correct. For, again, experience is not something going on inside somebody's head. Rather, it is one of the many things in which transactions in nature eventuate. This does not mean, of course, that natural processes eventuate in such traits when complex biological functions are not integral with them. Nature is certainly a different sort of thing with man in it than it would be if human beings did not exist. And the difference is clearly not simply the mere presence of a new sort of being. With the emergence of biological functions, nature possesses distinctively new and different kinds of relations, and thus displays novel powers and exhibits new features. With man interacting with it, nature reaches its fullest observable actuality.

> . . . it is reasonable to believe that the most adequate definition of the basic traits of natural existence can be had only when its properties are most fully displayed – a condition which is met in the degree of the scope and intimacy of the interactions realized.[31]

The distinctive character of the traits which we experience is a consequence of the interaction of the biological organism and its environment: There are functionally inseparable processes of organism and environment; and in the very interaction of these processes traits of nature emerge whose character depends in crucial ways on this interaction itself. Dewey strives to make clear that the various traits of experience are not produced by an isolated self; nor are they produced by wholly inanimate processes. Rather, in nature there are certain combinations of events which result in doubting, knowing, choosing, revering, etc. Na-

[31] *Ibid.*, p. 262.

ture is to be understood both as the sort of thing that produces such conditions and as possessing certain traits precisely because such processes occur. Thus the sense in which experience discloses or implies traits of nature is simply that these are real things in nature that are experienced. The experience of quality is direct evidence that there is quality in nature. Accordingly, a philosophy of experience is not psychology, but metaphysics; for it is the attempt to learn – not the mechanisms of experience – but the *traits* of experience, and these are the traits of nature.

Although Dewey's position ought to be clear and forceful, it is readily misconstrued. This is due in some measure to the considerable deficiencies in his prose style, but also to the preconceptions of his critics. Therefore, a number of further observations will be useful here. These will not only clarify what has been said, but will serve as well to introduce further important distinctions.

It should be observed that nature is not *identical* with experience. [32] That is, there are events in nature which occur independently of the kind of event we call experience. Clearly, however, as Dewey insisted, any knowledge which we might acquire of such events can only be *through* experience. It is by the methodical use of experience that we can learn that which is not subject to direct observation and determine the nature of those processes which terminate in experience. Stated most generally,

> Experience thus reaches down into nature; it has depth. It also has breadth to an indefinitely elastic extent. It stretches. That stretch constitutes inference.[33]

Science is the obvious example of such a process:

> . . . experience, if scientific inquiry is justified, is no infinitesimally thin layer or foreground of nature, but . . . it penetrates into it, reaching down into its depths, and in such a way that its grasp is capable of expansion; . . . . A geologist living in 1928 tells us about events that happened not only before he was born but millions of years before any human being came into existence on this earth. He does so by starting from things that are now the material of experience. Lyell revolutionized geology by perceiving that sort or thing that can be experienced now in the operations of fire, water, pressure, is the sort of thing by which the earth took

[32] The identity of experience and reality is the position imputed to Dewey by Santayana in the latter's "Dewey's Naturalistic Metaphysics," *The Journal of Philosophy,* XXII (December 1925), pp. 673-88.

[33] *Experience and Nature,* pp. 4a-1.

on its present structural forms. . . . Unless we are prepared to deny all validity to scientific inquiry, these facts have a value that cannot be ignored for the general thoery of the relation of nature and experience.[34]

Traditionally, philosophers have thought of "reason" as discontinuous with experience; and a number of recent philosophers (such as Russell) have argued that scientific knowledge is discontinuous with what Dewey calls experience. One of the many ways in which Dewey eliminated philosophic mysteries was to give clear and unmistakable evidence that science is continuous with "gross" or "primary" experience. The recognition of this continuity is another of the indispensable elements in Dewey's philosophy; so it is worthwhile to state in a little more detail for the time being the connection between knowledge and experience.[35] Primary experience is the experience of the qualitative world, while science is concerned with highly abstract cognitive experience in which the qualitatively individual and unique are not objects of knowledge. Scientific experience, as such, is largely ideational.

There can, however, be no absolute division between these two forms of experience. Such a division would constitute an utter breach between our immediate experience of the world and our scientific knowedge of it; it would suppose two altogether distinct and disconnected worlds, where, in fact, experience finds them to be one. For, when experience is examined in its integrity, it is clear that the products of scientific inquiry are insepara-

---

[34] *Ibid.*, pp. 3a-4a. (For the sake of clarity, I have changed the order of the sentences in the quotation. The sentence which I have put last in order actually occurs in the place marked by the first ellipsis.)

In this quotation Dewey seems to use "foreground" to suggest a screen between man and nature. He later used the term in a significantly different sense, stressing that experience is the foreground *of* nature and that use of this foreground is that with which we are conducted to the "background" – to further knowledge of nature. Cf. "Half-Hearted Naturalism," *Journal of Philosophy,* Vol. XXIV (1927), pp. 57-64; and "Experience and Existence: A Comment," *Philosophy and Phenomenological Research,* IX (1948-49), pp. 709-13. In the latter he says that "as good a summary of my actual position as could be stated in a few words" is " 'experience is the foreground *of* nature' " (p. 709).

[35] Among Dewey's many elaborate statements on this issue are *Experience and Nature,* Ch. 4; *The Quest for Certainty,* Chs. IV through VIII; "Common Sense and Science" *(The Journal of Philosophy,* XLV [April, 1948], pp. 197-208); *Logic,* especially Chs. IV and XXV; and most of the essays in *Essays in Experimental Logic.*

bly related to primary experience. Scientific concepts and theories are developed in order to explain, clarify, and control the phenomena of the experienced world, and it is their success in doing this that determines their validity.

> That the subject matter of primary experience sets the problems and furnishes the first data of the reflection which constructs the secondary objects is evident; it is also obvious that test and verification of the latter is secured only by return to things of crude or macroscopic experience – the sun, earth, plants and animals of common, every-day life. . . . The objects attained in reflection . . . *explain* the primary objects, they enable us to grasp them with *understanding*, instead of just having sense-contact with them.[36]

There is no breach between primary experience and knowledge, and there could be no such absurdity as asserting – as Russell has done – that if physics is true then experience is false. The remote reaches of theoretical physics make it possible for us to produce those mushroom clouds; and perhaps someday the equations of theoretical biology will permit us to end the experienced reality of cancer. More generally, it is clear that without an elaborated theory concerning the relation of experience to nature, the philosopher, as such, is helpless to explain how man's intellectual accomplishments can be of service to the compelling demands of experience.

Having provided some indication of this very important distinction between primary and refined experience, it can be pointed out that the traits that Dewey distinguishes in metaphysical analysis are those of primary experience. Ideas, as such, do not possess the same traits as gross experience. (But ideas functioning in gross experience are partial determinants of the traits of the latter, for they participate in providing cognitive structures in situations – what Dewey calls "the stable.") Metaphysical analysis attempts to describe the welter of primary experience in terms of its generic traits and their interrelations. What we find in this experience is a jumble of characteristics and events; and the metaphysician attempts to analyze these into common traits for all situations. It is from this "jumble" that refined, conceptual, experience eventually issues; and Dewey is able to analyze these conditions of refined experience with his metaphysical concepts. It will be seen that this kind of analysis both detects and fore-

---

[36] *Experience and Nature*, pp. 4-5.

stalls crucial errors in philosophic argument.

Another point that should be made clear is that an experience does not "speak for itself" in matters of truth and falsehood; for there is – beyond the matter of *what* is experienced – the further matter of interpreting such deliverances. Nature generates the gamut from superstition through poetry and science to piety. Thus nature's character is truly revealed. But this does not mean, of course, that superstitions are true. It simply means that nature is such that it can eventuate in superstition and must be understood as such:

> Now it is one thing to say that the world is such that men approach certain objects with awe, worship, piety, sacrifice and prayer, and that this is a fact which a theory of existence must reckon with as truly as with the facts of science. But it is a different thing to say that religious experience gives *evidence* of the reality of its *own* objects, [e.g., gods, supernal realms, etc.] or that the consciousness of an obligation proves the validity of its special object, or the general fact of duty carries within itself any deliverance as to its source in reality. . . . We must conceive the world in terms which make it possible for devotion, piety, love, beauty, and mystery to be as real as anything else. But whether the loved and devotional objects have all the qualities which the lover and the devout worshipper attribute to them is a matter to be settled by evidence, and evidence is always extrinsic.[37]

In all cognitive experience, it is the scientific method that determines truth or falsehood. This is the backbone of naturalism and instrumentalism, and Dewey should never be construed as holding otherwise.

A related point very much worthy of stress is that non-cognitive experience as such is never knowledge. In the context of the analysis of the nature of Dewey's metaphysics, the point is that, say, aesthetic, moral, or religious experience do not, *as such*, provide knowledge of the nature of nature. Rather, it is the *analysis* of such modes of experience that yields knowledge.

It should be sufficiently plain by now that Dewey's theory of nature is anything but reductive. Such notions as "nature is nothing but matter in motion," or "reality consists of nothing but the rational," or "nature is constituted of unrelated particulars" must be abhorrent to genuine empirical method. The necessary test of ideas (apart from logical consistency) is always in gross experience itself, never in theories of experience:

---

[37] *Experience and Nature* (first edition), pp. 17-8.

> The value of experience as method in philosophy is that it compels us to note that *denotation* comes first and last. . . . The value, I say, of the notion of experience for philosophy is that it asserts the finality and comprehensiveness of the method of pointing, finding, showing, and the necessity of seeing what is pointed to and accepting what is found in good faith and without discount. . . . We need the notion of experience to remind us that 'reality' includes whatever is denotatively found.[38]

It will, I believe, be clear in subsequent discussions in this book that Dewey's assumptions about the continuity of experience and nature and of primary and intellectual experience are vitally important. In brief, if Dewey's view is correct, all concerns of human experience are a function of nature, and as such they are subject to understanding and control by experimental intelligence.

3. Abuses and Uses of Experience

I have given some account of what naturalistic metaphysics is and of the method from which it is inseparable. To know these things, however, does not make one capable of using the method; nor does it show at once how it serves as a basis for further, more specific, studies (such as value theory). What remains to be done in the balance of this chapter is to discuss more particularly how the method of experience defines the aims of philosophizing and how it can be most effectively used. Such discussion will at the same time permit a fuller statement of the nature of Dewey's metaphysics. Also to be indicated are the subtle, yet devastating, ways in which empirical method has been subverted by a legion of philosophers. Indeed, it is this latter subject that I shall discuss next, leaving the aims and uses of the method of experience in metaphysics until last.

a. Abuses

Without making any assumptions about the nature and functions of experience, and using "experience" in its most inclusive possible sense, then it is obviously truistic that experience is the subject matter of philosophy. By the most inclusive sense I mean to include what has so frequently been distinguished from experience: reason, intuition, mystical union, aesthetic contemplation, moral insight, and the objects of such modes. Taken in this sense,

---

[38] *Ibid.*, pp. 10-1.

whatever philosophers wish to understand is something which is the subject of human experience, whatever it may be. In this inclusive sense, then, experience is what philosophy is about.

This last assertion may seem the ultimate in triviality. After all, isn't it a truism that all philosophers have been dealing with at least some kind of experience, however they might have named it – e.g., pure reason, sense of duty, or unity with God? There is an obvious sense in which it *is* a truism, but there is another sense in which it clearly is not. There is a clear and highly significant sense in which philosophers do not deal with experience, even in its inclusive meaning which I have outlined. The crippling difficulty has been that philosophers, deliberately or not, have carried on their reflections heedless of primary experience and its continuities with refined objects of thought. Indeed, the lack of attention to primary experience and its functions is a persistent feature in the history of modern philosophy, and professed empiricists have been among the worst offenders. And, so Dewey holds, insofar as this feature exists, philosophy is vain.

Consider again Dewey's distinction between gross, or primary experience on the one hand and reflective or refined experience on the other. The former is simply the ordinary commonsense experience of the workaday world; while the latter refers to the precisely conceptualized materials of the intellectual disciplines. The former tends towards the qualitatively immediate and individual; the latter toward the cognitively abstract and universal.

> This consideration of method may suitably begin with the contrast between gross, macroscopic, crude subject matters in primary experience and the refined, derived objects of reflection. The distinction is one between what is experienced as the result of a minimum of incidental reflection and what is experienced in consequence of continued and regulated reflective inquiry. For derived and refined products are experienced only because of the intervention of systematic thinking. The objects of both science and philosophy obviously belong chiefly to the secondary and refined system.[39]

It is the difference, at its extremes, between the swimmer's water which is cool, wet, rippling, and refreshing, and the H_2O of the chemist.

As we have seen in the preceding section, primary and derived

---

[39] *Experience and Nature,* pp. 3-4.

experience are continuous with one another. What we actually find in experience is what James called "the blooming, buzzing confusion," and from this are derived refined intellectual operations and products. The development of concepts of reflective experience is stimulated by events and problems of gross experience, and the value of such concepts is precisely in their efficacy to provide understanding and control of qualitatively diverse phenomena. In the sciences, the products of systematic thinking are continually tested by just that relation to experienced phenomena; and when they fail such tests, they are immediately challenged. Dewey cites the highly instructive consequences of the Michelson-Morley experiment:

> Thus when the Michelson-Morley experiment disclosed, as a matter of gross experience, facts which did not agree with the results of accepted physical laws, physicists did not think for a moment of denying the validity of what was found in that experience, even though it rendered questionable an elaborate intellectual apparatus and system. The coincidence of the bands of the interferometer was accepted at its face value in spite of its incompatibility with Newtonian physics. Because scientific inquirers accepted it at its face value they at once set to work to reconstruct their theories; they questioned their reflective premisses, not the full 'reality' of what they saw.[40]

In contrast with Dewey's emphatic attention to these relations within experience, modern philosophy has to a remarkable extent either severed or ignored the connections between primary and refined experience.[41] And it is precisely here where there is a significant sense in which philosophy works in isolation from experience. Philosophers adopt certain concepts – from whatever source – and become greatly enamored of them. They choose to deal with such concepts in and of themselves, thereby ignoring whatever connection they might have to primary experience; or they cling to such concepts in spite of the fact that they entail certain assumptions about the nature of experience which would make it altogether unlike what it is in fact found to be. Or

---

[40] *Ibid.*, p. 34.

[41] Further discussion of the continuity of primary and refined experience will occur in several places in the following chapters.

For a detailed analysis of the nature and use of Dewey's formulation of this distinction as it functions in inquiry, see Robert D. Mack, *The Appeal to Immediate Experience: Philosophic Method in Bradley, Whitehead and Dewey* (New York: King's Crown Press, 1945), pp. 51-68.

they might imply the outright denial of the reality of certain phases of experience. Lacking much notion of the character of intellectual history, they are unaware of the conditions under which and the purposes for which their favored concepts arose. Thus, rather than treat them as hypotheses like any other hypotheses – created to explain certain phenomena and to be tested by experience – they accept them as the axioms from which all truths must proceed. Such refined products are useless for every purpose save that of exciting the wits of philosophers. Such conceptual materials cannot play the same role that they do in the sciences: providing means of production and control of the things of gross experience and suggesting further inquiries to advance knowledge of the things of gross experience, upon which life and welfare depend.

The classic case of this philosophical futility is in the problems generated by the concepts of mind and body as formulated by Descartes, by which everyday events familiar to everyone become by definition either impossible or unintelligible: knowledge of nature, experience of the qualitative reality of nature, the experience of value in nature, and the deliberate movement of the body. Dewey repeatedly draws attention to both this process of uncritically adopting refined concepts and its attendant perplexities:

> Non-empirical method starts with a reflective product as if it were primary, as if it were the originally 'given.' To non-empirical method, therefore, object and subject, mind and matter (or whatever words and ideas are used) are separate and independent. Therefore it has upon its hands the problem of how it is possible to know at all; how an outer world can affect an inner mind; how the acts of mind can reach out and lay hold of objects defined in antithesis to them. Naturally it is at a loss for an answer, since its premisses make the fact of knowledge both unnatural and unempirical.[42]

These concepts, uprooted from their contexts, are frequently borrowed from the sciences.

> The trouble, then, with the conclusions of philosophy is not in the least that they are the results of reflection and theorizing. It is rather that philosophers have borrowed from various sources the conclusions of special analyses, particularly of some ruling science of the day, and imported them direct into philosophy, with no check by either the empirical objects from which they arose or those to which the

---

[42] *Experience and Nature,* pp. 9-10.

> conclusions in question point. Thus Plato trafficked with the Pythagoreans and imported mathematical concepts; Descartes and Spinoza took over the presuppositions of geometrical reasoning; Locke imported into the theory of mind the Newtonian physical corpuscles, converting them into given 'simple ideas'; . . . . When philosophers transfer into their theories bodily and as finalities the refined conclusions they borrow from the sciences, whether logic, mathematics or physics, these results are not employed to reveal new subject-matters and illuminate old ones of gross experience; they are employed to cast discredit on the latter and to generate new and artificial problems regarding the reality and validity of the things of gross experience. Thus the discoveries of psychologies taken out of their own empirical context are in philosophy employed to cast doubt upon even the reality of things external to the mind and to selves, things and properties that are perhaps the most salient characteristics of ordinary experience. Similarly, the discoveries and methods of physical science, the concepts of mass, space, motion, have been adopted wholesale in isolation by philosophers in such a way as to make dubious and even incredible the reality of the affections, purposes and enjoyments of concrete experience.[43]

Because of this uncritical and wholesale attachment to ideas framed for limited purposes, philosophers concern themselves almost exclusively with issues which ought to be museum pieces, but which instead provide the sport of pure dialectic and serve to persuade the gullible to deny what is most evident and what, indeed, must be the final test of ideas.

This development of concepts unrelated to the realities of primary experience is also the consequence of the philosopher's infatuation with certain phases of experience to the exclusion of others. Philosophers become preoccupied – for whatever reasons – with only one phase of experience, which they attempt to analyze in isolation from its related phases. Then, on the basis of the isolated experience, concepts and distinctions are developed which themselves are subsequently taken for primary subject matter. The result is that what is genuinely primary is severed from the "reality" presumably referred to by these distinctions, which are, therefore, incapable of describing in its primary integrity that experience from which they initially issued. These dis-

---

[43] *Ibid.*, pp. 33-5. It should be noted, on the other hand, that the sciences sometimes provide philosophers with concepts which can be generalized to have a wider and more fruitful application to existence than that which they initially possessed. For example, Dewey applies the strictly biological notions of organic interaction with the environment to provide a general account of the nature of mind and all phases of experience.

tinctions may come to be regarded as the *only* reality:

> Reflective analysis of one element in actual experience is undertaken; its result is then taken to be primary; as a consequence the subject-matter of actual experience from which the analytic result was derived is rendered dubious and problematic, although it is assumed at every step of the analysis.[44]

The philosopher's tendency to imprison his thought with self-defeating assumptions is evidently due in some measure to moral bias of some kind. Philosophical ideas and aims, Dewey urged, do not have a virgin birth in pure reason, but are responses to the problems and challenges of the environing world – whether scientific, religious, political, or social.

> . . . philosophy, like politics, literature and the plastic arts, is itself a phenomenon of humn culture. Its connection with social history, with civilization, is intrinsic. . . . The movement of time . . . exhibits as the work of philosophy the old and ever new undertaking of adjusting that body of traditions which constitute the actual mind of man to scientific tendencies and political aspirations which are novel and incompatible with received authorities. . . . Open your histories of philosophy, and you find written throughout them the same periods of time and the same geographical distributions which provide the intellectual scheme of histories of politics, industry or the fine arts. . . . However it may stand with philosophy as a revalation of eternal truths, it is tremendously significant as a revalation of the predicaments, protests and aspirations of humanity.[45]

The analysis of experience, whether primary or reflective, without assuming any particular theories about such things is

---

[44] *Ibid.*, p. 18. Dewey's point is that those analyses which in various ways call into question the actual data of experience depend for their presumed validity on these very data. Hence the arguments are self-contradictory. See, for illustration, Dewey's critique of Russell's skepticism, wherein Dewey shows in detail that Russell's arguments presuppose at several crucial points the objective reality of that experience about which Russell draws skeptical conclusions *(Essays in Experimental Logic* [New York: Dover Publications, n.d.], Chapter XI, "The Existence of the World as a Logical Problem").

Further examples of Dewey's critique of this faulty kind of analysis will be introduced shortly.

[45] *Philosophy and Civilization* (Capricorn Books; New York, 1963), pp. 3-4. Dewey's view might seem to be a precarious generalization. Yet for a full-scale implementation of this interpretation of the dynamics of intellectual history see J.H. Randall, Jr., *The Making of the Modern Mind* (Cambridge: Houghton Mifflin, 1954). Dewey himself frequently wrote brilliant pieces to show how specific philosophies reflected the pressing problems of the day, the dominant modes of experience of a certain class, or the personal aspirations of the philosopher. Sometimes philosophers explicitly avow their moral aims; for instance Spinoza or Kant, as well as Dewey himself.

notoriously difficult and uncommon. In seeing the world and the various ways men interact with it, all men commonly interpret their experience with preconceptions, certain moral beliefs and aspirations, and outright prejudice. It is difficult enough to persuade a thinker to go ahead and look at what he is talking about; and it is also difficult for him, when such a look is taken, to see things with objectivity, rather than selectively to fit a theory or fulfill a hope.

This procedure of creating separations in experience Dewey describes generically as the fallacy of selective emphasis: A selective choice of subject matter is made which is either not acknowledged or recognized to be such. Of course, special subject matters must be isolated for analysis; that is, selective choice is necessary for inquiry. But the results, the refined conclusions of systematic thinking, must be tested by reference to primary experience.

> Selective emphasis, choice, is inevitable whenever reflection occurs. This is not an evil. Deception comes only when the presence and operation of choice is concealed, disguised, denied. . . . Choice that is disguised or denied is the source of those astounding differences of philosophic belief that startle the beginner and that become the plaything of the expert. Choice that is avowed is an experiment to be tried on its merits and tested by its results.[46]

Philosophers are not alert to the effects of disguised choice and hence have come to ignore primary subject matter: ". . . they have failed to note the empirical needs that generate their problems, and have failed to return the refined products back to the context of actual experience, there to receive their check, inherit their full content of meaning, and give illumination and guidance in the immediate perplexities which originally occasioned reflection."[47] The philosopher takes a partial view of nature, ignores what is left out, and hence takes this simplified view as the sole reality. He equates selected phases of experience with the only true being, thus leading to a reductive or distorted philosophy which consigns the remaining traits of nature – if recognized at all – to a ghostly existence in some kind of neatly contrived realm altogether removed from nature.

There is a related, and most important, consequence of this

---

[46] *Experience and Nature*, pp. 29-30.

[47] *Ibid.*, pp. 32-3.

fallacy. In many instances it leads to taking the outcome of a process out of its context and treating it as a separate substance, discontinuous with the rest of existence. This is the

> . . . conversion of eventual functions into antededent existence: a conversion which may be said to be *the* philosophic fallacy, whether it be performed in behalf of mathematical subsistences, esthetic essences, the purely physical order of nature, or God.[48]

Further, these eventuations are erroneously treated as causes:

> The fallacy converts consequences of interaction of events into causes of the occurrence of these consequences. . . .[49]

As, for example, a presumed life principle might be regarded as the cause of life, mind the cause of thinking, or a bellicose instinct the cause of pugnacity. Philosophical idealism is a typical case:

> Idealism fails to take into account the specified or concrete character of the uncertain situation in which thought occurs; it fails to note the empirically concrete character of the subject-matter, acts, and tools by which determination and consistency are reached; it fails to note that the conclusive eventual objects having the latter properties are themselves as many as the situations dealt with. The conversion of the logic of reflection into an ontology of rational being is thus due to arbitrary conversion of an eventual natural function of unification into a causal antecedent reality; . . . .[50]

Thus philosophers, perhaps zealously admiring certain aspects of nature alone, distort our understanding of man's actual situation and remove it from rational analysis.

> Yet too commonly, although in a great variety of technical modes, the result of the search [for wisdom] is converted into a metaphysics which denies or conceals from acknowledgment the very characters of existence which initiated it, and which give significance to its conclusions.[51]

It would be difficult to overemphasize the extent to which Dewey holds the fallacy of selective emphasis to be at the root of philosophical problems and to be the chief impediment to genuine understanding of human existence. *Experience and Nature,*

---

[48] *Ibid.*, p. 29.

[49] *Ibid.*, p. 261.

[50] *Ibid.*, p. 68. The "eventual natural function" is a logically structured situation, which the idealist takes to be antecedently given as so structured.

[51] *Ibid.*, p. 59.

for example, is bulging with illustrations of this fallacy. Again and again Dewey finds philosophers omitting from their analysis of experience such traits as the precarious, novel, changing, qualitative characteristics of nature, which are so abundant in our experience, so crucial in understanding it. Yet philosophers relegate them to unreality, or set them rigidly apart from each other, establishing in separate realms of being the characteristics which in fact are so inextricably mixed.

To highlight Dewey's insights, it will be worthwhile to consider instances of this fallacy at greater length. Two crucial examples are what he calls "subjectivism" and "intellectualism." The former denotes the assumption that all we experience is our own ideas; hence experience is an impenetrable screen shutting each of us off from all external reality. This also carries with it the notion that mind is a discrete thing, substance, or realm of some sort. The latter (intellectualism) concerns the identification of reality exclusively with objects of cognition. Subjectivism has its origin, so Dewey asserts, when the experiencing subject itself is taken as an object of study (which is insofar a very desirable development) and this object (the act of experiencing) is taken to be complete in itself – functioning independently and exclusively. Thus mentalistic psychology develops:

> This great emancipation [recognition of the self as agent] was coincident with the rise of 'individualism,' which was in effect identical with the reflective discovery of the part played in experience by concrete selves, with their ways of acting, thinking, and desiring. The results would have been all to the good if they had been interpreted by empirical method. For this would have kept the eye of thinkers constantly upon the origin of the 'subjective' out of primary experience, and then directed it to the function of discriminating what is usable in the management of experienced objects. But for lack of such a method, because of isolation from empirical origin and instrumental use, the results of psychological inquiry were conceived to form a separate and isolated mental world in and of itself, self-sufficient and self-enclosed.[52]

Thus it is that "experience" loses its "double-barrelled" meaning and is presumed to refer only to *ways* of experiencing.

This subjectivism is greatly reinforced by intellectualism. Indeed, the two become intimately related. (Although the Greeks are held ultimately responsible for equating objects of cognition

---

[52] *Ibid.*, p. 15.

with true being, in the modern world it is Descartes who is primarily responsible for intellectualism.) Again, what Dewey has characterized as selective emphasis is evident in this development:

> Philosophy, like all forms of reflective analysis, takes us away, for the time being, from the things had in primary experience as they directly act and are acted upon, used and enjoyed. Now the standing temptation of philosophy, as its course abundantly demonstrates, is to regard the results of reflection as having, in and of themselves, a reality superior to that of the material of any other mode of experience. The commonest assumption of philosophies, common even to philosophies very different from one another, is the assumption of the identity of objects of knowledge and ultimately real objects. The assumption is so deep that it is usually not expressed; it is taken for granted as something so fundamental that it does not need to be stated.[53]

That is, the properties of objects, exclusively as they are characterized in, say, physics, are thought to be the *only* properties of such objects.

The assumption that all our encounters with genuine reality are a mode of knowing is a consequence of ripping cognitive experience out of its context. Thus, for example, Descartes, eager to defend the new science and to discredit qualitative science, fails to perceive the continuity and connections of gross and refined experience but, rather, supposes that knowing is a direct grasp of reality by "reason" – an error he shares with many others. The problem of epistemology arises from the failure to see that knowing is a consequence of selective operations performed on things of primary experience. These problems

> . . . spring from the assumption that the true and valid object of knowledge is that which has being prior to and independent of the operations of knowing. They spring from the doctrine that knowledge is a grasp or beholding of reality without anything being done to modify its antecedent state – the doctrine which is the source of the separation of knowledge from practical activity. If we see that knowing is not the act of an outside spectator but of a participator inside the natural and social scene, then the true object of knowledge resides in the consequences of directed action.[54]

Taken by this "spectator" theory, Descartes concludes that what matter "really" is is extension, and nature is nothing but this extension in motion: The whole reality of nature is disclosed by

---

[53] *Ibid.*, p. 19.

[54] *The Quest for Certainty*, p. 196.

physics. Accordingly, it is only our cognitive experience which discloses reality itself. The qualities hitherto thought to be in nature are only mistakenly attributed to objective things; they are really only in the mind:

> When real objects are identified, point for point, with knowledge-objects, all affectional and volitional objects are inevitably excluded from the 'real' world, and are compelled to find refuge in the privacy of an experiencing subject or mind.[55]

This line of reasoning that leads to dualism is a consequence of the failure to observe cognitive experience in its connections with primary experience. Expressed in the language of Dewey's metaphysics, this is a failure to see the connection between the stable and the other traits of experience – such as quality, the precarious, and histories.

The preceding discussion also reveals how intellectualism has come to be a support for subjectivism: The experience of qualities is (erroneously) assumed to be nothing but the experience of something in the mind – something "mental." It is further assumed (erroneously) that from these qualities all other ideas are formed – ideas are simply composite images. Hence it is concluded that ideas and not things are the object of experience; and mind is thus set apart from nature. Intellectualism and subjectivism are two sides of the same coin: If the external world is in reality a thing unto itself, then mind is severed from it; or if the mind is something complete and private in itself, then nature is totally apart from it.

> Since the psychological movement necessarily coincided with that which set up physical objects as correspondingly complete and self-enclosed, there resulted that dualism of mind and matter, of a physical and a psychical world, which from the day of Descartes to the present dominates the formulation of philosophical problems.[56]

It is highly instructive to see how these two hypotheses developed, for their genesis illustrates the fundamental philosophic fallacy; and it is abundantly clear that as hypotheses they don't stand the test of experience. Yet consider their enduring influence in modern philosophy! Throughout Dewey's work we find

---

[55] *Experience and Nature,* p. 24.

[56] *Ibid.,* p. 15.

him again and again drawing attention to the fact that a thinker has seized some favored portion of experience and has subsequently regarded it as autonomous, self-sufficient, unrelated to other phases of experience. Thus are "dualisms," "breaks," "non-interacting realms" introduced into nature and the character of the entire context distorted or unidentifiable. It is clear enough – as has been sufficiently indicated – that both subjectivism and intellectualism are gross distortions of what experience is found to be. (Moreover, they lead to all the puzzles involving the relation of mind to matter; and they have further pernicious effects, which will be indicated especially in Chapter IV.)

Dewey detects the working of selective emphasis in a variety of philosophical positions. The final chapter of the *Logic,* "The Logic of Inquiry and Philosophies of Knowledge," is a superb treatment of epistemological theories as instances of taking certain phases of experience out of context:

> The purposes of this chapter is, then, to consider some of the main types of epistemological theory which mark the course of philosophy with a view to showing that each type represents a selective abstraction of some conditions and some factors out of the actual pattern of controlled inquiry. It will be shown that this borrowing is what gives them their plausibility and appeal, while the source of their invalidity is arbitrary isolation of the elements selected from the inquiry-context in which they function.[57]

Similar problems occur in the analysis of aesthetic phenomena:

> . . . philosophies of esthetics have often set out from one factor that plays a part in the constitution of experience, and have attempted to interpret or 'explain' the esthetic experience by a single element; in terms of sense, emotion, reason, or activity; . . . . We can ask what element, in the formation of experience, each system has taken as central and characteristic. If we start from this point, we find

[57] *Logic: The Theory of Inquiry,* p. 514. The failure to identify the continuities of experience has been especially marked in philosophic analysis of inquiry and knowing. Dualisms, Dewey says, originate in "the erection of distinctions that are genetic and historic, and working or instrumental divisions of labor, into rigid and ready-made structural differences of reality" *(Essays in Experimental Logic,* p. 153). Dewey himself analyses the actual process (or "history," as he calls it) of inquiry indefatigably. What are in fact distinctive functions and phases of histories of all kinds philosophers have converted into separate realms of being.

Many other problems commonly called metaphysical arise because of the failure of philosophers to note the historical nature of inquiry. These are such problems as the nature of particulars and universals and the nature of conceptual categories. Dewey takes these up as a matter of course in his *Logic* and related articles.

> that theories fall of themselves into certain types, and that the particular strand of experience that is offered reveals, when it is placed in contrast with esthetic experience itself, the weakness of the theory. For it is shown that the system in question has superimposed some preconceived idea upon experience instead of encouraging or even allowing esthetic experience to tell its own tale.[58]

We have seen how philosophers get so far away from experience: They borrow concepts from the sciences, seizing upon them in their finished form (i.e., in their apparent exclusiveness of experience) and never reintegrate them into experience. Or they develop concepts of their own from only a limited, a favored, portion of experience taken out of its context and subsequently suppose that the nature of that experience is unrelated to other phases of experience. Accordingly, they develop theories of the nature of existence which bear little resemblance or relation to that experienced reality in which men must strive and suffer. To put it briefly, the most fundamental error in philosophy is in the artificial simplification of existence.

b. The uses of experience

The preceding section has indicated how philosophers manage to violate the realities of experience and nature. This is done chiefly by omitting fundamental traits from their view of nature. Philosophers have recurrently made the error of selecting only one part of experience as real, ignoring the rest of it. Subsequently, of course, they must in some way acknowledge the reality of what they have left out. Hence they devise for it a new realm of being, separating it absolutely from other phases of experience. The remedy for such procedure is partly in the recognition of choice and the insistence that concepts be faithful to gross experience. Clearly, moreover, both the development and criticism of philosophical positions can proceed much more surely and effectively if the philosopher is possessed of a carefully elaborated naturalistic metaphysics.

The last point can be made clear by approaching it with some of the ideas discussed so far: Philosophy, Dewey insists, must have an honest and thorough regard for experience; and naturalistic metaphysics is the attempt to discern, describe, and explain the function of the pervasive characteristics of experience. As

[58] *Art as Experience* (New York: G.P. Putnam's Sons, 1958), pp. 274-5.

Dewey sees it, these are also the most salient traits; and to leave them out of account is disaster for philosophy. If these traits are somehow left unnoticed in the analysis of certain kinds of experience, then such analyses are insofar deficient; and to the extent that philosophic systems disregard traits of nature, our experience appears unintelligible and anomolous. If it is indeed the case that philosophies have been vain principally because they have been insensitive to the nature of primary experience, then a careful discrimination and analysis of the generic traits of primary experience and their inter-relations would provide distinctions eminently useful in philosophic inquiries dealing with the characterization of any kind of experience. A remedy for philosophic analysis which unwittingly deals with only partial views of any kind of situation is a ready apprehension of those traits "sure to turn up in any universe of discourse." I quoted (on p. 9, above) Dewey's statement about the generic traits that "all important issues are concerned with their degrees and the ratios they sustain to one another." Similarly, he said that "the significant problems and issues of life and philosophy concern the rate and mode of conjunction" of these traits. (Quoted above at p. 10.) Thus what havoc do philosophers work when they seem above all given to ignoring most such traits in their own study of nature! Accordingly, a main function of metaphysics is to serve as what Dewey calls a "ground-map of the province of criticism."[59] The relation of metaphysics and criticism must be considered here in more detail.

There is considerable difficulty in discussing this relation, because Dewey's explicit remarks about criticism are unusually ambiguous, even for him. (See especially Chapter Ten of *Experience and Nature*.) Hence the following analysis is in part predicated on his specific statements on the subject, but even more so on the actual procedure he displays in his metaphysical analyses.

The notion of criticism can be divided into four parts: 1) the criticism of values; 2) the criticism of abstractions; 3) the analysis of the traits of particular kinds of experience (e.g., moral, cognitive, artistic); and 4) the analysis of events in experience as functional parts of an inclusive process. The fourth part is related not

---

[59] *Experience and Nature*, p. 413.

only to naturalistic metaphysics; it is also essential to what I have distinguished as philosophy of nature. Analysis of the fourth part will illustrate the intimate relation of the two inquiries.

1) Criticism of the first sort is a very complex and far-reaching activity, and a great deal will be said to characterize its various forms and functions in the course of this study. As Dewey argues in Chapter Ten of *Experience and Nature,* this criticism is the principal concern of philosophy. More fundamentally, philosophy is concerned with the clarification and development of all the assumptions and methods of criticism of value. Understood most comprehensively, criticism of value thus encompasses the three additional meanings of criticism to be introduced in the current discussion. (As I have suggested, however, the topic will be more manageable if four distinctions are made. These distinctions will clarify the nature of metaphysical analysis; and that is the immediate problem. Specific applications to value criticism will later be taken up at length.)

Most simply, criticism of value involves the analysis of the goods of experience in all their natural continuities. Inasmuch as value is a function of experience, even the most rudimentary forms of criticism must regard value as an objective part of nature, inseparably implicated with the traits of nature. Yet Dewey insists that the assumptions and procedures of criticism have been drastically obfuscated and impeded by the numerous forms of metaphysics which have claimed fixed ontological divisions where there is in fact continuity and organic intermixture. Thus nature has been regarded as bereft of value, and the functions of intelligence have been neglected. Dewey's objections will received their due attention. For the moment it need only be pointed out that a naturalistic metaphysics provides a "ground-map" of criticism in the obvious sense that it makes clear the continuities and intermixtures of the traits of nature and it displays their function in various kinds of experience. Thus – so we shall see – it makes criticism of values both intelligible and efficacious. If only implicitly, any coherent and effective theory of criticism must presuppose a metaphysics that characterizes nature at least as thoroughly and faithfully as that of Dewey. Speaking of such a metaphysics, Dewey says, "It will surrender the separation in nature from each other of contingency and regularity, the hazardous and the assured; it will avoid the relegation of them to distinct orders of Being which is characteristic of the classic tradition."[60]

2) Criticism of abstractions. In the sense intended here, abstractions are philosophic theories which are the outcome of committing the fallacy of selective emphasis. They are theories, that is, whose characterization of their subject matter either leaves out essential traits of that subject matter or treats it in such a way that it is isolated absolutely from other phenomena. The theory could be concerned with nature, mind, value, art, language, etc. – any distinctive subject matter. In any event primary experience is rendered unintelligible when this abstraction is offered as constituting a complete characterization of its subject matter.

In criticizing notions of this kind, Dewey indicates what traits of experience have been left out of the analysis, and he shows how this omission has resulted in misleading and obscure conclusions. I have indicated examples of this kind of criticism in the discussion of abuses of experience; and fuller examples will be provided in Chapters II and IV. Dewey regarded this kind of criticism as fundamental to his own work. Defending *Experience and Nature* in response to the critique of Santayana, he says,

> . . . a considerable part of my discussion of special topics is an attempt to show that characteristic traits of the subjects dealt with are to be accounted for as 'intersections' of 'interpenetrations' (I could think of no better words) of the immediate and the nexional or mediatory, just as my criticism of various philosophical theories rests on showing that they have isolated one phase at the expense of the other.[61]

And he had indicated in the same response that the novelty in *Experience and Nature* was in using his metaphysical method to "understand a group of special problems which have troubled philosophy."[62] Thus, for example (as we shall see in the next

---

[60] *Ibid.*, pp. 395-6.

[61] "Half-Hearted Naturalism," p. 61. In this quotation, "immediate" refers to what Dewey calls problematic, precarious, or contingent; and "nexional or mediatory" refers to known structures or relations: what Dewey calls the stable. Dewey's complaint is that philosophers have created hopeless perplexities by dividing the precarious and the stable into separate ontological realms; whereas in fact these two traits are always found together. Their "interpenetration" is, indeed, the source of all human endeavor and art. (See the first section of the following chapter, and Chapter III.)

[62] *Ibid.*, p. 59.

chapter), he removes the sources of the traditional mind-body problem by metaphysical criticism; and in Chapter III we shall see how he clarifies the nature of value by reference to generic traits. Art and science are also characterized by detecting the particular conjunctions of these traits of nature. Problems traditionally thought to be fundamental and even ultimate for philosophy are not so much solved, but eliminated, by pointing out that they are not somehow rooted in the very nature of things, but are in fact the creation of that incomplete analysis which arbitrarily introduces impassable separations into nature. By this sort of criticism, Dewey makes nature an intelligible whole and turns what had been the sport of dialecticians into subjects for scientific study.[63] And thus his philosophy passes the test of experience in a way equalled by few, if any, comprehensive philosophies of modern times. The function of the "ground-map" in all these criticisms is evident.

3) Criticism in the third sense is indispensable to criticism of the kind just indicated. Criticism of the third sort is of experience itself, not abstractions; and it is requisite to the formation of a "ground-map." As we shall see, the ground-map also becomes an effective instrument for the criticism of experience itself.

The traits of experience are not detected by examining nature-at-large, as it were; the subject matter must be more specific. Dewey examines particular kinds of experience and attempts to distinguish their traits. Then the attempt is made to determine what are the implications for metaphysics of such distinctive traits. That is, is there anything implied about nature by such experience which can be generalized in a way to characterize all situations? For example, doubting is something that occurs in situations of inquiry. There is some trait – or combination of traits – in nature which results in doubting. Can this trait be specified, and can it be generalized in its applicability to all subject matters? On Dewey's analysis, doubting implies (among other things) precariousness in nature; and precariousness is a trait which he regards as occurring in all situations. Likewise, valuing, when examined in its integrity, implies precariousness,

[63] More generally, much of what is commonly called metaphysics is simply a collection of problems that wouldn't even exist if experience were examined in its integrity.

structures, qualities, histories, and ends in nature. Of course, the test to determine whether such traits are really generic is simply to observe whether they occur in all situations. Presumably, the same sort of inquiry can be undertaken for any particular kind of event in experience. Insofar as the analysis of any subject matter turns up the same set of traits with other subjects, then their claim to be truly metaphysical is insofar strengthened. The set of traits taken to be generic is continually tested by its success as a "ground-map" for the further analysis of experience. Through such testing, it becomes elaborated and refined and becomes the more effective basis for criticism. Thus metaphysical analysis proceeds.

Metaphysical analysis concerns such obvious facts as cognitive experience, art and aesthetic experience, moral and religious experience, and attempts to discriminate their traits. As metaphysics, such endeavors are brought to their completion when these traits are seen to have implications for the traits of nature as nature. For any intelligible metaphysics, all separate analyses of experience must have common implications for the nature of nature; they must be indicative of the same generic characteristics. What is implied by the fact of thinking, of inquiry, of choice, of art? In every such case, Dewey attempts to understand the character of such events and attempts, further, to conclude how these events typify nature. That is, e.g., what are the traits of nature that elicit the phases of inquiry? How are these phases characteristic of nature?

> A naturalistic metaphysics is bound to consider reflection as itself a natural event occuring *within* nature because of traits of the latter . . . The interest of empirical and denotative method and of naturalistic metaphysics must wholly coincide. The world must actually be such as to generate ignorance and inquiry; doubt and hypothesis, trial and temporal conclusions; . . . The ultimate evidence of genuine hazard, contingency, irregularity and indeterminateness in nature is thus found in the occurrence of thinking.[64]

Indeed, Dewey says summarily in his rejoinder to Santayana's critique,

> If one generalizes this position, then the main features of human life (culture, experience, history – or whatever name may be preferred) are indicative of outstanding features of nature itself – of centers and perspectives, contingencies and fulfillments, crises and intervals, histories, uniformities, and particularizations.

[64] *Experience and Nature*, pp. 68-9.

> This is the extent and method of my 'metaphysics': – the large and constant features of human sufferings, enjoyments, trials, failures and successes together with the institutions of art, science, technology, politics, and religion which mark them, communicate genuine features of the world within which man lives.[65]

It is clear that Dewey tests his metaphysical formulations with his criticism of experience. It must be noted, in addition, that he also uses these metaphysical distinctions to aid in the criticism of experience itself. This is not a logically circular process. It is, rather, like the procedures of experimental science, in which hypotheses direct the inquirer to look for certain facts in experience; and these facts – when and if they do occur – frequently require some modification in the hypothesis. If, for example, the precarious is assumed to be a generic trait of experience, what constitutes the precarious and how does it function in moral experience, aesthetic experience, or inquiry? Hence Dewey deliberately looks for the precarious in, say, aesthetic experience. If he could not find it there, he might suppose his metaphysical formulations were in error.

As in fact happens, Dewey finds and characterizes the precarious in aesthetic experience. Thus his ground-map leads him to make a specific investigation of experience. Of course, insofar as his metaphysical distinctions are inclusive, his analysis of aesthetic experience (or any kind of experience) is apt to be more searching and complete.

Criticism by means of the generic traits includes for Dewey the determination of how the events characterized by these traits actually function. He endeavors to show how various kinds of experience arise in response to conditions described by the generic traits and their "interpenetrations"; and he shows as well how the specific nature of these experiences undergoes qualitative change as a consequence of the agent's interaction with the generically characterized traits of the situation.

Thus it is that criticism of experience proceeds both by means of determining the implications for metaphysics of the specific traits of situations and of using generic concepts as hypotheses for investigation. In respect to philosophy of value, metaphysical analysis would attempt to determine what are the specific charac-

---

65 "Half-Hearted Naturalism," p. 59.

teristics of moral situations; and it would attempt to determine what were the generic traits implied by the specific. In order to make valuing and moral experience intelligible as organic functions of nature, it would show how evaluation, judgment, and striving for value arise in response to the generic traits. The treatment of these issues includes the examination of how values and moral reflection can be more thoroughly and accurately characterized by looking for the presence and function of generic traits in moral situations. These considerations lead finally to the question of how actual moral reflection can be enlightened and made more efficacious by treating value as a trait of nature in continuity with other traits of nature. Dewey, as we shall see, deals very effectively with fundamental problems of value by treating these questions specifically.

4) The fourth kind of activity that is included in the notion of criticism is that of examining all events and processes of experience in their natural continuities. This means that the various distinctive situations of experience are analyzed in their development from initial, indeterminate and problematic stages to their settled, determinate, and consummatory stages. This means, for example, that one analyzes scientific inquiry from its initial to its final phases, noting all its constituents and traits in their actual sequential and functional connections with each other. Criticism in this sense means that whatever phenomena Dewey investigates are examined as functions of nature and experience. Experience itself is examined as a function of the interaction of organism and environment; so are language, self, mind, value, knowledge.

Criticism of this kind is another bulwark against the fallacy of selective emphasis. Notoriously, philosophy gets trapped in all sorts of blind alleys (no matter how euphemistically these alleys may be labeled) when it supposes that what is in fact a phase or an outcome of a natural process is an independent substance. When it is recognized that we are dealing with processes and not substances, natural science and its methods become far more efficacious in the discrimination and securing of human good. Consider, for example, the relevance of science when mind is understood as a functional part of nature, rather than as an essential entity of some kind. The same possibilities hold of value.[66]

---

[66] The functions of science will receive extended attention in subsequent chapters.

Dewey's substitution of an inclusive philosophy of process for dualistic philosophies of substance is not by any means an a priori postulate. He engages in prolonged analyses to argue that such things as mind, value, and self are natural functions; and in doing so he relies on the best-authenticated scientific assumptions. (See, herein, Chapters II and III.) This is not to say, of course, that Dewey's particular hypotheses are altogether accurate. On the other hand, to approach these phenomena as natural functions of some kind is a vastly more promising procedure than to take them as separate substances. The thinking substance theory, for example, clearly creates more problems than it solves. And, as we shall see in Chapter II, traditional notions of mind are supported only by theories in which the fallacy of selective emphasis is glaringly evident.

In these four modes of criticism, the distinctively metaphysical function is evident in the first three. The fourth mode is clearly organic to philosophy of nature. That is, from the kind of analysis involved in the fourth mode, conclusions readily follow concerning the concept of nature: The very characterization of nature must be of that which eventuates in such things as experience, mind, value, knowledge, etc.; and the conditions and character of this eventuation admit of being analyzed in detail.

There are evident connections between the fourth kind of criticism and naturalistic metaphysics: The analysis of the historical continuities of a given subject matter is not only useful on its own account; it is as well a source of formulations for metaphysical analysis. At the same time, the metaphysical ground-map is suggestive of traits which must not be overlooked if the description of these continuities is not to be arbitrarily simplified. The analysis of the stages of inquiry, for example, is important in itself; but it can also be utilized in the formation of metaphysical ideas. And these ideas also keep the philosopher alert to all the traits that might be discerned in the process of inquiry. Finally, the traits of nature discriminated in metaphysical analysis can be criticized as natural processes. It can be determined how quality, contingency, and ends arise in nature, how they are related to one another, and how they function in experience. In turn, nature is thereupon defined, in part, as that which produces in specified ways such things as quality, contingency, ends. As I stated in my Introduction, a fully elaborated metaphysics would state the traits of nature conceived as that which produces all the phenomena of experience.

This discussion of different kinds of criticism can be summarized by indicating their common function in philosophic studies. There are, of course, important ways in which analyses of art or science or valuation stand or fall on their own merits, without reference to more inclusive philosophical assumptions. (Dewey's political thought, for example, can be assessed in various ways without reference to his theory of nature.) It must be insisted upon, however, that such analyses – from any philosopher – do in fact imply certain assumptions about the nature of nature; and these analyses become distinctively and fundamentally philosophic when their implicit theory of nature is articulated. Especially in contemporary thought, a theory of nature is seldom even considered; but in the history of philosophy a great many particular studies about art or science or value have simply been made to conform to some preexisting theory of reality. (Examples abound: Spinoza, Hegel, etc.) It has also frequently happened that a special analysis of experience has been such that it could not possibly be correlated with the more inclusive and systematic theory of experience elaborated by the same philosopher. (The classical British empiricists are a principal example: Their sensationalistic philosophy of experience would, in the interest of consistency, forbid them to make assertions about anything at all.) To all conditions like these, Dewey's notion of criticism is applicable: It requires that the traits and continuities of experience be carefully observed. It demands thorough coherence to experience in any system of thought; and from any specialized analysis of experience it demands an intelligible continuity with ideas about the nature of nature. Its aim is the progressive enlightenment and enrichment of experience. "To note, register and define the constituent structure of nature is not then an affair neutral to the office of criticism. It is a preliminary outline of the field of criticism, whose chief import is to afford understanding of the necessity and nature of the office of intelligence."[67]

---

[67] *Experience and Nature,* p. 422. Both "It" and "whose" in the last sentence refer to the noting, registering, and defining of the first sentence.

The analysis of criticism provided here constitutes an elaboration of the meaning of the method of experience. It is clear that any conscientious and thorough application of the method must be "critical" in ways at least very similar to those indicated. Otherwise philosophy severs itself from primary experience and renders it opaque. Some final words are in order concerning the method of experience.

It has been suggested that what Dewey calls empirical method is no simple thing to pursue. It is important to see that the foundations of a sound empirical method involve considerably more, say, than the assumption that all propositions must somehow be related to observation statements. The method of experience both as a means of discovery and a means of test has a considerably wider meaning. Indeed, philosophies that have been traditionally known as empirical are alluded to by Dewey as being nonempirical:

> The first and perhaps the greatest difference made in philosophy by adoption respectively of empirical or non-empirical method is . . . the difference made in what is selected as original material.[68]
>
> Now the notion of experience, however devoid of differential subject-matter – since it includes all subject-matters –, at least tells us that we must not start with arbitrarily selected simples, and from them deduce the complex and varied, assigning what cannot be thus deduced to an inferior realm of being. It warns us that the tangled and complex is what we primarily find; that we work from and within it to discriminate, reduce, analyze; and that we must keep track of these activities, pointing to *them,* as well as to the things upon which they are exercised, and to their refined conclusions.[69]

Evidently any philosophy which accepts subjectivism or intellectualism, for instance, would not, in Dewey's sense, be empirical.

Previous discussion clearly indicates that when experience is made unintelligible by philosophical concepts, it is desirable to change the concepts rather than deny that which is their only possible test. Otherwise, philosophy exists in futile – if sometimes splendid – isolation from vital human experience; as such it presents the ludicrous spectacle of a presumably foundational discipline which is foundational to nothing. A good contrast between this approach and that of Dewey is seen in the latter's

---

[68] *Ibid.*, p. 10.

[69] *Experience and Nature* (first edition), p. 13.

scorn of the so-called "problem of knowledge." On Dewey's view we should not ask, for instance, Do we have knowledge? or Is knowledge possible? Rather, we should go to those situations which are distinguishable as cases of knowing and discover what characterizes them:

> There are two dimensions of experienced things: one that of having them, and the other that of knowing about them so that we can again have them in more meaningful and secure ways. It is no easy matter to know about the things we have and are, whether it be the state, measles, virtue or redness. Hence there *is* a problem of knowledge; namely the problem of how to find out about these things in order to secure, rectify and avoid being and having them.
>
> But a problem of knowledge in general is, so to speak brutally, nonsense. For knowledge is itself one of the things that we empirically *have.* While scepticism may be in place at any time about any specific intellectual belief and conclusion, in order to keep us on the alert, to keep us inquiring and curious, scepticism as to the things which we *have* and *are* is impossible.[70]
>
> A theory of knowledge in the sense of how to know most economically, liberally, effectively, a technique of instructive and rewarding inquiry is indispensable. But what has gone by the name of theory of knowledge has not been such an affair. It has been a discussion of whether we can know at all, a matter of validating or refuting wholesale scepticism (instead of how to conduct doubt profitably); of how far knowledge extends, what its limits are, limits not at a specific time and place, but inherent and final.[71]

Of course there are many issues concerning the nature and criteria of empirical knowledge. It is the wholesale denial of the very possibility of knowledge that Dewey ridicules. Obviously, it takes a lot of knowledge to design and build an automobile or a bomb, to send a rocket to the moon, to get from New York to Chicago, to make out an income tax return, or to perform a cornea transplant. Are we to doubt that such things happen? (And it is clear that to ask, "Is this really *knowledge*?" implies no more than a dispute about words. It does not imply any dispute about what actually occurs and is accomplished in experience.) The metaphysician should inquire into the nature of the world that such experiences do take place; he should not deny the experience of knowing itself:

> Everybody knows that the trend of modern philosophy has been to arrive at theories regarding the nature of the universe by means of theories regarding the

[70] *Ibid.*, p. 21.

[71] *Ibid.*, p. 19.

> nature of knowledge – a procedure which reverses the apparently more judicious method of the ancients in basing their conclusions about knowledge on the nature of the universe in which knowledge occurs.[72]

The point here is that philosophic inquiry is devoted to understanding and enlightening human experience as it in fact occurs, not to obscuring or denying it. Hence the existence of the presumed problem of knowledge evidently requires a change in its premises rather than acceptance of its conclusions. What characteristics of experience have been neglected such that knowing, as such, must be called into question? The changing of premises, however, is no arbitrary matter; it demands a more thorough and honest examination of experience. Any such examination might end in failure, but it is better to admit failure and try again rather than offer a "solution" which is patently misleading.

But how, specifically, is experience to be examined? This examination is that of criticism, as I have just explicated it. That discussion can be elaborated by making further reference to the interdependence of ideas and the direct analysis of experience. Thus the notion of the method of experience will become sufficiently detailed for present purposes. For successful inquiry into the nature of experience Dewey acknowledges that one may begin either with some theoretical assumptions or with a comparatively unprejudiced inspection of the primary subject matter. He emphasizes, however, that neither approach is self-sufficient: Ultimately, both must be used; and they must converge on a common result.

> There are two avenues of approach to the goal of philosophy. We may begin with experience in gross, experience in its primary and crude forms, and by means of its distinguishing features and its distinctive trends, note something of the constitution of the world which generates and maintains it. Or, we may begin with refined, selective products, the most authentic statments of commended methods of science, and work from them back to the primary facts of life.[73]

Each approach has its strengths and limitations. Scientific knowledge is indispensable (witness the use Dewey made of biology and physics), and – if there is any point at all to philosophizing – carefully formulated philosophical distinctions are equally val-

---

[72] *The Quest for Certainty,* p. 41.

[73] *Experience and Nature* (first edition), p. 2.

uable. Yet it is precisely these refined intellectual instruments, as we have seen, which will be readily accepted as final and axiomatic and which, consequently, may be such as to obscure genuine understanding.

The experiential approach, which begins "back of any science,"[74] is more fundamental, for it tries to see what experience is by direct observation rather than from an already established theory; and it is ultimately decisive. I quoted the following in another connection (p. 27 above):

> The value of experience as method in philosophy is that it compels us to note that denotation comes first and last. . . . The value, I say, of the notion of experience for philosophy is that it asserts the finality and comprehensiveness of the method of pointing, finding, showing, and the necessity of seeing what is pointed to and accepting what is found in good faith and without discount. . . . We need the notion of experience to remind us that 'reality' includes whatever is denotatively found.[75]

But the matter of discriminating the traits of experience is also the most difficult and exacting, for it is no simple matter to make honest judgments regarding what experience is:

> . . . the method which sets out with macroscopic experience requires unusual candor and patience. . . . Coarse and vital experience is Protean; a thing of moods and tenses. To seize and report it is the task of an artist as well as of an informed technician.[76]

Moreover, we cannot completely avoid bringing certain unacknowledged assumptions to our inquiry: "As the history of thought shows, the usual thing, a thing so usual as probably to be in some measure inevitable, is for the philosopher to mix with his reports of direct experience interpretations of it made by previous thinkers."[77]

Neither approach will work by itself. However honest an observer one may be, he would never get far in such criticism without introducing and employing some products of reflective thinking. Indeed, it is clear that these two "avenues" distinguish the extremes of a continuum:

> The two methods differ in starting point and direction, but not in objective or

---

[74] *Ibid.*, p. 6.

[75] *Ibid.*, p. 10-1.

[76] *Ibid.*, p. 3.

[77] *Ibid.*, pp. 3-4.

> eventual content. Those who start with coarse, everyday experience must bear in mind the findings of the most competent knowledge, and those who start from the latter must somehow journey back to the homely facts of daily existence.[78]

Any thorough study of experience in order to distinguish its traits and continuities must operate from these critical extremes, using them both as instruments of understanding, clarification, and criticism, neither of them being insulated from the insights and conclusions of the other. Philosophers may rely primarily on gross experience (F.H. Bradley exemplifies this procedure), or may begin with science and from it fill in a complete theory of nature (Whtehead is a good example); but exclusive dependence on one mode or the other is either to ignore the work and knowledge of others or to engage in sheer dialectic.

It should not be supposed that this method by any means involves a rejection of science. It is clear that Dewey effectively used both critical approaches; but the experiential approach is the more fundamental, for, as indicated, "denotation comes first and last." As in any inquiry, ideas function to indicate the focus of observation; they point out what the inquirer is to look for. Observation, in turn, requires the modification and elaboration of ideas. This process continues until theory and experience are — at least tentatively — correlated. Dewey, as we have seen, found that thinkers become ensnared exclusively in their refined products, slighting denotation. He even confessed to such a tendency himself:

> It is hardly necessary to say that I have not been among those to whom the union of abilities to satisfy these two opposed requirements, the formal and the material, came easily. For that very reason I have been acutely aware . . . of a tendency of other thinkers and writers to achieve a specious lucidity and simplicity by the mere process of ignoring considerations which a greater respect for concrete materials of experience would have forced upon them.[79]

And he says of *Experience and Nature:*

> If what is written in these pages has no other result than creating and promoting a respect for concrete human experience and its potentialities, I shall be content.[80]

---

[78] *Ibid.*, p. 2.

[79] "From Absolutism to Experimentalism," in *Contemporary American Philosophy,* edited by George P. Adams and William Pepperell Montague (New York: 1930), Vol. II, pp. 13-27; reprinted in Bernstein (ed.), *op. cit.*, pp. 3-18. Quotation is from pp. 8-9 in Bernstein.

[80] *Experience and Nature,* p. 39.

Philosophers, as Dewey made abundantly clear, tend to examine only one function of the situation in isolation from the other functions; and they contrive their distinctions on that limited basis. These distinctions thereafter serve as axiomatic assumptions concerning *all* matters pertaining to the situation from which the experience was arbitrarily separated. The aim, then, of the method of experience is to see situations *in their entirety;* and this means to detect all of the traits of the situation in their historical continuities, noting the connections and functions peculiar to the particular type of situation. It should employ no a priori assumptions about what does and does not belong to nature. Likewise, it should not proceed with dogmatic assumptions about what is knowledge, what is morality, etc. Of whatever nature the inquiry, the philosopher should examine these situations and discover what in fact their constituents are. He should, for example, examine moral experience in its integrity and *conclude* his inquiry by settling upon the most useful distinctions for understanding it, for distinguishing it from other situations, for controlling and enriching it, and for exhibiting its continuities with other modes of experience and with nature. The method of experience implies the thorough use of criticism. It is clear that this method is the means of seeing experience in its integrity – seeing the processes that man and nature carry on together in all their traits and phases. It is the method, then, of analyzing nature in all its richness and continuities, with the end in view of clarifying and guiding life experience.[81]

Finally, a further word is in order concerning the way in which the method of experience makes all phases of experience subject matter for scientific inquiry. As remarked earlier, this is accomplished by forbidding the division of existence into utterly separate realms: both by exhibiting the continuity of experience and nature and by providing a common set of traits generic to all situations of experience. There is also a more general sense in which Dewey applies intelligence to experience. His metaphysics

---

[81] Admonitions about method, it should be noted, apply equally well to explicitly nonempirical philosophies as well as to the professedly empirical. (As a matter of fact, it is a moot point as to which type of philosophy has been the more given to the use of a priori assumptions. Perhaps the empirical philosophies are in some ways the more insidious for their stated determination to reject and abhor all such assumptions.)

involves the highly fecund and positive function of explicating the "large and constant features" of human experience, rather than challenging or ignoring their very existence. Thus, for example, such things as knowledge and value are not matters to be denied, but facts of life to be understood.

It should be noted that the analysis of specific forms of experience occupies Dewey more than his deliberate attempts to formulate metaphysical distinctions. However – and this is of first importance – he always undertook his analyses and tested them with a view to discriminating all the traits of the subject matter and its continuities with nature. It was always essential to his philosophic enterprise to carry on his inquiries in the context of the theory of nature. *Experience and Nature* is Dewey's attempt to give explicit formulation to the assumptions about nature which were implicit in his more specifically delimited inquiries and to use these metaphysical formulations to expose the limitations of traditional analyses of experience.

This background is indispensable to Dewey's various philosophic conclusions; and, indeed, an understanding of this background is indispensable to understanding Dewey in any but a superficial way. Remarkably, however, the nature of Dewey's endeavor has not been preceived by most students of his philosophy. The works of J. H. Randall, Jr., display a keen appreciation of Dewey's accomplishments in metaphysics; but Randall has never made a systematic study of Dewey's metaphysics as such. By contrast, Sidney Hook implies that Dewey ultimately became an antimetaphysician. He notes Dewey's statement concerning the terms "metaphysics" and "metaphysical": "I derive what consolation may be possible from promising myself never to use the words again in connection with any aspect of any part of my own position."[82] Dewey's intention, however, was to protest the fact that his use of "metaphysical" was too frequently misread; and to avoid confusion he would never use it again.[83] He

[82] "Experience and Existence: A Comment," pp. 712-3. The remarks are quoted by Hook on p. 160 of his *The Quest for Being* (New York: St. Martin's Press, 1961.)

[83] Late in life Dewey wanted to give up much of the terminology he had habitually employed; for traditional language had impeded the grasp of new ideas. See *Knowing and the Known* (with A.F. Bentley; Boston: Beacon Press, 1949), throughout which decisive terminological changes are advocated. He even wanted to scrap "experience." (See the letter of July 15, 1949, from Dewey to Herbert W. Schneider, in the latter's *Ways of Being* [New York: Columbia University Press, 1962], pp. 42-3.)

was clearly not apoligizing for what I have described herein as his naturalistic metaphysics. Indeed, one sentence after that quoted by Hook, Dewey states, "And while I think the *words* used were most unfortunate, I still believe that that which they were used to name is genuine and important."[84]

Hook further asserts that Dewey wasn't really seeking what could legitimately be called generic traits of nature, but was actually involved in what could most accurately be described as philosophical anthropology.[85] This contention, it seems to me, so far as it is not merely a dispute about the meaning of "metaphysics," could be interpreted in a most unhappy way. That is, it could be taken to mean that when Dewey speaks of traits of experience he is *not* thereby speaking of traits of nature. This would clearly be a fatal misinterpretation; for it contradicts Dewey's most crucial assumption: the continuity of experience and nature. The persistent puzzles of modern philosophy can be avoided, and human problems addressed intelligently, only when it is understood that the traits of experience are traits *of nature.* (A champion of many of Dewey's views, Hook, of course, had no intention of inviting such a misinterpretation.)

Of course there are traits of nature independent of human life and experience, but Dewey's concern is with nature as it discloses itself most fully. I have already dealt with the most fundamental question at issue here (on p. 22). However, some further remarks in the same vein would not be out of place. Dewey has a sustained argument in defense of "the social" as a metaphysical category. It is such a category precisely *because* it is inclusive of physical, vital, and "mental" phenomena. Dewey's argument holds that the more numerous and varied the interactions in which a thing participates, the more we know of it; in more inclusive interactions things take on "new properties by release of potentialities previously confined because of absence of full interaction."[86] He further contends that the adequacy of "metaphysical description and understanding" is judged by "the extent to which that account is based upon taking things in the widest

---

[84] "Experience and Existence: A Comment," p. 713.

[85] Hook, *op. cit.*, p. 170.

[86] *Philosophy and Civilization*, p. 85.

and most complex scale of associations open to observation."[87] In social interactions the physical, vital, and mental enter into distinctively new and more complex interactions, hitherto unexampled. Thus "the social" eminently fulfills the criteria of metaphysical description.

The general point is simply that nature, so far as we know it, achieves the fullest realization of powers and properties in human life. It is not, be it noted, that the physical, vital, and mental

> have no describable *existence* outside the social, but that in so far as they appear and operate outside of that large interaction which forms the social they do not reveal that full force and import with which it is the traditional business of philosophy to occupy itself.[88]

Dewey's concern with metaphysics is clearly affirmed in an article of 1937, "Whitehead's Philosophy." He writes,

> Mr. Whitehead says that the task of philosophy is to frame 'descriptive generalizations of experience.' In this, an empiricist should agree without reservation. Descriptive generalization of experience is the goal of any intelligent empiricism.[89]

It is well to note here that naturalistic metaphysics obviously is neither cosmology nor dialectical speculation. Neither is it concerned to describe the peculiarities of every numerically distinct event that might happen to occur in the universe. To discriminate *only* those traits which are generic to *every* individual event in the universe – regardless of whether experience is manifest or not – would be to return to old-fashioned reductive metaphysics. Or (inasmuch as most events occur independently of experience), it would be to formulate an extremely uninteresting metaphysics. Dewey's metaphysics takes the more enlightening and useful form of discriminating the traits of nature generic to all occasions of primary experience.

In all Dewey's work the metaphysical basis is present and operative. In connection with the immediate concern with value theory, I do not contend that Dewey was thoroughly systematic in grounding his thinking in metaphysics. It is abundantly clear, however, that Dewey's work continually discloses, implicitly and

---

[87] *Ibid.*, p. 78.

[88] *Ibid.*, p. 86.

[89] Reprinted in *Problems of Men*, p. 410.

explicitly, that his thinking about the moral life was throughout informed with his naturalistic metaphysics – as well as with his philosophy of nature. In the chapters that follow, I will attempt to give this generalization something of its full meaning.

CHAPTER II

Man and Nature

When a reflective person considers the nature of human good and the conditions which attend it, a main determinant of his conclusions will be certain assumptions about the status of man in nature. Indeed, such assumptions will have decisive bearing on the conclusions regarding the very nature of value and the means of its secure attainment. As the history of philosophy profusely illustrates, moral systems are rooted in these basic conceptions; and thus it is these latter which impart much of the distinctive character to such systems.

The present chapter is concerned with some of Dewey's main findings relative to those conceptions which are basic to moral philosophy. What I will treat of this subject are three fundamental issues which Dewey analyzes at length. I will consider in order: 1) the continuity of experience and nature, 2) Dewey's analysis of the so-called mind-body problem and other issues linked with it, 3) the relation between individual and society. This will provide a rather general characterization of man's status in nature: dealing primarily with man at large, as it were.

It is clear that this kind of analysis belongs to what has been characterized herein as philosophy of nature. Dewey endeavors to examine and to understand these features of existence *as* interactions, as man functioning in and with nature. This attempt includes, of course, the discrimination of the variables and the instrumentalities of these interactions; and insofar as these analyses are successful, the concept of nature is enriched. More germane to the subject of this book, the analyses of these interactions will go far to show how various specific evaluations arise in nature and how they can in great measure be enlightened.

Dewey's treatment of these three fundamental interactions

includes a great deal of metaphysical analysis as well. Thus my discussion will include consideration of what, specifically, are the generic traits of experience and the use Dewey makes of them. Their nature and significance will be indicated in connection with the analyses of particular issues. (Their unique bearing on theory of value will not be analyzed until the next chapter.)

Relative to the three topics I have indicated are two further matters which will receive attention throughout: 1) the role Dewey assigns to science in these inquiries; 2) the significance of these issues for moral philosophy. The way in which these matters determine his inquiries into moral problems will receive more thorough notice in the balance of these chapters.

1. Experience and Nature

The notion of the continuity of experience and nature has already received some attention. What I mainly intend here is to elaborate my earlier discussion somewhat and, more important, to point out the moral implications of this continuity. Still, my discussion of experience and nature will be partially limited: Some issues which might deserve greater amplification will receive their appropriate consideration in the succeeding discussion of mind, body, and nature.

Were anyone to judge the matter without benefit of certain philosophical theories, the continuity of experience and nature would be readily admitted – indeed, insisted upon – and the continuity of experience and science would be open to no serious doubt. Yet philosophers have created dualisms, which in some traditions have enjoyed virtually axiomatic status. These dualisms are a consequence, as explained earlier, of arbitrary simplifications of nature. In other words, the implicit metaphysics in these positions is woefully inadequate. These dualisms are the consequence of an implied or explicit metaphysics which attributes but one generic trait to nature, leaving out at least four.

We have seen that subjectivism-intellectualism implies that the true nature of objective reality is exclusively in objects of cognition. In Dewey's metaphysical terminology, this is assigning the trait of "the stable" to nature, while denying, at least, "the precarious," "quality," "ends," and "histories." The stable alone is assigned to nature because philosophers have been insufficiently attentive to experience – failing to see how objects of cognition develop out of initially indeterminate situations in primary experience.

In rather summary fashion, the character of these traits will be indicated. Somewhat more will be said in the next section. The stable, in Dewey's thought, refers to whatever in the situation has a known structure, a cognitive status: "knowledge of the recurrent and stable, of facts and laws."[1] This trait implies, of course, that nature possesses relations and knowable structures. These are found in all situations of experience. But there are also in any situation, as experience attests, precarious elements; that is, there are confused, doubtful, and unpredictable features of the situation, with all the hazards to existence which these entail.

> A feature of existence which is emphasized by cultural phenomena is the precarious and the perilous. . . . Man find himself living in an aleatory world; his existence involves, to put it baldly, a gamble. The world is a scene of risk; it is uncertain, unstable, uncannily unstable. Its dangers are irregular, inconstant, not to be counted upon as to their times and seasons. Although persistent, they are sporadic, episodic. . . . Plague, famine, failure of crops, disease, death, defeat in battle, are always just around the corner, and so are abundance, strength, victory, festival and song. Luck is proverbially both good and bad in its distributions.[2]

The precarious (or contingent) exists because any object or condition is connected at some point with still further objects and conditions which are beyond our knowledge and control:

> The visible is set in the invisible; and in the end what is unseen decides what happens in the seen; the tangible rests precariously on the untouched and the ungrasped. The contrast and the potential maladjustment of the immediate, the conspicuous and focal phase of things, with those indirect and hidden factors which determine the origin and career of what is present, are indestructible features of any and every experience.[3]

Although the precarious is an obvious fact of experience, failure to acknowledge its full reality is almost universal in traditional philosophies. Hence what might seem a relatively trivial observation of experience is actually of great significance, because from such instances of selective emphasis stem the most decisive errors in philosophy.

---

[1] *Experience and Nature*, p. xi.

[2] *Ibid.*, p. 41.

[3] *Ibid.*, pp. 43-4.

> Upon their surface, the reports of the world which form our different philosophies are various to the point of contrariness. . . . These radical oppositions in philosophers suggest however another consideration. They suggest that all the different philosophies have a common premise. Variant philosophies may be looked at as different ways of supplying recipes for denying to the universe the character of contingency which it possesses so integrally that its denial leaves the reflecting mind without a clue, and puts subsequent philosophizing at the mercy of temperament, interest, and local surroundings. . . . The form assumed by the denial is, most frequently, that striking division into a superior true realm of being and lower illusory, insignificant or phenomenal realm which characterizes metaphysical systems as unlike as those of Plato and Democritus, St. Thomas and Spinoza, Aristotle and Kant, Descartes and Comte, Haeckel and Mrs. Eddy.[4]

The precarious and stable exist together in any situation; and it is precisely the existence of stable elements that makes it possible for men to adapt themselves to the precarious features of the environment at all. If all features of experience were exclusively and persistently precarious, life would be literally impossible. Hence the precarious traits of existence are those which are the problems, obstacles, and challenges for man, and the stable traits, the means of coping with them. It is precisely because of the omnipresence of these traits that man strives and endures, and even philosophizes:

> We live in a world which is an impressive and irresistible mixture of sufficiencies, tight completenesses, order, recurrences which make possible prediction and control, and singularities, ambiguities, uncertain possibilities, processes going on to consequences as yet indeterminate. . . . It is the intimate mixture of the stable and precarious, the fixed and the unpredictably novel, the assured and the uncertain, in existence which sets mankind upon that love of wisdom which forms philosophy.[5]

It is also true that the objects in the situation (as well as the situation as such) possess qualities. These are things taken in their immediacy. These qualities are not simply colors, sounds, tex-

---

[4] *Ibid.*, pp. 46-7; 59. The denial of full reality to the precarious originates in Greek philosophy: "With slight exaggeration, it may be said that the thoroughgoing way in which Aristotle defined, distinguished and classified rest and movement, the finished and the incomplete, the actual and potential, did more to fix tradition,. *the* genteel tradition one is tempted to add, which identifies the fixed and regular with reality of Being and the changing and hazardous with deficiency of Being than ever was accomplished by those who took the shorter path of asserting that change is illusory" *(Experience and Nature,* p. 49). Greek responsibility for modern dualisms will be discussed at greater length later on.

[5] *Ibid.*, pp. 47, 59.

tures, etc. (In fact, "simple" qualities – such as red or sweet – are perceived as a result of discrimination within a field of perception. Sensations are not the first data of perception.) The qualities of experience are more complex: objects and events are attractive or repulsive, beautiful or ugly, charming or daunting, lovable or hateful, fulfilling or defeating, and so on. Quality, too, is a generic trait of primary experience:

> In every event there is something obdurate, self-sufficient, wholly immediate, neither a relation nor an element in a relational whole, but terminal and exclusive. Here, as in so many other matters, materialists and idealists agree in an underlying metaphysics which ignores in behalf of relations and relational systems, those irreducible, infinitely plural, undefinable and indescribable qualities which a thing must *have* in order to be, and in order to be capable of becoming the subject of relations and a theme of discourse.[6]

There are also ends, conclusions, resident within any situation. The end might be a valued and anticipated outcome or simply the indifferent termination of the situation:

> We may conceive the end, the close, as due to fulfillment, perfect attainment, to satiety, or to exhaustion, to dissolution, to something having run down or given out. Being an end may be indifferently an ecstatic culmination, a matter of fact consummation, or a deplorable tragedy. Which of these things a closing or terminal object is, has nothing to do with the property of being an end.[7]

In any case – and this is the point – a qualitative change in the situation occurs to mark its distinguishable terminus. Because no state of affairs lasts forever, it is clear that ends are generic to all situations.

The fact that a situation moves – deliberately, successfully, or not – toward an end suggests still another generic trait: what Dewey calls histories, by which he refers to continuous processes of qualitative change.

> Acknowledgment of nature as a scene of incessant beginnings and endings, presents itself as the source of philosophic enlightenment. It enables thought to apprehend causal mechanisms and temporal finalities as phases of the same natural process, instead of as competitors where the gain of one is the loss of the other.[8]

---

[6] *Ibid.*, p. 85. To say that qualities are "undefinable and indescribable" refers to the fact that immediate experience is neither discursive nor cognitive; hence any conceptual description of that experience must be different than the experience in itself. When one talks about, or reflects upon, or in any way discriminates the quality of an immediate experience, that very act transforms the quality in question.

[7] *Ibid.*, p. 97.

[8] *Ibid.*, p. 98.

It is important to see that the various events which constitute a history are not discretely separated, but are discriminated parts of a continuous process. Thus the later events are a disclosure of the properties of earlier events, as these emerge in new relations and with new variables become qualitatively different. The later stages, while continuous with the earlier, have their distinctive nature and cannot be characterized as possessing nothing but the properties of earlier stages:

> Every event as such is passing into other things, in such a way that a later occurrence is an integral part of the *character* or *nature* of present existence. An "affair," *Res*, is always at issue whether it concerns chemical change, the emergence of life, language, mind or the episodes that compose human history. Each comes from something else and each when it comes has its own initial, unpredictable, immediate qualities, and its own similar terminal qualities. The later is never just resolved into the earlier. What we call resolution is merely a statement of the order by means of which we regulate the passage of an earlier into the later.[9]

The testimony of experience discloses that all things undergo qualitative transformation.[10] Histories are not cases of discrete and separate substances miraculously changing into still other such substances. There is, rather, a continuity of process marked by qualitatively different events.

It is Dewey's position that these five traits are characteristic of every situation. He insists that the generic traits of primary experience amount to these at least. The method of experience prohibits that we deny these traits of experience on the authority of a prior theory. Accordingly, once these traits are recognized, there is no justification for the argument which would separate experience and nature.

The argument for separation, as we have seen, is based on an incomplete analysis of the cognitive situation. It neglects, first of all, the precarious element in existence, which makes the situation indeterminate, creating and defining the tasks of inquiry.

---

[9] *Ibid.*, p. 111.

[10] "That even the solid earth mountains, the emblems of constancy, appear and disappear like the clouds is an old theme of moralists and poets. The fixed and unchanging being of the Democritean atom is now reported by inquirers to possess some of the traits of his non-being, and to embody a temporary equilibrium in the economy of nature's compromises and adjustments. A thing may endure *secula seculorum* and yet not be everlasting; it will crumble before the gnawing tooth of time, as it exceeds a certain measure. Every existence is an event." *(Experience and Nature,* pp. 70-1.)

The precarious elements demand that the activity of inquiry be undertaken in order that crucial features of the situation become cognitively meaningful. The very fact that this activity takes place implies that knowledge objects do not exist readymade in the situation.

The argument further neglects the fact that specific *ends* of inquiry are anticipated which dictate the way in which the features of the situation will be discriminated and manipulated. Thus, for example, in physics the immediate qualities and the terminal values of objects are ignored for considerations of causal sequences, measurements and correlations of space, time, mass, and velocity. Thus the knowledge object *qua* knowledge object (in its complete abstraction from experience) has no qualities; but this does not mean that the actual physical object in the various phases of experience is without qualities.

Clearly inquiry itself is not perceived as a history – a process of continuous change originating in a problematic situation and terminating in the possession of cognitive objects. Thus the acquisition of knowledge is seen as a discrete event, a direct grasp of reality by "the pure light of reason." (This notion of reason and its attendant feats of synthetic a priori knowledge is, obviously, not the *cause* of bad metaphysics, but the *result* of it.) When the procedures and conclusions of science are seen in their fullest context, there is no need to deny the objective reality of qualities, deposit them all in "mind," and thereupon consider experience to be exclusively of our own ideas.

Further, the objective reality of qualities should itself be regarded as the outcome of a history. Qualities are not, then, a separate realm of reality, disputing the field with scientific experience. For physical science is not a total characterization of reality and should not be regarded as fulfilling some such function. Rather it discriminates, measures, and correlates the *mechanisms* of nature; it correlates those processes of change which *terminate* in objects of experience.

> That heat is a mode of motion does not signify that heat and cold as qualitatively experienced are "unreal," but that the qualitative experience can be treated as an event measured in terms of units of velocity of movement, involving units of position and time, so that it can be connected with other events or changes similarly formulated. The test of the validity of any particular intellectual conception, measurement, or enumeration is functional, its use in making possible the

institution of interactions which yield results in control of actual experiences of observed objects.[11]

If objects which are colored, sonorous, tactile, gustatory, loved, hated, enjoyed, admired, which are attractive and repulsive, exciting, indifferent, and depressive, in all their infinitely numerous modes, are beginnings and endings of complex natural affairs, and if physical objects (defined as objects of physical science) are constituted by a mathematical-mechanical order; then physical objects instead of involving us in a predicament of having to choose between opposing claimants to reality, have precisely the characters which they should have in order to serve effectively as means for securing and avoiding immediate objects.[12]

Indeed, if qualities were unrelated to knowledge, the very notions of what knowledge is of would be embarrassingly vacuous:

Without immediate qualities those relations with which science deals , would have no footing in existence and thought would have nothing beyond itself to chew upon or dig into. Without a basis in qualitative events, the characteristic subject-matter of knowledge would be algebraic ghosts, relations that do not relate. To dispose of things in which relations terminate by calling them elements, is to discourse within a relational and logical scheme. Only if elements are more than just elements in a whole, only if they have something qualitatively their own, can a relational system be prevented from complete collapse.[13]

It would not be necessary to characterize the traits of nature precisely as Dewey does to see that the intellectualist-subjectivist position rests on unwarranted simplifications of nature. A thorough analysis of the cognitive situation could be undertaken without reference to traits *as* generic. Presumably, however, the irreducible traits of the situation are generic. Therefore, not only is an adequate metaphysics an effective instrument for criticizing such abstractions as intellectualism, but it also – and more important – is at the same time the "ground-map" which insures consistency, continuity, and integration of analysis from situation to situation. Thus metaphysics provides a unified characterization of nature which also constitutes a basis for analyzing all forms of converse of man and nature.

Naturalistic metaphysics insists on the reality of quality, but

---

[11] *The Quest for Certainty*, p. 129.

[12] *Experience and Nature*, pp. 141-2. An appraisal of the validity of Dewey's instrumentalist philosophy of science is irrelevant here. The only crucial point in this context is that physical science provides a characterization of reality as it is only *after* highly selective procedures of inquiry have been undertaken.

[13] *Ibid.*, pp. 86-7.

it falls to the sciences (primarily biology and physics) to explain what are the conditions in nature upon which the occurrences of qualities depend:

> Change the metaphysical premise: restore, that is to say, immediate qualities to their rightful position as qualities of inclusive situations, and the problems in question cease to be epistemological problems. They become specifiable scientific problems: questions, that is to say, of how such and such an event having such and such qualities actually occurs.[14]

The question of the relation of experience to nature and to science is no merely academic matter; rather, it entails issues of utmost practical consequence. These issues will be discussed in some detail in the subsequent chapters; so for the present only a rather general observation about the significance of continuity will be made. Of fundamental import in Dewey's theory of nature is his insistence that the world as disclosed by experience and the world as disclosed by science no longer present an unbridgeable dualism, but are continuous with one another. On the intellectualist point of view, the world is really nothing but a rational structure of matter in motion; while experience finds the world, by contrast, richly garbed with qualities, contingencies, histories, and ends. Thus, on the intellectualist view, if science is true, experience is false; and man is apparently condemned to dwell in two entirely separate realms. Reflective persons have found this separation unconscionable. Faced with the apparent impossibility of accepting the validity of both experience and science, many have embraced concrete experience with all its immediate values, rejecting science with all its instrumentalities. The dualism of experience and nature makes the latter something alien and foreign; man cannot feel at home in nature; he cannot with the sanction of science regard it as the medium of his existence:

> When nature was regarded as a set of mechanical interactions, it apparently lost all meaning and purpose. It glory departed. Elimination of differences of quality deprived it of its beauty. Denial to nature of all inherent longings and aspiring tendencies toward ideal ends removed nature and natural science from contact with poetry, religion and divine things. There seemed to be left only a harsh, brutal despiritualized exhibition of mechanical forces.[15]

---

[14] *Ibid.*, p. 265.

[15] *Ibid.*, p. 69.

The world disclosed by science is alien, and the sensitive soul is alienated by science. Romanticism flourishes, placing its faith in feeling, intuition, or tradition as guides to life, scorning the life of active reason. Accordingly, there is no place for intelligence as the instrument of criticism and direction and of the enrichment of the meanings of experience; and the actual conduct of affairs is managed by vested interests, prejudice, blind habit, religious authority.

> The modern world has suffered because in so many matters philosophy has offered it only an arbitrary choice between hard and fast opposites. . . . They are the logical consequences of the traditional opposition of Sense and Thought, Experience and Reason. Common sense has refused to follow both theories to their ultimate logic, and has fallen back on faith, intuition or the exigencies of practical compromise. But common sense too often has been confused and hampered instead of enlightened and directed by the philosophies proffered it by professional intellectuals. Men who are thrown back upon "common sense" when they appeal to philosophy for some general guidance are likely to fall back on routine, the force of some personality, strong leadership or on the pressure of momentary circumstances.[16]

Goethe's response to Holbach's *System of Nature* exemplifies the dilemma which this dualism has persistently occasioned:

> A system of nature was announced; and therefore we hoped to learn really something of nature – our idol. Physics and chemistry, descriptions of heaven and earth, natural history and anatomy, with much else, had now for years, and up to the last day, constantly directed us to the great, adorned world; and we would willingly have heard both particulars and generals about suns and stars, planets and moons, mountains, valleys, rivers and seas, with all that live and move in them. . . . But how hollow and empty did we feel in this melancholy, atheistical half-night, in which earth vanished with all its images, heaven with all its stars. There was to be matter in motion from all eternity; and by this motion, right and left and in every direction, without anything further, it was to produce the infinite phenomena of existence. Even all this we should have allowed to pass, if our author, out of his moved matter, had really built up the world before our eyes. But he seemed to know as little about nature as we did; for, having set up some general ideas, he quits them at once, for the sake of changing that which appears as higher than nature, or as a higher nature within nature, into material, heavy nature, which is moved, indeed, but without direction or form – and thus he fancies he has gained a great deal.
>
> If, after all, this book had done us some harm, it was this – that we took a hearty dislike to all philosophy, and especially metaphysics, and remained in that

---

[16] *Reconstruction in Philosophy* (Enlarged ed.; Boston: The Beacon Press, 1959), pp. 99-100.

> dislike; while, on the other hand, we threw ourselves into living knowledge, experience, action, and poetizing, with all the more liveliness and passion.[17]

This alienation from nature and the consequent disregard for intelligence is avoided when the dualism of experience and nature is exposed as a philosophic phantom.

> A philosophic reconstruction which would relieve men of having to choose between an impoverished and truncated experience on one hand and an artificial and impotent reason on the other would relieve human effort from the heaviest intellectual burden it has to carry.[18]

And Dewey says of *Experience and Nature:*

> I believe that the method of empirical naturalism presented in this volume provides the way, and the only way – although of course no two thinkers will travel it in just the same fashion – by which one can freely accept the standpoint and conclusions of modern science: the way by which we can be genuinely naturalistic and yet maintain cherished values, provided they are critically clarified and reinforced.[19]

2. Mind, Body, and Nature

Like the dualism of experience and nature, the separation of mind and body stemming from Descartes is a failure of metaphysics; and all of the philosophical assumptions which lead to the dualism are eliminated by metaphysical analysis. Moreover, beliefs about the subjectivity of meanings and of so-called mental processes are also rejected as a consequence of the analysis of "mind" as a joint operation or organism and environment – as the functioning of an inclusive situation.

Dewey holds, however, that belief in the mind-body dualism is not primarily a consequence of philosophical reflection, but is, rather, a reflex of cultural conditions. The philosophical formulations of mind and body as separate substances are in part a response to cultural conditions and in part a reinforcement to them. Accordingly, there is much that could be indicated regarding Dewey's insights into the social background of this dualism. The discussion of both the cultural background and implications of the dualistic position perhaps most appropriately belongs to the analysis of man and society. Hence a very brief account of

---

[17] Goethe, *Dichtung und Wahrheit*, Bk. XI, Oxenford tr. (quoted in Randall, *The Making of the Modern Mind*, p. 398).

[18] *Reconstruction in Philosophy*, p. 101.

[19] *Experience and Nature*, pp. ix-x.

them will be given later in the chapter. For the present I will provide only a preliminary statement of Dewey's argument in this connection, proceeding rather directly to the metaphysics underlying the explicit philosophical formulation of the mind-body problem.

To put the matter most generally, philosophers come to regard the individual mind as unrelated to nature when social conditions are such to make the individual *feel* unrelated and behave as if unrelated, or are such to make it politically expedient to regard the individual as unrelated. These conditions are reinforced by the Christian dogma of the essentially individual soul.

All of these conditions were eminently present in early modern history. The political and economic restructuring of western Europe put traditional social bonds and allegiances in turmoil; social reformers and revolutionaries, seeking the pivot and independent force with which to dislodge the "natural order" of archaic institutions, seized upon a concept of the individual as a being not essentially constituted by the conditions of his existence. In addition to this and to Christian dualism, when the philosopher confronts the fact of the new science, there is no further obstacle to an explicit and thoroughgoing isolation of the ego from nature. Referring to these social developments, Dewey says,

> The resource which offered itself was to place the mind of the individual as such in contrast to both nature and institutions. This historic fact, reinforced with the conspicuous assertion of medievalism that the individual soul is the ultimate end and ultimate subject of salvation or damnation, affords, it seems to me, the background and source of the isolation of the ego, the thinking self, in all philosophy influenced by either the new science or Protestantism. Descartes as well as Berkeley uses "self" as an equivalent of "mind," and does so spontaneously, as a matter of course, without attempt at argument and justification. If the given science of nature [Scholasticism] and given positive institutions expressed arbitrary prejudice, unintelligent custom and chance episodes, where could or should mind be found except in the independent and self-initiated activities of individuals? Wholesale revolt against tradition led to the illusion of equally wholesale isolation of mind as something wholly individual.[20]

From a technical philosophical point of view, this isolation is

[20] *Ibid.*, p. 224.

justified by interpreting the new science in a way which discredits Aristotelian metaphysics:

As long as the Aristotelian metaphysical doctrine persisted that nature is an ordered series from lower to higher of potentialities and actualizations, it was possible to conceive of the organic body as normally the highest term in a physical series and the lowest term in a psychical series. It occupied just that intermediate zone where, in being the actualization of the potentialities of physical bodies, body was also potentiality for manifestation of their ideal actualities. Aside from moral and religious questions, there was in medieval thought no special problem attaching to the relation of mind to body. It was just one case of the universal principle of potentiality as the substrate of ideal actuality. But when the time came when the moral and religious associations of spirit, soul, and body persisted in full vigor, while the classic metaphysics of the potential and actual fell into disrepute, the full burden of the question of the relation of the body, nature and man, of mind, spirit, and matter, was concentrated in the particular problem of the relation of the body and soul. When men ceased to interpret and explain facts in terms of potentiality and actuality, and resorted to that of causality, mind and matter stood over against one another in stark unlikeness; there were no intermediates to shade gradually the black of body into the white of spirit.[21]

The Aristotelian tradition persists, however, in Cartesian thought in a certain insidious way. For Descartes adopts the Greek theory of knowledge, the "spectator" theory. This theory, when held *with* the conclusions of the new science and *without* Greek metaphysics, leads inevitably to dualism. Inasmuch as the Greek theory of knowledge has had a decisive bearing on most of the problems plaguing modern philosophy – including fundamental problems of value – a brief outline of the theory is warranted. In the Greek view, knowing is direct grasp or beholding of the forms of things, totally unrelated to practical action:

Rational and necessary knowledge was treated, as in the celebrations of it by Aristotle, as an ultimate, self-sufficient and self-enclosed form of self-originated and self-conducted activity. It was ideal and eternal, independent of change and hence of the world in which men act and live, the world we experience perceptibly and practically.[22]

The knower contemplates a pure reality which is not affected by the activity of knowing:

Knowledge . . . is thought to be concerned with a region of being which is fixed in itself. Being eternal and unalterable, human knowing is not to make any difference in it. It can be approached through the medium of the apprehensions and

[21] *Ibid.*, pp. 250-1.

[22] *The Quest for Certainty*, pp. 17-8.

demonstrations of thought, or by some other organ of mind, which does nothing to the real, except just to know it.[23]

Thus pure knowing and practical arts correspond to separate realms or distinct levels of being:

"Pure activity" was sharply marked off from practical action, the latter, whether in the industrial or the fine arts, in morals or in politics, was concerned with an inferior region of Being in which change rules, and which accordingly has Being only by courtesy, for it manifests deficiency of sure footing in Being by the very fact of change. It is infected with *non*-being.[24]

This general theory of knowing has its origins in the belief that there are in nature pure, eternal forms, which exist antecedently to and independently of both their actualization in physical objects and the activity of knowing. This is True Being, ultimate reality; it is to be distinguished from that which is not true being: the transient and imperfect – privation of being. This changeless realm is the standard by which both to know and evaluate the world of mere process.

This ontological division, in turn, has its origins in the characteristic experience of Greek culture.[25] The Greek preoccupation with aesthetic experience, together with a rigid class structure which effected a sharp separation of overt activity from both rational and aesthetic contemplation, appear to be the proximate causes of the ontological division. Celebrating what is final and perfect, the aristocratic greeks were innocent of any notion that human contrivance was instrumental in creating the forms embodied in things of contemplation.

Labor, production, did not seem to create form, it dealt with matter or changing things so as to furnish an occasion for incarnation of antecedent forms in matter.[26]

---

[23] *Ibid.*, p. 21.

[24] *Ibid.*, p. 18.

[25] It would be extremely interesting to discuss in detail Dewey's remarkable insights concerning the effects of Greek life on Greek philosophy. Examining the roots of modern philosophy in Greek culture is one of Dewey's recurrent endeavors. See especially *Reconstruction in Philosophy,* Chs. I and V; *Experience and Nature,* Chs. Two and Three; and *The Quest for Certainty,* Ch. I. Evidently the most fundamental cultural fact was Greek religion. It provided an imaginative and moral account of nature; and so also, following the religious tradition, did Greek philosophy. The result was the unwitting transformation of moral preference into a description of existence. This took the form of identifying the good with a presumed perfect, necessary, changless and self-sufficient being, which, significantly, Aristotle identified with the divine.

[26] *Experience and Nature,* p. 91.

When this experience receives its philosophical formulation, objects of knowledge are thought to exist as such and without benefit of contriving activity. Accordingly, Plato's and Aristotle's theory of knowledge (as Dewey interprets it) involved a separation of experience and knowledge. In their conception, antecedently existing forms – not experimental operations – make knowledge and knowing possible.

> For the Greek community was marked by a sharp separation of servile workers and free men of leisure, which meant a division between acquaintance with matters of fact and contemplative appreciation, between unintelligent practice and unpractical intelligence, between affairs of change and efficiency – or instrumentality – and of rest and enclosure – finality. Experience afforded therefore no model for a conception of experimental inquiry and of reflection efficacious in action. In consequence, the sole notability, intelligibility, of nature was conceived to reside in objects that were ends, since they set limits to change. Changing things were not capable of being known on the basis of relationship to one another, but only on the basis of their relationship to objects beyond change, because marking its limit, and immediately precious.[27]

Thus were created the fundamental dualisms in Greek philosophy between sense and thought, opinion and knowledge. Derivative of a certain cultural experience, these are at the bottom of all modern dualisms. The Greeks are responsible for

> the introduction into nature of a split in Being itself, its division into some things which are inherently defective, changing, relational, and other things which are inherently perfect, permanent, self-possessed. Other dualisms such as that between sensuous appetite and rational thought, between the particular and the universal, between the mechanical and the telic, between experience and science, between matter and mind, are but the reflections of this primary metaphysical dualism.[28]

The Greek position is incorporated into the Christian tradition through Hellenistic philosophies and thus becomes embedded in western thought:

> Through this taking over of the conception of knoweldge as Contemplative into the dominant religion of Europe, multitudes were affected who were totally innocent of theoretical philosophy. There was bequeathed to generations of thinkers as an unquestioned axiom the idea that knowledge is intrinsically a mere beholding or viewing of reality – the spectator conception of knowledge. So deeply engrained was this idea that it prevailed for centuries after the actual progress of science had demonstrated that knowedge is power to transform the

---

[27] *Ibid.*, pp. 93-4.

[28] *Ibid.*, pp. 123-4.

world, and centuries after the practice of effective knowledge had adopted the method of experimentation.[29]

Hence,

Special theories of knowledge differ enormously from one another. Their quarrels with one another fill the air. . . . But they all make one common assumption. They all hold that the operation of inquiry excludes any element of practical activity that enters into the construction of the object known. Strangely enough this is true of idealism as of realism, of theories of synthetic activity as of those of passive receptivity. For according to them "mind" constructs the known object not in any observable way, or by means of practical overt acts having a temporal quality, but by some occult internal operation.[30]

It was this Greek theory of knowledge which combined with the new science. The consequence of this amalgam was that the cognitive objects of physics – matter in motion, quantitatively described – were regarded as the only objective reality. Over against this, impotent and inconsequential for nature, stood mind. For Aristotle, mind had been continuous with nature; and while for Aristotle there was in nature the active intellect, or *nous,* which makes pure knowledge possible, in moderns this power is taken to be subjective. There must be some special power or faculty possessed by the subject which effects this direct grasp of the antecedently existing structure of reality:

We are given to referring the beginnings of subjectivity to Descartes, with his *penseé* as the indubitable certainty, or to Locke with his simple idea as immediate object. Technically or with respect to later dialectical developments, this reference is correct enough. But historically it is wrong. Descartes' thought is the *nous* of classic tradition forced inwards because physical science had extruded it from its object. Its internality is a logical necessity of the attempt to reconcile the new science with the old tradition, not a thing intrinsically important. Similarly, Locke's simple idea is the classic Idea, Form or Species dislodged from nature and compelled to take refuge in mind.[31]

This negative condition, that the processes of search, investigation, reflection, involved in knowledge relate to something having prior being, fixes once for all the main characters attributed to mind, and to the organs of knowing. They *must* be outside what is known, so as not to interact with the object to be known.[32]

---

[29] *Reconstruction in Philosophy,* p. 112.

[30] *The Quest for Certainty,* pp. 22-3.

[31] *Experience and Nature,* p. 229.

[32] *The Quest for Certainty,* p. 23.

Thus, with qualities dismissed from objective reality and a special faculty needed for knowing, "mind" is created: repository of experience and agent of cognition.

This "abstract and technical" Cartesian dualism Dewey regards as in itself an "empty formalism," but it "found prepared for it a rich empirical field with which to blend," giving it "concrete meaning and substance."[33]

> The formalism and unreality of the problem remains, however, in the theories which have been offered as its "solutions." They range from the materialism of Hobbes, the apparatus of soul, pineal glands, animal spirits of Descartes, to interactionism, pre-established harmony, occasionalism, parallelism, pan-psychic idealism, epiphenomenalism, and the *elan vital* – a portentious array.[34]

The reason the "solutions" have preserved the "formalism and unreality" of the mind-body problem is that they all leave intact the Cartesian metaphysics of nature; they do not succeed in restoring the integrity of philosophical theory and gross experience, and philosophy continues to be baffled by the impossible separations of mind and matter, experience and reason, value and science. And philosophers, accepting these separations as axiomatic, must contrive (fantastic) theories to explain the obvious facts of experience. All such schemes accept "assumptions which first make a division where none exists, and then resort to an artifice to restore the connection which has been willfully destroyed."[35]

These assumptions *create* the mind-body problem, the solution to which is thereafter thought to be the veritable philosopher's stone itself. But the connection between mind and body is not (so it will be seen) a philosophical riddle, but a subject matter of empirical scientific inquiry. The genuine *philosophical* problem is, to speak properly, metaphysical:

> The diversity of solutions together with the dialectical character of each doctrine which render it impregnable to empirical attack, suggest that the trouble lies not so much in the solutions, as in the factors which determine statement of the problem. If this be so, the way out of the snarl is a reconsideration of the conceptions in virtue of which the problem exists. And these conceptions have primarily nothing to do with mind-body; they have to do with underlying metaphysical issues: – the denial of quality in general to natural events; the ignoring in

---

[33] *Experience and Nature,* p. 252.

[34] *Ibid.*

[35] *Ibid.*, p. 283.

particular of temporal quality and the dogma of the superior reality of "causes."[36]

The task of showing how metaphysical analysis does away with the controlling assumptions underlying this dualism has already been begun in pointing out how such analysis removes the basis for separating experience and nature: the necessity for removing qualities from nature to a presumed private abode in "mind" has been dissolved. Awareness of qualities is not a thing apart, but the terminus of natural processes in an inclusive situation. Much of the remaining analysis is all but explicit in what has been discussed thus far. The reality of qualities must be recognized. Also, any breach between experience and knowledge must be denied. This denial is a consequence of identifying the actual traits of experiences of inquiry and knowing and of recognizing that these traits are part of a history. That is, thinking and knowing are processes which begin with experience, in a situation where precarious or indeterminate elements demand the activity of inquiry, which itself involves active working with the materials of the situation: determining the specific constituents of the situation, settling on purposes, framing hypotheses, experimenting, testing – whether carried on crudely or professionally.

> A philosophy which accepts the denotative or empirical method accepts at full value the fact that reflective thinking transforms confusion, ambiguity and discrepancy into illumination, definiteness and consistency. But it also points to the contextual situation in which thinking occurs. It notes that that starting point is the actually *problematic*, and that the problematic phase resides in some actual and specifiable situation.
>
> It notes that the means of converting the dubious into the assured, and the incomplete into the determinate, is use of assured and established things, which are just as empirical and as indicative of the nature of experienced things as is the uncertain. . . . Generalizing from such observations, empirical philosophy perceives that thinking is a continuous process of temporal re-organization within one and the same world of experienced things, not a jump from the latter world into one of objects constituted once for all by thought.[37]

And the method of experience also requires that we accept these descriptive traits of thinking as indicative of the traits of nature:

---

[36] *Ibid.*, p. 252.

[37] *Ibid.*, pp. 67-8.

Reflection occurs only in situations qualified by uncertainty, alternatives, questioning, search, hypotheses, tentative trials or experiments which test the worth of thinking. A naturalistic metaphysics is bound to consider reflection as itself a natural event occurring *within* nature because of traits of the latter.[38]

The obvious traits of thinking, Dewey points out, include such things as "uncertainty, ambiguity, alternatives, inquiring, search, selection, experimental reshaping of external conditions."[39] Thus truth is not just antecedently "there" in nature to be witnessed; and the brute facts do not speak for themselves. Neither does the mind alone grasp eternal essences of being. The nature of valid knowing, is, rather, of a radically different character. It will be instructive to provide a brief sketch of the main features of this character, as Dewey sees it.

It is, first of all, altogether misleading to speak of a permanent structure of being; and the notion of an unchanging realm of being transcending the "realm" of change is wholly gratuitous. So far as all the sciences can determine, structures of all kinds are always subject to change and do indeed undergo change. The permanent and fixed, so far as we know, are ratios of change. That is, processes (themselves subject to change) interact with each other; and by means of experimental inquiry the scientist can determine with considerable accuracy how specified variations in one process correlate with specified variations in related processes. What we know as the outcome of such inquiries are interactions, functional relations – not an independent structure. We know, for example, that bodies attract each other directly with their mass and inversely as the square of the distance between them. This formula does not provide the form or essence of any object or set of objects; it simply expresses a relation of change. In addition, there is no need to postulate a realm of pure being to account for either the nature or possession of this know-

[38] *Ibid.*, p. 68. The activity of thinking to be sure, does involve what we call insight or intuition, but intuition can be false and misleading; it does not possess its own credentials of truth; and it is inseparable from the other phases of thinking. "In any case, the background of organized meanings can alone convert the new situation from the obscure into the clear and luminous. When old and new jump together, like sparks when the poles are adjusted, there is intuition. This latter is thus neither an act of pure intellect in apprehending rational truth nor a Crocean grasp by spirit of its own images and states." *(Art as Experience,* p. 266.)

[39] *Experience and Nature,* p. 69

ledge. The means by which these relations are determined are wholly experimental.

It is, however, no simple matter to determine these relations. We cannot know a priori the way one process varies with another, or even if processes are in fact related. To make such determinations requires – among other things – the institution of precise experimental conditions and the most exacting control and measurement of variables. The institution of conditions and manipulation of variables is determined by the hypothesis; and it is precisely in the institution of conditions and their controlled variation that the hypothesis is tested. The hypothesis is not in itself a case of knowledge. It is an imaginative idea subject to acceptance, rejection, or revision – depending on the outcome of experiment. The hypothesis states a relation between specified initial conditions and their expected consequences. Provided the hypothesis is confirmed, the knowledge acquired is exclusively concerned with the relations between conditions and their outcome, as expressed by the hypothesis.

To say this much is to indicate that inquiry is a form of directed and overt *activity.* Of course, the nature of this activity varies from science to science; and the manipulation of variables can sometimes be replaced by the manipulation of means of observation and measurement, or by signs representing objective processes. And, indeed, in rudimentary inquiries, perhaps only such simple activities as moving the body and looking may be involved. In every case, however, meaningful inquiry implies activity of some kind in selective interaction with materials of primary experience.

> There is no inquiry that does not involve the making of *some* change in environing conditions. . . . Even in the prescientific stage, an individual moves head, eyes, often the entire body, in order to determine the conditions to be taken account of in forming a judgment; such movements effect a change in environmental relations. Active pressure by touch, the acts of pushing, pulling, pounding, and manipulating to find out what things "are like" is an even more overt approach to scientific experimentation.[40]

It is evident, moreover, that human choice and contrivance play an indispensable part in determining the conceptual forms in which knowledge is stated and organized. These conceptual

---

[40] *Logic: The Theory of Inquiry,* p. 34.

forms are a function of inquiry. Nature apart from man has, to be sure, its regularities and uniformities, but it is only when events in nature enter into specific inquiries that concepts are formulated which are suitable for the subject matter at hand and for the aims of the peculiar inquiry.

> Scientific conceptions are not a revelation of prior and independent reality. They are a system of hypotheses, worked out under conditions of definite test, by means of which our intellectual and practical traffic with nature is rendered freer, more secure and more significant.[41]

The crucial issue in the present context is, of course, whether the notions of rationalistic knowing and objects of being, with their implied dualisms, have a warranted foundation. And Dewey concludes most emphatically that they do not, their only support consisting in an obviously mistaken analysis of the process of inquiry and knowing. It is difficult to imagine how the objects of knowledge acquired in the sciences could be developed in any way other than that of the inquirer actively involving himself in the processes of change under investigation. In addition, rationalistic "knowledge" – unlike that of the sciences – has proved notoriously unreliable in practice, incapable of settling disagreements of fact, anything but self-evident, and utterly impotent to lead to or control specifiable objects of experience. Hence pure forms of being seem to be simply gratuitous hypotheses. The entire issue can be stated tersely:

> If . . . it can be shown that the actual procedures by which the most authentic and dependable knowledge is attained have completely surrendered the separation of knowing and doing; if it can be shown that overtly executed operations of interaction are requisite to obtain the knowledge called scientific, the chief fortress of the classic philosophical tradition crumbles into dust.[42]

Dewey's repeated claim that knowing necessarily involves do-

---

[41] *The Quest for Certainty*, p. 165. The fundamental thesis of Dewey's *Logic* is that logical forms of all kinds are precisely those that develop in the process of inquiry: they are those forms that are functionally successful in inquiry. (See especially Chapter XIX in *Logic*.)

Dewey's position is necessarily given in great brevity in my text. For my immediate purposes, it has been sufficient to indicate his general point of view. An excellent summary analysis is to be found in Nagel's "Dewey's Reconstruction of Logical Theory" in *The Philosopher of the Common Man* (Copyright by Conference on Methods in Philosophy; New York: G.P. Putnam's Sons, 1940).

[42] *The Quest for Certainty*, p. 79.

ing is, in essence, simply to discard the spectator theory and to admit that knowledge is a result of inquiry, which involves selective operations on existential material, or else on written signs which designate such material; and knowing always involves experimental test. Clearly, the need for a special faculty for direct grasp of an antecedently given structure is dismissed; for knowledge is not acquired in that way and knowledge is not of that character. In dismissing the need for a special faculty, we dismiss with it the notion of an independent thinking substance, set in radical juxtaposition to its subject matter.

What has been done so far in this section is to show how the mixture of science and bad metaphysics produced modern dualisms. This unhappy mixture is fundamental in modern philosophy. But there remain further stages in Dewey's analysis of the metaphysics of dualism, and I will deal with these next.

Due to the fallacy of selective emphasis, the dualistic position disregards historic continuity and treats a phase of a continuous process as a separate substance with a being and a reality apart from that process. Specifically, experience and mind are isolated from the very conditions of their existence. An examination of Dewey's argument here requires a further elaboration of the traits "history" and "ends."

History is a generic trait of nature. This means that there are no things that are not parts of a continuous process; or, to put the matter differently, all things have histories, in which they undergo change and exhibit what they are in various interactions. Things are events in histories.

> There are no changes that do not enter into an affair, *Res*, and there is no affair that is not bounded and thereby marked off as a state or condition. . . . Such is the unbiased evidence of experience in gross, and such in effect is the conclusion of recent physics as far as a layman can see.[43]

This seems to be Dewey's way of saying that there are no discrete substances with inherent essences in nature, but that all things of human experience are known to come into existence from antecedent conditions and in interaction with other things undergo processes of change which distinguish them qualitatively from their initial character. This does seem to be a fact of experience and one to which contemporary physical theory attests.

---

[43] *Experience and Nature,* p. 101.

This notion of history entails also that ends are always ends *of a process.* They are not discontinuous substances or events existing independently in nature. Nor are they absolute endings; they are, rather, discriminated in experience as the terminus of a distinguishable state of affairs and as the beginning of a further state of affairs. If this notion be denied, the obvious connection of events must either be ignored or be accounted for by a notion of causation or relation which has no empirical warrant.

It should be noted further that endings are qualitative. Of the physical universe as it is described in physics alone, the notion of endings could have no meaning. An ending is only what is distinguished as such in experience; and what is thus distinguished is some event which for some purpose is marked off qualitatively from other events. This could be the end of an era or the end of an affair, the consummation of graduate study, running out of money or into a telephone pole.

A fact of importance to be recalled concerning ends is that none possess more reality or being than others. There is, in other words, no ontological hierarchy of ends. Any ranking of ends can only be according to their desirability, but such ranking does not make a quality more or less an end *as* end, *as* terminus. On this analysis, mind, as an eventual function, cannot be elevated to a higher ontological sphere of some kind. Finally, when we recall also that a history for Dewey means not simply continuity of process, but a process of *qualitative* change, then it is clear that the intellectualist-subjectivist metaphysics allows for neither ends nor histories in nature. On the latter view, qualities – hence ends and histories – are only something in the mind, and whose apparent implications with nature are totally unaccountable. This metaphysics positively forbids, therefore, that the qualitatively distinctive things called mind and experience be regarded as eventual functions – as the outcome of an inclusive set of natural processes.

As Dewey sees it, the failure to recognize the naturalistic traits of history and ends is not exclusively in the denial of quality to nature. It is also in assigning superior reality to causes, either efficient or final. Thus a spiritualistic metaphysics takes thought or thinking as the highest end or reality: in the Aristotelian sense, a final cause – that for the sake of which nature exists. A mechanistic world view, on the other hand, may be the consequence of the philosopher's being impressed by the transiency, instability, and waywardness of consciousness. Thus he regards material substance as possessing superior reality.

> One theory makes matter account for the existence of mind; the other regards happenings that precede the appearance of mind as preparations made for the sake of mind in a sense of preparation that is alleged to explain the occurrence of these antecedents. Mechanistic metaphysics calls attention to the fact that the latter occurrence could not have taken place without the earlier; that given the earlier, the latter was bound to follow. Spiritualistic metaphysics calls attention to the fact that the earlier, material affairs, prepare the way for vital and ideal affairs, lead up to them; promote them. Both statements are equally true descriptively; neither statement is true in the explanatory and metaphysical meaning imputed to it.[44]

Whether the focus of attention be final or efficient cause, one phase of a history is isolated, and that phase is by itself regarded as a different kind of being, outside the history itself. Accordingly, mind and matter are totally separate things. For the materialist, mind is regarded as an extraneous, supervening, ghostly phenomenon – a sort of by-product, irrelevant to the traits of natural processes. The spiritualist, by contrast, is above the concerns of the "material" world, thus neglecting the instrumentalities determining the very character of the so-called mental life.

Yet both positions must perforce recognize some connection between mind and matter; so it must be asserted that matter "causes" mind or that matter "exists for the sake of" mind. Because these are regarded as separated kinds of things, resort is taken to occult notions of causality:

> The notion of causal explanation involved in both conceptions implies a breach in the continuity of historic process; the gulf created has then to be bridged by an emission or transfer of force. If one starts with the assumption that mind and matter are two separate things, while the evidence forces one to see that they are connected, one has no option save to attribute the power to make the connection, to carry from one to the other, to one or the other of the two things involved.[45]

The same fallacy is common to both views:

> namely, the breaking up of a continuity of historical change into two separate

[44] *Ibid.*, p. 273.

[45] *Ibid.*, pp. 273-4.

parts, together with the necessity which follows from the breaking-in-two for some device by which to bring them together again.[46]

And the fallacy is metaphysical:

The problem is neither psychological nor epistemological. It is metaphysical or existential. It is whether existence consists of events, or is possessed of temporal quality, characterized by beginning, process and ending. If so, the affair of later and earlier, however important it is for particular practical matters, is indifferent to a theory of valuation of existence. It is as arbitrary to assign complete reality to atoms at the expense of mind and conscious experience as it is to make a rigid separation between here and there in space. Distinction is genuine and for some purposes necessary. But it is not a distinction of kinds or degrees of reality.[47]

The original error leading to the dualistic position was in failing to note the actual traits of thinking and inquiry and hence the actual traits of nature. Thus the Cartesian must burden himself with the notion of a substance in nature which yet cannot interact with nature. Rather than consult the evidence of experience and identify thinking as something man does with nature and possessing its distinctive historical sequences, the dualist postulates without empirical warrant a separate kind of substance *in which* this process of thinking takes place:

The idea that matter, life and mind represent separate kinds of Being is a doctrine which springs, as so many philosophic errors have sprung, from a substantiation of eventual functions.[48]

That to which both mind and matter belong is the complex of events that constitute nature. This becomes a mysterious *tertium quid,* incapable of designation, only when mind and matter are taken to be static structures instead of functional characters. It is a plausible prediction that if there were an interdict placed for a generation upon the use of mind, matter, consciousness as nouns, and we were obliged to use adjectives and adverbs, conscious and consciously, mental and mentally, material and physically, we should find many of our problems much simplified.[49]

Clearly, Dewey's analysis relies heavily on the notion of histories. A critic might well respond that Dewey has begged the

---

[46] *Ibid.,* p. 275.

[47] *Ibid.,* p. 110. The remarks quoted are unusually ambiguous. I take "consists of events or is possessed of temporal quality" to be providing alternative modes of stating the same notion and not to be expressing a disjunction. "Valuation of existence" does not refer to moral judgments but simply to naturalistic metaphysics.

[48] *Ibid.,* p. 261.

[49] *Ibid.,* p. 75.

question in asserting the generic character of history. Might not mind be just the thing that is not part of a history? Although such a thing is, perhaps, conceivable, it is useful to ask what positive support the notion has. That thinking is a qualitatively distinctive process hardly warrants the conclusion that it proceeds from a separate substance; nature is full of qualitatively diverse phenomena, but no one any longer postulates a separate "I know not what" to account for each. Indeed, all the assumptions which lead to the mind-substance theory have been shown to be the consequence of inadequate metaphysics. Denial of the continuity of mind and nature, as Dewey repeatedly mentions, is not based on empirical evidence but is dialectical, that is, derivative of a theory never called into question:

> A realist may deny this particular hypothesis that, existentially, mind designates an instrumental method of directing natural changes. But he cannot do so in virtue of his realism; the question at issue is what the real is. If natural existence is qualitatively individualized or genuine plural, as well as repetitious, and if things have both temporal quality and recurrence or uniformity, then the more realistic knowledge is, the more fully it will reflect and exemplify these traits.[50]

Recall that the dualist virtually admits Dewey's case by trying to put mind and body back together again by the use of *ad hoc* hypotheses. This sort of dialectical patching up might conceivably help the original theory survive a while longer. The necessity, however, for such exertions only suffices to make the basic assumptions more dubious. Moreover, in light of metaphysical analysis, it is difficult to see what it is in experience that might constrain one to accept the original (dualistic) view at the outset.

Not only is the dualistic view unsupported, but it takes on to itself the insuperable difficulties of accounting for the realities of human experience with a concept of mind which makes that experience by definition unintelligible; while, on the other hand, there seems to be no difficulty in treating mental events as events *of* nature:

> Qualities characteristic of sentiency are qualities *of* cosmic events. Only because they are such, it is possible to establish the one to one correspondence which natural science does establish between series of numbers and spatial positions on one hand and the series and spectra of sensory qualities on the other. The notion that the universe is split into two separate and disconnected realms of

---

[50] *Ibid.*, p. 160.

> existence, one psychical and the other physical, and then that these two realms of being, in spite of their total disjunction, specifically and minutely correspond to each other – as a serial order of numbered vibrations corresponds to the immediately felt qualities of vision of the prismatic specturm – presents the acme of incredibility.[51]

> The view of complete separation of existential consciousness from connection with physical things cannot be maintained in view of what is known of its specifiable connections with organic conditions, and of the intimate, unbroken connection of organic with extra-organic events. It can be maintained only by holding that the connection of consciousness in its varied forms with bodily action is non-natural. The only reason for asserting this position lies in the dialectic compulsion of denial of quality to natural events, and arrogation of superior existence to causal antecedents.[52]

How sane and fruitful is Dewey's approach, wherein the *assumptions* of the mind-body problem are reexamined, in light of an adequate "ground-map" of experience. Yet modern philosophy bears witness to strenuous and ingenious reasonings which take no heed whatever of these assumptions. Rather, virtually every approach holds without a moment's reflection that the problem consists in finding some conceivable relation between thinking substance and material substance. Dewey's contention that refined concepts are taken as original materials in philosophic inquiry finds no better illustration than in the repeated assaults at the mind-body problem which assume that the whole issue concerns the interaction of separate substances.[53]

Further, Dewey's approach to inquiry into the nature of mind is, in basic conception, very simple and intelligible: Mind is not regarded as an original being, independently responsible for "mental" functioning; it is not that *in which* and *by which* mental events occur. Rather, "mind" characterizes what happens, what goes on, when certain biological and environmental processes are united. What we call mind is, generally speaking, the activity of an inclusive situation. What some of the crucial consti-

---

[51] *Ibid.*, pp. 267-8.

[52] *Ibid.*, p. 343.

[53] In addition to the specific examples of such uncritical treatments of mind-body, seemingly countless discussions of "free will" assume, at least implicitly, a mind-body dualism.

tuents of this activity are will be considered next.[54]

There are evidently insuperable problems involved in regarding physical nature, life, and mind as separate substances. No such difficulties confront the notions of life and mind as eventual functions; indeed, experience evidently demands some such notion. Life is a quality of nature which emerges in more complex interactions of merely physical nature; mind invovles still more complex interactions. Thus the three levels are continuous, yet qualitatively different due to the nature of the interactions.

> The difference between the animate plant and the inanimate iron molecule is not that the former has something in addition to physico-chemical energy; it lies in the *way* in which physico-chemical energies are interconnected and operate, whence different *consequences* mark inanimate and animate activity respectively. . . . In general, three plateaus of such fields [of interaction] may be discriminated. The first, the scene of narrower and more external interactions, while qualititatively diversified in itself, is physical; its distinctive properties are those of the mathematical-mechancial system discovered by physics and which define matter as a general character. The second level is that of life. Qualitative differences, like those of plant and animal, lower and higher animal forms, are even here more conspicuous; but in spite of their variety they have qualities in common which define the psycho-physical. The third plateau is that of association, communication, participation. This is still further internally diversified, consisting of individualities. It is marked throughout its diversities, however, by common properties, which define mind as intellect; possession of and response to meanings. . . . The distinction between physical, psycho-physical, and mental is thus one of levels of increasing complexity and intimacy of interaction among natural events.[55]

From what has been quoted, it is implied that human communication is essential to nature functioning "mentally." This is precisely the next point of discussion, in which it will be seen that it is in communication that events in nature acquire meaning, significance; and these meanings are what make mind and discursive thought possible. (In the quotation, Dewey's reference to "intimacy of interaction" pertains to the distinctively human phenomenon of responding to objects remote in space and time due to their being part of the meaning of present events. Thus events widely separated in space and time become intimately related. This matter also comes up in the following discussion.)

---

[54] This discussion perhaps falls outside the intended scope of this study. However, it seems desirable to provide at least some notion of what are the positive assumptions with which Dewey would supersede the discredited thinking substance theory. It will not be possible to elaborate and analyze these assumptions; I will simply outline them. There will be occasion later to refer to some of Dewey's principal conclusions relative to this matter; so for this reason also it is necessary to make some minimal reference to them.

[55] *Experience and Nature,* pp. 253-4; 272; 261.

To deal specifically with mind and thinking: For Dewey, the constituents of thought are meanings. Meanings are perceived or known relations between things. The meaning of an object or event in our experience *is* the interactions known to us that it undergoes with other objects or events. Since anything may enter into a great variety of different relations, anything may acquire very complex meanings. The meanings of objects in human experience are almost exclusively in the consequences which are effected by the modes of interaction between these objects and human beings. That is, the meaning of an object is first of all the consequences of various ways of acting with that object. Scientific meanings, where frequently relations only between different physical events are distinguished, are a relatively late and uncommon occurrence, and they are an abstraction and refinement of meanings of direct experience. The meaning of an object, in any case, is not its qualitative immediacy, as such, but its connections with other things, "what it portends and gives evidence of."

> What a physical event immediately is, and what it *can* do or its relationship are distinct and incommensurable. But when an event has meaning, its potential consequences become its integral and funded feature. When the potential consequences are important and repeated, they form the very nature and essence of a thing, its defining, identifying, and distinguishing form. To recognize the thing is to grasp its definition. Thus we become capable of perceiving things instead of merely feeling and having them. To *perceive* is to acknowledge unattained possibilities; it is to refer the present to consequences, apparition to issue, and thereby to behave in deference to the connections of events.[56]

The last sentence of this quotation suggests – which is in fact Dewey's position – that to be in possession of a meaning is to be prepared to act with a given object in specifiable ways. Possession of meanings is a behavioral characteristic of an individual. To use the terminology of *Human Nature and Conduct,* meanings (as constituents of thought) are a class of habit.

Mind, as Dewey refers to it, is a system of meanings, and thinking takes place when precarious elements in existence stimulate a reorganization and enlargement of this system. Thinking is thus a manipulation of meanings; but this manipulation is not the activity of an ego. Rather, the way in which ideas are mixed, sorted out, connected and disconnected is a function of both

[56] *Ibid.,* p. 182.

explicit features of the environment and the existing fund of habits and their nature.

It is evident that meanings are neither psychic existences nor transcendental forms; they are relations *of* objective events *as* they enter into human action. But what process creates meanings? How does the system of meanings develop?

According to Dewey's theory, meanings are an emergent of social action. In the social context, there is the constant need for cooperative action. The conduct of individuals together, in and with an environment, must be adjusted and coordinated. To such an end, various objects and acts in the situation must have a function which is commonly understood by the participants. That is, if a community of endeavor is to be established, individuals must know how objects are to function in social action. If and when particular objects are thus understood, their function in the situation is their meaning. Hence it is that shareable meanings are derivative of social action.

The instrumentality which results in unified social action is language. Language is understood functionally: It is whatever succeeds in creating a community of action. Whatever cries or gestures succeed in effecting such action thereupon *become* language. The meaning of vocal acts, then, is precisely the interactions which the objects designated by them undergo in the social situation. These are the meanings denoted, represented, by language. The vocal acts which succeed in creating shared "use and enjoyment" of objects acquire the meaning of just those interactions of shared use and enjoyment. Thus it is that objects and the sounds making reference to them acquire at the same time the same shared and objective meanings to the participants in the situation. When the same sounds can be used effectively in reference to the same object in a different situation with new participants, then the meaning of the word has been communicated to other persons. Such meanings become more extensive, refined, and complex as the objects and actions denoted are used in a variety of situations.

It is essential to see that it is *social* action that creates shareable, common, communicable meanings. For vocal acts could never become language unless such acts were to occur in a context where at least two people respond to the sounds in the same way. In this situation each participant knows how the utterances function in the experience of the other. That is, the cries or signals which stimulate a specific action in an individual stimulate also an action in the other; and each is aware of what the role of the other will be: each knows what the sounds mean to the other. If the case were otherwise, distinctively social action, concerted action, could not ensue.

Language, in the sense Dewey intends, is communication. Persons do not simply make unintelligible noises at each other, as animals do. On the contrary, part of the meaning of one's vocal act is an understanding of what this act means to the hearer; and the hearer understands how the act functions in the experience of the speaker. Finally, each is aware that precisely this common situation exists. Language, again, is that which compels common understanding of the intended function of an object or act in a situation. Once the meaning of words is established, communication independently of overt action becomes possible.[57]

From this analysis, it is clear that meanings are not antecedent to the situation, but eventual of it. Moreover, efforts at communication in the situation do not *attach to* preexisting meanings, but are the very condition of their creation. This is a fundamentally important point; for, according to dualistic theories, meanings are psychic existences of some kind, inhabiting a mind; and communication is simply the attachment of sounds to preexisting meanings. There are insuperable difficulties in such theories in determining the relation of language to reality. When, however, language and meaning are recognized to be functionally inseparable and emergent of social action, the continuity between biological and mental functioning is established, and the relation between meanings and nature is removed from obscurity.

When events have meaning, man's relation to nature undergoes a most remarkable change; for man's contact with nature is removed from sheer immediacy into significance. Mere feelings are converted into signs of distant events which cannot be directly perceived. As objects function in a variety of different contexts, their meaning is constantly enlarged; and when such

---

[57] Dewey's theory of language, meaning, and communication as events of nature is presented in some detail in Chapter Five of *Experience and Nature.* A more concise and readable account is advanced in Chapter III of the *Logic,* especially pp. 45-9.

objects are matters of direct experience, their funded meaning makes events remote in space and time consciously significant in present experience. ". . . an environment both extensive and enduring is immediately implicated in present behaviour."[58] There is a vast increment in powers of human action when we can respond to and manipulate objects *as* meaningful.

Of course, some meanings develop without language, as, for example, animals learn to respond to some things as signs. But it is doubtful that animals do much in the way of what is distinctively communication, as characterized above. But when – as in human experience – meanings are represented by language, there is a vast qualitative increment in the powers of discursive thought. For language is readily manipulable, and its meanings have specifiable implications; hence reflection, hypothesis, and inference become possible. The more meanings one possesses, the more are the powers of thinking enhanced.[59] Moreover, language, once established, makes verbal communication possible. Ideas and information can be exchanged without individuals actually having to participate in the situations in which the meanings were generated. Thus it is that meanings can be collected, interrelated, enlarged, preserved, and transmitted across great stretches of time and space and brought into relation to daily experience with its demands for action in and with the world.

Language and meaning thus have this indispensable function in the creation of mind. We could not interact with nature beyond immediate experience if mere feelings were not convertible into significant events; and, furthermore, we would not have mind and we could not think without the linguistic meanings created in social action. What has been said regarding communication and its fruits is summarized in the following:

> As life is a character of events in a peculiar condition or organization, and "feeling" is a quality of life-forms marked by complexly mobile and discriminating

[58] *Experience and Nature,* p. 279.

[59] Any stage of thinking – any instance of the thought process – is the outcome of a history in nature. This history is constituted by the interaction of biological, psychological, and environmental processes. In respect to reflective thought, one of the most crucial functions in this history is that of meanings; for the content of successive meanings is a principal determinant of the sequence which the moments of thought follow.

responses, so "mind" is an added property assumed by a feeling creature, when it reaches that organized interaction with other living creatures which is language, communication. Then the qualities of feeling become significant of objective differences in external things and of episodes past and to come. This state of things in which qualitatively different feelings are not just had but are significant of objective differences, is mind. Feelings are no longer just felt. They have and they make *sense;* record and prophesy.[60]

When man's interactions with nature have this scope and complexity, when he responds to and manipulates meanings, he has mind, or functions mentally; the possession of meanings links the immediate to remote events, and their manipulation suggests many potentialities of nature. Novel relations are *instituted* in nature through the manipulation of meanings. That is, man hypothesizes and experiments. Mind is thus the consequence of this ability of the organism to enter into these distincitive interactions with nature, effected by the demands, interests, and needs of social action. The difference, then, between mind and body is a difference in the nature of interactions: when certain kinds of interaction of the body take place, the result is what has traditionally been called mind:

Body-mind simply designates what actually takes place when a living body is implicated in situations of discourse, communication, and participation. In the hyphenated phrase body-mind, "body" designates the continued and conserved, the registered and cumulative operation of factors continuous with the rest of nature, inanimate as well as animate; while "mind" designates the characters and consequences which are differential, indicative of features which emerge when "body" is engaged in a wider, more complex, and interdependent situation.[61]

Clearly, mind and thinking are not an activity of thinking substance; nor are they an exclusive property of the brain and nervous system. Brain and nervous system are but two of the conditions of an activity that is a function of more inclusive processes. Nor is mind "mental," because *what* man experiences is in nature; and the activity of thinking is an *inclusive* natural process. It might well be observed, in addition, that the expression "interaction of mind and body" is very misleading; for its suggests two different *entities* which interact. Whereas, in fact, as

---

[60] *Experience and Nature,* p. 258. Dewey's notions indicate that introspection and so-called private languages are always derivative of affairs of the public world.

[61] *Ibid.,* p. 285.

Dewey contends, there is one inclusive process which – in certain ways and under certain conditions – functions mentally: It undergoes those functions which we call mental or psychological. For purposes of analysis, distinguishable constituents of this process may be isolated; but *as* constituents of the entire process, they do not occur separately. The extent and way in which the biological organism enters into this process varies with the habits of the individual and the circumstances in which he is involved. That is, literally, more or less of the body is involved in the integrated process – organic action is more or less partial or more or less complete – depending on the meaning of the situation.

This section will be concluded by indicating how Dewey's findings determine the role of scientific inquiry into the relation of body and mind and the general moral import of determining the general nature of this relation. Before these topics are taken up, however, it remains to deal with a final problem suggested by the preceding exposition.

Dewey understands man in all his functions as wholly integral with nature. There is no separate ego; there is no encapsulated self, somehow shut off from natural processes. Experience is something that happens – goes on – in nature, and to appropriate it to one's "self" is not to change its traits. Although (as is perfectly obvious) all experience has its individualized character in a particular person, possession of experience does not make it disappear into "mind."

> It is absurd to call a recognition or a conception subjective or mental because it takes place through a physically or socially numerically distinct existence; by this logic a house disappears from the spatial and material world when it becomes *my* house. . . .
>
> Recognition of an object, conception of a meaning may be mine rather than yours; yours rather than his, at a particular moment; but this fact is about me or you, not about the object and essence perceived and conceived. Acknowledgement of this fact is compatible however with the conviction that after all there would be no *objects* to be perceived, no meanings to be conceived, if at some period of time uniquely individualized events had not intervened. . . . It is obvious . . . that a house can be owned only when it has existence and properties independent of being owned. The quality of belonging to some one is not an all-absorbing maw in which independent properties and relations disappear to be digested into egohood. It is additive; it marks the assumption of a new relationship. . . .
>
> Substitute "experience" for "house" and no other word need be changed. Experience when it happens has the same dependence upon objective natural

> events, physical and social, as has the occurrence of a house. It has its own objective and definitive traits; these can be described without reference to a self, precisely as a house is of brick, has eight rooms, etc., irrespective of whom it belongs to.[62]

Then, if mind is not an individual entity resident in a body, what is the self, or subject? Clearly, it too must be a discriminable quality of events of the organism interacting with the environment: "Personality, selfhood, subjectivity are eventual functions that emerge with complexly organized interactions, organic and social."[63] Experience is the outcome of inclusive natural processes; it happens; it occurs. The conscious appropriation, or ownership, of experience by an individual is an eventual function additional to the mere occurrence of experience. That is, the felt ownership of experience by a subject is a quality wrought within experience when certain further interactions between organism and environment occur:

> In some specifiable respects and for some specifiable consequences, these selves, capable of objective denotation just as are sticks, stones, and stars, assume the care and administration of certain objects and acts in experience. . . .
>
> To say in a significant way, "*I* think, believe, desire, instead of barely *it* is thought, believed, desired," is to accept and affirm a responsibility and to put forth a claim. It does not mean that the self is the source or author of the thought and affection nor its exclusive seat.[64]

---

[62] *Ibid.*, pp. 221-2; 232.

[63] *Ibid.*, p. 208.

[64] *Ibid.*, pp. 232-3. Dewey never explicitly discusses the self-conscious self as a social emergent. There could hardly be doubt that his thought on this matter would proceed much like that of G.H. Mead. The chapter "Nature, Communication and Meaning" in *Experience and Nature* evidently owes much to Mead. However, such indebtedness is not acknowledged. In that chapter Dewey says, "When the introspectionist thinks he has withdrawn into a wholly private realm of events disparate in kind from other events, made out of mental stuff, he is only turning his attention to his own soliloquy. And soliloquy is the product and reflex of converse with others; social communication not an effect of soliloquy. If we had not talked with others and they with us, we should never talk to and with ourselves. Because of converse, social give and take, various organic attitudes become an assemblage of persons engaged in converse, conferring with one another, exchanging distinctive experiences, listening to one another, over-hearing unwelcome remarks, accusing and excusing. Through speech a person dramatically identifies himself with potential acts and deeds; he plays many roles not in successive stages of life but in a contemporaneously enacted drama. Thus mind emerges." (p. 170.) Here the connection with Mead is most obvious, and Dewey's last sentence might equally well read, "Thus the *self* emerges." For, in Mead's analysis, it is only when we learn to take the role of others in imagination and thus see ourselves as object that we become a self-conscious self. (And this self, then, is one which exists *as* possessing certain relations to other persons.)

Although Dewey's writings on the emergence of the self and the process of becoming responsible for experience are rather sparse, he wrote extensively on the nature of the self and human agency. He accepted James's devastating critique of the ego as thinker and as unifier of experience[65] and even went James one better: In "The Vanishing Subject in the Psychology of James"[66] he attacked the notion of ego as will with essentially the same logic that James had applied to the notion of ego as thinker. In many other articles and books he attacked various forms of faculty psychology.[67] It would be well beyond the confines of the present work to analyze his contributions and criticism explicitly;[68] it will suffice merely to point out summarily his theory of the nature of the self and the corresponding explanation of will as habit.

The individual in his variations and distinctiveness is a crucial intermediary of natural processes. The self is neither an uncaused cause nor a simple and passive mirroring of events. It is, rather, an agency of reorganization and reconstruction:

> An adherent of empirical denotative method can hardly accept either the view which regards subjective mind as an aberration or that which makes it an independent creative source. Empirically, it is an agency of novel reconstruction of a preexisting order.[69]

Dewey's treatment of the explicit appropriation of experience to a self is rather limited. This is not matter for reservation in this context, however; what it more important is the denial of a preexistent ego which somehow emits or controls experience. It is a matter of experimental psychology to determine the specific ways in which experience comes to be experienced *as a possession.* Presumably, it is largely a matter of one's being treated *as* a responsible participant in experience, as Dewey's generalizations suggest.

[65] From James's *Principles of Psychology.*

[66] Reprinted in *Problems of Men*, pp. 396-409.

[67] Perhaps the most pioneering work here is "The Reflex Arc Concept in Psychology" *(Psychological Review,* 1896), in which he presents the theory of human behavior as an on-going, historical joint undertaking of person and environment. His "The Ego as Cause" *(Philosophical Review,* 1894) if read today would suffice to relegate much of current debate on free will to the status of undergraduate amateurism. It is worth noting that much of Dewey's work in psychology – as in everything else – proceeds by way of determining and criticizing the philosophy of nature implied in a psychological theory.

[68] The nature of personal freedom will receive attention in Chapter VII, "Intelligence and Value."

[69] *Experience and Nature,* p. 217.

More specifically, the self is a dynamic complex of habits.

A habit for Dewey is any way of interacting with the environment.[70] All action involves the presence of biological impulse. Impulse, however, becomes a structured way of behaving only in interaction with the environment; that is, only as it becomes part of habit. Hunger and the desire to appease it, for example, do not by themselves determine a way of getting food. The limitless ways that men acquire food are determined by the nature of their environment. Biological impulses interact with environment to create a specific mode of behavior – a habit. So it is with all habits: They are ways of organism and environment acting together. They are – as Dewey calls them – propulsive in nature, inseparably linked with impulse. What we call human nature, then, is not something original and fixed which individuals bring to their interaction with nature; it is, rather, the *consequence* of that interaction. As interaction goes on and individuals undergo differing histories, each individual is prepared to act with his environment in certain ways more or less unique to himself.

Habits do not function separately and in alternation. Rather, they function together in many combinations, depending upon the needs and demands of the situation. The character of each habit is qualified by the nature of its interaction with other habits in a concrete situation. Thus behavior does not necessarily become stereotyped, but can be uniquely suited to the conditions in which it occurs. On the other hand, each individual possesses a fund of habits distinguishable from that of others. The fact that habits function together, and in ways distinctive of a particular individual, accounts for the fact of "character" – of a more or less unified and dynamic composite of personality traits. This, indeed, is what Dewey means by the self: a dynamic organization of habits. Accordingly, the way that anyone behaves at any time is a function of the operative condition of his habits and the objective conditions of the environment. What is called "will" is the operation of habits in a specific situation.

> All habits are a demand for certain kinds of activity; and they constitute the self. In any intelligible sense of the word will, they *are* will. They form our effective

---

[70] Dewey's treatment of habit is found especially in *Human Nature and Conduct*, Part One, Chs. I and II.

desires and they furnish us with our working capacities. They rule our thoughts, determining which shall appear and be strong and which shall pass from light into obscurity.[71]

Although experience and mind are not hidden possessions of an isolated ego, it is also obviously true that mind as individualized is an empirical reality. Every individual is in many ways uniquely situated in the world; hence the body-mind has distinctive traits and is a distinctive history. Thus the common traits of experience are qualified, organized, and experienced in ways more or less peculiar to each individual. Such qualifications mean that there is something in virtually any experience which is uniquely individualized and hence "private." Individuation of this sort, however, should not be misinterpreted:

Romanticism has made the best and the worst of the discovery of the private and incommunicable. It has converted a pervasive and inevitable color and temper of experience into its substance. In conceiving that this inexpugnable uniqueness, this ultimate singularity, exhausts the self, it has created a vast and somnambulic egotism out of the fact of subjectivity.[72]

The foregoing general discussion of mind-body and related matters implies that empirical science has the same role in this field that it has in dealing with purely physical processes. It is a matter of experimental inquiry to determine what are the specific constituents of the inclusive processes which result in specific ways of experiencing. As in any science, theories may be contrived which link together experimental laws; and variables may be manipulated in order to regulate the occurrence of phenomena. Scientific procedures may thus be directed to explanation, prediction, and control of particular phenomena. In such inquiries the great advances in biology are of enormous use, and Dewey himself exploited them to the limits of his capacity.[73] Although experience attests to the organic relation of subject and object, the mechanisms of this relation and of the derivation of the complex forms of experience from the rudimentary could not be known until biology became a highly developed science. In reference to the understanding and management of particular

---

[71] *Human Nature and Conduct* (New York: The Modern Library, 1930), p. 25. Somewhat more about the dynamics of behavior will be outlined in the next section and in Chapter VII.

[72] *Experience and Nature,* p. 243.

[73] It can be said with justice that it belongs to Dewey more than to any other thinker to have perceived and developed the implications of biological evolution for a theory of experience, of morals, art, and science. This is a singular achievement.

kinds of experience, the conditions of their occurrence can in principle be determined by the methods of experimental inquiry, and nature can be turned to human account.

> Every discovery of concrete dependence of life and mind upon physical events is therefore an addition to our resources. If life and mind had no mechanism, education, deliberate modification, rectification, prevention and constructive control would be impossible.[74]

As we have seen, in connection with the general problem of the relation between mind and nature Dewey assigns a crucial function to language. Accordingly, the study of language as mode of social interaction, means of communication, as condition of distinctively intellectual behavior, would be of decisive importance. Its possible contributions to behavioral psychology and learning theory and hence to social change would seem to be of great magnitude.

The interactions in nature which eventuate in distinctively human nature are extremely complex; and inquiries into this subject are, accordingly, both exacting and vast in scope. In this connection, I will provide a further statement from Dewey which not only suggests the possibilities of empirical inquiry, but provides as well a general characterization of its moral implications:

> Those who talk most of the organism, physiologists and psychologists, are often just those who display least sense of the intimate, delicate and subtle interdependence of all organic structures and processes with one another. The world seems mad in pre-occupation with what is specific, particular, disconnected in medicine, politics, science, industry, education. In terms of a conscious control of inclusive wholes, search for those links which occupy key positions and which effect critical connections is indispensable. But recovery of sanity depends upon seeing and using these specifiable things *as* links functionally significant in a process. To see the organism *in* nature, the nervous system in the organism, the brain in the nervous system, the cortex in the brain is the answer to the problems which haunt philosophy. And when thus seen they will be seem to be *in*, not as marbles are in a box but as events are in history, in a moving, growing never finished process. Until we have a procedure in actual practice which demonstrates this continuity, we shall continue to engage in appealing to some other specific thing, some other broken off affair, to restore connectedness and unity. . . . Thus we increase the disease in the means to cure it.[75]

---

[74] *Ibid.*, p. 263.

[75] *Ibid.*, p. 295-6.

Man exists in a staggeringly complex and changing system of relations. Thus to isolate a certain mode of activity – say, the religious – and try to understand it as an unrelated phenomenon, and hope to exploit it alone to usher in a Golden Age, is not only impossible but self-defeating as well. We find Dewey again and again complaining that both practical proposals and philosophical formulations of practical problems presuppose such arbitrary isolation.

The moral implications of the conclusions reached about the relation of mind and nature are enormous. Some of these implications will be better dealt with in the discussion which terminates this chapter. For the present, the point of consequence to be indicated is that Dewey's position puts the methods and conclusions of scientific inquiry directly in the service of human experience. Even this matter, however, I will not discuss further, for it more properly comes after an analysis of the status of value in nature and of the relation between facts and values. These are topics of later chapters, so the moral importance of science will not be examined at this point. It is sufficient here merely to point out that a most significant *issue* has been discriminated. Perhaps, as many philosophers hold, there is no connection between facts and values. Accordingly, there would be no *moral* consequence of the fact that human experience is wholly subject to scientific investigation. On the other hand, if value can be validly identified with certain phases of experience, then the import of science for morals is incalculably great.

3. Individual and Society

It is plain from the positions delineated thus far that there can be no dualism of individual and society. All phases of human experience are the product of organically united processes of "the live creature" and his surroundings; and clearly, the social environment is the most decisive feature of these surroundings. Whatever may be the gladness, sorrows, freedoms, or frustrations man undergoes in society, they are not contingent upon whether or not the individual is related to society, but *how* he is related.

Earlier, in pointing out the distinctively metaphysical character of Dewey's philosophy, I noted his assertion that "the social" is a metaphysical category because it incorporates and transforms the physical, the vital, and the psychic, bringing them into more complex interactions and novel outcomes.[76] The continuity of individual and social might conceivably be admitted, however, while regarding the social as an extension of individual human nature or – at the other extreme – regarding the individual as but an extension of, say, the will of the state. Actually, both these positions are invalidated by implication by the discussion of mind in the preceding section; and Dewey has a great deal of importance to say about the philosophies surrounding such positions. I must, unfortunately, be very sparing on these matters. However, enough must be said to elucidate Dewey's main assumptions regarding the relation of individual and society and to establish certain conclusions which will have a direct bearing on subsequent discussions.

The notion of independent laws of human nature or laws of thought evidently does presuppose an ego or will isolated from nature, or even a fixed essence or species of man. All such notions are incompatible with the implications of Darwinian theory. The rejection of the notion of fixed and inherent species is a rejection of an essence of man or of any unalterable characteristic of man, cultural or biological.

Perhaps more scientifically respectable, however, is the notion that all behavior is determined by instincts which in themselves fix patterns of action. If the notion of instinct is that of a separate power or force somehow resident within the individual, it is

---

[76] Regrettably, Dewey does not indicate specifically what the status of the social is relative to those traits so effectively discriminated and employed in *Experience and Nature.* My judgment is that the social is logically subsequent to them; i.e., a metaphysical analysis of nature effectively removes whatever intellectual supports there are for the various dualisms. Thus to insist on the social as a category is a way of indicating the continuities and inclusiveness of experience and nature. Indeed, "the social" can evidently be substituted for "experience"; so we could legitimately speak of various phases, or traits, of the social. These traits of the social occur in varying degrees and conjunctions, resulting in, say, moral, aesthetic, or cognitive situations. Thus the social is the most inclusive category of experience. There are, of course, events which occur independently of the social. Again, however, the generic traits, as Dewey understands them, are clearly not descriptive of all numerically distinct events that happen to occur in the universe. Naturalistic metaphysics is the attempt to describe what *kind* of thing nature is in its fullest disclosure of powers; it does not attempt to describe or explain the peculiarities of every particular event that happens to occur in the universe.

not intelligible. Yet if instincts are construed as simply a fixed function of physiological organization, the notion is not inherently absurd. Moreover, it is clearly a question subject to settlement by experimental science.

In *Human Nature and Conduct* (especially Part Two) Dewey mounts a very forceful attack on any notion of instinct as a fixed pattern of behavior. Perhaps Dewey's confidence might not have been fully warranted by the knowledge available to him in 1921. Nevertheless, he succeeded at least in showing that theories of immutable instinct have a great deal of evidence against them and, moreover, employ a lot of bad logic.

Evidence against any concept of instincts as fixed forms of behavior is the evidently endless variety of human nature – modes of conduct, temperament, objects of value, diversity of institutions – between which there are numberless distinctions, subtle or pronounced. (Moreover, of course, the character of a given individual often undergoes significant changes.)

> At some place on the globe, at some time, every kind of practice seems to have been tolerated or even praised. How is the tremendous diversity of institutions (including moral codes) to be accounted for? The native stock of instincts is practically the same everywhere. Exaggerate as much as we like the native differences of Patagonians and Greeks, Sioux Indians and Hindoos, Bushmen and Chinese, their original differences will bear no comparison to the amount of difference found in custom and culture. Since such a diversity cannot be attributed to an original identity, the development of native impulse must be stated in terms of acquired habits, not the growth of customs in terms of instincts. The wholesale human sacrifices of Peru and the tenderness of St. Francis, the cruelties of pirates and the philanthropies of Howard, the practice of Suttee and the cult of the Virgin, the war and the peace dances of the Comanches and the parliamentary institutions of the British, the communism of the south sea islander and the proprietary thrift of the Yankee, the magic of the medicine man and the experiments of the chemist in his laboratory, the non-resistance of Chinese and the aggressive militarism of an imperial Prussia, monarchy by divine right and government by the people; the countless diversity of habits suggested by such a random list springs from practically the same capital-stock of native instincts.[77]

Against all this diversity, instinct theories seem highly implausible. (A presumed "territorial" instinct, for example, which accounts for aggressive behavior, is evidently helpless to explain the characteristic temperament and conduct of Eskimos, the Ituri Pygmies, or the ghetto Jews of Europe.)

---

[77] *Human Nature and Conduct*, pp. 91-2.

The bad logic of those who hold that human behavior is the working of instincts takes at least two forms. First, such reasoning is frequently reductive; it supposes that one's conduct in an environment is not at least in part determined by appraisal of objective conditions (is not "intelligent") or by other forms of interaction. Secondly, such thinking is evidently an instance of converting an eventual function into a substantial cause: the results of a history are regarded as a separate entity which *caused* the history:

> No social institution stands alone as a product of one dominant force. It is a phenomenon or function of a multitude of social factors in their mutual inhibitions and reinforcements. If we follow an infantile logic we shall reduplicate the unity of result in an assumption of unity of force behind it – as men once did with natural events, employing teleology as an exhibition of causal efficiency. We thus take the same social custom twice over: once as an existing fact and then as an original force which produced the fact, and utter sage platitudes about the unalterable workings of human nature or of race. As we account for war by pugnacity, for the capitalistic system by the necessity of an incentive of gain to stir ambition and effort, so we account for Greece by power of aesthetic observation, Rome by administrative ability, the middle ages by interest in religion and so on. We have constructed an elaborate political zoology as mythological and not nearly as poetical as the other zoology of phoenixes, griffins and unicorns.[78]

As Dewey points out, these "accounts" of behavior are no more informative than accounting for the dormitive effects of opium by its dormitive potency.

If the diversity of human nature were explained by an argument that instincts somehow worked *through* the social environment and were thereby distorted by force, it would seemingly be the responsibility of the instinct theorist to show that his assumptions were not gratuitious – were not a useless postulation of some occult power which serves no function in explanation. In 1971, the fashion among those with pretensions to science is to reduce all behavior to aggression. In 1939 Dewey wrote, " 'Love of power,' to which it is now fashionable to appeal, has a meaning only when it applies to everything in general and hence explains nothing in particular."[79] To reduce all human action to love of power or to aggression is at best an abuse of language. One might wish to say, for some reason, that the conduct of both

[78] *Ibid.*, p. 111.

[79] *Freedom and Culture* (New York: Capricorn Books, 1963), p. 113.

a Martin Luther King, Jr., and a Josef Stalin is "aggressive" or is accounted for by "aggression." But as an explanation, such notions are vacuous: They entail nothing; they have no experimental meaning. Hence also, they are of no scientific use. King and Stalin are drastically different people. It is vital to know what makes the difference between them. Simply to explain their conduct by innate aggression is an unconscionable vanity.

Further illustration of the meaningless use of instincts as presumed explanatory devices abound. Say, for example (as many do), that man behaves sexually because of his sex instinct. As such, this is at best a mere description of behavior: Man behaves sexually because there is something about him that causes him to behave sexually. Unfortunately, the word "instinct" works a spell on most minds; so men suppose they have an explanation where in fact they have nothing of the sort; and inquiry is replaced by sage complacency. This is not to say, of course, that the word "instinct" could not be employed to denote certain mechanisms of behavior which are capable of operational definition. But until we deal precisely with such mechanisms, we have not advanced at all beyond the logic of essences and other occult potencies.

If human behavior is explicable without recourse to a theory of fixed instincts, then such a theory is gratuitious. Dewey prefers "impulse" to "instinct," and of these impulses he argues that they are, in themselves 1) unstructured, 2) plastic, and 3) in each instance of their occurrence qualitatively unique: 1) Fear, anger, hate, lust, etc. obviously do not by themselves determine any particular form of behavior; they are not in themselves "serviceable powers." This is empirically evident. 2) Impulses, therefore, can take many forms of action, depending on their incorporation with habits, which are interactions with the environment.

> Any impulse may become organized into almost any disposition according to the way it interacts with surroundings. Fear may become abject cowardice, prudent caution, reverence for superiors or respect for equals; an agency for credulous swallowing of absurd superstitions or for wary skepticism. A man may be chiefly afraid of the spirits of his ancestors, of officials, of arousing the disapproval of his associates, of being deceived, of fresh air, or of bolshevism.[80]

[80] *Human Nature and Conduct,* p. 95.

3) Finally, any instance of the occurrence of an impulse varies with the existing biological-psychological condition of the organism and with the nature of the affective environment: When one is tired or rested, hot or cold, sick or well, hungry or filled to repletion; anxious, preoccupied, in unfamiliar surroundings, concentrated, relaxed, mindless, or elated – when one is in any possible combination of such conditions (which admit of infinite variety); and when one is in a qualitatively distinctive environment, then the occurrence of any impulse will be qualitatively unique.

> In reality, when one is afraid the whole being reacts, and this entire responding organism is never twice the same. . . . It is only mythology which sets up a single, identical psychic force which "causes" all the reactions of fear, a force beginning and ending in itself. . . . There is no one fear having diverse manifestations; there are as many qualitatively different fears as there are objects responded to and different consequences sensed and observed. . . . Cowardice, embarrassment, caution, and reverence may all be regarded as forms of fear. They all have certain physical organic acts in common – those of organic shrinkage, gestures of hesitation and retreat. But each is qualitatively unique. Each is what it is in virtue of its total interactions or correlations with other acts and with the environing medium, with consequences.[81]

An impulse, then, is not a separate entity, but is itself an eventuation of some combination of circumstances. What we refer to as instincts are, on Dewey's view, eventuations of a situation. Particular biological, psychological, and environmental conditions combine to *produce* anger, fear, lust, and such things. Anger, fear, and lust recur, of course; but this is not the same resident power cropping up again. This is the recurrence together of somewhat similar biological-psychological-environmental conditions. Situations are never twice identical; so impulses are always qualitatively unique.

Thus, as Dewey understands the matter, it is *habit* – and not instinct – that is the conservative element in conduct. Behavior *becomes* fixed due to impulse being forced into channels already established, and insisted upon, by social authorities of various sorts. And it is precisely this socially enforced fixity of habit (social customs) that results in antisocial behavior. Whenever the accepted forms of social action are such that they cannot readily

---

[81] *Ibid.*, pp. 154-5.

be incorporated into the conduct of individuals, or when they are too limited to accommodate the diversity of human energies, impulsive desires do not vanish; they are pent up. Desires and interests are sacrificed to the requirements of the status quo, and individuals suffer frustration, until they must seek an outlet which is not socially condoned.

> Instinctive reactions are sometimes too intense to be woven into a smooth pattern of habits. Under ordinary circumstances they appear to be tamed to obey their master, custom. But extraordinary crises release them and they show by wild violent energy how superficial is the control of routine. . . . At critical moments of unusual stimuli the emotional outbreak and rush of instincts dominating all activity show how superficial is the modification which a rigid habit has been able to effect. . . .
>
> There always exists a goodly store of non-functioning impulses which may be drawn upon. . . . Rigid custom signifies not that there are no such impulses but that they are not organically taken advantage of. As matter of fact, the stiffer and the more encrusted the customs, the larger is the number of instinctive activities that find no regular outlet and that accordingly merely await a chance to get an irregular, uncoordinated manifestation.[82]

If impulses are not innate patterns of conduct, there is no inherent necessity in their being denied in the interest of social control. On the contrary, when the biological vitalities of human beings find available a variety of forms of fulfillment, occasion for their deviation into hostility and destruction need not arise. Depending on the character of the social medium, a naturally energetic and aggressive person could become anything from a hoodlum to a social reformer, or a completely incapacitated neurotic. Accordingly, social control would seem to be a function, among other things, of the freedom and resources of the community. Instead of persons vacillating between various forms of either extreme individualism or total submission, they could develop and share the values of participative social intercourse; in many instances, authoritarian control could be happily dismissed for the habits of voluntary cooperation in the pursuit of shared interests.

Dewey's general approach to understanding human nature has the notable advantage over instinct theories that it can, among other things, account for both the regularities and singularities in behavior. Of course it is true that human beings exhibit enor-

---

[82] *Ibid.*, pp. 100-3.

mous hostility, destructiveness, and irrationality. These can be understood as the persistence in society of particular structural characteristics (perhaps created and perpetuated at one time by necessities of survival, or by ruling elites, etc.). For every postulated instinct, on the other hand, there are numerous counterexamples; and these can be explained as the occurrence of irregular circumstances. In any society freakish circumstances may occur to permit a more generous or a more vile development of human nature, and we find indisputable examples of each. Dewey was strongly of the opinion that manipulation of the social determinants of human behavior is in principle sufficient to create an integrated, creative, and cooperative individuality. Even if it were true, however, that he overemphasized social determinants of ways of behaving, it remains nonetheless true that there is nothing inherently inaccessible or unalterable about human nature; for the biological functions of man are by no means immutable. They are physico-chemical processes subject to physico-chemical change. Hence to speak of inherently unchangeable instincts is to journey into the occult. Fundamentally, the only meaningful question is *How* does human nature change? – not Is it changeable?

The arguments in favor of an unalterable and autonomous human nature are unpersuasive. I have been considering Dewey's position relative to the view that in some way society is but an extension of individual human nature; and it is clear that he finds no warrant for such a conclusion. As for the other view – that the individual is but a microcosm of society – it suffers variously from two erroneous assumptions: First, supposing that the individual is wholly passive, having no impulses demanding some form of fulfillment not already accessible in the society; and/or second, supposing society to be a wholly unified, monistic entity, which imposes its mold universally on all individuals. In respect to the first point the error seems quite clear: insofar as one is in any sense opposed to society, he cannot be considered simply an extension of it. The second assumption ignores the fact that societies are not uniform and monistic. Rather, societies are in some measure pluralistic; they consist of a variety of different and variously related – or unrelated – groups.

> Society is one word, but many things. Men associate together in all kinds of ways and for all kinds of purposes. One man is concerned in a multitude of diverse

> groups, in which his associates may be quite different. It often seems as if they had nothing in common except that they are modes of associated life. Within every larger social organization there are numerous minor groups: not only political subdivisions, but industrial, scientific, religious, associations. There are political parties with differing aims, social sets, cliques, gangs, corporations, partnerships, groups bound closely together by ties of blood, and so in endless variety. In many modern states, and in some ancient, there is great diversity of populations, of varying languages, religions, moral codes, and traditions. From this standpoint, many a modern political unit, one of our large cities, for example, is a congeries of loosely associated societies, rather than an inclusive and permeating community of action and thought.[83]

It is primarily in interaction with such groups that the individual human nature is determined. Thus the individual does not bear the exclusive stamp of the state, nor the church, nor family, nor any single institution. By interaction in this multifarious context, the biological energies of the individual are incorporated into habits and human nature is formed. It is this dynamic, historical, *inter*action of the biological organism and its environment (mainly the social environment) that constitutes – literally creates – human nature.

It is the *inter*action with the social environment – with all its modes of action, both institutionalized and novel – that forms the mind, the habits of thought and conduct of the individual, and also forms his standards of behavior and taste, and his virtues and vices:

> Because of his physical dependence and impotency, the contacts of the little child with nature are mediated by other persons. Mother and nurse, father and older children, determine what experiences the child shall have; they constantly instruct him as to the meaning of what he does and undergoes. The conceptions that are socially current and important become the child's principles of interpretation and estimation long before he attains to personal and deliberate control of conduct. Things come to him clothed in language, not in physical nakedness, and this garb of communication makes him a sharer in the beliefs of those about him. These beliefs coming to him as so many facts form his mind; they furnish the centres about which his own personal expeditions and perceptions are ordered. Here we have "categories" of connection and unification as important as those of Kant, but empirical not mythological.[84]

To Dewey it is foolishness to ask whether morals are social or

---

[83] *Democracy and Education* (New York: The Macmillan Company, 1916), pp. 94-5.

[84] *Reconstruction in Philosophy*, p. 92.

whether they ought to be social. For the fact is that they *are* social and could be nothing else. What is intended here is to say that moral beliefs and habits *originate* in social behavior and that moral action acquires its meaning in social behavior. It is not meant that particular moral requirements are *justified* simply because they are a social fact.[85]

> Some activity proceeds from a man; then it sets up reactions in the surroundings. Others approve, disapprove, protest, encourage, share and resist. Even letting a man alone is a definite response. Neutrality is non-existent. Conduct is always shared; this is the difference between it and a physiological process. It is not an ethical "ought" that conduct *should* be social. It *is* social, whether good or bad.[86]

> The resistance and the cooperation of others is the central fact in the furtherance or failure of our schemes. Connections with our fellows furnish both the opportunities for action and the instrumentalities by which we take advantage of opportunity. All of the actions of an individual bear the stamp of his community as assuredly as does the language he speaks. Difficulty in reading the stamp is due to variety of impressions in consequence of membership in many groups. The social saturation is, I repeat, a matter of fact, not of what should be, not of what is desirable or undesirable. It does not guarantee the rightness or goodness of an act.[87]

Moral conduct is always relative to other persons, directly or indirectly. The response which one's conduct brings from others becomes part of the funded meaning of that conduct – as snatching at food becomes rudeness or greediness. The various consequences of behavior are its meaning; and anyone contemplating a certain form of action responds in imagination to both the funded meaning of the act and also to the particular consequences expected of the act.

> In language and imagination we rehearse the responses of others just as we dramatically enact other consequences. We foreknow how others will act, and the foreknowledge is the beginning of judgment passed on action. We know *with* them; there is conscience. An assembly is formed within our breast which discusses and appraises proposed and performed acts. The community without becomes a forum and tribunal within, a judgment-seat of charges, assessments and exculpations. Our thoughts of our own actions are saturated with the ideas that others

---

[85] At this point it may seem to be begging the question to say that *morals* are social. Unavoidably, I must deal with this aspect of Dewey's philosophy before dealing with the status of value in nature. As subsequent discussions in this book will make clear, it is essential to understand the social nature of morality.

[86] *Human Nature and Conduct,* pp. 16-7.

[87] *Ibid.,* p. 317.

entertain about them, ideas which have been expressed not only in explicit instruction but still more effectively in reaction to our acts.[88]

The cumulative experience of social interaction yields certain standards of behavior, which are but statements of those ways of doing things which the given culture (or authoritative elements within it) have found to be effective in promoting certain desired results. Specific virtues and vices are not psychic powers; neither are they disembodied ideals. Rather, they are ways of acting with the environment which are especially distinguished for producing notably good or bad consequences.

> Honest, chastity, malice, peevishness, courage, triviality, industry, irresponsibility are not private possessions of a person. They are working adaptations of personal capacities with environing forces.[89]

It is important to emphasize that moral practices and norms – of whatever sort – originate in social interaction; for this entails that prior to any such interaction there could be no such things as moral standards or rules. The importance of this conclusion is not simply in that it contradicts theories of natural law and divine commandment; for it also has very positive implications for Dewey's substantive ethical and social theories. Discussion of these, however, must be postponed to later chapters.

In noting the general role played by social interaction in producing mind, morals, and habits of conduct, a derivative but extremely important point should be introduced. This is that intelligence is a social phenomenon. "Social intelligence," as Dewey calls it, has at least three important meanings. The first of these is all but explicit in the foregoing: Whatever effective habits of intelligence an individual possesses are the product of the peculiarities of his interaction with society. Highly significant, of course, is the nature of the cultural and educational institutions. In addition, the quality of countless further sorts of interactions is also crucial to the development of intelligence. To state something about these is to state the second meaning of social intelligence: Inquiry itself is obviously a social process. As is manifest in any intellectual discipline, the work of any individual is to a very great extent a matter of communication with other inquir-

---

[88] *Ibid.*, p. 315.

[89] *Ibid.*, p. 16.

ers. Each draws upon the funded achievements of others; there is a community of learning, testing, criticizing, and intellectual stimulus. Any claim to knowledge must be such that it can, among other things, be confirmed by the community of qualified individuals. The sophistication and effectiveness of inquiry depend on both the funded knowledge made available by institutions of various sorts, and also by the freedom, availability, and vitality of the instruments and procedures of communication. Great intellectual achievements may be chiefly associated with a few names, but the achievements are essentially social.

> The individual inquirer has not only the right but the duty to criticize the ideas, theories and "laws" that are current in science. But if we take the statement in the context of scientific method, it indicates that he carries on this criticism in virtue of a socially generated body of knowledge and by means of methods that are not of private origin and possession. . . . Consider what is involved in the production of steel, from the first use of fire and then the crude smelting of ore, to the processes that now effect the mass production of steel. Consider also the development of the power of guiding ships across trackless wastes from the day when they hugged the shore, steering by visible sun and stars, to the appliances that now enable a sure course to be taken. It would require a heavy tome to describe the advances in science, in mathematics, astronomy, physics, chemistry, that have made these two things possible. The record would be an account of a vast multitude of cooperative efforts, in which one individual uses the results provided by him by a countless number of other individuals, and uses them so as to add to the common and public store. A survey of such facts brings home the actual social character of intelligence as it actually develops and makes its way.[90]

Clearly, in this second sense, social intelligence is not an additive concept. That is, it is not simply the conglomeration of individual intelligences, but implies the qualitative improvement of individual intelligences and their products. It is at once a process which enormously enhances the effectiveness of the individual intelligence and by which the necessarily ineffectual efforts of isolated intelligences are transformed into creative, reliable, and cumulative inquiry.

The third meaning of social intelligence is simply that intelligence can be embodied in social institutions. Institutions are more or less permanent ways of doing things. These ways may be intelligent, or inappropriate, or harmful. In any case, these ways of doing things are fixtures of social action, and individuals ac-

---

[90] *Liberalism and Social Action* (New York: Capricorn Books, 1963), pp. 67-9.

cordingly tend to adopt these ways, whether intelligent or not. When institutions are embodiments of intelligence, those who are nurtured by them learn to employ an intelligence simply by habit which was once the work of genius:

> The level of action fixed by *embodied* intelligence is always the important thing. . . . A mechanic can discourse of ohms and amperes as Sir Isaac Newton could not in his day. Many a man who has tinkered with radios can judge of things which Faraday did not dream of. It is aside from the point to say that if Newton and Faraday were now here, the amateur and mechanic would be infants beside them. The retort only brings out the point: the difference made by different objects to think of and by different meanings in circulation. A more intelligent state of social affairs, one more informed with knowledge, more directed by intelligence, would not improve original endowments one whit, but it would raise the level upon which the intelligence of all operates.[91]

Descartes might have thought that by himself alone he excogitated eternal verities, but in this assumption he was completely mistaken.

Although the individual and society are in a fundamental sense organically united, it is clear that individuals frequently don't *feel* any such unity and, indeed, are in open conflict with society. What is perhaps a seeming contradiction must be explained. In order to see that there is no contradiction here, the crucial fact to be understood is that society is not a bloc at large. Societies, as remarked earlier, consist of numerous groupings. These are various and multiform, with countless purposes, methods, and modes of organization, overlapping and intersecting in nature, function, and membership. There are in many cases legal or informal relations of authority between groups; and in other cases there are groups which function in comparative independence of any outside authority. Individuals are nurtured by and belong to a variety of such groups. Since this is almost universally the case, a person is simply mistaken in saying he is opposed to "society." In reality he is opposed to certain groups or authorities within the society. These may, of course, be considerable in number and power; but even in the most extreme cases the individual has faithful allegiance and participation in some social grouping simply in virtue of his oppositions: There are thousands of hippies; and there is, at the other extreme, an American Nazi

---

[91] *The Public and Its Problems* (Denver: Alan Swallow, 1927), p. 210.

Party. And American Nazis belong to other groups as well – religious, recreational, familial, racist, professional, etc. Thus to point out that individuals are in conflict with certain features of their society provides no evidence that the individuals' habits were not socially determined. Even the complete anchorite, if he has a mind, acquired it in social interaction. What, then, is here the significant subject of inquiry is the sources of conflict (and unity) *within* a society.

Dewey has much to say concerning the way in which ruptures between the individual and significant social groups have affected philosophical conceptions of the nature of man and how they affect the experience of the individual. In the present context, only a summary account of his views can be provided. Some such account is, however, requisite to further discussions of value. The present study is concerned with exhibiting how value and valuing are made intelligible and are illuminated in the context of nature. Accordingly, examination of the effects of various traits of the social environment on human beliefs and values seems pertinent.

Something on this subject has already been said: Dewey has argued that the mind-body and related dualisms are fundamentally a reflex of social conditions. In various contexts throughout his writings he indicates several examples of such conditions. These could be classified into perhaps three general types: 1) conditions wherein individuals have found their surroundings obdurately resistant or alien to their desires and interests, 2) any rigid distinctions of social class which enforce sharp cleavages between activities regarded as purely mental and activities regarded as purely physical, 3) conditions wherein social allegiances, authorities, and groupings are in a state of flux, making the individual seem to be essentially unrelated to anything in society. Of course, these types can occur together.

Such conditions are principally responsible for various forms of otherworldliness, or withdrawal of social interest including – notably – the "inner life" of the romantic. When the individual is unable to act successfully with his surroundings, he must either directly resist objects or completely submit to them. In either case he regards the environment as something overwhelming and alien, against which he may struggle or else make wholesale withdrawal to some other realm where the impediments of the world seem to have no consequence. Thus is created an acute sense of sharp division between man and the world. The relation to nature and society is not experienced as one of selective participation with natural processes; to the agent, on-going activity is apparently not maintained by cooperation with the environment. Rather, his experience is that he is a separate entity, and nature at large is antagonistic and alien.

> Every type of culture has experienced resistance and frustration. These events are interpreted according to the bias dominating a particular type of culture. To the modern European mind they have been interpreted as results of the opposed existence of subject and object as independent forms of Being. The notion is now so established in tradition that to many thinkers it appears to be a datum, not an interpretative classification. But the East Indian has envisaged the same phenomena as evidence of the contrast of an illusory world to which corresponds domination by desires and a real world due to emancipation from desires, attained through ascetic discipline and meditation.[92]

> This resort to an objectivism which ignores initiating and re-organizing desire and imagination will in the end only strengthen that other phase of subjectivism which consists in escape to the enjoyment of inward landscape. Men who are balked of a legitimate realization of their subjectivity, men who are forced to confine innovating need and projection of ideas to technical modes of industrial and political life, and to specialized or "scientific" fields of intellectual activity, will compensate by finding release within their inner consciousness. . . . Philosophical dualism is but a formulated recognition of an impasse in life; an impotence in interaction, inability to make effective transition, limitation of power to regulate and thereby to understand.[93]

Technical philosophies evidently reflect the actual experience of a culture. I have given some brief indication of social conditions which, according to Dewey, conduce to explicit and formal dualisms. It must also be noted what these conditions do to the experience of the individual. Generally speaking, it is clear enough what the consequences are: Individuals are, variously, frustrated in their endeavors, limited to only certain kinds of experience, shut off from many of the resources of the community, without common values, and without a sense of participating in, contributing to, or being supported by, social action. All of these ills are a consequence of a community life in which there are arbitrary barriers and limitations, where life activities are di-

---

[92] *Experience and Nature*, pp. 238-9.

[93] *Ibid.*, pp. 241-2.

vided into strictly demarcated compartments, where there is little communication and shared experience, where there are lacking enduring, trustworthy, and intimate allegiances.

It will be necessary here to provide in outline Dewey's thought concerning the form of social life which would be both remedy to such ills and the condition of integrated individuality in persons. Even apart from the intrinsic interest of this subject, it has an important bearing on discussions of value to come later. In general, Dewey's ideals of democracy and individuality portray the conditions and values which would prevent the evils of fixed social barriers and provide the medium for the enhancement of experienced human goods. In Dewey's view, the concepts of individuality and democracy have common implications. Consider first his notion of individuality.[94]

On Dewey's grounds, individuality involves nothing so foolish as separating oneself in a wholesale way from all forms of society. Neither does it involve separating one's existence into fixed divisions of social and non-social, or duty and interest, confining individuality to the exclusively private realm. Nor does the individual offer himself up to his station and its duties for the glory of the state. Rather individuality is a matter of the *way* one functions *in* and *with* society. Individuality is realized in and through society – or, to speak more accurately – in and through a variety of different forms of associated life. A person discovers, develops, and fulfills his various powers and interests by interaction with groups and individuals:

---

[94] Dewey's works of immediate pertinence to social philosophy are *Democracy and Education, Reconstruction in Philosophy, Human Nature and Conduct, The Public and Its Problems, Individualism Old and New, Liberalism and Social Action,* and *Freedom and Culture,* as well as numerous articles. The positions elaborated in these works require, in Dewey's own estimate, a comprehensive philosophical basis. This basis is found to a large extent in those works themselves, but most fundamental of all is *Experience and Nature.* In response to Morris Cohen's critique of *Experience and Nature,* Dewey said, "Finally, while I am grateful and deeply appreciative of Cohen's approval of my personal Liberalism, I must add not only that this Liberalism is definitely rooted in the very philosophy to which he takes exception, but that any theory of activity in social and moral matters, liberal or otherwise, which is not grounded in a comprehensive philosophy seems to me to be only a projection of arbitrary personal preference." ("Nature in Experience," in Bernstein, *op. cit.,* p. 255.) Cohen's critique is in *The Philosophical Review,* XLIX (1940): "Some Difficulties in Dewey's Anthropocentric Naturalism."

> To learn to be human is to develop through the give-and-take of communication an effective sense of being an indivdually distinctive member of a community; one who understands and appreciates its beliefs, desires and methods, and who contributes to a further conversion of organic powers into human resources and values. . . . A *distinctive* way of behaving in conjunction and *connection* with other distinctive ways of acting, not a self-enclosed way of acting, independent of everything else, is that toward which we are pointed.[95]

And in a related context:

> Liberty is that secure release and fulfillment of personal potentialities which takes place only in rich manifold association with others: the power to be an individualized self making a distinctive contribution and enjoying in its own way the fruits of association.[96]

The value of particular associations depends upon the range of values which the association realizes and upon the extent to which one embraces and shares in these distinctive values. One's character becomes many-sided, one enjoys a diversity of values and qualities of experience, precisely because of the diversity of participation in various groups. In addition, certain important ideas, attitudes, and habitual responses are developed and reinforced: The individual comes to think of himself in large measure *as* a participant in these forms of associated life; he comes as a matter of course to consider his own aims and actions as a function of the aims and activities of the group. In the same instance, he regards the person of others in a like manner, that is, as participants in the conjoint activities of association. This is not an ideal of conformity. It is an ideal of democratic equality; and it manifests itself in the individual not only in his recognition of the interests of others as having the same status as his own, but also in his willing and habitual regard for these interests. At the same time, he is aware that he enjoys precisely the same full stature and recognition as an individual in the eyes of the other members of the group. He is a "sustained and sustaining member

[95] *The Public and Its Problems*, pp. 154, 188. In my judgment, Dewey gives insufficient attention to the effects on individuality from sources not immediately social, such as that derived from literature of various kinds. But this is a difference in emphasis, for literature is itself a usufruct of social intelligence.

[96] *Ibid.*, p. 150.

of a social whole."[97] Such habits are of inestimable importance. When, as a customary expression of his personality, an individual approaches and deals with other persons with the honest presumption that they are to be consulted, understood, and appreciated without prejudice and with the assumption that they have something to contribute, then the richest sort of values accrue to the experience of the individual and the life of the group. This is one of the principal values of democracy, of genuine shared experience. It should be added here that as the individual personality develops and forms, the greater is the distinctive part played in social interaction by that individual. (On Dewey's view, the expression of mere impulse is the least individuated form of behavior. Distinctiveness of human nature is a matter of the character, direction, and growth of habits.)

The values in each form of participation are enriched and broadened by the experience each person brings from his other associations.

> Now in any social group whatever, even in a gang of thieves, we find some interest held in common, and we find a certain amount of interaction and cooperative intercourse with other groups. From these two traits we derive our standard [of the worth of any given mode of social life]. How numerous and varied are the interests which are consciously shared? How full and free is the interplay with other forms of association? . . . If we take . . . the kind of family life which illustrates the standard, we find that there are material, intellectual, aesthetic interests in which all participate and that the progress of one member has worth for the experience of other members – it is readily communicable – and that the family is not an isolated whole, but enters intimately into relationships with business groups, with schools, with all the agencies of culture, as well as with other similar groups, and that it plays a due part in the political organization and in return receives support from it. In short, there are many interests consciously communicated and shared; and there are varied and free points of contact with other modes of association. . . . These more numerous and more varied points of contact denote a greater diversity of stimuli to which an individual has to respond; they consequently put a premium on variation in his action. They secure a liberation of powers which remain suppressed as long as the incitations to action

[97] *Individualism Old and New* (New York: Capricorn Books, 1962), p. 88. This should not be taken as an argument that *all* groups should function according to the principles of social democracy. *Being* democratic, as such, is obviously not the purpose of many groups which enjoy shared and valued aims; and strictly democratic decision-making procedures may well be injurious to these aims. (This is a cautionary word to forestall the [a priori] assumption that Dewey would extend participatory democracy to all forms of associated living. See footnote 100, this chapter.)

are partial, as they must be in a group which in its exclusiveness shuts out many interests.[98]

To describe the character of this interaction is to describe essentially what Dewey meant by democracy. His discussion of democracy was infrequently directed toward the procedures of political competition and decision-making. Rather, he concerned himself with the qualities of associated living:

> Democracy is much broader than a special political form, a method of conducting government, of making laws and carrying on governmental administration by means of popular suffrage and elected officers. It is that, of course. But it is something broader and deeper than that. The political and governmental phase of democracy is a means, the best means so far found, for realizing ends that lie in the wide domain of human relationships and the development of human personality. It is, as we often say, though perhaps without appreciating all that is involved in the saying, a way of life, social and individual. The keynote of democracy as a way of life may be expressed, it seems to me, as the necessity for the participation of every mature human being in formation of the values that regulate the living of men together: which is necessary from the standpoint of both the general social welfare and the full development of human beings as individuals.[99]

The essentials of democracy, in this fundamental sense, consist largely in the life of so-called face-to-face groups – at any rate, in face-to-face groups of a specific sort: Those groups in which communication is vital and meaningful, where everyone's role is participative and is induced by perception of shared aims rather than coerced by authority, and where requirements of efficient organization are subordinated to the values of genuine association.

Social unity is a function of – among other things – the nature of the interactions within and among such groups. When the individual possesses a plurality of allegiances, he shares in some measure in the values of other individuals in the society who likewise possess diversified loyalties. In this way it happens that individuals who oppose each other or are indifferent to each other in respect to some aims are yet agreeable and cooperative in respect to other aims; and hence it happens that their shared aims are often such to discourage outright disruption between

---

[98] *Democracy and Education,* pp. 96-7, 101.

[99] "Democracy and Educational Administration," reprinted in *Intelligence in the Modern World,* edited and with an introduction by Joseph Ratner (New York: The Modern Library, 1939), p. 400.

them despite their differences. In such a context, it is much easier for individuals to convert blind conflict into accommodation and adjustment. Certainly it is a frequent experience that one is willing to listen to and attempt to appreciate the position of another when a measure of mutual interest has been enjoyed in respect to other values. On the other hand, fanatical and unyielding antagonisms are the product of totally self-enclosed, noninteracting groups.

It is clearly of utmost importance to a society to encourage a rich variety of values, endeavors, and associations, but, it must be emphasized, a pluralism of this kind is valuable only if individuals possess free access to such groups. In a free, pluralistic society (a democratic society), both the individuality of persons is developed and expressed and at the same time social unity is fostered. A society in which certain kinds of persons are systematically excluded from certain kinds of activity is at once a society in which individuality cannot flourish and in which violent social conflicts between wholly compartmentalized and stagnating units are inevitable.

> Segregated classes develop their own customs, which is to say their own working morals. As long as society is mainly immobile these diverse principles and ruling aims do not clash. . . . But mobility invades society. War, commerce, travel, communication, contact with the thoughts and desires of other classes, new inventions in productive industry, disturb the settled distribution of customs. . . .
>
> Each class is rigidly sure of the rightness of its own ends and hence not overscrupulous about the means of attaining them. One side proclaims the ultimacy of order – that of some old order which conduces to its own interest. The other side proclaims the rights to freedom, and identifies justice with its submerged claims.[100]

---

[100] *Human Nature and Conduct,* pp. 82-3. Any particular organization has its own purposes and its changing problems and values; and these will determine the balance between democracy and other values. A random listing of groups suggests the differences in aims and values which they can embody: athletic teams, armies, labor unions, religions, schools of all kinds, recreational groups, political parties, economic organizations, political units. As Dewey himself insists, there is no absolute and permanent way of dividing liberty and authority.

In the present context, however, Dewey's point needn't be endlessly qualified. It is sufficient to point out that democracy as both end and means is one of our most precious values; and it can never thrive until it becomes social habit. And to the extent that persons are limited in their movements, associations, and activities, individuality has little prospect. (More on this in Chapter VII.)

For Dewey, to say that a society is of this democratic nature is to say that social intelligence is operative throughout it. One of the topics of the last chapter will be consideration of the relation of democracy and social intelligence; hence present remarks will be brief. Social intelligence implies a full and free flow of communication in which all may enter; it implies an absence of dogmatism, of arbitrary authority, and of intolerance of novel views. Thus democracy and social intelligence are, as social facts, inseparable.

Clearly, in Dewey's perception of the matter, the concepts of democracy and individuality are likewise inseparable: either concept implies the other. In a democratic society human energies, rather than being suppressed, find free access to constructive modes of fulfillment; social groupings are determined by perception of common interests and ends; and individuals develop the habits of participative social action. There are no class distinctions or impassable social barriers of any kind, and the collective goods of the community are available to all. Above all, it is a society in which the values of social intelligence are fully acknowledged, and all institutions make them flourish. The point of it all is that the individuals in and through their shared social existence bring to enduring reality in each the inclusive and richly funded meanings of experience which the intelligent interaction with nature can afford.[101]

> Democracy as compared with other ways of life is the sole way of living which believes wholeheartedly in the process of experience as end and as means; as that which is capable of generating the science which is the sole dependable authority for the direction of further experience and which releases emotions, needs, and desires so as to call into being the things that have not existed in the past. For every way of life that fails in its democracy limits the contacts, the exchanges, the communications, the interactions by which experience is steadied while it is also enlarged and enriched. the task of this release and enrichment is one that has to be carried on day by day. Since it is one that can have no end till experience itself comes to an end, the task of democracy is forever that of creation of a freer and more humane experience in which all share and to which all contribute.[102]

[101] Contrary to popular belief, Dewey had no abounding confidence that his democractic ideals would actually be accomplished. What he did want to insist upon, however, is 1) that there are no intrinsic limitations in human nature to such a state of affairs, and 2) that whatever the difficulty of our social problems, the method of intelligence is the only one promising hope of solving them. (See the concluding section of this book.)

[102] "Creative Democracy – The Task Before Us," in *The Philosophy of the Common Man,* p. 228.

It has been one of the themes of this section that philosophical dualisms are of much more than simply academic concern. Not only are they symptomatic of genuine social problems, but, in turn, they also render philosophy impotent to deal with the realities of existence: social thought is burdened, for example, with a theory of atomistic individualism which can account for neither the nature, the values, the problems, nor the needs of associated life; and, moreover, man is set apart from scientific investigation. Worse, when dualisms are once accepted as somehow inherent in the very nature of things, social institutions are deliberately arranged to perpetuate them. Thus we have, for example, disastrous theories of education, in which intelligence as a process (that is, as the social practice of inquiry) is completely neglected for the direct inculcation of information into the pre-existing "minds" of the students. Such information must be accepted on authority – that of the existing vested interests of the community. Thus are deceit and prejudice perpetuated, and habits of intelligence discouraged. Similarly – to provide another example of disastrous separations – we have "art" in museums and elsewhere we have ugliness.

These last remarks suggest the topics which will complete this final section of the chapter: It remains to show how Dewey's conclusions about man and society determine the character and role of scientific inquiry into this field, and to suggest something of the moral import of Dewey's position.

As regards scientific inquiry, it will be sufficient to make but two points. The first is simply to remark that all that was said in this connection about mind and body is equally appropriate here. The second point can be introduced by explaining the sub-title of *Human Nature and Conduct:* "An Introduction to Social Psychology." The sub-title is misleading, for one might expect a primer on the subject of social psychology. What Dewey does, however, is to write a book on individual psychology *as social.* He argues firmly against individual psychology as such, and insists that human nature is the product of social interaction. Thus Dewey sets the tasks of social psychology proper: to discover the social determinants of individual (and group) behavior.[103] Indi-

[103] Since behavior is biological-environmental, complete explanations of behavior would also require knowledge of biological mechanisms. Accounts of human behavior must also consider the nonhuman determinants in the environment.

vidual psychology as such is an impossibility; persistence in it can only be misleading, and Dewey never tired in his criticisms of endeavors of any kind which try to deal with man as a discrete entity. Not only moralists, theologians, and various sorts of professed dualists persist in such endeavor, however, but scrupulous scientists as well. (See above, pp. 97-8.) The consequence of this truncated science is a complete inability to undersand the most distinctive features of human nature.

> We are far from having reached the point in which it is seen that the whole difference between animal and human psychology is constituted by the transforming effect exercised upon the former by intercourse and association with other persons and groups of persons. For, apart from unconditioned reflexes, like the knee-jerk, it may be questioned whether there is a single human activity or experience which is not profoundly affected by the social and cultural environment. . . .
>
> I do not believe I am going beyond the implications of these passages when I say that the operation of "living situations created by human contacts" is the only intelligible ground upon which we can distinguish between what we call the *higher* and the *lower* (the physical on one side and the ideal and the "spiritual" on the other) in human experience. . . .
>
> Take the case of those who revolt against the old dualism, and who because of their revolt imagine they must throw away and deny the existence of all phenomena that go by the names of "higher," intellectual and moral. Such persons exist. They suppose they are not scientific unless they reduce everything to the exclusively somatic and physiological. This procedure is a conspicuous instance of what must happen when observation, description and interpretation of human events are confined to what goes on under the skin to the exclusion of their integrated interaction with environmental conditions, particularly the environment formed by other human beings. Knowledge of strictly somatic organs and processes is certainly necessary for scientific understanding of "higher" phenomena. But only half-way science neglects and rules out the other factor.[104]

Again, of course, there is in Dewey's position utmost moral significance in making all phases of social experience subject matter for social intelligence. More particularly, the assertion that morality itself is a phenomenon of social interaction implies at the least that the conditions of moral conduct and beliefs can be investigated by experimental procedures. Moreoever, there are crucial implications in the assumption that man is essentially a social (if not always sociable) being and that his nature is not

---

[104] *Intelligence in the Modern World,* pp. 825-7. There will be in Chapter VII further discussion of the nature of social science and the role of the social scientist.

fixed in rigid patterns by instincts. If the social variables in the determinations of human nature can be accurately discriminated, then it is clear that manipulations of these variables will bring predictable changes in behavior. (The same, of course, is true of biological variables. The biological and environmental, indeed, function together.) Assumptions concerning a presumed antithesis of individual and society, or – by contrast – a presumed identity of the two, or concerning the "unalterable workings of human nature," can only prevent a clear perception of the problems of the individual and of social control, and of the values resident in shared experience.

Many of the presumably moral implications of Dewey's analysis of man and society have already been remarked in the course of indicating the rudiments of that analysis. Rather than rehearse these points, I will simply conclude with Dewey's more general observations pertaining to the lessons to be learned from a just appreciation of man's status in nature.[105]

Dewey has a conception of natural piety and spirituality much like that expressed in Greek literature and articulated explicitly by Santayana. Piety involves, in Santayana's own words, ". . . man's reverent attachment to the sources of his being and the steadying of his life by that attachment."[106] The sources of our being are all in nature. When an individual comes to a vivid awareness of his own vital and supportive connections with nature, the consequence is a deeply felt natural piety. This piety, for Dewey, is mostly owing to the community, the idea of which is his fundamental religious symbol:

> Infinite relationships of man with his fellows and with nature already exist. The ideal means, as we have seen, a sense of these encompassing continuities with their infinite reach. This meaning even now attaches to present activities because they are set in a whole to which they belong and which belongs to them. Even in the midst of conflict, struggle and defeat a consciousness is possible of the enduring and comprehending whole. . . . Within the flickering inconsequential acts of separate selves dwells a sense of the whole which claims and dignifies them. In its presence we put off mortality and live in the universal. The life of the community

[105] In the succeeding chapters there will be occasion to deal at greater length with some of the moral issues introduced in the present chapter.

[106] George Santayana, *The Life of Reason,* Vol. III: *Reason in Religion* (New York: Collier Books, 1962), p. 125.

in which we live and have our being is the fit symbol of this relationship. The acts in which we express our perception of the ties which bind us to others are its only rites and ceremonies.[107]

Moreover, what we find in nature fragile, transient, incomplete, adulterated, muted, is capable of ideal fulfillment. That is, the precarious suggestions of nature can with the cooperation of human imagination and art be transformed into secure values and enduring ideals. Spirituality, in distinction from piety, consists precisely in devotion to the ideal possibilities of nature. The genuinely democratic community is such an ideal.

Yet it is equally true that nature is also the source of suffering, evil, and defeat; however much intelligence may minimize their incidence, they are nevertheless a permanent part of existence as human. It should be clear, then, that either a wholesale piety or a wholesale antagonism to nature at large is both inappropriate and factitious. Nevertheless, historic philosophies, when they have had any regard for nature at all, have frequently shuttled between these exclusive positions. [108] Apart from the outright falsehood of such views, they fail to provide a basis for the activity of intelligent interaction with nature – either wholly embracing or wholly resisting it; they either forbid any piety whatsoever or make it such that forbids moral distinctions.

Militant atheism is also affected by lack of natural piety. The ties binding man to nature that poets have always celebrated are passed over lightly. The attitude taken is often that of man living in an indifferent and hostile world and issuing blasts of defiance. A religious attitude, however, needs the sense of a connection of man, in the way of both dependence and support, with the enveloping world that the imagination feels is a universe. Use of the words "God" or "divine" to convey the union of actual with ideal may protect man from a sense of isolation and from consequent despair or defiance.

In any case, whatever the name, the meaning is selective. For it involves no miscellaneous worship of everything in general. It selects those factors in existence that generate and support our idea of good as an end to be striven for. It excludes a multitude of forces that at any given time are irrelevant to this function. Nature produces whatever gives reinforcement and direction but also what occasions discord and confusion. The "divine" is thus a term of human choice and aspiration.[109]

---

[107] Dewey, *Human Nature and Conduct,* pp. 330-2.

[108] Bertrand Russell finds nature wholly alien and hostile in the highly representative "A Free Man's Worship," while Bergson, at the other extreme, regards human good as ultimately identified with the cosmic process as such.

[109] *A Common Faith* (New Haven: Yale University Press, 1960), pp. 53-4.

Moreover, men invite, alternately, hopeless disappointment, isolation from experience, and needless ineffectuality when they regard themselves either as beings who can somehow escape nature or as creatures wholly submissive to it.

> Men move between extremes. They conceive of themselves as gods, or feign a powerful and cunning god as an ally who bends the world to do their bidding and meet their wishes. Disillusionized, they disown the world that disappoints them; and hugging ideals to themselves as their own possession, stand in haughty aloofness apart from the hard course of events that pays so little heed to our hopes and aspirations. But a mind that has opened itself to experience and that has ripened through its discipline knows its own littleness and impotencies; it knows that its wishes and acknowledgments are not final measures of the universe whether in knowledge or in conduct, and hence are, in the end, transient. But it also knows that its juvenile assumption of power and achievement is not a dream to be wholly forgotten. It implies a unity with the universe that is to be preserved. The belief, and the effort of thought and struggle which it inspires are also the doing of the universe, and they in some way, however slight, carry the universe forward.[110]
>
> Nature's place in man is no less significant than man's place in nature. Man in nature is man subjected; nature in man, recognized and used, is intelligence and art.[111]

---

[110] *Experience and Nature,* pp. 419-20. Dewey's use of "universe" in this quotation is highly infelicitous. It gives the impression that he is being recaptured by his one-time objective idealism. The word "nature" would have been far more appropriate, implying that what man is and does is organic with the characteristic forces of nature as these are operative in distinctive ways in particular situations. This notion is to be sharply distinguished from the view that all the different things which actually happen to exist in the universe are in some significant sense constitutive or determining of man's nature and striving. The following quotation employs a more apt expression.

[111] *Experience and Nature* (first edition), p. 28.

CHAPTER III

Nature and Value

> The more sure one is that the world which encompasses human life is of such and such a character (no matter what his definition), the more one is committed to try to direct the conduct of life, that of others as well as of himself, upon the basis of the character assigned to that world. And if he finds that he cannot succeed, that the attempt lands him in confusion, inconsistency and darkness, plunging others into discord and shutting them out from participation, rudimentary precepts instruct him to surrender his assurance as a delusion; and to revise his notions of the nature of nature till he makes them more adequate to the concrete facts in which nature is embodied.[1]

To enter upon an analysis of Dewey's philosophy of value is certainly one of the most formidable tasks one could undertake in connection with his thought. It is clear that Dewey was centrally concerned with value and that his philosophy was ultimately practical. He was, moreover, persuaded that a study of value necessarily involved a theory of nature. Indeed, Dewey held that one can discuss value intelligibly *only* in the context of nature. The issues surrounding value were, in Dewey's estimate, so inextricably related to fundamental philosophical issues that he could say that "no great difficulty would attend an effort to derive all the stock issues of philosophy from the problems of value and their relationship to critical judgment."[2] Because Dewey held these convictions and because his aim was to serve practical ends, he had a profusion of illuminating and eminently useful things to say about value in nature.

My program in the present chapter will be divided into two

---

[1] *Experience and Nature,* pp. 413-4.

[2] *Ibid.,* p. 402.

parts: first, an exposition of Dewey's position regarding the nature of value and its status in nature; second, an analysis of conduct as art. The second topic is essential to understanding what are the inclusive processes in nature which are richest in value. I should make it clear at this point that this chapter will not be concerned with the actual procedures of evaluation, moral judgment, or justification of claims. Much that will be said in the present chapter has, of course, a crucial bearing on these issues, which will receive attention in the final chapter. Any division of such a complicated subject matter seems inevitably to require the postponement of discussions otherwise germane to the question at hand.

1. The Metaphysics of Value

In accordance with the method of experience, it is essential to see value in all its implications with nature. Thus – so it will be shown – the events designated as values are continuous with natural processes; and the experience of value is continuous with gross experience. Moreover, when moral situations are examined in all their phases, it will be clear that characteristically moral experience is also organic to cognitive experience, aesthetic experience, and to religious experience as well. [3] It will also be clear that none of these facts can be made intelligible without full acknowledgment of those realities of nature which Dewey has characterized as the generic traits of experience.

To understand values and valuing in nature, it is essential to exhibit them as they actually occur in life experience. Value is neither an isolated entity, nor a phantom of subjective mind, nor a transcendent form; but it is an eventual function in nature, produced with the contrivance of intelligence and activity. Experienced values, as we shall see, are always eventual of a situation. That function of experience and nature which Dewey designates by the term "value" is the consummatory phase of a situation which is initially problematic. Accordingly, the analysis shall be-

[3] The connections with so-called religious experience will not be made explicit until the sixth chapter. However, the discussion of piety and spirituality briefly introduced at the conclusion of Chapter II suggests that Dewey has no difficulty in understanding and clarifying religious experience with naturalistic assumptions.

gin by characterizing the problematic situation. (There are notable merits in studying values in the context of concrete situations. What these merits are will be made evident in several subsequent analyses. Many would claim, of course, on a variety of grounds, that values are not organic to situations. Dewey criticizes these views at length. See especially Chapter IV.)

Such situations arise when the on-going activity of an individual is impeded, disrupted, or is in some significant way unsatisfactory. In anyone's activity there are inherent obstacles as well as external distractions and impediments. Thus difficulty, frustration, confusion, and perplexity inevitably punctuate the course of on-going activity. In short, a fundamental fact of experience is the recurrence of the problematic situation. This is true in the study, the laboratory, the playing field, the business endeavor, the studio, and so forth. These situations may involve immediately only one person, or several, or thousands.

> We compare life to a traveler faring forth. We may consider him first at a moment where his activity is confident, straightforward, organized. He marches on giving no direct attention to his path, nor thinking of his destination. Abruptly he is pulled up, arrested. Something is going wrong in his activity. From the standpoint of an onlooker, he has met an obstacle which must be overcome before his behaviour can be unified into a successful ongoing. From his own standpoint, there is shock, confusion, perturbation, uncertainty. For the moment he doesn't know what hit him, as we say, nor where he is going. But a new impulse is stirred which becomes the starting point of an investigation, a looking into things, a trying to see them, to find out what it going on.[4]

Because these situations arise in the course of activity of some kind, the way in which the agent analyses the situation and formulates his aims in it will be largely determined by the specific nature of the activity which has been interrupted.

In life experience we are recurrently faced with the problem of converting problematic situations into restored activity and — one hopes — in a manner which provides satisfactions and fulfillments of some kind. Dewey attempted to formulate distinctions which would enlighten this process. Inasmuch as he was deeply absorbed in the analysis of value, it is remarkable that the terminology which he employs to make distinctions in this subject matter is exceptionally careless. It is safe to say that his highly am-

[4] *Human Nature and Conduct,* p. 181.

biguous language here is largely responsible for the almost total misunderstanding of his basic views.[5] Even in such a mature work as *Experience and Nature* there is a lamentable inattention to consistency and precision in usage. In *The Quest for Certainty* and in the relatively late *Theory of Valuation* (1939), as well as in a number of articles, there is a conscientious attempt to introduce greater clarity. Nevertheless, the carelessness is never wholly eradicated; and Dewey compounds this problem by trying out some new terms, rather than clarifying the old. In spite of all these difficulties, however, it can be made clear what distinctions in the primary subject matter Dewey was making. The following analysis will attempt precisely that clarification.

We have already seen how Dewey establishes the reality of quality in nature. It is from this reality that the interaction of man and nature produces, under specifiable conditions, what is called value. In any situation, including the problematic, an individual is surrounded by objects in nature which present numberless qualities; they are attractive and repulsive in countless ways and constitute stimuli for pursuit and avoidance of all kinds. Each of the objects presenting such qualities can be treated in various ways, in order to undertake further interactions with it if attractive or avoid it if unattractive. Obviously, what possibilities of the problematic situation appear to be most eligible will depend in large measure on whatever the actual aims and activities were which became impeded. This would seem to be an indisputable fact of experience. It is in this immediate experience of quality that value is rooted; but Dewey persistently emphasizes that these immediate experiences are to be distinguished from what he calls the consummatory phase of experience: value proper. This distinction will be made clear shortly.

As I have noted, the vocabulary Dewey uses to mark such distinctions is very much lacking in precision. Immediately attractive qualities he calls, among other things, "immediate values," "immediate goods," "problematic goods," "enjoyments," "desires," "likings," "apparent goods," "direct valuings," "valuings," "prizings," and even (regrettably) "values." When, how-

[5] The most typical misunderstandings will be examined briefly in this and later chapters. Not the least cause of misunderstanding is in critics imputing to Dewey their own assumptions and aims.

ever, he is signifying his distinctions cautiously, he withholds the name "values" from these events. That Dewey declines to call these immediate qualities values does not mean that they are valueless; nor does it mean that values proper are detached from nature. There is, as Dewey insists, an intrinsic appeal and attraction in all immediate goods. That is, immediate qualities are prized in and for themselves.

It must be pointed out, however, that in any situation each of the immediately attractive objects or aims which is presented is itself problematical. Qualitative events are objective realities in nature. To act with them in any way is to become subject to still further events in nature. What these events will in fact be is doubtful, and they might or might not be welcome:

> All experienced objects have a double status. They are individualized, ... whether in the way of enjoyment or of suffering. They are also involved in a continuity of interactions and changes, and hence are causes and potential means of later experiences. Because of this dual capacity, they become problematic. Immediately and directly they are just what they are; but as transitions to and possibilities of later experiences they are uncertain.[6]

It is clear, to put the matter briefly, that problematic goods are an instance of what was identified in Chapter II as the precarious character of nature.

A prizing in itself and as such does not and cannot specify any course of conduct; it provides no means for determining what the conditions and consequences of pursuing it will be; and it can provide no means of comparing it in any way to other prizings. For, again, a prizing is an object experienced only in its immediacy, out of relation to other objects. It is obvious, then, that prizings as a mode of experiencing are not evaluations. It should be equally obvious that it is a matter of utmost practical importance that there be some effective means developed to discriminate between problematic (precarious) objects.

> First and immature experience is content simply to enjoy. But a brief course in experience enforces reflection; it requires but brief time to teach that some things sweet in the having are bitter in after-taste and in what they lead to. Primitive innocence does not last. Enjoyment ceases to be a datum and becomes a problem.[7]

---

[6] *The Quest for Certainty*, p. 236.

[7] *Experience and Nature*, p. 398.

With activity arrested, and in the presence of a number of problematic goods (and problematic evils as well), some kind of a choice has to be made to set the agent on a course of action appropriate to his circumstances. Clearly, at such times the agent is not in a state of indifference, but deals with real problems and real alternatives.

> It is a great error to suppose that we have no preferences until there is a choice. We are always biased beings, tending in one direction rather than another. The occasion of deliberation is an *excess* of preferences, not natural apathy or an absence of likings. We want things that are incompatible with one another; therefore we have to make a choice of what we *really* want. . . .[8]

The situation demands a choice. Some particular way of acting with a discriminated feature of the situation must be selected. It is at this stage that the procedures of judgment, evaluation, must be initiated. It is clear that the actual processes of evaluation utilized by different persons differ radically from one another. The procedure recommended by Dewey is that which he calls the method of intelligence. This will receive detailed examination in the concluding chapter. In the present context the important thing to note is that this method requires, among other things, the use of cognitive structures in the situation. That is, the use of the stable traits of the situation is indispensable to evaluation. Immediately precarious goods exist in a system of relations; and, depending on what actions might be taken with them, they will function as conditions to a variety of further possible events in which the agent and others will be implicated. These events may be very welcome or very disagreeable; so it is vital to have knowledge of their relations and to inquire into their possible functions. These actual and potential relations, insofar as they are known, are the stable elements of the situation.

The evaluative process must be undertaken in order to transform an initially problematic situation into a determinate one, wherein an immediate good, or some combination of goods (or goods and evils) is somehow distinguished and pursued in preference to others. To make such a selection implies that in some way, however rudimentary and implicit, a plan of action has been devised – a way of acting with discriminated features of the

---

[8] *Human Nature and Conduct,* p. 193.

environment has been settled upon. Thus a particular consequence is expected to ensue from undertaking a certain course of action. This anticipated relation of means-end can be formulated in a hypothesis: if such and such action is undertaken, such and such an end will result.

Dewey frequently used the same expression to refer to both the *plan* of action and that to which action is specifically directed, namely, "end-in-view." He not only used "end-in-view" ambiguously in this way, but he also used the expressions "idea of value" and "value" in place of "end-in-view." Moreover, he commonly used "end" both for "end-in-view" and for "value." This astonishing carelessness permitted a confusion of ends-in-view with values. But values, as we shall see, are not ends-in-view, even when the latter are actually achieved. Consummatory experience is to be distinguished from the achievement of the end-in-view, as such. Dewey's remarkably loose language, however, has permitted students and critics of his philosophy to assume that an end-in-view, when accomplished, is a value.[9]

Both to indicate his various usages and – in due course – to clarify the distinction between ends-in-view and values, it can also be noted that in *Human Nature and Conduct* Dewey characterizes the notion of object of desire in such a way that it has precisely the same meaning as end-in-view, in the sense of specific interaction. In various writings, he also used "moral judgment," "value judgment," and "proposition of appraisal" to denote the hypothesis which formulates a plan of action. The latter notions will receive sustained attention in the last chapter.

This conceptual imprecision need not delay us, for the nature of the distinctions Dewey intends can be made clearly and consistently. In this study I will never refer to the hypothesis of means-end with "end-in-view."[10] "End-in-view" will be used exclusively to denote the intended specific interaction with specific

---

[9] All studies of Dewey's value theory or ethical theory of which I am aware have made the mistake of identifying end-in-view and value. It will be made clear that such analyses are in error. It is also clear, however, that Dewey himself must share responsibility for such confusions. The usage in "The Construction of Good" in *The Quest for Certainty* particularly encourages the error indicated here.

[10] A difficulty with Dewey's treatment of the hypothesis will be brought up after the notion of value has been introduced. (See footnote 14.)

features of the situation. What is meant by value will be indicated shortly and eventually elaborated in detail. Before proceeding with that, however, it will be useful to clarify the topics already introduced.

What must be noted is that Dewey insists on the difference between the mere occurrence of an attractive quality and the end-in-view, which has been selected by some process of inquiry and reflection. There is also a difference between a situation which transpires merely by force of inertia and one which proceeds with specific goals and deliberate action. All situations move toward termination, but the situation which contains an end-in-view has at least some element of felt continuity and rational control:

> Every situation or field of consciousness is marked by initiation, direction or intent, and consequence or import. What is unique is not these traits, but the property of awareness or perception. Because of this property, the initial stage is capable of being judged in the light of its probable course and consequence. There is anticipation. Each successive event being a stage in a serial process is both expectant and commemorative. What is more precisely pertinent to our present theme, the terminal outcome when anticipated (as it is when a moving cause of affairs is perceived) becomes an end-in-view, an aim, purpose, a prediction usable as a plan in shaping the course of events.[11]

It would be seriously misleading to regard the end-in-view as an object in itself. Rather, it is a particular way of interacting with selected features of the environment. End-in-view, then, as purpose or aim, is a proposed interaction in which *both* the agent and his surroundings would be necessarily and intimately involved. There should, therefore, be no lurking assumption that ends-in-view are in some way independent of natural transactions and without import for the nature of nature. When Dewey's position is understood, it becomes entirely legitimate to speak of purposes in nature. (Dewey is very emphatic in distinguishing his position from Greek teleology, which – in his view – assumed fixed and predetermined purposes in nature existing independently of human preference and intelligence. He also sharply

---

[11] *Experience and Nature,* p. 101. This quotation is exemplary of Dewey's ambiguity.

rejects the view that purposes are merely subjective.[12])

A problematic situation is in any case a very complex affair. The individual brings to it a number of interests and aims; and the affective environment has many elements in it which present a variety of different potentialities for action. The situation possesses obstacles, conflicts, doubtful and confusing factors, and competing attractions. The most welcome outcome for the individual implicated in such circumstances would be to transform the situation in such a way that competing desires are unified, conflicts removed, obstacles overcome or turned to account, and the resources of the situation utilized to initiate or restore inherently satisfying interaction. Whenever Dewey is careful to make accurate distinctions, it is always to this creative integration of the entire situation that he refers with the term "value."

The end-in-view is the specific action which is expected to function in a way to unify the operative elements of the situation. The end-in-view accomplishes this unification, but it is not itself the unification. This distinction *has* been made clearly by Dewey, except that he uses "end" instead of "value":

> The attained end or consequence is always an organization of activities, where organization is a co-ordination of all activities which enter as factors. The *end-in-view* is that particular activity which operates as a co-ordinating factor of all other subactivities involved.[13]

An uncomplicated example will illustrate this distinction: Suppose a cook happily engaged in the preparation of a stew. He runs out of salt. Thus there is a problematic situation, and he has to find a way to resume his activities. In this case, his end-in-view would be to acquire in some way some salt. Possession of the additional salt would not itself be a value, but it is a necessary condition for creating a value – creating a reunified situation. In most situations, obviously, the formulation of an end-in-view is hardly so easy; but the point here is simply to distinguish that activity which will coordinate the powers of the situation from that coordination itself. This is the distinction between end-in-view and value. The same distinction is expressed in different language in *Human Nature and Conduct:*

---

[12] Criticism of some main theories of ends and values will be undertaken in the next chapter.

[13] *Theory of Valuation,* pp. 48-9.

> The object desired and the attainment of desire are no more alike than a signboard on the road is like the garage to which it points and which it recommends to the traveller. Desire is the forward urge of living creatures. When the push and drive of life meets no obstacle, there is nothing which we call desire. There is just life-activity. But obstructions present themselves, and activity is dispersed and divided. Desire is the outcome. It is activity surging forward to break through what dams it up. The "object" which then presents itself in thought as the goal of desire is the object of the environment *which, if it were present,* would secure a re-unification of activity and the restoration of its ongoing unity. The end-in-view of desire is that object which were it present would link into an organized whole activities which are now partial and competing.[14]

Although Dewey's use of the term "value" is not wholly consistent, whenever he is at all cautious about his language the word never refers to either immediate goods or what Aristotle called "adventitious charms": prized events which do not occur as a consequence of both intelligence and deliberate action:

> *Only* as these objects are the consequence of prior reflection, deliberate choice and directed effort are they fulfillments, conclusions, completions, perfections. A natural end which occurs without intervention of human art is a terminus, a de facto boundary, but it is not entitled to any such honorific status of completions and realizations as classic metaphysics assigned them.[15]

It may be, of course, that the end-in-view does not function as anticipated. If, however, the end-in-view succeeds in integrating the situation, this integration is what Dewey also calls the consummatory phase of experience: "Values are naturalistically interpreted as intrinsic qualities of events in their consummatory

---

[14] Pp. 249-50. Dewey evidently should have made more distinctions pertaining to means-ends hypotheses. As he envisions the procedure of the problematic situation, there seem to be at least two kinds of hypotheses that pertain to the consummatory event: First, that a particular act will in fact suffice to remove obstacles, unite disparate energies, etc.; second, that certain means are a condition of that act (e.g., the cook predicts that the salt will restore the on-going process of preparing the stew; and he also predicts that he will find some salt in the pantry). Dewey sometimes refers to the first sort and sometimes to the second without any suggestion that they are in fact different. Hence in a more thorough and careful account he should have indicated that the agent must try to determine whether his alternative ends-in-view will in fact do what he wants them to do, and that the agent must also try to foresee what actions are requisite to the ends-in-view.

Of course, in situations of complexity it would be the case that a number of hypotheses about the potentialities of the situation would have to be formulated. That problem is not of present concern, however.

[15] *Experience and Nature,* p. 102.

reference."[16] The consummatory phase is a species of what Dewey has described generically as ends. It has presumably been established that ends are real events in nature; so it is equally evident that consummatory events (values) are also an eventual function in nature.

Because the word "value" is usually such a vague and general term – in Dewey's writings and in common usage – and because its very generality is frequently useful, I will hereafter use the expression "consummatory value" to refer particularly to the unification of situations by means of intelligent interaction. Later in this chapter and at subsequent junctures in this work the notion of consummatory value will be elaborated in detail, and the instrumentalities of achieving it will also be closely examined. At this stage, however, additional concepts which Dewey utilizes in his analysis of value and valuing must be presented.

The development of the situation described so far is clearly a history: a continuous process of qualitative change, which, in the kind of experience referred to, begins with a problematic situation in which there are a variety of immediate goods and terminates in a consummatory experience (or possibly in disappointment, frustration, and failure). Thus, Dewey says, "the foundation for value and the striving to realize it is found in nature, because when nature is viewed as consisting of events rather than substances, it is characterized by *histories,* that is, by continuity of change proceeding from beginnings to endings."[17] This history, like any other, is an inclusive process involving the organic interaction of organism and environment. The traits of the history are neither in objects by themselves nor in the subject by himself, nor in a relation between antecedently determinate subject and objects. The history is their joint product, and in which they both undergo transformation. The conditions of the history are open to scientific investigation at every stage.

It is no exaggeration to say that most of Dewey's writings on value have to do with elaborating the character of this history and in assessing various instrumentalities for prosecuting it successfully. Ideally, this history becomes what Dewey calls art.

---

[16] *Ibid.,* p. xvi.

[17] *Ibid.,* pp. xi-xii.

Indeed, when a history is art, the entire process is one of the fundamental goods of human existence. Although Dewey distinguishes one phase of such a history as *consummatory* value, he emphasizes that the continuous activity itself constitutes one of the most fulfilling and intrinsically precious traits of experience.

It may be noted that a certain vagueness has so far attended this analysis of value. What Dewey has distinguished as a value is the consummation of intelligent conduct. However, conduct admits of great variation in degree as to its intelligence. Clearly, then, what is called a consummatory value cannot be distinguished absolutely; it marks a distinction, not a division. As we shall see in the next section, to the extent that conduct is art, the end of conduct is a consummatory value.

At this stage the distinctions developed can be readily summarized. Prizings, problematic goods, etc., are the immediately attractive qualitative features of the environment; these can be acted with in a variety of ways to produce various ends. When some one (or more) of these immediate goods is by some intellectual procedure selected for some form of interaction, this intended interaction is called an end-in-view. Purposes imply plans of action; and the expected relation between means and ends in the intended action can be stated in hypotheses. "Value," in the most honorific sense, refers to the actual consummation of a history in which intellectual procedures have been operative and have directed an action (which is the end-in-view) which succeeds in unifying the energies of the situation. What have been distinguished are the problematic goods, plan of action formulated as a hypothesis, end-in-view and consummatory value.

There is a difference between an end occurring casually and one which is a genuine fulfillment. There is also a crucial difference between goods in their precarious immediacy and a good which has been subject to evaluation of some kind. They are also different states of affairs in which an end-in-view is anticipated and in which it is actually realized; and, finally, there is an obvious difference between situations in which the end-in-view functions according to expectations and in which it does not. Again, it should be stressed that immediate qualitative experiences possess their intrinsic appeal or repulsion; but it is precisely because so many features of the environment are at the same time directly appealing or repugnant and linked with further consequences that some means of selection must be instituted. Action on the first impulse is almost certainly doomed to failure, and promises little fulfillment in any case. Thus it is obviously important to preserve all the distinctions hitherto presented in order to distinguish the office of intelligence in moral life and discriminate the phases of moral experience that are subject to practical control.

Before proceeding it will be well to remark the connection between Dewey's characterization of value and valuing, as we have it so far, and his naturalistic metaphysics. As the method of experience requires, Dewey analyzes value in its context and continuities; and it is clear that the traits of nature which he calls quality, the precarious, the stable, ends, and histories are indispensable to his analysis. These traits are very much in evidence in situations in which one has to choose a course of action in order to meet existing problems. Accordingly, any metaphysics which rejected or ignored such traits would seem to be utterly helpless to provide or guide a consistent analysis of valuation. Indeed, as the next chapter will indicate, Dewey criticizes many philosophies of value precisely because they render moral experience unintelligible by denying its most salient traits. Thus it is that reflection on moral experience must acknowledge, by some name, these traits. Moreover, as Dewey steadfastly insists, it won't do to recognize any of these traits as belonging only to a separate realm of being. Unless they are regarded as traits of nature, mingled together in every situation, then metaphysical reflection cannot provide the slightest enlightenment for actual human predicaments, but can only render them unintelligible. The traits of nature are what give rise to these predicaments and must be analyzed and managed in their interdependencies for any endeavor to be successful.

It should also be pointed out that an analysis of valuational experience commits a philosopher to a theory of nature: Explicitly or not, he is making claims about what does and does not characterize nature, about man's relation to nature, and about the inherent potentialities and/or limiations of nature. If there *is* an explicit metaphysics, it is frequently the case that it is so reductive and dualisitic that it is incompatible with the implied or explicit theory of value. Or – in the interest of consistency –

moral experience is arbitrarily simplified. (See the section "Experience and Nature" in the preceding chapter, and see the following chapter.)

Unlike most philosophers, Dewey deliberately attempted to integrate his metaphysical views and his theory of value; and he did so in a way which at the same time provides a full account of value *and* of nature. Each inquiry provides observations and distinctions which enhance the other. Each inquiry is carried on in a way to make them mutually clarifying and enriching; and the two theories tend to become wholly integrated. Hence the "ground-map of criticism" is effective both in analyzing value in its context in nature and in examining theories of value; and it is itself developed and clarified by close attention to experiences of valuation. As I have suggested, it is difficult to see how any thorough and useful theory of value could be developed without an analysis of nature at least as perceptive and searching as Dewey's.

More reference to the critical use of metaphysics will be made shortly, but the discussion is now at a stage where a crucial misinterpretation of Dewey's views should be brought to attention. It concerns the meaning and function of the distinctions introduced pertaining to the transformation of situations from problematic to consummatory.

As indicated, Dewey insists on the distinction between an immediate good and an end-in-view. The difference between the statement that interaction with an object is an immediate good and the statement that it is an end-in-view Dewey has designated by the terms *de facto* and *de jure* judgments.[18] This terminology has proved to be highly misleading, for it suggests that Dewey is detailing a procedure with which to convert descriptive statements into normative statements – trying to derive "ought" statements from "is" statements. This is the interpretation given

---

[18] This is the distinction used in *The Quest for Certainty*, Chapter X, "The Construction of Good." Lamentably, in this book Dewey uses the terms "value" and "idea of value" to designate, respectively, the end-in-view and the hypotheses which state the expected means-end relations. His particular choice of language will not obscure the point at issue, however.

to Dewey's discussion by Morton White,[19] who takes it for granted that Dewey is engaged in some such enterprise; and he finds that the presumed attempt is a failure. If "The Construction of Good" were taken in isolation, it could plausibly be read in this way; but it cannot be so taken if it is examined in the context of the book of which it is a part, or in connection with the philosophy of value which Dewey develops in so many additional articles and books.

The distinctions which Dewey introduces are not for the sake of establishing formal relations between different propositions, or for determining the existential conditions which would presumably justify the sudden appearance of an "ought" in a statement. This is not the nature of the problem at all. What Dewey *is* trying to do is designate notably different phases of inquiry in the problematic situation and to point out the efficacy of such inquiry for directing the situation to consummatory value. The inherent value of consummatory experience as the outcome of a situation initially frustrated and problematic is not itself questioned.

By the use of *"de facto"* and *"de jure"* Dewey is calling attention to a special instance of the continuity between primary and refined experience. He is referring to the difference between an immediate good experienced as such and a specific plan of action formulated as a consequence of systematic inquiry into the nature of the situation. Here, as elsewhere in Dewey's philosophy, we have no dualisms – just distinctions. There is a continu-

---

[19] Morton G. White, "Value and Obligation in Dewey and Lewis" *(The Philosophical Review,* LVIII, 1949, pp. 321-9); and *Social Thought in America* (New York: The Viking Press, 1949), Chapter XIII.

Sidney Hook seems to hold much the same interpretation of Dewey's views, for his defense of Dewey's ethical theory against White's criticisms is largely based on showing that Dewey's philosophy does indeed provide a means of producing a normative sentence from a descriptive one. (See Hook's article, "The Ethical Theory of John Dewey" which originally appeared in *John Dewey: Philosopher of Science and Freedom,* which Hook edited. [New York: The Dial Press, 1950.] This article was reprinted in Hook's *The Quest for Being.* See especially pp. 57-9 in *The Quest for Being.)*

Indeed, I know of only one exception to this stereotyped treatment of "The Construction of Good." It is provided by R.W. Sleeper in "Dewey's Metaphysical Perspective: A Note on White, Geiger, and the Problem of Obligation" *(The Journal of Philosophy,* LVII, 1960, pp. 100-15). This is the most enlightening analysis available of what Dewey was attempting to accomplish in "The Construction of Good."

ity between the experience of prizing and the formulation of an interaction which is an end-in-view. The use of *"de jure"* and *"de facto,"* then, denotes different kinds of apprehension of the situation: those that follow critical inquiry and reflection and those that do not. It is obviously important to distinguish judgments which are the outcome of inquiry, for such judgments constitute a far more reliable basis for action than judgments which are merely first impressions.

Dewey's notion of *de jure* judgment pretends to introduce no basis for action additional to what is discovered in exclusively experimental inquiry. That is, such judgments have no "ought" words in them. Contrary to White's assumptions, Chapter X of *The Quest for Certainty* is not concerned with the status of statements of moral obligation (statements with "ought" in them.)[20] For anyone accustomed to believing that all moral philosophy hinges on the presumed "is-ought" problem, this will be a difficult fact to accept.

Dewey has explicitly affirmed that the difference between these two judgments is simply in that they are outcomes of notably different stages of inquiry into the problematic situation:

> The answer to the question I raised in my original list of "Questions" as to whether the distinction between direct valuings and evaluations as judgments is one of separate kinds or one of emphasis is, accordingly, answered in the latter sense. I am the more bound to make this statement because in some still earlier writings I tended to go too far in the direction of separation. I still think the reason that actuated me is sound. In current discussion, traits distinctive of valuing are frequently indiscriminately transferred to valuation. But the resulting

---

[20] Discussions in subsequent chapters will show that *de jure* judgments have a normative *function,* but they have it exclusively in that they disclose to the individual the implications of proposed lines of conduct.

There is a further meaning to the distinction between *de facto* and *de jure* judgments, weakening White's interpretation still more. For a *de facto* judgment refers to a present (or past) prizing, while a *de jure* judgment has reference to future events, namely, the end-in-view. On Dewey's view, it is only by the anticipation of events that conduct is subject to guidance by intelligence. The concern is not with what *has* happened, but with what *will* happen. Hence a judgment is called *de jure* not only to indicate that it is the result of inquiry, but also to signify that it is the kind of judgment that has a decisive bearing on conduct. The point is not that such a judgment *ought* to have such bearing, but that it *in fact* has such a bearing. This issue will receive detailed examination in the last chapter, "Intelligence and Value."

confusion can be escaped by noting the distinction to be one of phase in development.[21]

It is evident, of course, that a *de jure* judgment could in no way be derived from a *de facto* judgment. That would be deducing the *results* of inquiry from the experiences which *initiate* inquiry. But Dewey is not in the least concerned with the formal relations between such judgments or, by means of devising an operational definition of "ought," transforming one kind of proposition into another. He is interested in the actual transformation of *situations* and in formulating concepts which will enlighten that process. There is no mistaking this point: The problem Dewey is trying to explicate and clarify has nothing to do with either the formal relations between statements or the definition of ethical terms. Rather, it concerns the discrimination of different phases of the situation and how the awareness of these differences furnishes means of dealing effectively with its actual predicaments. Thus it is that White's analysis of logical fallacies is altogether irrelevant to the arguments which Dewey was in fact presenting. I will return to this issue in later chapters, where the import of Dewey's arguments for traditional problems of moral philosophy will be examined. At present, the exposition of Dewey's general characterization of value must be resumed.

What I have summarized so far leaves much to be developed. What has been done, however, is to show that on Dewey's view the entire process of valuation and the entire reality of value lie wholly within nature. It has also been shown that his naturalistic metaphysics is integral to his theory of value. To establish that value and valuation are inclusive processes intrinsic to nature was a result which Dewey regarded as crucially important. The concept of nature must be such that it includes the notion of value as an irreducible trait; for if value and valuation are to be subject to experimental intelligence and if our knowledge of them is to be put in the service of human needs, they must be understood in their continuities in nature. Dewey states the issue decisively:

---

[21] "The Field of 'value'," in Lepley (ed.), *Value: A Cooperative Inquiry* (New York: Columbia University Press, 1949), p. 75. It is noteworthy also that Dewey uses the *de facto-de jure* distinction to indicate the difference between untested and tested knowledge claims *(Experience and Nature,* p. 402).

Philosophy, then, is a generalized theory of criticism. Its ultimate value for life-experience is that it continuously provides instruments for the criticism of those values – whether of beliefs, institutions, actions or products – that are found in all aspects of experience. The chief obstacle to a more effective criticism of current values lies in the traditional separation of nature and experience, which it is the purpose of this volume to replace by the idea of continuity.[22]

Dewey's analysis of value in nature makes further explicit use of his metaphysical distinctions. The balance of this chapter will be devoted to further indication of the explicit use of the generic traits to clarify value and also to the characterization of art as practice by reference to traits of nature.

Somewhat has already been said to indicate at least in part the indispensable character of the notions of quality, precariousness, the stable, ends, and histories to Dewey's theory of value. Analysis of value in terms of these traits can continue with further investigation of qualities.

All values are necessarily qualitative. "The realm of immediate qualities contains everything of worth and significance."[23] And many kinds of events can acquire this immediate quality. "It is conceivable that just because certain objects are immediately good, that which secures and extends their occurrance may itself become for reflective choice a supreme immediate good. . . . Even the utility of things, their capacity to be employed as means and agencies, is first of all not a relation, but a quality possessed, immediately possessed . . . ."[24]

Qualitative events, however, are also the most precarious:

Whatever depends for its existence upon the interaction of a large number of independent variables is in unstable equilibrium; its rate of change is rapid; successive qualities have no obvious connection with one another; any shift of any part may alter the whole pattern. . . . Thus the things that are most precious, that are final, [are] . . . just the things that are unstable and most easily changing . . . . The richer and fuller are the terminal qualities of an object the more precarious is the latter, because of its dependence upon a greater diversity of events.[25]

Prizings and values of all kinds are both qualitative and precarious. This much being so, it is clear that our cognitive experience,

---

[22] *Experience and Nature,* p. xvi.

[23] *Ibid.*, p. 114.

[24] *Ibid.*, pp. 107-9.

[25] *Ibid.*, pp. 114-7.

as cognitive, is not consummatory, but instrumental. Values are the consummations of histories and – to anticipate later discussions – such histories can be deliberately initiated and their consummations secured when the conditions of their occurrence are known and subject to control; and this requires utilization of the stable features of the situation.

> While "consciousness" as the conspicuous and vivid presence of immediate qualities and of meanings, is alone of direct worth, things not immediately present whose intrinsic qualities are not directly had, are primary from the standpoint of control. For just because the things that are directly had are both precious and evanescent, the only thing that can be thought of is the conditions under which they are had. The common, pervasive and repeated *is* of superior rank from the standpoint of safeguarding and buttressing the having of terminal qualities. . . . In truth, the universal and stable are important because they are the instrumentalities, the efficacious conditions, of the occurrence of the unique, unstable and passing.[26]

Thus it is that the stable has value, but not in itself and as such, but insofar as it is instrumental.[27]

In explaining why it is that events are prized and valued, Dewey has important observations to make about the functioning of the precarious and the stable:

> The union of the hazardous and the stable, of the incomplete and the recurrent, is the condition of all experienced satisfaction as truly as of our predicaments and problems. While it is the source of ignorance, error and failure of expectation, it is the source of the delight which fulfillments bring. For if there were nothing in the way, if there were no deviations and resistances, fulfillments would be all at once, and in so being would fulfill nothing, but merely be. It would not be in connection with desire or satisfaction. Moreover when a fulfillment comes and is pronounced good, it is *judged* good, distinguished and asserted, simply because it is in jeopardy, because it occurs amid indifferent and divergent things. . . . The constant presence of instability and trouble gives depth and poignancy to the situations in which are pictured their subordination to final issues possessed of calm and certainty.[28]

Indeed, various conjunctions of the precarious and stable elements are determinants of all human problems. That is, there is a structured, determinate, on-going course of events, which is always being disrupted in some way and hence calling for novel

---

[26] *Ibid.*, pp. 115-6.

[27] Of course the act of knowing can be valued in itself, but the *enjoyment* of knowing, as such, is not a cognitive transaction with nature.

[28] *Ibid.*, pp. 62, 89.

redirection. Any intelligible metaphysics must recognize this organic relation of the precarious and stable; any philosophy which fails to do so can provide only bafflement.[29]

The importance of the precarious for understanding experience can be further illustrated. In concerning himself with the theory of nature underlying democratic ideals, Dewey insists on the reality of the precarious:

> A philosophy animated, be it unconsciously or consciously, by the strivings of men to achieve democracy will construe liberty as meaning a universe in which there is real uncertainty and contingency, a world which is not all in, and never will be, a world which in some respects is incomplete and in the making, and which in these respects may be made this way or that according as men judge, prize, love and labor. To such a philosophy any notion of a perfect or complete reality, finished, existing always the same without regard to the vicissitudes of time, will be abhorrent.[30]

It is only because of the precarious that men have alternatives and choices. (Otherwise, action would go on unimpeded.) Thus also men can, with foresight and imagination, contrive and construct a future of which their own desires and intelligence are essential conditions. More generally, if all the processes of nature were complete in and of themselves without human participation, then nature would seemingly preclude any change in its course initiated by human action.[31] But Dewey's fundamental thesis is that the distinctive human traits are organically implicated with nature and thus are determinants of the course of nature. This is not to say that Dewey is defending "free will." He is simply insisting on the fact that it is the precarious events in nature which stimulate human beings to redirect natural processes in ways determinable by whatever happen to be the given desires and abilities of the persons involved.[32]

---

[29] See above, Chapter I, pp. 9-11 and *passim*.

[30] "Philosophy and Democracy," in *Characters and Events*, Vol. II, p. 851, edited by J. Ratner (New York: Henry Holt and Company, 1929).

[31] The notion that nature works independently of man is evidently contradicted by experience, but it has frequently been held, by, e.g., fatalistic philosophies, forms of absolute idealism, and philosophies holding that there are antecedently fixed patterns for human behavior existing independently in nature to which men have no choice but to conform. These philosophies must refer to the workings of desire and intelligence as appearance, illusion, or as an inferior grade of being. It is apparent that such philosophies are forced into such a position by holding some form of reductive metaphysics.

[32] Intelligent experience is, accordingly, the most creative medium of natural processes. See the concluding quotation of Chapter II.

There is a further distinctive sense in which democracy implies the precarious. Dewey's notion of democracy implies that in any situation there are genuine moral alternatives; and democracy is a way of determining these alternatives.[33] Again, without the occurrence of the precarious in nature, the fact of alternatives just would not arise; and democracy as a means of forming and choosing alternatives just would not exist. In moral philosophies which deny full status to the precarious (such as rationalism and idealism) there can be no such thing as a choice between moral alternatives: The absolute moral law stands perfect, unqualified, and immutable; and the only choice is whether to conform to it.

Finally, the precarious and stable are crucially important in moral experience – as in all other experiences – because they are necessary conditions for the occurrence and activity of intelligence. If precarious events did not occur, there would be no such thing as problems – no interferences in ongoing activity. Thus such activity would be mindless. It is precisely the fact that nature eventuates in problematic situations that gives rise to thinking, reflective imagination.

> Unless there were something problematic, undecided, still going-on and as yet unfinished and indeterminate, in nature, there could be no such events as perceptions. . . . It were, conceivably, "better" that nature should be finished through and through, a closed mechanical or closed teleological structure, such as philosophic schools have fancied. But in that case the flickering candle of consciousness would go out.[34]

Yet it is not the precarious elements alone that are necessary for thought. There must also be stable features of existence which can be utilized in order to convert precarious events to such a nature that on-going activity can be sustained:

> Unless nature had regular habits, persistent ways, so compacted that they time, measure and give rhythm and recurrence to transitive flux, meanings, recognizable characters, could not be. But also without an interplay of these patient, slow-moving, not easily stirred systems of action with swift-moving, unstable, unsubstantial events, nature would be a routine unmarked by ideas.[35]

---

[33] There will be further discussion of value theory and democracy, mainly in Chapter VII.

[34] *Experience and Nature*, p. 349.

[35] *Ibid.*, p. 351.

At this point consideration can be directed to some further characteristics of ends which will be seen to have great significance for theories of value. (These remarks will in part draw attention to issues previously raised.) Some elementary but very important observations are in order: Ends are always transitive; what for one situation is an end is for another situation a beginning. There are no lapses in the continuity of natural processes, no absolute beginnings or absolute endings:

> Every end is as such static; this statement is but a truism; changing into something else, a thing is obviously transitive, not final. Yet the thing which is a close of one history is always the beginning of another, and in this capacity the thing in question is transitive or dynamic. . . . Empirically . . . there is a history which is a succession of histories, and in which any event is at once both beginning of one course and close of another; is both transitive and static.[36]

In reference to those ends which are the consummatory events in nature, it is likewise true, of course, that they too are at the same time both endings and beginnings. More concretely, whenever an end is achieved, this condition does not mark the completion or termination of all activity. It is, of course, intrinsically valuable; but it is also transitional to further endeavors and consummations. When, for example, one has earned a diploma, this is a consummatory experience; but it is also the beginning of new experiences in which the state of affairs represented by the diploma will enter into new interactions and consummations. Similarly, there could be no stage in human development where the self was perfected and finished. Simply to have accomplished certain ends is at the same time to have acquired new powers and possibilities — to be, in other words, a different self to enter into new interactions and qualify them in novel ways. There is no antecedently existing form of the self or an ideal self which simply awaits to be realized in static perfection. The process of growth is, of course, limited by the necessities of nature. The point is that there could be no stage in the development of the self where it would be by definition completed or perfected. (Hence, also, the good of man does not lie in some remote, still-unrealized perfection for which we toil now in preparation. "Perfection

---

[36] *Ibid.*, p. 100.

means perfecting, fulfillment, fulfilling, and the good is now or never."[37])

Looking at the same issue from a world-historical perspective, there is no basis for assuming that human history will reach a point where there is nowhere else it can go; for the process of history itself produces novel powers and possibilities, novel problems and solutions. Teleological philosophies of history misrepresent the nature of process.

> There is something pitifully juvenile in the idea that "evolution," progress, means a definite sum of accomplishment which will forever stay done, and which by an exact amount lessens the amount still to be done, disposing once and for all of just so many perplexities and advancing us just so far on our road to a final stable and unperplexed goal.[38]

Thus it is just as it is with any end in nature: There are no final and absolute consummations in human experience. The notion, however, of absolute ends has been dominant in the history of philosophy; and Dewey's criticism of this notion will be taken up in the next chapter. Clearly, such a notion arises when ends, or values, are thought to be something apart from nature.

What has been said about ends, when combined with the concept of histories, suggests a fundamental notion about the relation of means to ends. Ends are not isolated entities discontinuous with natural processes. Rather, means and ends are organically related; they constitute an inclusive whole; and the difference between means and ends is simply a matter of emphasis and attention, or a significant redirection of events. A continuous process possesses some features of more importance than others, and some stages have a pivotal character not enjoyed by others. Receiving the diploma, again, is regarded as especially significant, and it marks a pivotal stage in human career, but this by no means sets it outside the historical continuity. (Indeed, as earlier discussion has indicated, an end-in-view should not be regarded as an arrest or closure of conduct, but, on the contrary, should be regarded as precisely that activity which will maintain, integrate, and enhance the on-going history.)

---

[37] *Human Nature and Conduct,* p. 290. A detailed discussion of the nature and values of growth will appear in Chapter VI.

[38] *Ibid.,* p. 285.

The significance of the organic connection of means-ends will be elaborated in subsequent discussions. For the present, I will confine myself to two further points: 1) The assertion of the inclusive unity of means-ends by no means eliminates the distinction between intrinsic and extrinsic value. 2) Evaluation of ends is inseparable from evaluation of means, and means from ends: means and ends can only be evaluated together.

1) The intrinsic-extrinsic distinction is not abandoned; it is simply better understood. [39] It has already been indicated that all events have an irreducible intrinsic quality which is attractive (or repulsive) as such. But this fact hardly entails that the event is not also the condition of still further events and the occurrence of still further qualities. In this latter capacity, the event could be said to have extrinsic quality: it is instrumental for the occasion of further events. The only way, it seems, in which both intrinsic and extrinsic quality could be denied to the same event would be to stipulate that "intrinsic" means "out of relation to anything else"; and Dewey ridicules this notion:

> The words 'inherent,' 'intrinsic,' and 'immediate' are used ambigously, so that a fallacious conclusion is reached. Any quality or property that actually belongs to any object or event is properly said to be immediate, inherent, or intrinsic. The fallacy consists in interpreting what is designated by these terms as out of relation to anything else and hence as absolute. . . . A quality, including that of value, is inherent if it actually belongs to something, and the question of whether or not it belongs is one of *fact* and not a question that can be decided by dialectical manipulation of the concept of inherency. . . . Relational properties do not lose their intrinsic quality of being just what they are because their coming into being is *caused* by something 'extrinsic.' The theory that such is the case would terminate logically in the view that there are no intrinsic qualities whatever, since it can be shown that such intrinsic qualities as *red, sweet, hard,* etc., are causally conditioned as to their occurrence.[40]

2) Nothing seems to earn Dewey's scorn so much as the assumption that ends are to be valued independently of means. The

[39] Brand Blanshard not only holds that insistence on the continuity of activity precludes any notion of intrinsic value, but he evidently assumes that this is Dewey's position as well. In reference to this continuity Blanshard asks, "Does this imply that there are no such things as intrinsic values, or ends in themselves? Yes, Dewey would answer – . . . this *is* what it implies. . . . He will admit no ends whose value is not determined by the fact that they are also means." *(Reason and Goodness;* London: George Allen and Unwin Ltd., 1961; pp. 172-3.)

[40] *Theory of Valuation,* pp. 26-8.

seamless continuity of means-ends does not imply, of course, that given a certain end, there is only one means of achieving it; but it does imply that *some* means is necessary to achieving it. This being the case, the value of an end is linked of necessity to the value of means, and its value will vary with alternative means: The value of a proposed means is an inextricable part of the value of the means-ends continuum. The means is organic to the end; so the value of the means is organic to the value of the end. Likewise, a means can only be assessed relative to the ends it is expected to serve. Clearly, then, it would seem that means-ends combinations must be evaluated together. This view is inescapable when values are recognized to be eventual functions in nature – rather than transcendent forms or subjective feelings. Thus Dewey rails against moralists who wish to treat ends as things that both can and should be judged apart from what is organic to them.

> It is impossible to form a just estimate of the paralysis of effort that has been produced by indifference to means. Logically, it is truistic that lack of consideration for means signifies that so-called ends are not taken seriously. It is as if one professed devotion to painting pictures conjoined with contempt for canvas, brush and paints; or love of music on condition that no instruments, whether the voice or something external, be used to make sounds. The good workman in the arts is known by his respect for his tools and by his interest in perfecting his technique. The glorification in the arts of ends at the expense of means would be taken to be a sign of complete insincerity or even insanity. Ends separated from means are either sentimental indulgences or if they happen to exist are merely accidental. The ineffectiveness in action of "ideals" is due precisely to the supposition that means and ends are not on exactly the same level with respect to the attention and care they demand.[41]

The fact that means-ends are inseparable for valuation carries the implication that there is no dualism of moral goods and nonmoral goods. Thus a presumed nonmoral good, like health, is endowed with the value of the ends which it enhances, such as benevolence. Dewey insists that we must do away "once for all with the traditional distinction between moral goods, like the virtues, and natural goods like health, economic security, art, science and the like."[42] Thus intelligence and intellectual re-

---

[41] *The Quest for Certainty,* p. 279. Although there is continuity of means-ends, there is no requirement to judge means-ends indefinitely. This matter is discussed in Chapter VII.

[42] *Reconstruction in Philosophy,* p. 172.

sources of all kinds would have moral value to the extent that they promote so-called moral ends or any of the goods of experience:

> When physics, chemistry, biology, medicine, contribute to the detection of concrete human woes and to the development of plans for remedying them and relieving the human estate, they become moral; they become part of the apparatus of moral inquiry or science. . . . At the same time that morals are made to focus in intelligence, things intellectual are moralized.[43]

This is another way of bringing attention to the fact that human values are natural functions and can only be effectively understood and pursued as such.

The foregoing pages have indicated to some extent the use Dewey makes of his metaphysics in his criticism of value. Not only does he argue convincingly that certain traits of nature must be acknowledged in some form if the experience of human beings is to be made intelligible, but he also analyses these traits and their interactions in such a way to indicate their actual function in moral experience. Consequently, he is also able to provide considerable enlightenment about the means by which concrete problems can be addressed. In this vein, the following section pursues still further Dewey's analysis of value in nature. Before proceeding to that, however, it is appropriate to make one comment in reference to the implications of what has thus far been said about value.

Values, we have seen, do not have either their origin or their locus in some transcendental law, divine commandment, supernatural realm, the absolute, or anything of the sort. Rather, values are distinguishable experiences of individual human beings interacting with their environment. Recall as well that morals, on Dewey's view, are social. Whatever their content may be, moral norms are the outcome of the attempts – rational, deliberate, or not – of members of groups to adjust and unite their aims (and perhaps to oppress and exploit some of their number). Thus it is that moral norms, so-called, are derivative of such experiences and expectations of individual human values as they occur in the social medium. It is out of these basic experiences of value in society that moral norms are developed. Accordingly, there are

[43] *Ibid.*, pp. 173-4.

no prior moral laws – no moral laws antecedent to such kinds of experience – which could in any way give priority of right or advantage to one person or group as opposed to others. That is, on Dewey's theory of value there can be no justification for anyone to assume that he is on his own account inherently invested with a morally privileged status relative to other persons. This idea is fundamental to Dewey's philosophy of democracy, and the latter is inseparable from his ethical theory. Indeed, as we shall see in Chapter VII, his ethical theory *is* his philosophy of democracy.

There are many further implications of the theory of value developed to this point, and they will receive attention in due course; but, having noted this much, I return to Dewey's analysis of the status of value in nature. The discussion will be devoted to conduct as art, which is that experience, according to Dewey, in which consummatory value is produced. His treatment of this subject involves analyses in both metaphysics and philosophy of nature.

2. Conduct as Art

As a preliminary generalization, it can be said that art is that process in nature in which 1) the meaning of *all* phases of a history are unified in *each* of its phases; 2) the different functions of experience (e.g., thinking, sensing, acting) are all distinctively constitutive of the unified process; and 3) the meanings of interactions with nature are enlarged and intensified. Dewey has this way of putting it:

> The doings and sufferings that form experience are, in the degree in which experience is intelligent or charged with meanings, a union of the precarious, novel, irregular with the settled, assured, and uniform – a union which also defines the artistic and the aesthetic. For wherever there is art the contingent and ongoing no longer work at cross purposes with the formal and recurrent but commingle in harmony. And the distinguishing feature of conscious experience, of what for short is often called "consciousness," is that in it the instrumental and final, meanings that are signs and clews and meanings that are immediately possessed, suffered and enjoyed, come together in one.[44]

1) In art the precarious becomes an integral part of an inclusive whole. It becomes such because it is utilized rather than

[44] *Experience and Nature*, pp. 358-9.

avoided, circumvented, or permitted to obstruct. It is, rather, converted into a means; the precarious becomes instrumental when it is deliberately put to advantage, and thus it is harmonized in a whole. Experience as art is then freed of the irrelevant, the casual, or the discordant which so characterize our usual experience. Moreover, whatever is instrumental in art possesses the meaning of whatever is consummatory; and the consummatory phases possess not only their own unique qualities, but the meaning of the instrumental qualities as well: "The theme has insensibly passed over into that of relation of means and consequence, process and product, the instrumental and consummatory. Any activity that is simultaneously both, rather than in alternation and displacement, is art."[45] That is, when a consummatory end (a value) is deliberately pursued with full awareness and appreciation of the means organic to it (the end-in-view), then the active involvement with the means is consciously invested with the value and significance of the end. The experience of the end, likewise, is invested with the value and significance of the means.

It should be noted further that the consummatory experience possesses the additional meaning of quickening the very capacity to participate in further experiences of enhanced quality:

> A consummatory object that is not also instrumental turns in time to the dust and ashes of boredom. The "eternal" quality of great art is its renewed instrumentality for further consummatory experiences. . . . Any activity that is productive of objects whose perception is an immediate good, and whose operation is a continual source of enjoyable perception of other events exhibits fineness of art. . . . They are their own excuses for being just because they are charged with an office in quickening apprehension, enlarging the horizon of vision, refining discrimination, creating standards of appreciation which are confirmed and deepened by further experiences.[46]

2) The unification of experience called art encompasses more than the conversion of the precarious into the instrumental and the integration of the meanings of the instrumental and consummatory phases of experience; for it also implies the unification of the various functions in experience. That is, it unifies sense, thought, action, impulse, imagination. Indeed, this unification is

---

[45] *Ibid.*, p. 361.

[46] *Ibid.*, pp. 365-6.

such that the qualities of each function of experience are heightened by the qualities of the others.

The various kinds of experience of human beings are not the work of separate and independent faculties. That is, for example, cognitive experience is not the work of Reason; and aesthetic experience is not the work of a singular faculty which (miraculously) comes into play when (and only when) we encounter a "work of art." Rather, such experience is composed of a certain ordering of the functions just indicated in interaction with the environment.[47] In experience as art (distinguished from aesthetic experience), this ordering is particularly felicitous. Inasmuch as it is activity, it involves impulse; and of course it involves sense.[48] It also involves what Dewey calls aesthetic experience, and intelligence and imagination as well. Dewey uses "aesthetic" to mean *any* consummatory or otherwise intrinsically valuable experience. "Aesthetic objects" are all things "immediately enjoyed and suffered," "things directly possessed."[49]

> A passion of anger, a dream, relaxation of the limbs after effort, swapping of jokes, horse-play, beating of drums, blowing of tin whistles, explosion of firecrackers and walking on stilts, have the same quality of immediate and absorbing finality that is possessed by things and acts dignified by the title of aesthetic. . . . Delightfully enhanced perception or aesthetic appreciation is of the same nature as enjoyment of any object that is consummatory. It is the outcome of a skilled and intelligent art of dealing with natural things for the sake of intensifying, purifying, prolonging and deepening the satisfaction which they spontaneously afford.[50]

In what generically is called art, it is imagination and intelligence which have the function of bringing sense, impulse, action, and aesthetic quality into inclusive form that is "charged with meanings capable of immediately enjoyed possession."[51] The nature of this process can best be indicated by reference to the problematic situation. We have seen that such situations arise when existing activities become frustrated in some way. The spe-

---

[47] See especially the first three chapters of *Art as Experience.*

[48] The peculiar way in which experience as art involves sense will be indicated under point 3, following. As we shall see, what is said there of sense could equally well be said of any experience which is in Dewey's sense aesthetic.

[49] *Experience and Nature,* p. 87.

[50] *Ibid.,* pp. 80; 389.

[51] *Ibid.,* p. 358.

cific character – the specific problems – of such situations are organic to the situation itself: Although in some particulars a situation will resemble other such occasions, even these particulars are part of a larger context; so they *occur* uniquely. Hence it is that all situations are singular, unique. These facts could hardly be questioned by anyone sensitive to experience. (It follows also that the specific nature of the consummatory phase of the situation will be as unique as the situation itself. We will find in later discussions that the uniqueness of value is a matter of some consequence.)

In order to resolve the specific existing difficulties and to integrate diverse elements, some new course of action must be settled upon. That is, an end-in-view must be discriminated and a plan of action formulated. Inasmuch as the constituents of the situation differ from those of other situations, the means of meeting its problems will likewise differ from the means of other situations. Moreover, the situation admits of an indefinite number of possible outcomes, depending on what action is taken. Therefore there neither are nor can be any ready-made plans of action exactly suited to the particular situation. Alternative plans of action do not and cannot exist antecedently to such situations; they are not part of some presumed inherent structure of reality. Rather, the plan and the end-in-view are created in the situation itself. In other words, the end-in-view – if it is to be pertinent and efficacious – must be uniquely appropriate to the specific situation: it must issue from the situation itself. Rather than existing in some sense antecedently to particular activity, it arises from within activity itself; and it is contrived for the sake of restoring or redirecting on-going activity:

> Ends are foreseen consequences which arise in the course of activity and which are employed to give activity added meaning and to direct its further course. They are in no sense ends *of* action. In being ends of *deliberation* they are redirecting pivots *in* action.[52]

It is, then, the task of intelligence to analyze the situation and also to function imaginatively to contrive alternative plans of action; and it is necessary that each such plan be appraised in

---

[52] *Human Nature and Conduct,* p. 225.

imagination according to its merits.[53] When choice is made and action undertaken, selected features of the situation are manipulated and ordered to integrate means and ends and bring the inclusive whole into existence. Thus it is that intelligence and imagination are instrumental in producing and enhancing the qualitative meaning of the whole.[54] Moreover, the use of imagination and intelligence itself has an enhanced meaning because it is imbued with the values and rewards which it produces. Intelligence and imagination are valued for the consummations of experience which they promise. As this procedure tends toward the ideal limit of successfully integrating all the elements of the situation and directing them toward a consummatory end, this process is art:

> The existence of art is the concrete proof of what has just been stated abstractly. It is proof that man uses the materials and energies of nature with intent to expand his own life, and that he does so in accord with the structure of his organism – brain, sense-organs, and muscular system. Art is the living and concrete proof that man is capable of restoring consciously, and thus on the plane of meaning, the union of sense, need, impulse and action characteristic of the live creature. The intervention of consciousness adds regulation, power of selection, and redisposition.[55]

3) So-called objects of sense admit of indefinite variation in

---

[53] The nature of this process will be considered in detail in Chapter VII.

[54] The entire experience as integrated has its own unifying quality or emotion – its distinctive general character: "A piece of work is finished in a way that is satisfactory; a problem receives its solution; a game is played through; a situation, whether that of eating a meal, playing a game of chess, carrying on a conversation, writing a book, or taking part in a political campaign, is so rounded out that its close is a consummation and not a cessation. Such an experience is a whole and carries with it its own individualizing quality and self-sufficiency." (*Art as Experience,* p. 35.)

[55] *Art as Experience,* p. 25. As suggested by this quotation, Dewey regards experience as art as the chief verification of his theory of nature, for it is that experience in which interaction with nature is most conspicuous in transforming crude experience into refined and meaningful experience, and in which the generic traits are all clearly in evidence within the same inclusive situation. (Actually, it would be more accurate to say that art is both a source and a verification of theory of nature, for the philosopher can learn much of what nature is from his examination of arts. The analyses of experience and the formulation of its "ground-map" always stand in critical relation to each other.) If there were a proper understanding of what Dewey calls art, philosophical dualisms would have no footing. "Thus would disappear the separations that trouble present thinking: division of everything into nature *and* experience, of experience into practice *and* theory, art *and* science, of art into useful *and* fine, menial *and* free." *Experience and Nature,* p. 358.)

their use and meaning in the situation. This is a fact of great importance; in order to specify that importance it is necessary to return to the subject of meanings. Meanings, it will be recalled, are the connections, the relations, of objects. The meaning of an object is the various interactions that it enters into with other objects. As indicated earlier, most meanings refer to the consequences of acting with objects in various ways. The events of primary experience become known in their relations to other events, and thus the experience of any such event becomes informed with meanings. These relations constitute the funded meaning of an object, and the object becomes a sign for related objects.

It is clear that any object admits of indefinitely ramifying meanings, for it admits of an indefinite plurality of interactions in nature. Dewey provides a homely example:

> Thus an existence identified as "paper," because the meaning uppermost at the moment is "something to be written upon," has as many other explicit meanings as it has important consequences recognized in the various connective interactions into which it enters. Since possibilities of conjunction are endless, and since the consequences of any of them may at some time be significant, its potential meanings are endless. It signifies something to start a fire with; something like snow; made of wood-pulp; manufactured for profit; property in the legal sense; a definite combination illustrative of certain principles of chemical science; an article the invention of which has made a tremendous difference in human history, and so on indefinitely.[56]

A matter of consequence to be remarked at this point is that the events which are related in the meaning of an existential object all possess qualitative traits: All the objects with which a given object interacts are each possessed of qualities which make them immediately attractive, repulsive, beautiful, hateful, delightful, and so on. Hence the meaning of an object is funded with all these various immediate values. (We should also take note that the various senses reinforce each other in the growth of meanings, as, for example, experiences of touch, taste, and smell are part of the meaning of what is seen.) A meaning is, in other words, a complex of these immediate qualities existing in specifiable relations. Hence, also, the value of any object or event will be a function of its meanings – of its existential relations to

[56] *Experience and Nature,* pp. 319-20.

other objects and events of value. That is, the actual felt value of an object for an individual depends upon the meaning with which that object is funded for that individual. This is the case whether the object is directly experienced or is merely present in imagination.

It would be incorrect to regard the concepts of meaning and value as coextensive. (Not all meanings are consummatory values; and many meanings – such as those in theoretical science – are at a considerable remove from the immediacies of gross experience.) It is true, however, that anything possessing value of any kind beyond its sheer immediacy is an amalgam of qualitative meanings; and – inasmuch as quality is a generic trait of experience – a meaning is an amalgam of immediate values. To put the matter in more precise terminology: The meaning of an object is a complex of prizings (and/or rejections) presumed to exist in certain unified relations contingent upon specified forms of action with that object.[57] Indeed, in many contexts Dewey uses "meanings" and "values" interchangeably.

It was emphasized earlier that value of any kind is continuous with primary experience. We now see that a thing of value is in part such because it interacts with a number of prized events. Its meaning is its value. Thus, say, good health has its immediate qualities, but it is valuable in a discriminated sense because of its connections with the qualities of a host of related events. In no sense, therefore, is a valued event an isolated entity. In its actual occurrence, it is an event *experienced in its continuities with other events;* and all of these events have some intrinsic qualitative appeal. Some of these events will also be disagreeable; but, as we have seen, as conduct becomes art, such traits are minimized.

I have been discussing the qualitative aspect of meanings. At this point it must be added that objects and acts are perceived *as* meaningful. Dewey observes (contrary to the dogmas of British empiricism) that events are perceived *as* meaningful. Experience is not made up of so-called sense-data, but of meanings: "Consciousness in a being with language denotes awareness or percep-

---

[57] It is well to be reminded here that in much of human conduct many of these prizings and aversions are traits of anticipated interactions with other persons. The meaning of action to an individual is largely dependent upon the social responses he expects from it.

tion of meanings; it is the perception of actual events, whether past, contemporary or future, *in* their meanings, the having of actual ideas."[58]

> The discussion has explicitly gone on the basis that *what* is perceived are meanings, rather than just [isolated] events or existences. . . . Objects are precisely what we are aware of. For objects are events *with* meanings; tables, the milky way, chairs, stars, cats, dogs, electrons, ghosts, centaurs, historic epochs and all the infinitely multifarious subject-matter of discourse designable by common nouns, verbs and their qualifiers. So intimate is the connection of meanings with consciousness that there is no great difficulty in resolving "consciousness," as a recent original and ingenious thinker has done, into knots, intersections or complexes of universals.[59]
>
> "This," whatever *this* may be, always implies a system of meanings focused at a point of stress, uncertainty, and need of regulation. It sums up history, and at the same time opens a new page; it is record and promise in one; a fulfillment and an opportunity. It is a fruition of what has happened and a transitive agency of what is to happen.It is a comment written by natural events on their own direction and tendency, and a surmise of whither they are leading.[60]

This does not mean that one literally and physically witnesses all at once all the relations into which an object enters. Rather, the meaning of an object is gradually built up in experience: As one familiarizes himself more and more with an object, the object comes to stimulate a more and more complex response in him:

> We find also in all these higher organisms that what is done is conditioned by consequences of prior activities; we find the fact of learning or habit-formation. In consequence, an organism acts with reference to a time-spread, a serial order of events, as a unit, just as it does in reference to a unified spatial variety. Thus an environment both extensive and enduring is immediately implicated in present behaviour.[61]

One need not explicitly rehearse in imagination all the things an object means in order to experience the object as "charged with meanings" or to respond to it appropriately. Whatever the mechanisms of this process may be, its occurrence is an obvious fact of experience. Take for example the familiar experience of seeing a friend: This is not an instance of seeing a bundle of shapes, colors, and movements, for clearly the experience is immediately

---

[58] *Ibid.*, p. 303.

[59] *Ibid.*, pp. 317-9.

[60] *Ibid.*, p. 352.

[61] *Ibid.*, p. 279.

abundant with meanings.

In the present context, the significance of the fact that objects are directly experienced as meaningful is that so-called intrinsic values are capable of becoming qualitatively richer. The quality of experience is not a fixed thing, but it admits of being indefinitely improved; experience admits of being fuller, more significant, inherently more valuable. There are great qualitative differences in the values of experience.

When histories are characterized by what Dewey calls art, disparate and unrelated events are brought into a unity, features of the environment which were initially impoverished of meanings acquire significance in the transformed situation. As objects examined and manipulated by intelligence are seen in new uses and additional connections, ". . . qualities cease to be isolated details; they get the meaning contained in a whole system of related objects; they are rendered continuous with the rest of nature and take on the import of the things they are now seen to be continuous with."[62] Thus it is that such histories enlarge and intensify the intrinsic meanings of man's interaction with nature. The process which effectively accomplishes this goal is art, and its product is rightly a work of art:

> Thus to be conscious of meanings or to have an idea, marks a fruition, an enjoyed or suffered arrest of the flux of events. But there are all kinds of ways of perceiving meanings, all kinds of ideas. Meaning may be determined in terms of consequences hastily snatched at and torn loose from their connections; then is prevented the formation of wider and more enduring ideas. Or, we may be aware of meanings, may achieve ideas, that unite wide and enduring scope with richness of distinctions. The latter sort of consciousness is more than a passing and superficial consummation or end: it takes up into itself meanings covering stretches of existence wrought into consistency. It marks the conclusion of long continued endeavor; of patient and indefatigable search and test. The idea is, in short, art and a work of art. As a work of art, it directly liberates subsequent action and makes it more fruitful in a creation of more meanings and more perceptions.[63]

Art, in Dewey's sense, is clearly a more generic character of existence than what is called fine art. Indeed, Dewey insists upon the more inclusive sense of art precisely to show that it is continuous with experience and nature, including what are called prac-

---

[62] *Ibid.*, p. 5.

[63] *Ibid.*, p. 371.

tical – or even menial – arts. Art is to be distinguished from mindless routine at one extreme and complete disorganization at the other. With the use of intelligence, any form of practice is subject to becoming excellent.

> The limiting terms that define art are routine at one extreme and capricious impulse at the other. It is hardly worthwhile to oppose science and art sharply to one another, when the deficiencies and troubles of life are so evidently due to separation between art and blind routine and blind impulse.[64]

Given the subjectivisitic biases of modern thought, a further reminder at this point might be appropriate: That peculiar interpenetration of traits of experience called art is not something going on "inside the subject," but most eminently involves on-going participation of man and nature. (While this fact may [one hopes] be obvious if taken in reference to conduct, it is also true of activity in what are commonly called the fine arts. [65])

According to the views so far presented in this book, any value is a function of nature; but consummatory value occurs when nature functions as art. To the extent that conduct is art, experience is transformed from a brute, existential sequence of unrelated events into a unity of meaning. Not only is the consummatory experience a wealth of value, but the entire process is funded with value; it constitutes an undivided whole, valuable throughout, whose continuities are keenly appreciated. This sort of history is not one which consists alternately of valueless means and valuable ends. Nor is it one in which the end is mere closure, having embodied nothing of the means; and it is not a mere series of events having no intrinsic connections in experience. It is, rather, a good in itself precisely because of its felt continuities and connections. Art is that natural process which is most heavily laden with values and most productive of value. It is the name given to those occasions when human powers cooperate with nature to bring the potentialities of both into their happiest and most harmonious fruition. Art is nature's consummation: ". . . art . . . is the complete culmination of nature". [66]

Somewhat more remains to be said about the nature and

---

[64] *Ibid.*, p. 361.

[65] See especially *Art as Experience*, Chapter IV.

[66] *Experience and Nature*, p. 358.

value of this process. Dewey also has more to say concerning how, specifically, conduct in nature can become art, and hence most valuable. I will attempt to do justice to his views in the last two chapters. The concern of the present discussion has been primarily to characterize the concept of art in order to indicate its pertinence to understanding value in its context in nature. At this juncture, I will turn to an examination of Dewey's criticism of theories of value alternative to his own. This examination will provide further illustration of the uses of theory of nature in this field. It will at the same time both clarify Dewey's own position and urge its validity in comparison to notable treatments of this subject, ancient, modern, and contemporary.

CHAPTER IV

The Method of Experience in Moral Philosophy

The preceding chapter has been intended to elucidate Dewey's views on the status of value in nature. His metaphysical distinctions appear to be well suited to the characterization and understanding of moral experience. The present chapter will be devoted to Dewey's methodological assumptions as they pertain to value theory, and to his critique of the assumptions—both metaphysical and methodological—underlying some other main forms of value theory.

1. The Problem of Value

It was seen in the first chapter that one of Dewey's main assumptions — the most fundamental assumption in all his philosophy — is that the aim of all philosophizing is to make human experience in all its phases and connections intelligible: Philosophy should attempt to elucidate and illuminate experience and in so doing increase human capacity to control experience and to enrich its meanings. With this end in view, Dewey made the all-important distinction between primary subject matter and the intellectual concepts developed to clarify and explain that subject matter; and he drew attention to the persistent compulsion of philosophers to take the derivative subject matter as primary and forsake any relevance to primary experience. Thus he ridiculed, for example, the problem of knowledge: Philosophers could become so isolated from experience that they could deny one of its most obvious characters—namely, knowing. Philosophers could become drawn into a dialectic of concepts so happily and thoroughly that their ruminations there could define knowledge right out of existence. (Thereafter, of course, philosophers are incapacitated to render service to the actual procedures of inquiry and to determine how these procedures could be extended to other fields, such as morals.)

All these considerations apply equally well to the problem of value. Thus, in a crucial sense, there can be no problem of value in general; it is nonsense to ask whether there are values, whether values exist: For it would be difficult to discover any more outstanding feature of experience than the fact that man values and that there are specifiable things valued.

> Our constant and unescapable concern is with prosperity and adversity, success and failure, achievement and frustration, good and bad. Since we are creatures with lives to live, and find ourselves in an uncertain environment, we are constructed to note and judge in terms of bearing upon weal and woe—upon value.[1]
>
> Affections, desires, purposes, choices are going to endure as long as man is man; therefore as long as man is man, there are going to be ideas, judgments, beliefs about values. Nothing could be sillier than to attempt to justify their existence at large; they are going to exist anyway. What is inevitable needs no proof of its existence.[2]

The philosophical problem, therefore, is not to question the reality of value and valuation, but to understand and illuminate them. The philosopher's role is neither to invent nor legislate values. Rather, it is to learn the status of value in nature so that the instrumentalities to secure, enrich, and extend values may also be determined. And just as the philosopher should attempt to clarify and criticize the procedures and criteria of inquiry and knowing, so also he should determine how existing norms, principles, and ideals are derived from immediate goods, intellectual and practical habits, and beliefs about value. He does this primarily with a view to making distinctions between effective and ineffective means of transforming problematic situations into consummatory. This task includes analysis of various recommended methods of formulating value judgments and reaching decisions about conduct. And, of course, this process is carried out in reference to the social context: The task is not to determine how one man can most successfully exploit another, but

---

[1] *Experience and Nature*, p. 28.

[2] *The Quest for Certainty*, p. 299.

how the richest and most inherently satisfying life activity can be shared, as much as possible, by all. (Recall that there is no justification in moral philosophy for regarding some persons, a priori, as inherently entitled to advantage. In any case, Dewey's reflections were guided by his love of democratic values.)

In the same vein, a recurrent and familiar experience is that which could be called the moral situation; and by this is simply meant those occasions when we are faced with practical problems of what to do in some context where our actions will have a bearing on the weal and woe of others, and ourselves as well. Given this fact, ethical theory is not concerned with whatever puzzles philosophers might contrive in dialectic. Rather, the concern must be with the moral situation as it is experienced: What is fixed and what is variable? What are the problems which such situations pose, and what are the operations which will clarify and solve these problems? Prior to his analysis, the philosopher should not have already fixed his notions of what morality, responsibility, right, duty, and freedom are. He should not have a priori standards of moral reasoning, validity, or justification. Rather, he must learn what nature is and can provide on such issues. And when he distinguishes the various ways in which ethical situations function, *then* he should endeavor to formulate his ethical distinctions. According to the method of experience, the philosopher should examine the features of the moral situation and from that analysis determine the methods of ethical reasoning.[3]

Simply to take this approach hardly guarantees, of course, that all problems of moral theory will instantly be solved. On the other hand, there is an absurdity in bringing to the analysis of the moral life an a priori concept of, say, moral good, hoping there will be some application for it. The result is that the philosopher despairs of morality; or perhaps in his egotism he advocates a morality at the expense of experienced well-being.

All that has been said so far is unmistakably entailed by the assumptions outlined in Chapter I. Except for Chapter Ten of

[3] It must not be forgotten that in the enterprise of examining moral experience, the thinker should make critical use of whatever scientific knowledge is pertinent to understanding the phenomena in question.

Experience and Nature, Dewey rarely undertook systematic treatment of these implications of the method of experience for moral philosophy. It is abundantly clear in all his works, however, that these were the assumptions that informed his every inquiry. Thus when Dewey speaks of what is good or not good, what men ought to do or ought not to do, he is not issuing a proclamation based on authority, pure reason, or revelation; he is specifying those conditions which, if met, would seem to intelligence to go furthest toward enhancing the goods that are already present in human experience.

The work of philosophy is not to deny the values resident in experience; it is the criticism of "goods which are accepted as goods not because of theory but because they are such in experience."[4]

> There are values, goods, actually realized upon a natural basis – the goods of human association of art and knowledge . . . . We need no external criterion and guarantee for their goodness. They are had, they exist as good, and out of them we frame our ideal ends.[5]

Accordingly, philosophical criticism of values

> starts from actual situations of belief, conduct, and appreciative perception which are characterized by immediate qualities of good and bad, and from the modes of critical judgment current at any given time in all the regions of value; these are its data, its subject matter. These values, criticisms, and critical methods, it subjects to further criticism as comprehensive and consistent as possible. The function is to regulate the further appreciation of goods and bads; to give greater freedom and security in those acts of direct selection, appropriation, identification and rejection, elimination, destruction which enstate and which exclude objects of belief, conduct and contemplation . . . . For as philosophy has no private score of knowledge or of methods for attaining truth, so it has no private access to good. As it accepts knowledge of facts and principles from those competent in inquiry and discovery, so it accepts the goods that are diffused in human experience. It has no Mosaic nor Pauline authority of revelation entrusted to it. But it has the authority of intelligence, of criticism of these common and natural goods.[6]

What has been said about experience in moral philosophy invites several questions. One of the foremost concerns what are, in fact, the instrumentalities and criteria of criticism. This ques-

---

[4] *Experience and Nature,* pp. 432-3.

[5] *A Common Faith,* p. 48.

[6] *Experience and Nature,* pp. 403-4; 408. See alsp p. 412 of the same volume and p. 51 of *A Common Faith.*

tion will receive due notice in later chapters. Other questions concern – among other things – the status of rival theories of value. These I will take up next. My discussion will include some observations concerning the position that there are no strictly moral or normative propostions.

2. Abuses of Experience

I do not intend to canvas all the remarks that Dewey made relative to the profusion of theories of value. Most theories of value will, however, be dealt with at least by implication. I will indicate in order: 1) the consequences for any theory of value predicated upon the intellectualist-subjectivist metaphysics, 2) the consequences of misconstruing the nature of ends or of ignoring the organic relation of means-ends, and 3) the consequences of mistaking conceptual materials for primary subject matter.[7] This third topic occasions a discussion of moral language, in which a return is made to further considerations of Dewey's methodological assumptions in moral philosophy.

1) It is clear that the intellectualist-subjectivist view invites dire problems concerning the nature of value:

> The isolation of traits characteristic of objects known, and then defined as the sole ultimate realities, accounts for the denial to nature of the characters which make things lovable and contemptible, beautiful and ugly, adorable and awful. It accounts for the belief that nature is an indifferent, dead mechanism; it explains why characteristics that are the valuable and valued traits of objects in actual experience are thought to create a fundamentally troublesome philosophical problem.[8]

Hence, value, presumably no longer in nature, must either belong to some ideal realm which transcends actual human striving and is grasped by reason alone; or it must be merely subjective – the mere capricious liking or disliking of a private, unrelated self; or it must be a real entity in itself, organic to nothing and yet –

[7] Dividing the subject-matter in this way will entail that certain theories of value will be subject to criticism on more than one of the selected issues. Indeed, much of the material to be considered in the second topic constitutes an elaboration of materials to be introduced in the first. However, a philosophy can maintain a discontinuity of means and ends without entertaining the intellectualist-subjectivist metaphysics. The latter point of view is a distinctly modern phenomenon, while the notion of absolute ends goes back to ancient Greek philosophy. Therefore, the division into separate discussions seems justified.

[8] *Experience and Nature*, p. 21.

unaccountably – intruding itself into existence at crucial turnings in experience:

> Poignancy, humor, zest, tragedy, beauty, prosperity and bafflement, although rejected from a nature which is identified with mechanical structure, remain just what they empirically are, and demand recognition. Hence they are gathered up into the realm of values, contradistinguished from the realm of existence. Then the philosopher has a new problem with which to wrestle: What is the relationship of these two "worlds?" Is the world of value that of ultimate and transcendent Being from which the world of existence is a derivation or a fall? Or is it but a manifestation of human subjectivity, a factor somehow miraculously supervening upon an order complete and closed in physical structure? Or are there scattered at random through objective being, detached subsistences as "real" as are physical events, but having no temporal dates and spatial locations, and yet at times and places miraculously united with existences?[9]

And Dewey adds at once that such problems are wholly unnecessary:

> Choice among such notions of value is arbitrary, because the problem is arbitrary. When we return to the conceptions of potentiality and actuality, contingency and regularity, qualitatively diverse individuality, with which Greek thought operated, we find no room for a theory of values separate from a theory of nature.[10]

Moral philosophy crippled by reductive metaphysics is at best irrelevant to experience and impotent to aid actual human endeavors. Its actual consequences are in fact a positive evil. It is irrelevant because it is isolated from experience. It is impotent because it assumes a dualism of experience and nature and hence also of experience and science: Both subjectivistic and transcendental philosophies exclude actual experiences of value from scientific explanation and control. On the one hand, the "self" does not partake of natural processes; so its features cannot be a variable in any theory or experiment in nature; and knowledge of nature has no bearing on knowledge of value. Those who hold the mentalistic theory of value "endow this quasi-gaseous stuff with powers of resistance greater than are possessed by triple-plate steel."[11] When man and nature are regarded as independent entities, the possibilities of an inclusive science go unheeded.

---

[9] *Ibid.*, p. 394.

[10] *Ibid.*, p. 395. The Aristotelian notions of potentiality and actuality are, with some differences, implied by Dewey's notion of histories.

[11] *Problems of Men*, p. 281.

On the other hand, transcendental philosophies entail the equally great practical difficulties which issue from placing the good the true and the beautiful beyond nature and experience, there to scintillate untouched by human hands; for in the transcendental realm such things are not amenable to human production and management. The same criticisms could easily be extended to realistic theories as well.

As we shall see in greater detail later on, these theories are harmful in that their philosophic assumptions impede constructive criticism of values, and they often represent a disguised rationale for the value system of an elite established in power.

These criticisms of nonempirical theories of value may be elaborated. For instance, when values are not an integral part of experience, it is difficult to see what makes them valuable, for they are discontinuous with the delights and aspirations of experience. Of what, indeed, are they fulfillments? What are their meanings? What activity can be undertaken in their behalf? If a value is a disconnected entity, how can it be enriched with meanings and related to other values? What role can intelligence play in the criticism of values if its function is no more than simply to grasp them as such? In truth, one may sincerely ask of such values, What *good* are they? Further, when values are regarded as "above" mere experience, the latter is slighted and even despised. "The elevation of the ideal above and beyond immediate sense has operated not only to make it pallid and bloodless, but it has acted, like a conspirator with the sensual mind, to impoverish and degrade all things of direct experience." [12]

The tragedy of such metaphysics with their theories of knowledge and value is that "intelligence is divorced from aspiration."[13] The genuinely life-and-death issues of human experience are regarded as somehow inferior; and the goods of experience remain insecure, fleeting, occurring only at random. Philosophers, it is notorious, are much given to seeking and perhaps contriving some great truth which will save them from the exertions, uncertainties, and anxieties of temporal life. The consequence is that those intellectual assumptions and distinctions are not developed which could be effective in discriminating, enrich-

---

[12] *Art as Experience*, p. 31.

[13] *Reconstruction in Philosophy*, p. 212.

ing, and securing the goods of experience; and the values and meanings resident in natural existence are unnoticed and uncultivated. Or (as in the case of much current reflection) philosophers go to the opposite extreme and fret about the justification of value as such. But the result is the same: the instrumentalities for the criticism of specific values are neglected. All this is so much vanity:

> Is there not reason for believing that the release of philosophy from its burden of sterile metaphysics and sterile epistemology instead of depriving philosophy of problems and subject-matter would open a way to questions of the most perplexing and the most significant sort? . . . Would not the elimination of these traditional problems permit philosophy to devote itself to a more fruitful and more needed task? Would it not encourage philosophy to face the great social and moral defects and troubles from which humanity suffers, to concentrate its attention upon clearing up the causes and exact nature of these evils and upon developing a clear idea of better social possibilities; in short upon projecting an idea or ideal which, instead of expressing the notion of another world or some far-away unrealizable goal, would be used as a method of understanding and rectifying specific social ills.[14]

There has been in many modern philosophies an enchantment with a presumed realm of changeless perfection, which is adored both in itself and as providing the standard by which the things of experience are to be known and measured. Hence the notion that experience itself could yield instrumentalities for discriminating, judging, and securing values has been given little credence. Disregard of experience has discouraged men about the very possibility of utilizing experience for human fulfillment:

> The most serious indictment to be brought against non-empirical philosophies is that they have cast a cloud over the things of ordinary experience. They have not been content to rectify them. They have discredited them at large. In casting aspersion upon the things of everyday experience, the things of action and affection and social intercourse, they have done something worse than fail to give these affairs the intelligent direction they so much need. It would not matter much if philosophy had been reserved as a luxury of only a few thinkers. We endure many luxuries. The serious matter is that philosophies have denied that common experience is capable of developing from within itself methods which will secure direction for itself and will create inherent standards of judgment and value. No one knows how many of the evils and deficiencies that are pointed to as reasons for flight from experience are themselves due to the disregard of experience shown by

---

[14] *Ibid.*, pp. 126, 124. The sequence of the remarks has been inverted simply for the sake of clarity. There is no alteration in meaning.

> those peculiarly reflective. To waste of time and energy, to disillusionment with life that attends every deviation from concrete experience must be added the tragic failure to realize the value that intelligent search could reveal and mature among the things of ordinary experience. I cannot calculate how much of current cynicism, indifference and pessimism is due to these causes in the deflection of intelligence they have brought about.[15]

Not just for the sake of an intelligible philosophy of value, but for the sake of human good, our problems and aims must be properly located in nature.

Modern subjectivist philosophies have not done better in providing assumptions which would unite intelligence and aspiration. They have held that experience consists of atomic sensations, which are intrinsically unrelated to each other and to nature. Sensations are held together, according to this theory, only by the presumed laws of the association of ideas. Hence the notion of criticizing problematic goods in their actual continuities in nature, and the notion of contriving consummatory values, are altogether foreign.

I will not elaborate further on these theories at the present time, for they will receive renewed attention in connection with the following topic.

2) An assumed or implied discontinuity of means and ends has taken a variety of forms in the history of philosophy. (It has done so not least in connection with the metaphysics just examined.) At one extreme is the view that ends are final causes, somehow determining the nature of natural processes, or at any rate constituting the standard by which such processes are known and judged. Such ends are not a contrivance of human imagination and effort; and their existence is in no way dependent upon human preferences. At the opposite extreme is subjectivism, for which ends are merely private – unrelated wishing and willing. Hence nature, if this view is taken seriously, has no connection as means to the nature of such ends. Dewey rejects both views,

---

[15] *Experience and Nature,* p. 38. Although Dewey aims this remark at ancient and modern philosophies, it is pertinent to contemporary philosophies as well. Existentialism – with all its literary, religious, and quasi-intellectual followers – has scorned intelligent direction of experience. And much of English-speaking philosophy has simply turned its back on the problems Dewey regards as most fundamental, not, in this case, for a "higher" truth, but on the assumption that there are no legitimate philosophical issues related to moral experience proper.

because the reality of ends necessarily involves *both* nature and man; and thus also interactions of man and nature are organic as means to such ends. The former position, which Dewey regards as historically and socially by far the more influential of the two, will be examined first.[16]

This view derives primarily from the Greeks.[17] According to Plato and Aristotle, all natural processes, inclusive of the human, are regulated by antecedently and independently existing forms, or characters.[18] For Plato, these are the Forms, which, apparently, have an existence apart from their embodiment in objects of experience. For Aristotle, these are the so-called final causes, which, apparently, have no disembodied existence, but which are in some sense inherent in natural processes, determining their character and outcome. All natural processes strive toward the fulfillment of an end whose nature is predetermined. Thus also with human ends:

> If the changes in a tree from acorn to full-grown oak were regulated by an end which was somehow immanent or potential in all the less perfect forms, and if change was simply the effort to realize a perfect or complete form, then the acceptance of a like view for human conduct was consonant with the rest of what passed for science. Such a view, consistent and systematic, was foisted by Aristotle upon western culture and endured for two thousand years.[19]

---

[16] It should not be surprising that these apparently opposite views are frequently predicated on common metaphysical assumptions: the denial to nature of qualities, the precarious, ends, and histories. One school then seeks value in the transcendent; the other in the subjective.

[17] In regard to many issues in metaphysics, Dewey had a keen admiration for the Greek approach: The Greeks never denied the facts of experience; their aim was always to explicate the world in which there was such experience. Dewey's severe qualifications of Greek philosophy were invariably directed against their explications. So it was with ends.

His criticism of Greek philosophy should not be allowed to conceal the fact that Dewey's own thought is remarkably like that of Plato and Aristotle. Dewey's ethics has no closer historical precedent than that of Aristotle; and Dewey's concept of art in nature also finds its best precedent in Aristotle. Dewey's fundamental concern with the separation of knowledge and action and with the assumption of fixed and self-sufficient ends, or forms, in nature obscures such similarities.

It is true, of course, that the Greek theory of ends is not predicated on an intellectualist-subjectivist metaphysics. This latter theory is the special burden of modern philosophers.

[18] See in Chapter II, above, the discussion of the Greek theory of knowing, in Section 2, pp. 70-3.

What I am providing here, of course, is Dewey's rendering of their view; and Dewey's interpretation could be qualified in important ways, especially in relation to Aristotle. However, his view of their theory of ends seems to be the same as that which has been attributed to them historically and which has been widely followed.

[19] *Human Nature and Conduct*, p. 224.

These forms are the standard of truth and perfection; and it is in reference to them that the outcomes of natural processes are to be assessed. They are also regarded as Ultimate Being, the divine; and the highest good is in the direct rational grasp of these forms. "Pure contemplation of these forms was man's highest and most divine bliss, a communion with unchangeable truth."[20]

Given the value imputed to the intellectual possession of these forms, and given their presumed relation to events of experience, such forms have historically been regarded as ends in the most honorific and exclusive sense. In various philosophies the character of the realm of changeless perfection has been understood in different ways. There has, however, been a persistent assumption that there is some such realm and that it constitutes the ultimate norm of conduct and striving. In Greek philosophy, in Scholastic thought, natural law theories, and various forms of idealism, the changing and transient are always referred to something absolute and eternal which transcends experience. In most cases, these assumptions presuppose some form of ontological division. When Dewey refers in general to the classical theory of ends, it is this tradition which he has in mind.

Much has been said in this research to indicate that Dewey rejects this classical conception on a variety of grounds. I will not go over them again; but I will, rather, consider in greater detail the various ways in which this originally Greek conception hinders the analysis, criticism, and pursuit of value. In this reference, Dewey's objections can best be seen by recalling some points introduced in the preceding chapter. It was pointed out there that ends-in-view arise within activity. When activity is balked for whatever reason, the situation becomes problematic. Then some plan must be devised to utilize the various energies of the situation so that activity may be reintegrated; and the end (consummatory value) envisaged is precisely the institution of unified activity. The value of the end-in-view is that it integrates the on-going interaction of organism and environment and enhances the qualities of that interaction – not that it brings activity to a close. Neither the plan of action nor the consummatory value exists in any sense antecedently to the situation; and the consum-

[20] *The Quest for Certainty*, pp. 15-6.

matory phase itself is not an absolute ending, but is also a prelude to further activity.

This view is radically in contrast with the view that ends are forms of Ultimate Being, utterly removed from "mere" experience and overt endeavor. Dewey became increasingly convinced that the latter assumptions were the crucial impediment to the actual criticism of values. In fact, *The Quest for Certainty* is essentially devoted to showing the error of the Greek view and to arguing that ends (whether ends-in-view, or consummatory values) are discriminated *in* experience and made secure by intelligence and action. If, by contrast, ends are beyond experience and endeavor, then they are not only separated from consideration by experimental intelligence, but they are also, presumably, made secure simply by knowing them. The superempirical faculty of reason has simply to make direct grasp of these forms and thereby make them a secure possession. Of course, knowledge of the objects and events of the "material" world, and manipulations of such things, are irrelevant to this process.[21]

In various guises the Greek theory of ends – just as the Greek theory of knowing, of which it is derivative – has been adopted in modern philosophies. Thus there is the persistent assumption that somehow the end lies beyond action and change and is secured through simply mental endeavors of some kind. This way of thinking about values is fundamentally apologetic. That is, if the ends which determine the nature of things are standards of perfection, then whatever is by their nature must be good. Greek thought regards only "*good* objects as natural ends, *bad* objects and qualities being regarded as mere accidents or incidents, regrettable mechanical excess or defect." Hence Greek metaphysics is "apologetic, justificatory of the beneficence of nature, it has been optimistic in a complacent way."[22] There has been a succession of such philosophies which assume that the good in its full and perfect form is somehow already present in reality just as we find it, if only we can know it properly. The good is not a product of our interaction with nature; it is not something which

[21] A brief analysis of the presumed intrinsic value of absolute ends will be presented later on.

[22] *Experience and Nature,* p. 103.

we create with such interaction. Rather, it is simply antecedently given: Somehow, there is a way of apprehending reality – some secret of existence, perhaps – which will show that the way things really are is "really" right and good.

This notion is fundamental in objective idealism, which holds that in the Absolute all evils are negated; they are disclosed as mere appearance. Hence one must simply comprehend the Absolute. Lacking the philosophic genius to do so, one need only accept, or will, his station in the scheme of things in order to realize the good. This profoundly apologetic and conservative point of view was certainly one of the first and strongest inducements to Dewey to rethink the premises of the philosophic idealism which he early espoused. It is a philosophy in which creative intelligence, selecting and contriving ends, striving for that which is not yet in being, have no meaning. Against this background, Dewey's phrase "the *construction* of good" is especially significant.

What, in actual fact, philosophers have been apologists for has frequently been special interests of some kind. These can be made immune to criticism if they are presumed to be embodiments of the ideal. Seemingly, philosophers have been much given to the elaboration of pristine, ideal goods. This often represents – so Dewey holds – special pleading for entrenched traditional values, or for the values of a particular class or nation. Chapter I of *Reconstruction in Philosophy* is chiefly devoted to explicating the notion that philosophy has, historically, been primarily apologetic:

> It became the work of philosophy to justify on rational grounds the spirit, though not the form, of accepted beliefs and traditional customs. . . . The result has been that the great systems have not been free from party spirit exercised in behalf of preconceived beliefs.[23]

The result of placing ends in an ideal realm is not simply that philosophy has been so much inconsequence, but that deliberately productive activity has been regarded as inferior, and irrelevant to value:

---

[23] *Reconstruction in Philosophy,* pp. 18-20. As I indicated in Chapter I, Dewey frequently displayed exceptional gifts in disclosing the moral preconceptions of various philosophies.

> The result is the depreciated meaning that has come to be attached to the very meaning of the "practical" and the useful. Instead of being extended to cover all forms of action by means of which the values of life are extended and rendered more secure, including the diffusion of the fine arts and the cultivation of taste, the processes of education and all activities which are concerned with rendering human relationships more significant and worthy, the meaning of "practical" is limited to matters of ease, comfort, riches, bodily security and police order, possibly health, etc., things which in their isolation from other goods can only lay claim to restricted and narrow value. In consequence, these subjects are handed over to technical sciences and arts; they are no concern of "higher" interests which feel that no matter what happens to inferior goods in the vicissitudes of natural existence, the highest values are immutable characters of the ultimately real.[24]

From such views it follows also that the knowledge yielded by science of the processes of the natural world has no connection with the determination of value. The rejection of the presumed separation of ends and nature provides for philosophy what is perhaps its greatest challenge and greatest responsibility:

> Man has beliefs which scientific inquiry vouchsafes, beliefs about the actual structure and processes of things; and he also has beliefs about the values which should regulate his conduct. The question of how these two ways of believing may most effectively and fruitfully interact with one another is the most general and significant of all the problems which life presents to us. Some reasoned discipline, one obviously other than any science, should deal with this issue. Thus there is supplied one way of conceiving of the function of philosophy. But from this mode of defining philosophy we are estopped by the chief philosophical tradition. For according to it the realms of knowledge and practical action have no inherent connection with each other.[25]

Pertinent to the discussion of absolute ends is an analysis of their value. They seem desirable only when insufficiently examined: "We long, amid a troubled world, for perfect being. We forget that what gives meaning to the notion of perfection is the events that create longing, and that, apart from them, a 'perfect' world would mean just an unchanging brute existential thing."[26] Although hardly expressed with comparable literary brilliance, Dewey's insights resemble those of Nietzsche, who repeatedly claimed that man's love of heaven was a consequence of failure in earthly endeavors. Dewey observes that where frustrations and

[24] *The Quest for Certainty*, p. 32.

[25] *Ibid.*, pp. 18-9. The realm of knowledge referred to in the quotation is the realm of forms or of True Being beyond experience. In the passage, Dewey was attacking the spectator theory of knowing and its results.

[26] *Experience and Nature*, p. 63.

impositions are overwhelming, mere cessation of activity may be regarded as the ultimate good:

> What in effect is love of ease has masqueraded morally as love of perfection. A goal of finished accomplishment has been set up which if it were attained would mean only mindless action. It has been called complete and free activity when in truth it is only a treadmill activity or marching in one place . . . . Some forms of Oriental morals have united this logic with a profounder psychology, and have seen that the final terminus on this road is Nirvana, an obliteration of all thought and desire . . . . Because a thirsty man gets satisfaction in drinking water, bliss consists in being drowned.[27]

An exhausted man dreams of transcendent values and static perfection, but, upon reflection, it is difficult to see how a person possessed of normal vitalities and arts could long endure the changeless tedium of "bliss." But heaven may take many forms; and with seemingly prophetic insight into the maunderings of existentialists about the infinite possibilities of man's absolute freedom, Dewey says,

> The philosophy which holds that the realm of essence subsists as an independent realm of Being also emphasizes that this is a realm of possibilities; it offers this realm as the true object of religious devotion. But, by definition, such possibilities are abstract and remote. They have no concern nor traffic with natural and social objects that are concretely experienced. It is not possible to avoid the impression that the idea of such a realm is simply the hypostatizing in a wholesale way of the fact that actual existence has its own possibilities. But in any case devotion to such remote and unattached possibilities simply perpetuates the other-worldliness of religious tradition, although its other-world is not one supposed to exist. Thought of it is a refuge, not a resource.[28]

The foregoing discussion suggests that, on Dewey's view, the quest for Ultimate Reality cannot be traced exclusively to Greek metaphysics, Hellenized Christianity, or sophisticated rationalizations for special interests. The love of Ultimate Reality seems also to be a reflex of practical impotence:

> It would be plausible to argue (and, I think, with much justice) that failure to make action central in the search for such security as is humanly possible is a survival of the impotency of men in those stages of civilization when he had few means of regulating and utilizing the conditions upon which the occurrence of consequences depend. As long as man was unable by means of the arts of practice

[27] *Human Nature and Conduct*, pp. 173-5.

[28] *The Quest for Certainty*, pp. 305-6.

to direct the course of events, it was natural for him to seek an emotional substitute.[29]

Ends conceived according to the traditional notion as changeless, perfect, and ultimate Dewey refers to in general as fixed ends. The idea of fixed ends finds its way, in a great variety of forms, into many theories of value and into many practical institutions. This is true, remarkably, even of utilitarianism. Before proceeding to Dewey's analysis of subjective ends and to his criticism of the utilitarian theory of ends, I will pursue still further what he regarded as the actual practical liabilities of belief in fixed ends. My discussion will be directly concerned with Dewey's criticisms of social institutions and practices as embodiments of fixed ends.

A brief summary of the deficiencies of fixed ends will be a useful beginning: Fixed ends are conceived as somehow given prior to activity; they exist independently, antecedent to the situation; and somehow activity must conform to them willy-nilly. It is clear that such ends neither function to unify and release the potentialities of the situation; nor are they such unifications. They are not consummations; they cannot possess the meaning of antecedent activities or of prospective activities. When the notion of fixed ends is taken seriously, no measure is taken to discover and fulfill the goods actually resident in the situation. This notion of fixed ends, then, actually precludes the use of intelligence and imagination, directed action, and consummations in experience. (In addition, adherence to fixed ends breeds fanaticism: One end – in isolation from all the consequences of action – is alone regarded as significant; and action is accordingly judged by one consequence in itself, rather than by all the consequences which the action happens to produce.) Where human good is concerned, fixed ends are evidently self-defeating: As separated from activity, they are impossible of fulfillment; and they suppress the development of the values actually resident in

[29] *Ibid.*, p. 33. In this connection see the discussion in Chapter II, above, pp. 69-70, 111-3, where Dewey's view is presented that philosophical dualisms are ultimately rooted in social conditions. See also *Reconstruction in Philosophy*, Chapter V. Dewey's various explanations for the belief in the ideal realm of ends are not incompatible with each other. Certainly the technical, or philosophical, rationale for such belief lies in the assumption of the spectator theory of knowledge.

natural existence, abandoning man to his recurrent perplexities.[30]

This adherence to fixed ends – so sedulously taught by philosophy and cultivated by religion – has all-too-tangible manifestations in practical institutions. There are, of course, numberless instances of social authorities arbitrarily imposing ends from without upon the activities of individuals. Thus the individuals are effectively prohibited from pursuing their own interests and realizing the potential meanings of activity peculiarly suited to themselves. In respect to the defense of such conditions, philosophers have not been without guilt. Whatever the role of philosophy, however, it is clear that social life is plagued by separations of ends and means. Dewey recurrently seizes on both educational and industrial practices. In both instances the "ends" served are not fulfillments of the activity itself; so the activity is without intrinsic meaning, its possible values unrealized, its problems untouched. "Education" is seldom other than indoctrination, wherein the process of inquiry, intellectual development, and the consummations attendant to them are wholly neglected in favor of direct imposition of existing intellectual and moral doctrine:

> Education furnishes us with a poignant example. As traditionally conducted, it strikingly exhibits a subordination of the living present to a remote and precarious future. To prepare, to get ready, is its key-note. The actual outcome is lack of adequate preparation, of intelligent adaptation. The professed exaltation of the

---

[30] It is of interest to point out one of Dewey's principal criticisms of the Marxist theory of ends. Dewey shows that the Marxist theory of social practice (as articulated by Trotsky) clearly implies a discontinuity of means and ends. The presumed means to Marxist socialism is revolutionary class struggle. In that ideology, alternative means are not considered; and the assumption that these means will (or even could) in fact achieve the expected end is not questioned. Consequently, Marxists regard themselves as absolved from the responsibility of considering the actual consequences of promoting class conflict. (Dewey goes on to argue, indeed, that the Marxists can make no *moral* case consistently with their own premises. For if history leads by an inevitable sequence to an inevitable end, there is no determination of either ends or means by way of discrimination and selection, whether enlightened or not. The end is no more the outcome of procedures of judgment than is the "end" of water spilling over a dam.) See "Means and Ends: Their Interdependence, and Leon Trotsky's Essay on 'Their Morals and Ours' " *(The New International,* IV, August, 1938, pp. 232-3). Trotsky's essay is in *The New International,* IV, June, 1938.

future turns out in practice a blind following of tradition, a rule of thumb muddling along from day to day. . .[31]

Similarly, it is notoriously the case in modern industries that work is essentially meaningless. The presumed requirements of production permit no expression of individuality, and the individual worker creates no product. There is no end inherent in the work; there is only terminus. Moreover, and more fundamentally, economic life as a whole is regarded as something apart from moral significance or ends:

The present state of industrial life seems to give a fair index of the existing separation of means and ends. Isolation of economics from ideal ends, whether of morals or of organized social life, was proclaimed by Aristotle. Certain things, he said, are conditions of a worthy life, personal and social, but are not constituents of it. The economic life of man, concerned with satisfaction of wants, is of this nature. Men have wants and they must be satisfied. But they are only prerequisites of a good life, not intrinsic elements in it. Most philosophers have not been so frank nor perhaps so logical. But upon the whole, economics has been treated as on a lower level than either morals or politics. Yet the life which men, women and children actually lead, the opportunities open to them, the values they are capable of enjoying, their education, their share of all the things in art and science, are mainly determined by economic conditions. Hence we can hardly expect a moral system which ignores economic conditions to be other than remote and empty.

Industrial life is correspondingly brutalized by failure to equate it as the means by which social and cultural values are realized.[32]

I doubt whether a more momentous *moral* fact can be found in all human history than just this separation of the moral from other human interests and attitudes, especially from the "economic."[33]

Economic and educational institutions are just two of the best examples of what is so commonplace in modern life: the derogation of practical matters to a status wholly removed from "ideal" or "moral" matters. Life is neatly divided into practical concerns and ideal concerns; the former are largely bound up with material efficiency; the latter are either other-worldly or the values of traditional authorities. In either case, what function as ends in society are not fulfillments, but impositions.

When ends, or values, are thought to be discontinuous with activity, the result has two inseparable aspects. First, the mo-

[31] *Human Nature and Conduct,* pp. 269-70. With many writers, the term "alienation" is used to refer to much the same phenomena that Dewey analyses as separations of means and ends.

[32] *The Quest for Certainty,* p. 282.

[33] "Liberating the Social Scientist," *Commentary,* IV (October, 1947), p. 383.

mentous consequences for human weal and woe of all "practical" institutions are not regarded as subject to distinctively moral evaluation; for the moral life, its criteria and its rewards, is determined independently of such things. Second, the presumed moral ends are not subject to criticism and control in light of the experienced realities of human need and aspiration as these are found concretely in social existence. Dissolve this wholly factitious and pernicious boundary, and the traits of practical life are at once subject to analysis and criticism in terms of both their intrinsic value and their human consequences; and what have hitherto been regarded as pure moral values must also at once become subject to appraisal for their actual worth in guiding and giving meaning to life experience.

The means-ends division has the consequence of confining intelligence to certain limited spheres of activity. Much of what Dewey recommends as procedure for criticizing value *is* in some measure utilized in the interest of such things as economic efficiency, material success, and the acquisition of power. People frequently *are* intelligent in the *pursuit* of such ends. But Dewey's procedures are *not* utilized in the criticism of the ends themselves and of their implications for actual social conditions and social policy.

Dewey's disdain for such divisions has already been indicated. It is accurate to say that Dewey regarded the acceptance of the philosophical rationale for this dualism as an insuperable impediment to intelligent examination of contemporary life; and it is impossible to grasp the full import of many of his writings without recognizing that he is addressing himself to the eradication of the assumptions which justify the radical division between means and ends in society. His writings return incessantly to considerations of various dualisms; and a superficial reading would indicate that he alternates almost capriciously from the damnation of one dualism to another as being at the bottom of modern intellectual difficulties. Thus he seizes now on body and mind, and then on theory and practice, and yet again on ends and means, art and science, experience and nature, and so on. But this is surely not, however, the impulsive lashing out at whatever dualism occurs to him first, for they are at bottom all instances of the same dualism; and this can be most fundamentally expressed as the separation of knowing and doing. Assume (for whatever reasons) a bifurcation of knowledge and action, and then all the other dualisms follow. For knowing, unattended by activity, presupposes a fixed and static realm of True Being utterly divided from the world of process, yet somehow constituting the standard for judging processes of change. And all these dualisms imply the same result: rendering in principle all human endeavor (including experimental science) irrelevant to the all-important human concern with value.

When Dewey urges the method of intelligence for the criticism of values, he is not primarily engaged in displaying wit and insight to fellow philosophers. He is demanding the end – in both theory and practice – to the separation of means and ends in human life, and he is demanding the consequent appraisal of all human institutions and ideals for their bearing on experienced human good. It is only in this context that Dewey's remarks can be understood and appreciated:

> The social and moral effects of the separation of theory and practice have been merely hinted at. They are so manifold and so pervasive that an adequate consideration of them would involve nothing less than a survey of the whole field of morals, economics and politics. . . .This issue involves nothing less than the problem of the directed reconstruction of economic, political and religious institutions.[34]

The subjectivist notion of ends can be dealt with more briefly. This theory presupposes a dualism of man and nature, with all its attendant problems, and hence also a certain discontinuity of means and ends. That is, man and nature are conceived as independently functioning systems, each with its own inherent laws. Thus their relation is purely external and mechanical; the inherent nature of neither "substance" is affected by this mechanical action. This notion necessarily combines with the notion that values are exclusively mental events.

It is clear that this theory, which belongs to classical British empiricism, has serious deficiencies.[35] It cannot consistently offer any idea of how nature can be efficacious in the realization of value, and it cannot provide any intelligible notion of consummatory experience. According to the theory, ideas, or mental

---

[34] *The Quest for Certainty*, pp. 283; 259.

[35] For Dewey's analysis and critique of classical empiricism, see especially "The Need for a Recovery of Philosophy" and "An Empirical Survey of Empiricisms," both of which are reprinted in Bernstein (ed.), *op. cit.*

events, are discrete and separate entities – intrinsically unrelated to each other or to nature. Hence, according to the theory, a "value" must occur "in the mind" according only to presumed inherent laws of association of ideas.

Guided by such assumptions, the British empiricists not only could not develop an intelligible theory of value, but their practical proposals were severely limited as well. They did not begin to investigate the possibilities of criticizing problematic goods by considering their continuities in nature; and they did not develop any notion of the construction of consummatory value by means of inquiry, reflection, and overt action.

> They resolved mind into a complex of external associations among atomic elements, just as they resolved society into a similar compound of external associations among individuals, each of whom has his own indepentently fixed nature .... The conception of intelligence as something that arose from the association of isolated elements, sensations and feelings, left no room for far-reaching experiments in construction of a new social order.... The theory of mind ... did not arrive at the idea of experimental and constructive intelligence.[36]

Dewey holds that empirical theories continue to carry much the same burdens:

> Equally significant is the fact that empirical theories retain the notion that thought and judgment are concerned with values that are experienced independently of them [independently of thought and judgment]. For these theories, emotional satisfactions occupy the same place that sensations hold in traditional empiricism. Values are constituted by liking and enjoyment; to be enjoyed and to be a value are two names for one and the same fact. Since science has extruded values from its objects, these empirical theories do everything possible to emphasize their purely subjective character of value. A psychological theory of desire and liking is supposed to cover the whole ground of the theory of values; in it, immediate feeling is the counterpart of immediate sensation.... .The objection is that the theory in question holds down value to objects *antecedently* enjoyed, apart from reference to the method by which they come into existence; it takes enjoyments which are casual because unregulated by intelligent operations to be values in and of themselves.[37]

By implication, if not in intent, subjectivist theories have also been apologetic: In failing to provide adequate assumptions and instrumentalities of criticism, they are in theory committed to the acceptance of values just as they happen to occur.

---

[36] *Liberalism and Social Action*, pp. 42-3.

[37] *The Quest for Certainty*, pp. 257-8.

> The serious defect in the current empirical philosophy of values, the one which identifies them with things actually enjoyed irrespective of the conditions upon which they depend, is that it formulates and in so far consecrates the conditions of our present social experience.[38]

In Chapter III I mentioned that many might find Dewey's insistence on the situational character of values objectionable. Some indication of the merits of Dewey's view has been provided. (And the issue will be raised again.) An individual can, of course, desire fixed ends of some sort and guide his conduct by what he believes they dictate; but their intrinsic worth and their efficacy in experience are altogether questionable. On the other hand, the notion of value as unrelated sensations of pleasure and pain is not of the sort to enlighten experience as we actually find it. Of course, Dewey cannot insist that only consummatory experience can rightly be designated by the word "value." One may use the word as he pleases. That is a matter of little account. The important matter is that individuals perceive the difference in experience between that which Dewey calls value, and fixed ends, and mere sensations.

The criticisms Dewey makes of the arbitrary wrenching apart of means and ends find many targets in philosophical and theological writings, as well as in social practice. It might seem, however, that the utilitarian moral philosophy would be safely removed from his attacks. But such is not the case. Utilitarianism is in significant ways infected with the classical assumptions, and Dewey had subtle insights regarding its deficiencies.[39] (Of course, what has been said of the limitations placed on a theory of value by the classical empiricist philosophy of experience applies to classical utilitarianism.)

To Dewey, the uppermost deficiency of utilitarianism – as of all classical empiricism – is its failure to develop a theory of the

---

[38] *Ibid.*, p. 285. It appears to be Dewey's principal objection to Perry's theory of value that it does not sufficiently concern itself with the instrumentalities for criticizing problematic goods and for the construction of consummatory values. Although there may be some weight in this objection, it is by no means clear that Dewey ever gave Perry a careful reading. Perry is obviously not vulnerable to the most decisive criticisms that can be leveled, for example, against Hume.

[39] See especially the many references in *Reconstruction in Philosophy, Human Nature and Conduct, Ethics, The Public and Its Problems,* and *Liberalism and Social Action.*

creative functions of social intelligence in the construction of values. To calculate anticipated pleasures and pains is by no means to contrive organic consummations in experience. My concern here, however, will be to indicate Dewey's treatment of happiness (or pleasure) as an end.

Obviously, Dewey is anything but opposed to human happiness; and the utilitarians gained his profound respect for insisting that goods are the goods of human experience:

> To utilitarianism . . . belongs the distinction of enforcing in an unforgettable way the fact that moral good, like every good, consists in a satisfaction of the forces of human nature, in welfare, happiness.[40]

Despite their genuine sympathies for experienced human well-being and their determination to put ethical theory in its service, the utilitarians did not develop their assumptions in a way which would illuminate the procedures by which men might actually share in a more generous measure of happiness. This failure is largely due to treating happiness itself as the *terminus* of activity – as a fixed end. After praising utilitarianism in *Reconstruction in Philosophy,* Dewey goes on:

> But it was still profoundly affected in fundamental points by old ways of thinking. It never questioned the idea of a fixed, final and supreme end. It only questioned the current notions as to the nature of this end; and then inserted pleasure and the greatest possible aggregate of pleasures in the position of the fixed end.[41]

Regarded as a fixed end, the idea of happiness, as such, could not perform the functions of enriching, directing, and unifying ongoing activity. In contexts of practical action, or even in those of conceptual distinction, "happiness" is an abstraction, a disguise, and a distraction from the kinds of inquiry requisite to consummatory experience.

Dewey's objection can be clarified by dividing it into five points: 1) Happiness, or pleasure, is not – contrary to the utilitarian assumption – a thing in itself or an independent process of some kind. Rather, it is a quality of behavior. And this quality, indeed, is not a fixed, invariable trait which is somehow additive

---

[40] *Human Nature and Conduct,* p. 211

[41] *Reconstruction in Philosophy,* pp. 180-1. Some of this discussion of utilitarianism anticipates topics which will be covered in some detail in Chapters VI and VII.

to the properties of behavior. Rather, the pleasure of any particular activity is a quality of that activity as such in its uniqueness:

> If we still wish to make peace with the past, and to sum up the plural and changing goods of life in a single word, doubtless the term happiness is the one most apt. But we should again exchange free morals for sterile metaphysics if we imagine that "happiness" is any less unique than the individuals who experience it; any less complex than the constitution of their capacities, or any less variable than the objects upon which their capacities are directed.[42]

2) Given the fact that pleasure is a quality of activity, the idea that pleasures or happiness are given entities which in and of themselves are ends simply mistakes the nature of these things. Properly understood, happiness is not in any specific sense an end at all; but it is something which *attends* an end. Happiness, Dewey says,

> . . . is not directly an *end* of desire and effort, in the sense of an end-in-view purposely sought for, but is rather an end-product, a necessary accompaniment, of the character which is interested in objects that are enduring and intrinsically related to an outgoing and expansive nature.[43]

It follows, therefore, 3) that happiness conceived as a fixed end can never function as a guide to conduct. In itself it offers no clue to what must be done in a particular situation in order to develop the most value in it.

> The proper business of intelligence is the discrimination of multiple and present goods and of the varied immediate means of their realization; not search for the one remote aim. . . .We may anticipate that the aboliton of *the* final goal ... in morals will quicken inquiry into the diversity of specific goods of experience, fix attention upon their conditions, and bring to light values now dim and obscure.[44]

4) Conceived as a fixed end, happiness is removed from the con-

---

[42] *The Influence of Darwin on Philosophy* (Bloomington: Indiana University Press, 1965), p. 69. Dewey was aware that J.S. Mill had insisted on the qualitative differences in pleasures. But Mill had not sufficiently considered the implications of his position. For inasmuch as pleasure is a unique quality of activity, pleasure *as such* cannot be in any sense a serviceable goal. Certainly, in any case, Dewey's critique of utilitarianism is not equally weighty against Mill as against his predecessors.

[43] *Ethics* (Revised Edition; New York:Henry Holt and Company,1936),p. 214.This book was written jointly with James H. Tufts. The quoted portion, however, was written exclusively by Dewey; and all further quotations from the *Ethics* in this study will be from the chapters written by Dewey.

In my sixth chapter, considerable attention will be given to the nature of happiness, which, indeed, Dewey sharply distinguishes from pleasure.

[44] *The Influence of Darwin on Philosophy*, pp. 68-70.

tinuity of means-ends. That is, Dewey regards the utilitarian conception as placing happiness beyond activity, rather than within it. In accordance with this conception, the conditions of happiness are "mere" means, are without value in themselves. Hence the notion of conduct as art, in which intrinsic value is realized throughout, eludes the utilitarians. Utilitarianism presents an idea of conduct as a sequence of valueless means and valuable ends. "Such a point of view treats concrete activities and specific interests not as worthwhile in themselves, or as constituents of happiness, but as mere external means to getting pleasures." [45] To make it a matter of policy to put yourself in a way of giving up present satisfaction for future rewards implies a lack of awareness of the nature of experience as art. The full import of this idea (experience as art) will not be evident until the sixth chapter; but it can be observed here that failure to appreciate it means that the best possibilities of value pass unnoticed. Dewey regards the utilitarians as having failed to recognize the possibilities for value in a proper analysis of the continuities of means-ends. This shortcoming is not only a blindness to the potentialities of experience; it also conceives means and ends in such a way that ends are made unnecessarily insecure. This is the fifth point.

5) Happiness as a state to be achieved beyond present activity rather than within it is precisely that condition which is most difficult to predict and secure:

> Future pleasures and pains are influenced by two factors which are independent of present choice and effort. They depend upon our own state at some future moment and upon the surrounding circumstances of that moment. Both of these are variables which change independently of present resolve and action. They are much more important determinants of future sensations than is anything which can now be calculated. Things sweet in anticipation are bitter in actual taste, things we now turn from in aversion are welcome at another moment in our career. . . . Future pleasures and pains, even of one's own, are among the things most elusive of calculation. Of all things they lend themselves least readily to anything approaching a mathematical calculus. And the further into the future we extend our view, and the more the pleasures of others enter into account, the more hopeless does the problem of estimating future consequences become.[46]

---

[45] *Reconstruction in Philosophy,* p. 181.

[46] *Human Nature and Conduct,* pp. 202-3. More will be said on the relation of future to present in Chapter VI.

It would seem that on Dewey's view utilitarianism was really but a beginning of a genuinely experimental moral philosophy. "The idea of a fixed and single end lying beyond the diversity of human needs and acts rendered utilitarianism incapable of being an adequate representative of the modern spirit."[47]

Further things might be said about the nature and function of ends. (In fact, the subject will receive further attention in the sixth chapter.) Enough has been said, however, to display the vital importance of having a clear conception of the actual character of ends and means in nature. The next abuse of experience in moral philosophy to be discussed is the mistaking of conceptual materials for primary subject matter.

3) Many examples of this sort of abuse can be adduced. A classic instance is the Kantian insistence that a distinctively moral act is such that cannot be motivated by ordinary desire. Regardless of the (erroneous) ways in which Kantians regard desire, the self, and responsibility, the basic fallacy here is in making an a priori assumption of what morality must be. Suppose it is reliably concluded that all voluntary acts are determined by desire. Then the poor Kantian despairs of morality! But what a silly plight that would be! For it would remain as urgent as ever to understand and distinguish various kinds of behavior – hitherto called moral and immoral – and to determine procedures for enhancing and widening certain kinds of experience and discouraging others. Experience and its values do not change one bit by the Kantian decision to grant or withhold the term "moral" to certain features of them; and the practical importance of inquiring into such features is not in the least diminished.

A variant of the same kind of error stems from selective emphasis: Dewey finds a predilection in philosophers to convert reflective insight into goods into reductive metaphysics. Thus the good becomes also the exclusively real. Dewey speaks of a "bias toward treating objects selected because of their value in some special context as the 'real,' in a superior and invidious sense. . ."[48]

---

[47] *Reconstruction in Philosophy*, p. 183. And utilitarians seem too much pervaded by the Puritan spirit: "Consider the utilitarians how they toiled, spun and wove, but who never saw man arrayed in joy as the lillies of the field. Happiness was to them a matter of calculation and effort, of industry guided by mathematical book-keeping." (*Experience and Nature*, p. 78.)

[48] *Experience and Nature*, p. 27.

> When philosophers have hit in reflection upon a thing which is stably good in quality and hence worthy of persistent and continued choice, they hesitate, and withdraw from the effort and struggle that choice demands: – namely, from the effort to give it some such stability in observed existence as it possesses in quality when thought ot. . . .Hence they transmute the imaginative perception of the stably good object into a definition and description of true reality in contrast with lower and specious existence, . . .[49]

Thus what at first appears as the vanities of transcendental metaphysics becomes on reflection a record of human aspirations:

> Instead of the disputes of rivals about the nature of reality, we have the sense of human clash of social purpose and aspirations. Instead of impossible attempts to transcend experience, we have the significant record of the efforts of men to formulate the thingsof experience to which they are most deeply and passionately attached. Instead of impersonal and purely speculative endeavors to contemplate as remote beholders the nature of absolute things-in-themselves, we have a living picture of the choice of thoughtful men about what they would have life to be, and to what ends they would have men shape their intelligent activities.[50]

Rather than catalogue various historical instances of the attempt to superimpose categories on experience or to substitute categories for experience, I will deal with just one more case of such a fallacy. This is so-called noncognitivism in ethics. As championed by A.J. Ayer and C.L. Stevenson, it received specific attention from Dewey.[51] Although Dewey's critique was in many ways pertinent, it is fair to say that he missed a crucial point of what Ayer and Stevenson were saying. His analysis, however, is not incorrect, but incomplete. This incompleteness does not stem from inherent defect in Dewey's moral philosophy, and it can be remedied exclusively be reference to his own fundamental

---

[49] *Ibid.*, p. 53.

[50] *Reconstruction in Philosophy*, pp. 25-6. In this connection it deserves mention that the bulk of evaluative criticism suffers from a different form of selective emphasis: Appraisals of experience simply fail to give a full account of the values at issue. This can stem both from failure to consider the possible range of consequences and from the resolute refusal to acknowledge values that obviously exist. This latter failure is witnessed very much of late: in the typically crude assertion, for example, that liberalism is totally corrupt, totally bankrupt, etc. Any doctrinaire position in morals and politics evidently suffers from selective emphasis, favoring only certain groups and values.

[51] The argument of Chapter VI of Ayer's *Language, Truth and Logic* is dealt with in Dewey's *Theory of Valuation* (especially pp. 6-13); and Dewey published a discussion of Stevenson's *Ethics and Language:* "Ethical Subject-Matter and Language," *The Journal of Philosophy*, XLII (1945), pp. 701-12.

assumptions. It seems likely that if Dewey had grasped the full import of the noncognitivist position, he would readily have dismissed it as inconsequential for experience, and essentially on the basis of assumptions which I have already introduced. (See above, pp. 161-5 .) Considering the current vogue for noncognitivism in ethics, and considering that noncognitivism is regarded as an impasse in ethics, it seems altogether suitable to enlarge upon Dewey's specific remarks on this subject by utilizing more general considerations he has introduced in other contexts. Thus it will be shown that the noncognitivist position is a case of having become mired in conceptual problems which are irrelevant to experience.

It is very important to have a clear notion of what it is, in fact, that the noncognitivist is asserting. When the din has calmed and the dust has settled, the central thesis of noncognitivism comes to this: It is never a contradiction to deny any definition of any ethical term, and hence, also, any ethical predicate. If one attempts to define "good" in terms of pleasure and absence of pain, there is no inherent abusrdity in denying that pleasure and absence of pain are good. This is because pleasure does not *mean* good; and neither does absence of pain. The same analysis could be extended to more complex and highly qualified attempts to define moral terms. Accordingly – at least as Ayer sees it – one could not deny that grass is green in the same way that he could deny that pleasure is good.[52] If this is so, then it follows that there can never be any intersubjectively verifiable meaning of "good", or of any other presumed moral term. Accordingly, moral predicates are in reality meaningless, and moral propositions are not genuine cognitive claims. Moral propositions are pseudopropositions.[53]

---

[52] This analysis is not limited to so-called naturalistic definitions; it applies to any attempt whatsoever. It also has direct application to arguments which hold that there is a good, but that it is unanlyzable. For where would there be a contradiction in withholding the word "good" from Moore's presumed nonnatural, unanalyzable quality?

[53] Of course a moral claim can be cognitive if a certain moral principle is presupposed. Thus it is true, e.g., that giving food to a person miserable from starvation is good if it is presupposed that it is good to aid people in misery. The noncognitivist points out, however, that such an example simply puts the problem at one remove; for – inasmuch as "alleviating misery" does not *mean* "good" – it is not self-contradictory to say that it is not good to help persons in misery. Appeal to still further standards is simply to initiate an infinite regress.

In the sense in which noncognitivists intend this argument, the position may well be valid. Subsequent to Ayer, more sophisticated analyses of moral language were provided; yet the noncognitivists continue to hold the seemingly crucial thesis that there is an unbridgeable dualism between the descriptive and normative meanings of ethical words. Stevenson is included in this group. In all this dispute, interest has centered almost exclusively about whether or not the noncognitivist argument is valid; for there has evidently been uniform agreement that *if* it is true, normative ethics could not possibly be an empirical discipline. From the persepctive of Dewey's philosophy, however, the noncognitivist argument could be granted as valid, but nevertheless dismissed as inconsequential. That is, even if the noncognitivists' argument about moral language is correct, its significance for moral philosophy is virtually nil. A further examination of the issue will indicate why this is so.

As Ayer points out, the noncognitivist position simply explicates a fact of our language. [54] That is, the linguistic rules of English happen to be such, presumably, that any distinctively ethical predicate can be appended to any factual characterization of any state of affairs without thereby either affirming or denying any of the facts in question. In other words, moral terms have no uniquely determinable meaning or reference. If moral terms are used simply as substitutes for wholly descriptive terms, no one is obliged by either facts or linguistic conventions to accept that substitution.

This state of affairs can be illustrated: One may call benevolence good. But there isn't any intersubjectively verifiable test for goodness; there is only a test for the behavioral characteristics of benevolence, or for the functioning of benevolence. Likewise, one may call benevolence bad. Again, however, there isn't any test for badness. There are precisely the same tests for the nature and functions of benevolence, and the results are precisely the same. There could be no proofs or demonstrations of any kind

[54] See p. 105 of Ayer's *Language, Truth and Logic* (New York: Dover Publications, n.d.). Ayer's emotivism, closely allied with his thesis of noncognitivism, will not be examined herein. Dewey has much to say about it, however, in *Theory of Valuation,* where he exposes the fact that the emotive theory of ethical language is a gross distortion of experience.

that benevolence is good. Such efforts are futile. All that inquiry can determine is that benevolence has such and such characteristics, or that something is an instance of benevolence, or that benevolence has certain conditions and tends to have certain consequences. Hence it is that the definitions of all moral words are exclusively stipulative. And however one stipulates the use of such terms, no one else is in any way bound to adopt this usage. Anyone may use "good" where someone else uses "bad." The point is that one may choose whatever moral predicates he likes. *In doing so, he introduces no new qualities and alters no verifiable facts.* Even if it were true that he violates certain linguistic habits, in no verifiable way does he violate extralinguistic fact; and this is the decisive conclusion. Thus, to repeat and sum up, any so-called moral predicate can be denied without at the same time denying any matter of fact. [55] One could say "Benevolence is good"; another could say "Benevolence is bad"; and there need be no dispute whatever between them about any of the facts of benevolence.

These are conclusions about moral language; they are *not* conclusions about the nature of human desires, feelings, or values. The controversy surrounding these conclusions (by those who understood them) has been carried on within the confines of linguistic analysis: analysis of the "jobs" which moral language presumably accomplishes. Ayer's emotivism, accordingly, was justly challenged as misleading in certain ways; and the most intelligent critiques of the sophisticated forms of noncognitivism have questioned the argument that descriptive and normative meanings are so neatly separable. [56] But in any case it must be noted that the entire controversy concerns language and its uses,

---

[55] Dewey did not understand that Ayer was making precisely this point. It is here, then, that the argument escaped him. When Ayer argued that cognitive claims in ethics could not be made, Dewey supposed that the argument was predicated exclusively on the assumption that feelings are wholly subjective, having no reference whatever to objective states of affairs. There does seem to be some such assumption in Ayer's thought, but his conclusion does not depend upon it.

The most uniquely useful feature of Dewey's critique of Ayer is in his account of the way specific situations determine the meaning of the language used in them.

[56] See, for example, the perceptive articles by Philippa Foot: "Moral Beliefs," *Proceedings of the Aristotelian Society*, LIX (1958); "Moral Arguments," *Mind*, LXVII (1958); and "Goodness and Choice," *Proceedings of the Aristotelian Society*, suppl. vol. XXXV (1961).

actual and permissible.

Having said this much, let me return the discussion to the import of noncognitivism for moral philosophy. Whatever may be the truth of the noncognitivist argument, it is crucially important to see that a foolish conclusion is *drawn* from the argument. I refer to the conclusion that ethics is nonsense. This conclusion is foolish because it presupposes that "ethics" is, or must be, a certain sort of discipline. With apparently no reflection on the ways in which ethics can be construed as an intellectual discipline, it assumes a priori what ethics must be. What Ayer evidently regards as the model for ethics (if ethics were to be possible) will be indicated in Chapter VII. For the present it need only be observed that there appears to be a presumption among noncognitivists (as well as among many others), that ethics, strictly speaking, and exclusively experimental inquiries are mutually exclusive disciplines. Determining, however, that there can be no such thing as ethics in this sense, philosophers offer the weighty judgment that ethics is nonsense.

It is clear that what was said a short time ago relative to Kantian preconceptions about morality is equally pertinent here.[57] At this point I shall elaborate somewhat. (There will be in the concluding chapter as well a thorough analysis, in the context of Dewey's philosophy of nature, of the peculiar functions of so-called moral discourse. The present discussion will anticipate that chapter in some particulars.) At present, the decisive point to bear in mind is that moral terms do not predicate additional qualities to situations, or add or substract any facts in a way which could not be accomplished by strictly descriptive language. While Ayer, for one, regards this as making nonsense of ethics, Dewey regards this as precisely the necessary condition of any effective theory of ethics. Although little of his explicit position can be presented in the balance of this chapter, the generalization can be made that, on Dewey's view, all the functions of

[57] I mentioned earlier that the noncognitivist position was almost wholly inconsequential. I said "almost," because it must be granted that this position banishes the use of unverifiable moral language; and this, of course, is a useful result. However, one doesn't have to be a noncognitivist to reach that result. Any conscientious pragmatist reaches the same conclusion; but he doesn't on that account dismiss the whole enterprise of normative ethics.

moral inquiry, analysis, discourse, argumentation, justification, and conciliation not only can, but must, be carried on in empirically verifiable language. This is true, at any rate, if moral philosophy is construed as a discipline in the service of understanding, enriching, and uniting actual human values, enlightening human aims, guiding conduct and mediating the actual clash of values. On these assumptions, the presumed need for distinctively ethical terms just vanishes. Consequently, the alleged indefinability of ethical terms is simply *irrelevant* to the enterprise of moral philosophy. To put it another way: There is nothing that so-called ethical words can do that strictly descriptive words cannot; while there is much that descriptive words can do that ethical words cannot. As we shall see in due course, Dewey is not himself begging any questions about what ethics ought to be. The question of what ethics or moral philosophy ought to be is not to be decided by philosophic predilections, definition, or conceptual analysis. Moral philosophy as a discipline exists because there is in nature a massive subject matter which demands acute intellectual attention, namely, human needs, values, conflicts, aspirations, and the corresponding requirements for information, guidance, methods of inquiry, and procedures for social reconciliations.

From Dewey's point of view it is clear that the noncognitivist argument can be granted and at the same time dismissed as trivial. The argument implies that there is no way in which the usage of terms like "good" and "right" can be enforced; that is, there is no logical impediment to anyone's using these terms in any way that pleases him. What all recent critics have failed to observe, however, is that it is a matter of no importance that such definitions can't be verified. For regardless of what names are used to describe it, human experience with its demands and aspirations will remain what it is. It will still be true that it is of utmost importance to all human beings that certain kinds of experience be enhanced and secured and other kinds avoided. Thus it will be equally vital to know the conditions of such experience.

The important matter for human life is whether the pursuit of value is blind and ignorant or informed and intelligent. It is crucially important to everyone to know how to discriminate between different kinds of experience, to enlarge the meanings of experience, and to learn the conditions and consequences of their varied transactions with nature. Above all, it is important for men to learn the conditions and consequences of their interaction with other men in society and to be able to discern alternative possibilities of life experience. Whatever lexicon be adopted is of little moment; the important matters will retain their importance nonetheless: The nature of, say, shared experience will remain what it is, and persons will continue to treasure it and strive for it. It is not consequential what terminology is used to make these claims and distinctions, so long as we know and can communicate what claims and distinctions are being made. Thus there is some awkwardness, but no essential impediment to human well-being, in saying, for example, that shared experience is not good. Enlightened men will seek and cherish it nonetheless. The important matter is that we know what in fact are the qualities and conditions and rewards of shared experience. About all such matters of human experience it is entirely clear that an indefinite number of cognitive claims can be made and tested; and it is precisely the information provided in such claims that is so vital to human well-being. The intellectual discipline which is concerned with this general subject matter is correspondingly valuable.

Perhaps it is objected that considerations and inquiries of the kind suggested do not bear on the problem of prescription. What is the problem of prescription, however, is not at all clear. Dewey's views on the subject will be given later on in this section in connection with his discussion of the views of C. L. Stevenson, and still later, in the last chapter. At present only one point need be introduced: Prescription, for Dewey, functions to direct behavior; and the best direction for behavior issues from the agent's thorough awareness of the factual possibilities, implications, and alternatives which confront him in any concrete situation. In brief, conduct is best guided by precisely the factual considerations that have been alluded to in these pages.

Of course it can always be claimed that Dewey hasn't any absolute justification for asserting that what he is concerned with is rightly called ethics or moral philosophy. But not only is such an argument merely about words, but it readily invites a question as to the importance of any ethical theory that has no direct bearing on experienced weal and woe; for it is these that men are concerned with. Clearly, men have believed that their good has been essentially connected with things with which it in fact has not been connected, but in any case the concern has been with real or anticipated weal and woe. That there are many goods of experience is undeniable, but their interrelations in nature are often obscure, the methods for discriminating them ineffectual, and the policies for dealing with their conflict benighted. Hence the matters for inquiry concern the kind of world in which such goods do occur, the nature of their occurrence in such a world, and the conditions of their selection, control and expansion. In this connection, recall Dewey's remarks (quoted above) pertaining to the importance of enlightening human aims and endeavors with our actual knowledge of nature: "Some reasoned discipline, one obviously other than any science, should deal with this issue. Thus there is supplied one way of conceiving the function of philosophy." No matter what name the inquiry, it is essential that it be undertaken:

> What does knowledge indicate about the authoritative guidance of our affections, desires and affections, our plans and policies? Unless knowledge gives some regulation, the only alternative is to fall back on custom, external pressure and the free play of impulse. There is then need of theory on this matter. If we are forbidden to call this theory philosophy by the self-denying ordinance which restricts it to formal logic [or whatever is the mode of the day], need for the theory under some other name remains.[58]

On Dewey's view,

> Philosophy recovers itself when it ceases to be a device for dealing with the problems of philosophers and becomes a method, cultivated by philosophers, for dealing with the problems of men.[59]

Again, the issue is not how "philosophy" and "ethics" are to be defined; that is a trivial matter. Problems of men, however, are not trivial; and such problems are the ones with which Dewey is concerned. In light of such obviously important considerations, it seems that the presumed impasse of noncognitivism is a result of losing sight of the primary subject matter and focusing instead on

---

[58] *The Quest for Certainty,* p. 67.

[59] *Creative Intelligence: Essays in the Pragmatic Attitude,* edited by Dewey, A.W. Moore, H.C. Brown, G.H. Mead, *et al.* (New York: Henry Holt, 1917). The quotation is from Dewey's essay in this volume, "The Need for a Recovery of Philosophy," p. 65.

the linguistic conventions current in an elite subculture. Without any subject matter in primary experience, philosophers have the vain task of carrying out their conceptual analyses with neither aim nor test in primary experience. The subject matter of Dewey's moral philosophy is not the analysis of "good" and "ought," as if we had to get these concepts clear as a necessary preliminary to applying them to some subject matter. The primary task is to understand the experience to which such words might usefully be applied.

If the distinction between gross and refined experience is a valid one, then it is clear that all too frequently the conceptual subject matter in ethics is treated in isolation from experience. If value theory begins "back of any science," including any hoped-for moral science, and if we consider the various subject matters of nature – the various kinds of experience in nature or transactions with nature, then it is clear that there is a legitimate and important subject matter of human weal and woe. There is, however, no primary subject matter of good and evil; these latter are refined intellectual concepts used, presumably, to explain and clarify gross experience. Hence we must develop appropriate meanings for them relative to primary subject matter. There is an absurdity in *beginning* the analysis of man and nature with a concept of moral good, hoping there will be a place for it, or in having such criteria for the definition of moral science that it is logically impossible to undertake distinctively moral inquiry. Rather, we should go to man's experience in nature as it actually occurs and determine how it can be understood, guided, and enriched. Thus we use such words as "good," "right," or "ought" in whatever ways will fill these aims. There indubitably are many things or events in nature for which such terms could be employed to make distinctions, indicate relationships, and summarize facts. There need be nothing whatsoever in this procedure that is in any sense arbitrary. About many such events and experiences it will be entirely possible to use so-called moral terms to make cognitive claims. Of course, any set of conventional signs could be contrived for these purposes; and what the particular vocal and written peculiarities of these signs might be are of no consequence. The test of these terms, whatever they might be, is whether they really succeed in their function; and the test of the propositions in which such terms occur are the familiar experimental procedures.

"Ethical naturalism" is usually used to mean that normative terms are translatable without loss of content into factual terms – i.e., are definable without use of further normative terms; and thus the notion entails also that moral claims are cognitive. It is clear, then, that Dewey is an ethical naturalist. He is so, however, in a special way, for he makes no claims to dictate the definitions of moral terms. His "definitions" can be regarded as unashamedly stipulative, and his only concern is that they be effective tools of communication. We shall find that in most discourse of moral import Dewey prefers that moral language not be used at all. It is probably dangerous, therefore, even to introduce the expression "ethical naturalism," because the accounts of its meaning (such as the stereotype provided by G. E. Moore) are oversimplified in a way to make the position look moronic. From Dewey's point of view, it is clearly impossible to provide even stipulative definitions of normative terms in a wholesale way and once and for all; for such terms will take on different meanings in every situation. The specific characters of the events denoted by moral terms are unique to each particular situation; and Dewey's moral vocabulary is used to do no more than denote the verifiable meanings of these events. [60] (This point will be elaborated in subsequent chapters.)

If there were universal and necessary definitions for so-called moral terms, then, presumably, the need for investigation into the specific goods of the situation would be unnecessary. Apart from being highly injurious to human well-being, such sacrifice of inquiry would be, to repeat Dewey's phrase, to "exchange free morals for sterile metaphysics." The mania for problems of definition seems to represent an atavism of that sterile metaphysics which seeks changeless perfection, and an ignoring of primary subject matter.

Given the unfortunate stereotypes of ethical naturalism, it would be clearer – if a label is to be of any use – to characterize Dewey's position as naturalism in ethics. For Dewey's naturalism

---

[60] See, for example, Chapter II of *Theory of Valuation,* where this idea is explicitly illustrated in considerable detail.

is of a more fundamental sort than ethical naturalism. I allude to his assumption (elaborated in the first chapter) that philosophy must be faithful to experience. Thus his moral philosophy is but an instance of this basic philosophical naturalism. At any rate, all the moral distinctions in Dewey's thought refer exclusively to events in nature. A number of the distinctions that Dewey uses have already been introduced. The discussion of the nature of the good will be undertaken in the sixth chapter, and the nature of moral judgment and justification will be explicated in the last chapter; so further distinctions in the primary subject matter which Dewey makes with value terms will not be indicated at this point. What is pertinent right now are some of the practical implications of Dewey's naturalism in ethics; and these display its existential value.

The primary concern of Dewey's moral philosophy, as we have seen, is with the fulfillments, negations, joys, and miseries of human experience – about which much of crucial importance can be learned and asserted. Whether we call these things "goods" or "bads" is simply a matter of determining if such words can be used to make useful distinctions in the subject matter. It is *not* a question of whether some prior and independent meaning of such terms may legitimately be applied, or whether there is justification in using so-called moral terms to characterize this experience at all. Of course, the assertion of naturalism in ethics does not automatically solve all the problems of moral philosophy. Presumably, however, it provides an empirical subject matter subject to empirical tests. At the same time, therefore, it frees moral philosophy both from obscurantism and from being hopelessly truncated in scope.

One practical implication of Dewey's naturalism is that the resources of scientific intelligence are placed at once at the disposal of all human aims. Much has been said on this theme already, and more will be said in later chapters. To conclude the present section, I will simply concern myself with a preliminary examination of the function of factual claims in the guidance of conduct. (This theme, too, will receive extended attention in the last chapter.)

While noncognitivism truncates the realm of ethical inquiry, many traditional moral philosophies have treated values and obligations as something originating beyond experience and nature and in most cases as finding their justification and fulfillment in that presumed transcendental sphere. Accordingly, there has also been a very strong reliance on superhuman authority in moral doctrine: God, Reason, The State, etc.; and with this reliance has developed the (outrageous) assumption that the good life should be subordinated to abstract laws and principles, rather than that laws and principles should be developed for the sake of the good life. There is, therefore, a very strong tradition – perhaps subtly influencing even the most rigorous empirical thinkers – that somehow moral terms ought to have some kind of occult, secret, mysterious, or otherwise superempirical meaning; and if they don't have such a meaning it is unfortunate. At least – as it is often held nowadays – moral language has functions which cannot be accomplished by any other means, explicit or covert. This is an obscure idea. The feeling seems to be, nevertheless, that purely natural and descriptive meanings somehow aren't enough for morals: Perhaps they lack the authority that moral situations seem to require. At any rate, ordinary experimental meanings don't seem to have the *force* expected of such terms as "good" and "ought."

> It is unfortunately true that many moral *theories*, some of them of considerable prestige in philosophy, have interpreted moral subject-matter in terms of norms, standards, ideals, which, according to the authors of these theories, have no possible factual standing. "Reasons" for adopting and following them then involve a "reason" and "rational" in a sense which is expressly asserted to be transcendent, *a priori*, supernal, "other-wordly." According to theorists of this type, to give reasons of the kind found in inquiries and conclusions in other subjects eliminates what is genuinely moral, reducing it, say, to the "prudential" and the expediently "politic." On this basis, ethics can be "scientific" only in a sense which gives the word "science" a highly esoteric significance – a sense in which some writers hold philosophy to be *the* supreme science, having methods and depending upon faculties that are beyond the possible reach of humbly subordinate "natural" sciences.[61]

Dewey, however, can only rejoice in whatever diminutions occur in the presumed superempirical meanings of moral terms, for men cannot guide their conduct in the world toward inclusive values unless they are aware of the actual facts of their situation.

---

[61] "Ethical Subject-Matter and Language," p. 711.

Not occult powers but observable and predictable events are the conditions of intelligent conduct. Not only is Dewey satisfied with "merely" naturalistic predicates, but he insists on them. For the sake of human good (as well as for the sake of empirical truth, which is organic to it), he resists notions of nonnatural qualities, categorical imperatives, the disclosures of pure reason, divine commandment, emotive meanings, etc. Indeed, any consistent naturalist should be entirely willing to do away with all so-called moral terms. Dewey doesn't *want* to introduce more than verifiable meanings. If he uses moral terms, he does so because they are functional, and he desires no occult power from them. The meaning and "force" of, say, "Murder is wrong" is not divine. It means that murder has such and such consequences: pain, grief, anxiety, social disorder, etc.; and the specific wrongness of a specific murder consists in whatever consequences it has for ill, and in nothing else. To expect more is to evoke a "ghostly queerness" and to obscure what it is important to know. The force, or authority, in "Murder is wrong" is simply in the response one has to all the consequences entailed by murder. The authority is not transcendent, but is a function of human nature.[62] The notion of an autonomous or categorical "ought" represents simply an authoritarian command or an emotional outburst of some kind, and it is completely helpless in the task of directing behavior by knowledge of objective conditions. Recall in this connection the discussion of meanings in the last section of the preceding chapter. The growth in the meaning of actions and events should not be by way of interlarding them with obscurities. Rather, it should more accurately and thoroughly reflect the realities and potentialities of nature. In this manner, meanings become qualitatively richer and more affective; and they are at the same time more reliable guides to conduct.

It is clear, in fact, that Dewey regarded it as preferable that factual statements about consequences be utilized rather than simply summarizing them with vague and emotive moral terms. Otherwise, the meanings of such terms should be specified. Rather than moral terms *qua* moral being nonreferential, it is

---

[62] Thus a person who likes murder will agree that it has certain consequences,but he presumably is not repelled by them. This situation will receive amplification shortly, and extended treatment in the last chapter.

precisely when such terms are *not* referential that they are at the same time *not* moral – not conducive to human good.[63] In his review of Stevenson, Dewey objected strenuously to the assumption that there is an emotive meaning to genuinely ethical terms. Speaking of "genuinely ethical sentences," he says,

> Their use and intent is practical. But the point at issue concerns the means by which the result is accomplished. It is, I repeat, a radical fallacy to convert the end-in-view [the *purpose* of the ethical sentence] into an inherent constituent of the means by which, in genuinely moral sentences, the end is accomplished. To take the cases in which "emotional" factors *accompany* the giving of reasons as if this accompaniment factor were an inherent part of the judgment is, I submit, both a theoretical error and is, when widely adopted in practice, a source of moral weakness. . . .Stevenson says "Ethical terms cannot be taken as fully comparable to scientific ones. They have a quasi-imperative *function.*" Now . . . the point at issue does not concern the last of the two sentences quoted. Nor does it concern the correctness of the statement that "Both imperative and ethical sentences are *used* more for encouraging, altering, or redirecting people's aims and conduct than for simply describing them." The point at issue is whether the facts of *use* and *function* render ethical terms and sentences not fully comparable with scientific ones as respects their subject matter and content. As far as concerns *use* it would not, I believe, be going too far to say the word "more" in the above passage is not strong enough. Of ethical sentences as ordinarily used, it may be said, I believe, that their *entire* use and function of ethical sentences is directive or "practical." The point at issue concerns another matter: It concerns how this end is to be accomplished if sentences are to possess distinctively and genuinely *ethical* properties.[64]

It is true that ethical sentences have the *function* of directing behavior, but this function is best fulfilled by disclosing as many facts as possible about the probable consequences of acting (or living) in a certain way. This is the decisive point, the point of repeated emphasis in Dewey's writings. Hence Dewey summarizes:

> The theoretical view about ethical sentences which is an alternative to that put forward by Stevenson is, that as far as non-cognitive, extra-cognitive, factors enter into the subject-matter or content of sentences purporting to be legitimately

---

[63] Thus R.L. Holmes's interpretation is precisely the opposite of what Dewey intended. Holmes claims that Dewey "denies that moral terms (at least qua moral) are property-referring and that the primary job of moral judgments is to convey knowledge. . . ." ("John Dewey's Moral Philosophy in Contemporary Perspective," *The Review of Metaphysics,* XX, No. 1, September 1966; p. 55.)

[64] "Ethical Subject-Matter and Language," pp. 703, 709. (Dewey's quotations refer, respectively, to pp. 36 and 21 of *Ethics and Language.* Italics were not in original text from Stevenson, but were added by Dewey.)

ethical, those sentences are by just that much deprived of the properties sentences should have in order to be genuinely *ethical*. . . .

Extra-cognitive devices are without doubt employed to effect a result which in consequence is moral only in the sense in which the word "*im*moral" is included in the scope of "moral." Many propositions which are now taken to be immoral have had positive moral property ascribed to them at former times. There is here a strong indication that extra-rational factors played an undue part in forming the earlier propositions and getting them accepted.[65]

And all of this seems to be by and large true when "moral" or "ethical" refers to experienced human goods. Dewey provides a perfectly clearcut example of the kind of difference he has with Stevenson by the analogy with legal argument:

The practices, often resorted to by a skilled lawyer in defending a client charged with a criminal act, often contain non-cognitive elements and these may sometimes be more influential, more directive, of what the jury does than evidence of the matter-of-fact or descriptive sort. Would one say in this case that these means, such as intonations, facial expressions, gestures, etc., are a *part* of legal propositions *qua* legal? If not in this case, why in the case of ethical propositions?[66]

The reason for denying the predicate "ethical" to emotive meanings is simply that such meanings obscure human good, while factual claims clarify it. Direction by facts is presumably more humanly desirable than direction by such ejaculations as "Stealing, Bah!" and "Promise-keeping, Yippee!" Likewise, direction by facts is ultimately more "moral" than direction by mere commands, such as "Do not steal," or "You ought to keep your promises." To state it most abstractly, men must function in and with nature. and it is clear that nature is – as it were – hospitable to certain kinds of behavior and inhospitable to others. Accordingly, there is an obvious and fundamental sense in which nature itself is directive, or regulative, of conduct; and the more knowledgeable men are about nature, the more their conduct will be of a welcome and even precious sort.

Objections to such a throughgoing naturalism are inevitable. Many, of course, would be based on precisely the erroneous theories of value already discussed. Still others would result from a priori assumptions about what moral terms ought to mean and what moral discourse ought to accomplish, and also about what

---

[65] *Ibid.*, pp. 709-10.

[66] *Ibid.*, pp. 710-1.

means are necessary to certain assumed ends; and still others might result from simply unreflective predilection for moral terms. In addition to what has already been suggested, considerably more explanation of Dewey's views on the nature and function of moral judgment will be presented in the concluding chapter. For now, one particular criticism may be anticipated. A presumably crippling question that might be leveled at Dewey's naturalism assumes the context of an imagined debate with a hoodlum, a Nazi, a Klansman, etc. What instrumentalities of argument and moral persuasion can the naturalist employ against such people?

We must remember here that the hoodlum, the Klansman, and the Nazi have no legitimate grounds for invoking meaningless moral terms. That is, their claims, like any others, must, if they are to have any meaning whatever, be expressed in terms which denote intrinsic properties and actual consequences. Therefore, with whatever rhetoric, myth, or moral predicates they arm themselves, it is nevertheless true that the nature and consequences of their deeds are of a specifiable character; and those consequences can be readily distinguished from those of acting, say, democratically. If it is true that the only legitimate way to talk about good is in terms of the actual goods of human experience, then it follows unmistakably that the Nazi behavior entails far less good and far more evil than democratic behavior. Relative to actual human interests, what more appropriate way to compare fascism and democracy than in terms of human consequences, however they might be named?

Assuming that the Nazi were willing to engage in rational discussion, what might be said to him to persuade him to adopt another course of action? How could his preferences, his values, be altered? A number of arguments are open to the naturalist: First of all, the lack of factual support for Nazi myths could be adduced; and both the war aims of the *Führer* and the rationale for the Nazi's own actions could thereby be undermined. The Nazi would be hard put to provide justification for the arrogation of the right to rule the world. Whatever genuine problems beset his nation could be assessed in light of alternative means of dealing with them. In addition, he might be made more sensitive to certain values if the full meaning – the full implication – of his actions could be made thoroughly clear to him. One could, moreover, seek to discover what the problems were which the Nazi himself suffered and suggest alternative, less vile, forms of conduct which might bring satisfactory values into the man's life. Different ideals of life might arouse in him the idea of new possibilities for himself and new ways of relating to other persons. Finally, of course, the naturalist might simply convict the Nazi of logical inconsistency. (Such inconsistencies are a common feature of moral discourse – as we find in experience and in the Socratic dialogues.) The Nazi, for example, might espouse a certain principal of conduct together with certain criteria for applying it. It might be found that he was making an exception to that principal in his own case (or in the case of another), and it might also be found that his own criteria of application did not warrant that exception. Thus the presumed rationale for his actions vanishes.

There might be more resources in rational discourse, but I do not know what they could be if they were not statable in verifiable propositions. One could call the Nazi's behavior "wrong," "evil," "barbaric," "hideous," "loathesome," etc.; but I don't know what such words could mean apart from reference to the verifiable character of this behavior as it affected all those who were in any way subject to it or aware of it. The Nazi's acts could also be called unjust or immoral. Again, however, what could such terms mean except, say, "making an exception in favor of one's self" or "regarding one's own claims as inherently possessing priority over the claims of others?" Or perhaps a more elaborately articulated concept of justice or of morality is set forth, and the Nazi is accordingly called unjust or immoral. This is to say that certain conditions have to be satisfied for an act to be moral or just. The issue is again the same: To be meaningful, these conditions must be stated in experimentally verifiable language. Hence in this case, as in any case, when such actions are called – say – immoral, one cannot mean more with this locution than precisely a violation of the conditions specified. "To be immoral" would mean "to fail to satisfy the conditions specified," and no more – however elaborate the conditions might be. My point in this is to indicate that "immoral" cannot denote anything more than can be stated in descriptive language; it adds no meaning to that language.[67] The consequence is that the use in rational discourse of such words as "unjust" and "immoral" in no way constitutes an instrument of argumentation and proof surpassing the capabilities of naturalism. This – once more – is not to cite an inherent defect in moral philosophy as an intellectual discipline. For Dewey, a thoroughgoing experimentalism is the prime virtue of the discipline and of practical moral discourse as well.

We know, of course, that the Nazi is in all likelihood not the least concerned with rational discourse. He might be threatened, coerced, or deceived into abstaining from visiting agony on persons. Perhaps the mere authority of someone – a priest, an officer, a father-figure – would prevent the Nazi from continuing. Or the conditions of his existence might be altered in a way to reconstruct his personality in a significant way. Although actions of this sort would be welcome under the circumstances, they would not constitute rational persuasion or moral argument. It seems clear, therefore, that the problem in this example is not to contrive different meanings for moral words; for there is nothing to be accomplished, established, or in any way proved thereby that could not be done as well or better by intelligent inquiry and discourse concerning verifiable characteristics of experience. This issue will be brought up again in subsequent discussions. It may be concluded for the present that it is obvious that men are plagued in various ways by moral problems of all sorts; and it is by no means clear what to think or do about many of them. It does seem clear, however, that work on such problems will not be advanced by philosophers who are unwilling to make a com-

---

[67] So-called performative utterances do not constitute an exception to this claim. The entirety of what is both meant and done in saying, for example, "I promise" can be stated in descriptive language. To promise is to make a declaration of intent to perform a certain action; and the action is regarded as possessing a very high order of priority relative to alternative possible actions. Thus one can and does count upon the fulfillment of the intent, and the parties to the promise assume that failure of fulfillment is normally deserving of blame. If promising is regarded as placing oneself under an obligation, then the meaning of "placing oneself under an obligation" would be the same as I have suggested for "I promise."

Discussions of promising are the most recent manifestation of the predilection of philosophers to tell us what we "really" mean or what we are "really" doing when we use certain words. Much of the treatment of moral language takes the form of simply imposing on experience the results of armchair philosophic analysis.

pletely forthright assessment of what are in fact the relevant resources and liabilities of experience.

Moral discourse has functions additional to that of providing the weapons to argue with Hitler. There are many persons who are not bent on evil; they are in significant measure humane, charitable, honest, and even aspiring. They hope for a better life for themselves and others. They want to develop some conception of the good life, to know how to implement it, and to know how to make more inclusive, enduring, and widespread the goods of experience. With such people moral philosophy has an indispensable office. Dewey's conception of the good life will be indicated in some fullness in the sixth chapter. Before getting to that important matter, however, it remains to elaborate an issue of decisive importance in moral philosophy: the relation of values to facts.

CHAPTER V

Fact and Value

If one assumes that nature is nothing but matter in motion, then he has insuperable problems about the relation of facts to values; for on such assumptions the realm of nature and the realm of value are wholly separate, and empirical science must be concerned wholly with the former.

> The new science, it is said, has stripped the world of the qualities which made it beautiful and congenial to men . . . and presented nature to us as a scene of indifferent physical particles acting according to mathematical and mechanical laws.
>
> This effect of modern science has, it is notorious, set the main problems for modern philosophy. How is science to be accepted and yet the realm of values to be conserved? . . . Philosophers have been troubled by the gap in kind which exists between the fundamental principles of the natural world and the reality of the values according to which mankind is to regulate its life.[1]

Likewise, if one assumes that moral conceptions are not identical with statements about experienced human goods and evils, then, again, there are insuperable problems about the relation of values to facts. Thus, if one holds the noncognitivist view, "It follows that ethics does not depend *logically* on facts about man and the world, empirical or non-empirical, scientific or theological."[2]

Philosophers who hold such views and yet at the same time have some sensitivity to experience may even undertake the ab-

---

[1] *The Quest for Certainty,* p. 41.

[2] William K. Frankena, *Ethics,* (Englewood Cliffs, N.J.: Prentice-Hall, Inc., 1963), p. 84.

surd endeavor to show how value statements might be *deduced* from purely factual statements! Or they might take a less hopeless and arbitrary approach and attempt to exhibit a less rigorous but nonetheless logical relation between descriptive and normative statements. The pinnacle of philosophic wisdom would be that trick of logic which could produce an "ought" where mere "is" has been. As indicated earlier (above, pp. 137-8), this endeavor has been imputed to Dewey himself. On Dewey's assumptions, however, there is no problem, logical or ontological, of *deriving* values from facts, or of deriving value statements from factual statements. We have seen that Dewey's naturalistic metaphysics requires that we acknowledge values to be as real a part of nature as any fact. Problematic goods are immediate and original data in nature, and consummatory experiences are eventual functions of complex natural processes. Operations of inquiry, imagination, and action convert a problematic situation into art. And as we have already seen, the difference between a problematic good and a value is not an absolute difference between "is" and "ought," but simply designates the noteworthy differences in the situation occurring at its origin and its consummation. Thus Dewey has no concern with the wholly artificial problem of puzzling over how values can possibly exist in a world exclusively composed of mere facts; for the world is not of that sort to begin with. Neither is he concerned with deducing normative statements from descriptive.

There *is* a difference, of course, between the normative and the descriptive; but this difference is determined exclusively by the specific nature of actual concrete situations. The status of a state of affairs as an indifferent fact is a consequence of the relation which that affair bears to the problematic situation: if it has no apparent bearing on its conduct or outcome, then it is in that context valueless. In a different situation, a similar state of affairs might be crucially important. The fact, for example, that one of the members of a gathering is a medical doctor will in many contexts be of no consequence; but when someone at the gathering is injured, such a fact becomes extremely valuable. Likewise, whether a statement is simply descriptive or is normative as well depends upon its function in the problematic situation. The formulation in propositions of the presumed facts about the actual and potential functions of problematic goods in specific situations creates what Dewey calls moral judgments. "If Jones is a doctor, then Jones can aid the stricken man" is such a judgment. The question of the nature of moral judgment and its normative function will be treated at length in Chapter VII; so I will not concern myself with it further at this time.

It is clear that what Dewey seeks are the facts *about* values and the means of discriminating them and constructing them in experience. The most fundamentally important facts about value concern its status in nature. When such status can be determined, it is then possible to carry on intelligible inquiry into more particular problems: What functional coalescence of human and environmental factors determines the nature of particular goods and evils? What are the relations that goods and evils sustain to each other? What are the conditions of their occurrence and the probable consequences of pursuing them in various ways? What are the alternative methods and means of mediating the clash of values? Dewey insists, indeed, that knowledge of such events in their relations is the only means of subjecting them to critical appraisal. All such inquiries are wholly experimental. They may concern the predicaments of an individual or the bewilderingly complex problems of the stagnation and degradation of American cities. As Dewey sees it, upon such inquiries, and upon the full communication of the information which they produce, human welfare – and even survival – depend.

At this point much might be said about the intelligent construction, criticism, and pursuit of value with the use of appropriate facts and methods. Although this chapter will give brief attention to these issues, detailed examination of them is reserved for the final chapter. What has been made clear, nevertheless, is that on Dewey's view moral terms are not necessary to moral discourse, in any of its functions. Saying just this much does not, of course, provide much indication of the positive nature of moral discourse (again, a matter to come in Chapter VII); but it at least makes clear that moral judgments and moral statements – whatever they might be in Dewey's conception – are at any rate verifiable. Just to establish this much makes it possible to deal intelligibly with a matter of foremost concern to Dewey: the relation of science to value. Therefore, what I intend to undertake here is an elaboration of the continuity of cognitive and moral experience in nature, leaving until the concluding chapter a specific analysis of how science can be used to criticize and enhance values, and how the model of experimental reasoning is applicable to moral deliberation.

It has already been shown that Dewey's metaphysics insists on the reality of qualities, the precarious, the stable, ends, and histories, all of which are natural events and all of which are so fundamental to the understanding of value. But Dewey's philosophy of nature accomplishes more than this. For properly to exhibit the relation of cognitive and moral experience requires not only that the nature of value be clarified, but that the nature of science be clarified as well. Accordingly, most of what Dewey writes about science is organic to his theory of nature. That is, his "philosophy of science" is not primarily devoted to analyzing and criticizing the particular problems of scientific explanation, but to 1) understanding science as a purposive activity of experience in and with nature, in which verifiable propositions about nature are produced and tested, 2) determining what nature is such that science is a fact of experience, and 3) determining the relations – the continuities – between science and other modes of experience (such as primary experience, valuation, conduct as art). As previous analyses have indicated, Dewey's theory of nature and philosophy of science are inseparable. Much has been made explicit about his theory of nature. It remains here to examine further the implications of his philosophy of science and elucidate its relation to his analysis of value.

A great deal could be written about Dewey's efforts in this vein – the analysis of science in all its continuities in nature. The concern here must be confined to his conclusions as they bear on problems of value. In this area, there are two general points of fundamental importance: First, the subject matter of science is not some presumed reality forever hidden from us by immediate consciousness. Rather, our scientific formulations are ultimately determined by the world as we experience it. Second, science is not an affair of some presumed faculty of Reason. It is, rather, a practical activity. Neither of these points require much in the way of introduction at this point, for the continuity of nature, experience, and science has already been discussed at some length; so has the concept of science as activity, together with the bankruptcy of the notion of a priori Reason. It will be worthwhile, however, to elaborate somewhat on the relevance of these continuities to value theory. In regard to the first point, special emphasis should be given to the instrumental or mediatory character of scientific theories: Experienced phenomena pose specific problems for inquiry; "scientific" concepts and laws are developed to provide the desired explanation and the possibility of prediction and control. Scientific hypotheses are tested by undertaking experiments which will yield precisely the phenomena which will confirm or deny the hypotheses. The relations and entities proposed by hypotheses are not a reality to rival that of experience. Rather, they state the conditions upon which the occurrence of experienced things depend.

It happens, of course, that scientific laws, theories, and concepts frequently make no use of predicates denoting qualities; but this abstract character of science is not at all a denial of the reality of qualities. On the contrary, it is a procedure which greatly enhances our knowledge of qualitative events. The aims of science are incalculably advanced by expressing qualitative properties in terms of quantitative variations of specified physical processes. (Thus, for example, sounds are understood, in part, as the consequence of variations in the mechanical force transmitted by longitudinal pressure waves in a material medium.) The fact that the conditions of the occurrence of qualities can be stated quantitatively makes it possible for highly diverse qualitative phenomena to be explained by common physical principles. Hence, also, by mathematical manipulation the characterizations of the conditions of diverse phenomena are interconvertible. Thus it is that the occurrence of any particular event can be characterized in such a way that a large body of scientific knowledge is made immediately relevant to understanding and – more important – manipulating that event. Clearly, the elimination of qualities from consideration is an intermediate step in inquiry, and this elimination – or, more properly, abstraction – far from eliminating qualities as subject matter for scientific investigation, is what makes quantitative science so eminently powerful an instrument for explanation, prediction, and control of qualitative events. Scientific abstractions are framed "in pursuit of realization of a certain interest – that of the maximum convertibility of every object of thought into any and every other."[3]

> As long, for example, as water is taken to be just the thing which we directly experience it to be, we can put it to a few direct uses, such as drinking, washing, etc. Beyond heating it there was little that could be done purposefully to change its properties. When, however, water is treated not as the glistening, rippling object with the variety of qualities that delight the eye, ear, and palate, but as something symbolized by H_2O, something from which these qualities are completely absent, it becomes amenable to all sorts of other modes of control and adapted to other uses.[4]

And Dewey says that science "is the example, *par excellence,* of the liberative effects of abstraction. . . ."[5]

The occurrence of any qualitative event constitutes, therefore, an occasion and problem for inquiry. Qualities in themselves provide neither knowledge nor explanation: "They are the materials of problems not of solutions. They are *to be* known, rather than objects of knowledge."[6] The instrumental, or mediatory, character of scientific ideas consists in the fact that they are formulated to understand problems originating in primary experience, and they specify the conditions upon which these events in primary experience depend. In addition, they lead to still further and various events in primary experience hitherto regarded as unrelated to the phenomena which first occasioned inquiry. Thus scientific laws about H_2O lead to discoveries that could never be made by studying water, as such.

Before considering the relevance of this first point to moral philosophy, some reference to the second point (science as activity) will be made. Knowing is initiated in gross experience. Some hypothesis is imaginatively conceived to account for the occurrence and/or variations of a particular event. Normally, the hypothesis is framed as a prediction: If such and such conditions are instituted, then certain consequences will follow (where the consequences are the event in question). The hypothesis, in turn is tested by overt experiment. In experimentation, the inquirer measures (if possible) what he takes to be the various constitu-

---

[3] *The Quest for Certainty,* p. 136.

[4] *Ibid.,* p. 105.

[5] *Knowing and the Known,* p. 282. This article, "Common Sense and Science," originally appeared in *The Journal of Philosophy,* XLV (April, 1948), pp. 197-208.

[6] *The Quest for Certainty,* p. 103.

ents in the process to be explained. In any case, he introduces specific and controlled changes in these presumed variables to determine how changes in given features of the subject matter produce change in other features. (As, for example, determining how the pressure in an enclosed volume of gas changes with variations in the temperature; or – say – determining how quantitative intelligence varies with verbal abilities in given control groups.) If the variations are in fact what the hypothesis predicted, the hypothesis is at least *prima facie* confirmed; then – and only then – is knowledge acquired. (A more complex analysis of what constitutes confirmation of a hypothesis is not relevant to this discussion.)

It is clear in this procedure that the warranted scientific idea can be produced only by activity; knowing is not immediate grasp of the forms of an independent, changeless reality, Rather, what is known of the subject matter are correlations of processes of change. Each variable in the subject matter is a process of some kind.[7] As various specifiable processes enter into various interactions, a variety of outcomes are effected. So-called laws of nature state the relations of change between such interacting processes upon which specifiable outcomes are conditional.

> In the old scheme, knowledge, as science, signified precisely and exclusively turning away from change to the changeless. In the new experimental science, knowledge is obtained in exactly the opposite way, namely, through deliberate institution of a definite and specified course of change. *The* method of physical inquiry is to introduce some change in order to see what other change ensues; the correlation between these changes, when measured by a series of operations, constitutes the definite and desired object of knowledge.[8]

The pertinent implications of these fundamental characteristics of science can now be presented. The abstractive character of science has a clear bearing on the understanding of the conditions and management of values. Both immediate goods and values, we have seen, are inclusive qualitative events in nature. No more does the color red pop up in nature *ex nihilo* than does a good exist independently, discretely separated from a complex of ante-

---

[7] The notion of inherent, unchanging substance has lost all standing in scientific inquiry. Pressure and temperature, for example, are processes – not substances or essences.

[8] *Ibid.,* p. 84.

cendent conditions. And no more than colors do goods possess a nature independently of the processes of which they are a function. To think of a good as something miraculously autonomous in nature – or set apart from nature – is as erroneous as to think similarly of red. And just as we do not have knowledge of an object of sense until we know something about the relations which it sustains to other things, we do not have knowledge of an immediately experienced good until we know the relations which *it* sustains to other things:

> To assume that anything can be known in isolation from its connections with other things is to identify knowing with merely having some object before perception or in feeling, and is thus to lose the key to the traits that distinguish an object as known. It is futile, even silly to suppose that some quality that is directly present constitutes the whole of the thing presenting the quality. It does not do so when the quality is that of being hot or fluid or heavy, and it does not when the quality is that of giving pleasure, or being enjoyed.[9]

Valued events, as we have seen, are qualitative in character. Rather than being exempted from scientific analysis on that account, they are in fact subject to all the powers of investigation and control possessed by quantitative physical science. Insofar as the conditions for the occurrence of values can be treated as quantifiable variables in the laws of the biological and physical sciences, the instrumentalities for securing such values are enormously enhanced. (This does not mean, of course, that exclusively quantitative methods are alone applicable to such inquiries. In considering the relevance of science to value, we must keep clearly in mind Dewey's urgent endeavors to eradicate any justification for cutting off ends from means. Thus the actual consequences of all modes of associated living are to be understood as goods [or evils], yet of a problematic sort. This being so, the economist, sociologist, psychologist, political scientist, etc. – even when quantitative techniques have not been developed – can provide information of utmost moral significance; for their disciplines can provide essential information about the conditions and consequences of institutionalized forms of behavior. That is, it can be learned what are the actual values occasioned [or sacrificed] by these modes.)

---

[9] *Ibid.*, p. 267.

Experimental knowledge, again, is the outcome of specified forms of activity. When it is recognized that science, knowing, inquiry, are activities, in which objects of immediate experience are manipulated in various ways in order to understand them as correlated in certain ways with further processes, then it is also recognized that inquiry and science are arts. Dewey makes a special point of exhibiting knowing as an art, as practice:

> Thought, intelligence, science is the intentional direction of natural events to meanings capable of immediate possession and enjoyment; this direction – which is operative art – is itself a natural event in which nature otherwise partial and incomplete comes fully to itself; so that objects of conscious experience when reflectively chosen, form the "end" of nature.[10]

It is clear, in other words, that scientific inquiry is a means of acting with the environment in specific ways in order to explain and control the events of primary experience and to enrich their meanings by determining their relations to other events of primary experience. Such inquiries begin, clearly enough, with problematic situations, which define the general subject matter and aims of inquiry. Hypotheses concerning the constituents and outcome of inquiry are formulated. These imply carefully specified plans of action for conducting and controlling inquiry. Hypotheses involve determinations of relevant and irrelevant materials and dictate action in accordance with which the materials of the situation are manipulated. They also determine the kind of evidence the inquirer is specifically to look for; they determine the kind of observations he is to make. In experimentation, then, irrelevant materials are discarded or avoided and the precarious features are converted into instrumentalities. The consummatory phase of experience ensues if experimentation in fact yields the result anticipated by the hypothesis. Such an endeavor is an art, its product a work of art. (See above, p.158, quotation from *Experience and Nature,* p. 371.)

Not only is the practice of science an art carried on in and with nature, but it possesses the same intrinsic values as any art. Such "intellectual" endeavor has its distinctively consummatory phase, which is organic to the instrumental phases, both giving them meaning and possessed of their meaning:

---

[10] *Experience and Nature,* p. 358.

> Thinking is pre-eminently an art; knowledge and propositions which are the products of thinking, are works of art, as much so as statuary and symphonies. Every successive stage of thinking is a conclusion in which the meaning of what has produced it is condensed; and it is no sooner stated than it is a light radiating to other things – unless it be a fog which obscures them.[11]

> There are absorbing inquiries and speculation which a scientific man and philosopher will recall as 'experiences' in the emphatic sense. In final import they are intellectual. But in their actual occurrence they were emotional as well; they were purposive and volitional. Yet the experience was not a sum of these different characters; they were lost in it as distinctive traits. No thinker can ply his occupation save as he is lured and rewarded by total integral experiences that are intrinsically worthwhile.[12]

It should be obvious that science must be distinguished from other arts in terms of its requirements for logical method and extrinsic empirical tests. As an *activity,* however, what distinguishes science from other arts are its materials, its intent, and its uses:

> Hence *an* experience of thinking has its own esthetic quality. It differs from those experiences that are acknowledged to be esthetic, but only in its materials. The material of the fine arts consists of qualities; that of experience having intellectual conclusion are signs or symbols having no intrinsic quality of their own, but standing for things that may in another experience be qualitatively experienced.[13]

> It is not possible to divide in a vital experience the practical, emotional, and intellectual from one another and set the properties of one over against the characteristics of the others. . . . The most elaborate philosophic or scientific inquiry and the most ambitious industrial or political enterprise has, when its different ingredients constitute an integral experience, esthetic quality. . . .
>
> Nevertheless, the experiences in question are dominantly intellectual or practical, rather than *distinctively* esthetic, because of the interest and purpose that initiate and control them. In an intellectual experience, the conclusion has value on its own account. It can be used in its independent entirety as a factor and guide in other inquiries. In a work of art there is no such single self-sufficient deposit. The end, the terminus, is significant not by itself but as the integration of the parts. It has no other existence.[14]

It is unnecessary to go into detailed investigation to determine how closely the actual work of scientists approximates to con-

---

[11] *Ibid.,* p. 378.

[12] *Art as Experience,* p. 37.

[13] *Ibid.,* p. 38.

[14] *Ibid.,* p. 55.

duct as art; for enough has been said to show that scientific inquiry is a mode of practice in and with nature, beginning and ending with the rich and variegated materials of primary experience. This is the essential fact to be apprehended and appreciated. It is important to take note here that Dewey uses "science" primarily to denote activity, procedure, *according to a certain method.* When understood in this fundamental sense, it is properly distinguished from that body of knowledge – laws, theories, concepts – which is usually called science. The so-called body of knowledge is clearly derivative of the method; it has been the main product of the method. We shall learn, however, that it is not the only possible product – or, indeed, the most intrinsically valuable product – of the method of experimental intelligence.

It is of the first importance to see that science is both concerned with the experienced world and is set in the context of art-as-practice. This awareness revolutionizes man's active relationship with nature:

> The remarkable difference between the attitude which accepts the objects of ordinary perception, use and enjoyment as final, as culminations of natural processes and that which takes them as starting points for reflection and investigation, is one which reaches far beyond the technicalities of science. It marks a revolution in the whole spirit of life, in the entire attitude taken toward whatever is found in existence. When the things which exist around us, which we touch, see, hear and taste are regarded as interrogations for which an answer must be sought (and must be sought by means of deliberate introduction of changes till they are reshaped into something different), nature as it already exists ceases to be something which must be accepted and submitted to, endured or enjoyed, just as it is. It is now something to be modified, to be intentionally controlled. It is material to act upon so as to transform it into new objects which better answer our needs. Nature as it exists at any particular time is a challenge, rather than a completion; it provides possible starting points and opportunities rather than final ends.[15]

The difference between science as rationalistic knowing and science as art is the difference between "the art of acceptance and the art of control." [16] Precarious events in nature need not occur casually; men need not indulge in rites and supplications to save themselves; nor need they seek a presumed changeless Being as a refuge from earthly tests; and there is no necessity simply to

[15] *The Quest for Certainty,* p. 100.

[16] This is the title of Chapter IV of *The Quest for Certainty.*

endure events in nature fatalistically:

> But apart from the exercise of intelligence which yields knowledge, the realities of our emotional and practical life have fragmentary and inconsistent meanings and are at the mercy of forces beyond our control. We have no choice save to accept them or to flee from them. Experience of that phase of objects which is constituted by their relations, their interactions, with one another, makes possible a new way of dealing with them, and thus eventually creates a new kind of experienced objects, not more real than those which preceded but more significant, and less overwhelming and oppressive.[17]

It is clear that this awareness of science as art has a fundamental importance: It has been precisely the misunderstanding of the processes of science that has provided philosophical justification for the dualisms of knowing and doing, experience and nature, and – most important – ends and means. [18]When such misunderstandings are disclosed, the intellectual rationale for these dualisms vanishes. This is a matter of intense practical importance, for it liberates the manifestly enormous powers of social, experimental intelligence to the service of genuine human concerns. When science is regarded as a thing apart from the doings and sufferings of ordinary experience, then it is at the same time a thing apart from actual human values; and scientific method is confined to exclusively physical matters.

> The failure to recognize that knowledge is a product of art accounts for an otherwise inexplicable fact: that science lies today like an incubus upon such a wide area of beliefs and aspirations. . . . Science . . . becomes brutal and mechanical, while criticism of values, whether moral or esthetic, becomes pedantic or effeminate, expressing either personal likes and dislikes, or building up a cumbrous array of rules and authorities. The thing that is needed, discriminating judgment by methods whose consequences improve the art, easily slips through such coarse meshes, and by far the greater part of life goes on in darkness unillumined by thoughtful inquiry.[19]

In brief, to understand science as art is to realize that statements about values *are* logically dependent on facts about man and the world. This is so, at any rate, when values are identified with certain phases of experience; for then it is possible to undertake scientific investigation of these goods. The truth of any verifiable statement about values – such as those concerning

---

[17] *Ibid.*, pp. 219-20.

[18] See above, pp. 24-5, 28-9, 64-6, 76-80, 179-80.

[19] *Experience and Nature*, pp. 382-3.

means to ends – is dependent upon facts about nature. Accordingly, when the means-consequences at issue pertain to values, the validity of the statement of these relations depends as much upon natural facts as any other experimental hypothesis. If Y is a value, and X is its presumed condition, then the proposition "If X, then Y" is an experimental hypothesis in full standing. As we shall see in Chapter VII, what Dewey refers to as moral judgments are such statements of means-consequences.

For those who assume that the fact-value problem centers about the task of deducing normative from descriptive propositions, this argument will have little relevance. However (again to anticipate the last chapter), Dewey is not in the least concerned to demonstrate any moral truths. His moral science is not one which terminates in theorems. Rather, it is simply devoted to providing as much information about goods and evils as possible. In moral discourse, the issues surrounding any provisional good are confined to determining its potential functions *in the situation.* It is precisely the situation and its functions that make particular interactions valuable; and what is valued in one situation will not be in another. In reference to a concrete predicament, a course of conduct is devised which will deal with the actual problems at hand. It is difficult to see how anything whatsoever can be evaluated apart from any context whatever – real or imagined. What is a presumed good in a situation can be judged as a functional part of an inclusive system of relations incorporating many qualitative meanings. Thus it is determined what are the relations of dependence which sustain this good and which separate it from, or unite it with, other goods and bads, contingent upon specifiable actions. At the same time it is determined how such actions (in various alternatives) would suffice to meet the actually existing problems of the situation. (As we shall see in Chapter VII, a crucially important consideration in all reflection about alternative courses of conduct is the assessment of the effects action will have on one's habits, or character. This, above all, is the kind of knowledge upon which the quality of the moral life depends.)

Of course, even when men understand the full meaning of what they do, and change their conduct accordingly, there will still be conflicts of value. But these, on Dewey's grounds, are not to be adjudicated by some supposed moral law but – insofar as possible – by democracy. For goods are always the goods of individual human beings, and there are no a priori moral rights or powers to justify the presumed intrinsic superiority that might be claimed by particular individuals. To those who hold that critical judgment can proceed only with the use of abstract and independent standards, Dewey's position may seem an invitation to moral chaos. Nevertheless, it is worthwhile to suggest here but one consideration in Dewey's defense: If we attempt to rid our thoughts of religious and philosophical teachings, might we not reasonably conclude that the good of man, in this world in which we all share, depends of necessity on our knowing – on all men knowing – what are the actual facts of our actual situation? – on our knowing the full implications of what we are doing? And these implications cannot be determined apart from communication in that context where actions find their full meaing and effect: in society. Whatever the merits of Dewey's theory of moral deliberation, its practice can never be fully effective if carried out by individuals in isolation; and Dewey never supposed otherwise. Indeed, if deliberation were regarded as an essentially individual process, rather than a collective one, it simply would not be moral deliberation in the sense Dewey intended. We shall learn that it is in the democratic community alone where moral discourse can find its full meaning and value. Human behavior is largely self-defeating, and a good part of our futility is a consequence of ignoring the real character of our acts, responding at once to every transient desire, remaining ignorant of alternative possibilities of conduct, or of trusting blindly in presumably authoritative moral dictates. For these Dewey would substitute cooperative social intelligence. Men might even come to prefer democracy to both stubborn self-seeking and intransigent commandment.

My concern at present, however, is neither to elaborate nor justify Dewey's views on the uses of science, scientific methods, and democracy in procedures of evaluation and the adjustment of conflicting ends. More thorough characterization of the nature and function of moral discourse and moral judgment will receive due attention later. It is nonetheless clear that there is an indefinite plurality of ends in human experience which are both precious and shareable. (In many cases they are precious *because* they are shareable.) Hence, regardless of what subsequent analyses may show, it is unmistakable that all the scientific information we can acquire about the occurrence of these ends in nature constitutes an inestimably important condition for human wellbeing.

These latter comments suggest further points of significance in understanding the nature of science: Experimental laws are not statements which classify or characterize the nature of the ends which nature somehow must actualize. The old teleological science presumed to discover those immutable and perfectly definite ends which all things by nature strive to realize. By contrast, experimental laws simply state the outcomes conditional upon specified interacting processes. It is important to recognize that the possible interacting processes can be varied in an indefinite number of ways; so an indefinite plurality of outcomes can be effected. The point is that there are not just so many possible ends in nature, eternally fixed by nature's laws. Nature's "laws" do no such thing. Finally, it must be stressed that (contrary to traditional views) scientific inquiry is creative: Not only is the very formulation of hypotheses a creative activity, but such hypotheses also indicate ways in which natural interactions can be restructured. Hence with knowledge of nature and with imagination, man might contrive and realize ends without limit in conformity with both his cherished interests and his varied ideas about the possibilities of human nature.

It will be instructive to summarize the discussion of science and value as it has progressed to this point by making explicit use of metaphysical distinctions: The qualitative and precarious in experience are not such that they are ontologically separated from the stable and from ends; and hence we need neither to acquiesce to the qualitative and the precarious just as they occur, nor do we need to make some dialectical leap into true being in order to rid ourselves of their defects. Rather, by determining and utilizing stable instrumentalities, the precarious and qualitative can be reordered and enriched to construct inclusive consummatory ends. This process is historical in nature, and its constituents are historically linked. It is accomplished by means of directed inquiry and activity. Taken in its entirety, this process constitutes art; and in it we find the traits of nature clearly exemplified and inextricably interrelated.

At this point it is suitable to provide an analysis of the ways in which our understanding of the nature of science can make experimental inquiry specifically adaptable to moral concerns. To ward off typical misgivings, however, it will be necessary first to draw attention to what the use of science in the moral life is *not.* Dewey is not advocating a society whose values and institutions are dictated by "scientists," whose goals are efficiency, regimentation, and personal aggrandizement. The notion of a society programed by scientists is surely appalling.[20] More detailed attention to the function of scientists and their works will be provided in Chapter VII; but it may be said here, at least, that in Dewey's conception of the good society, they have no powers of prescription. Rather, they are the providers of vitally important information for value formation, adjustment, and achievement.[21]

One of the basic problems in making effective use of experimental procedures in practical difficulties is that of language. Scientific language, it is well known, is very different from ordinary language. The former is highly abstract, possessing only meanings which permit valid and consistent inference; while the latter is highly emotive and saturated with cultural bias. It is, moreover, frequently so vague, ambiguous, and indeterminate in meaning that it limits inference and makes it unreliable and inconsistent.

> The primary meanings and associations of ideas and hypotheses are derived from their position and force in common sense situations of use-enjoyment. They are expressed in symbols developed for the sake of social communication rather than to serve the conditions of controlled inquiry. The symbols are loaded with meanings that are irrelevant to inquiry conducted for the sake of attaining know-

---

[20] For scientists or science to prescribe values would be only the most modern version of establishing fixed and antecedent ends.

[21] In "Means and Ends: Their Interdependence, and Leon Trotsky's Essay on 'Their Morals and Ours,' " Dewey says, "No scientific law can determine a moral end save by deserting the principle of interdependence of means and end. . . . To be scientific about ends does not mean to read them out of laws, whether the laws are natural or social" (p. 233). Knowledge of laws suggests various means of securing various ends. But laws as such do not determine ends. A law expresses correlations of change, but it can of itself in no way establish the desirability of outcomes effected by processes of change. There is, moreover, an indefinite plurality of possible ends in nature: As variables are changed, so also are ends, though the laws remain constant. Hence there is not a uniquely appropriate end corresponding to each law. In the context of the article on Trotsky, Dewey's point was that even if there were laws of history, these laws could of themselves neither determine historical outcomes nor assign a value to them. To suppose that they could is simply to misunderstand the nature of scientific laws.

> ledge as such. These meanings are familiar and influentially persuasive because of their established associations. The result is that the historic advance of science is marked and accompanied by deliberate elimination of such terms and institution in their stead of a new set of symbols constituting a new technical language.[22]

Abstraction, as we have seen, is what makes science such an effective instrument in understanding and controlling qualitatively diverse events; it is a necessary condition for any sophisticated science. Obviously, then, for science to be an effective instrument of inquiry into practical affairs of social interaction, where human good is to be realized or destroyed, a technical and abstract language must be developed for use in such inquiries. The language of politics and morals and special interests is clearly detrimental; and Dewey felt that there was an urgent need to develop a far more precise and abstract terminology, as free of emotional associations as possible:

> The extreme remoteness of the subject matter of physical science from the subject matter of everyday living is precisely that which renders the former applicable to an immense variety of the occasions that present themselves in the course of everyday living. . . . Negative illustration, if not confirmation, may be supplied by the backward state of both knowledge and practice in matters that are distinctively human and moral. The latter in my best judgment will continue to be a matter of customs and of conflict of customs until inquiry has found a method of abstraction which, because of its degree of remoteness from established customs, will bring them into a light in which their nature will be indefinitely more clearly seen than is now the case.[23]

In his chapter on social inquiry in the *Logic*, Dewey stresses the importance of developing an appropriate technical language:

> Serious social troubles tend to be interpreted in *moral* terms. That the situations themselves are profoundly moral in their causes and consequences, in the genuine sense of moral, need not be denied. But conversion of situations investigated into definite problems, that can be intelligently dealt with, demands objective *intellectual* formulation of conditions; and such a formulation demands in turn complete abstraction from the qualities of sin and righteousness, of vicious and virtuous motives, that are so readily attributed to individuals, groups, classes, nations. . . . For such procedure is the only way in which they [moral problems] can be formulated objectively or in terms of selected and ordered conditions. And such formulation is the sole mode of approach through which plans of remedial procedure can be projected in objective terms.[24]

---

[22] *Logic: The Theory of Inquiry*, p. 425.

[23] "In Defense of the Theory of Inquiry," in Bernstein (ed.) *(op. cit.)*, p. 147.

[24] *Logic: The Theory of Inquiry*, pp. 494-5. A recent example of the kind of social inquiry most welcome to Dewey is Jay W. Forrester's *Urban Dynamics* (Cambridge,

It can well be remarked that too often even when one supposes he is inquiring into conditions and consequences, he severely limits himself in various ways – by unacknowledged ignorance, by lack of thoroughness and exactitude, by the merely sentimental preference for certain ends or policies, by limitation in will or courage to uncover and examine his prejudices. These limitations are in evidence in all forms of "knee-jerk" or "ritualistic" social advocacies, whether of the left, right, or center. There is an obvious sense in which the best moral inquiry is wholly scientific and unsentimental.

Of course, a highly refined and logical language could not of itself serve to assimilate the procedures of practical problem solving to those of science. In addition, it must be shown that the most effective means of solving such problems is identical in logic to that employed in the sciences proper. Inquiry in the physical and social sciences and inquiry into the resolution of moral problems are not conceived by Dewey to be inherently different in terms of procedure. In each case there is the same experimental logic. It is a noteworthy characteristic of Dewey's *Logic* that it is not exclusively concerned with what are normally referred to as the sciences. Rather, the concern is more generic: it is the theory of inquiry. And he defines inquiry functionally:

> Inquiry is the controlled or directed transformation of an indeterminate situation into one that is so determinate in its constituent distinctions and relations as to convert the elements of the original situation into a unified whole.[25]

> All controlled inquiry and all institution of grounded assertion necessarily contains a *practical* factor; an activity of doing and making which reshapes antecedent existential material which sets the problem of inquiry.[26]

By Dewey's analysis, not only do the physical and social sciences fit this definition, but moral inquiry, deliberation, and judgment

---

Massachusetts: M.I.T. Press, 1969). Forrester has made extensive use of mathematical models and computer simulation to try to discover the almost infinitely complex correlations of interaction that determine the life of the American cities. The hypotheses resulting from the study are frequently novel; and they contradict many current notions about the ways in which the variables of city life actually function. This kind of work is of great moral importance because it tries to explain how in fact cities work. This kind of knowledge is plainly indispensable if the problems of the cities are ever to be solved; and it is acquired precisely because it uses a very technical apparatus of inquiry, measurement, and correlation.

[25] *Ibid.*, pp. 104-5. In the original, the entire statement is italicized.

[26] *Ibid.*, p. 160.

do so as well. (This will be indicated in Chapter VII.)

To develop an inclusive theory of inquiry in its continuities in nature Dewey regarded as a matter of acute practical importance. To display the continuity of cognitive and moral experience meets a conspicuous need in contemporary life, for modern culture is distinguished for the effects of science on everything *but* moral thought and belief. To present such an inclusive theory in a sustained treatise is the task Dewey set himself in his *Logic*. He says,

> On the one hand the outstanding problem of our civilization is set by the fact that common sense in its content, its "world" and methods, is a house divided against itself. It consists in part, and that part the most vital, of regulative meanings and procedures that antedate the rise of experimental science in its conclusions and methods. In another part, it is what it is because of application of science. This cleavage marks every phase and aspect of modern life. . . . It is for this reason that it is here affirmed that the basic problem of present culture and associated living is that of effecting integration where division now exists. The problem cannot be solved apart from a unified logical method of attack and procedure. The attainment of unified method means that the fundamental unity of the structure of inquiry in common sense and science be recognized, their difference being one in the problems with which they are directly concerned, not in their respective logics.[27]
>
> Science has . . . affected the actual conditions under which men live, use, enjoy and suffer much more than . . . it has affected their habits of belief and inquiry. Especially is this true about the uses and enjoyments of final concern: religious, moral, legal, economic, political. The demand for reform of logic is the demand for a unified theory of inquiry through which the authentic pattern of experimental and operational inquiry of science shall become available for regulation of the habitual methods by which inquiries in the field of common sense are carried on; by which conclusions are reached and beliefs are formed and tested.[28]

Notably, there is a very technical treatment of experimental method in its explicit applicability to value in Chapter IX of the *Logic*: "Judgments of Practice: Evaluation." This chapter does not constitute a digression in the book, or even a special subject matter unrelated to other topics, but it is regarded by Dewey as an integral part of any thorough study of the theory of inquiry.

---

[27] *Ibid.*, pp. 78-9. The very thorough analyses of inquiry in the *Logic* culminated thirty-six years of reflection and writing on this subject, and he continued to write extensively on it for more than a decade following.

[28] *Ibid.*, pp. 97-8. Further discussion of the relation of science to culture will be undertaken later in this chapter.

What has been said here does not deal with the question of how ends are selected and justified. Dewey's treatment of this matter will eventually be set forth. What has been indicated will not receive its full meaning, of course, until the discussions of Chapter VII have been presented; and those discussions will rely in part on the assumptions introduced here. It is sufficient for the time being to remark that at no point in the process of determining moral conduct does Dewey recommend resort to other than experimental methods.

The present analysis of the application of science to moral subject matter can be concluded by making explicit the sharp contrast between Dewey's views and those which he regarded as having the greatest impact on both philosophy and social practice. (This constitutes an elaboration, from a different perspective, of some of the ideas presented in the preceding chapter.)

The Greek conception of science, which was not discredited until the rise of modern science, was altogether appropriate to their theory of ends: Objects of true knowledge and ultimate ends were one and the same thing: the eternal and perfect forms. When Greek science vanished, however, the theory of ends did not vanish with it. Thus was created the total gulf between science and value:

> For centuries, until, say, the sixteenth and seventeenth centuries, nature was supposed to be what it is because of the presence within it of *ends*. In their very capacity as ends they represented complete or *perfect* Being. All natural changes were believed to be striving to actualize these ends as the goals towards which they moved by their own nature. Classic philosophy identified *ens, verum,* and *bonum* and the identification was taken to be an expression of the constitution of nature as the object of natural science. In such a context there was no call and no place for any *separate* problem of valuation and values, since what are now termed values were taken to be integrally incorporated in the very structure of the world. But when teleological considerations were eliminated from one natural science after another, and finally from the sciences of physiology and biology, the problem of value arose as a separate problem.[29]

> When the notion [of inherent regulative ends] was expelled from natural science by the intellectual revolution of the seventeenth century, logically it should also have disappeared from the theory of human action. But man is not logical and his intellectual history is a record of mental reserves and compromises. He hangs on to what he can in his old beliefs even when he is compelled to surrender their

[29] *Theory of Valuation*, pp. 2-3.

> logical basis. So the doctrine of fixed ends-in-themselves at which human acts are – or should be – directed and by which they are regulated if they are regulated at all persisted in morals, and was made the cornerstone of orthodox moral theory. The immediate effect was to dislocate moral from natural science, to divide man's world as it had never been divided in prior culture.[30]

Indeed, social sciences have persisted in various ways in the ancient logic:

> Classical political economy, with respect to its logical form, claimed to be a science in virtue, first, of certain ultimate first truths, and, secondly, in virtue of the possibility of rigorous "deduction" of actual economic phenomena from these truths. From these "premises," it followed, in the third place, that the first truths provided the norms of practical activity in the field of economic phenomena; or that actual measures were right or wrong, and actual economic phenomena normal or abnormal, in the degree of their correspondence with deductions made from the system of conceptions forming the premises. . . . Any attempt to regulate economic phenomena by control of the social conditions under which production and distribution of goods and services occur was thereby judged to be a violation of natural laws, an "interference" with the normal order, so that ensuing consequences were bound to be as disastrous as are the consequences of an attempt to suspend or interfere with the working of any physical law, say, the law of gravitation.[31]

In various writings Dewey pointed out as well that many social sciences were still preoccupied with the classificatory assumptions and techniques of Greek and Scholastic science.

> Hence our social and moral "sciences" consist largely in putting facts as they are into conceptual systems framed at large. Our logic in social and humane subjects is still largely that of definition and classification as until the seventeenth century it was in natural science.[32]

The debate continues today as to whether social sciences can be

---

[30] *Human Nature and Conduct,* p. 224.

[31] *Logic: The Theory of Inquiry,* pp. 504-5. Dewey adds, "The members of this school, from Adam Smith to the Mills and their contemporary followers, differed of course from the traditional *rationalistic* school. For they held that first principles were themselves derived inductively, instead of being established by *a priori* intuition. But once arrived at, they were regarded as unquestionable truths, or as axioms with respect to any further truths, since the latter should be deductively derived from them" (p. 504). In addition, of course, the assumptions from which such laws were deduced were erroneous. Such assumptions pertained to various presumed laws of individual human nature; and these, as such, must be discarded when the organic unity of man and nature is understood.

[32] *The Quest for Certainty,* p. 251. For sustained analyses, see, for example, Part II of *Human Nature and Conduct.*

genuinely experimental. Those who deny empirical status to social sciences appear to do so on some kind of radically dualistic assumptions about man and nature. Needless to say, Dewey's *Logic* (as well as other writings) tried to indicate how the social sciences could be conducted in full experimental equivalence to the natural sciences.

It was the crippling belief in this gulf between science and value (whether construed subjectively or transcendently) that Dewey was attempting to remove; and he attempted further to indicate specifically the uses of experimental knowledge and techniques in moral problems. To undertake that task implies, of course, that one must develop an inclusive theory of nature, science, and value. To anyone unaware that this was Dewey's sustained enterprise, most of Dewey's writings will be virtually impossible to understand.

Ends, or values, regarded as the changeless limit and perfection of all processes of change, were once regarded as the object of knowledge *par excellence*. As Dewey understands knowing, however, relations of change are what is known. The constituents of these processes of change are indefinitely variable. Hence, also, there is an indefinite plurality of possible outcomes, or ends. If science has given up the idea of unchanging essences, or fixed ontological structures, morality cannot in any way be integrated with experimental procedures, with all their efficacy for inquiry and for creation and control of ends, until it does likewise.

Science is a monumental fact of the modern world. To one who would understand that world, science can be tolerated, abhorred, exploited, but never ignored or misconceived. It can also, if we are willing to undertake "the discipline of experience," be the greatest liberator of human values. Dewey repeatedly argued that in our modern world there is a special urgency to recognizing the full potentialities of experimental intelligence. He repeatedly drew attention to the fact that while we live in a civilization profoundly affected (and afflicted) throughout by science and technology, we are living with *moral* assumptions and methods from a prescientific era. The particular dualisms dating from the early modern period left science wholly separate from moral or "spiritual" matters, and ancient authorities continued to be dominant in the latter:

> The hypothesis here offered is that the upsets which, taken together, constitute the crisis in which man is now involved all over the world, in all aspects of his life, are due to the entrance into the conduct of the everyday affairs of life of processes, materials and interests whose origin lies in the work done by physical inquirers in the relatively aloof and remote technical workshops known as laboratories. It is no longer a matter of disturbance of religious beliefs and practices, but of every institution established before the rise of modern science a few short centuries ago. The earlier "warfare" was ended not by an out-and-out victory of either of the contestents but by a compromise taking the form of a division of fields and jurisdictions. In moral and ideal matters supremacy was accorded to the old. They remained virtually immutable in their older form.[33]

It is the experimental method which has given to man the enormous control of nature which permitted him to spawn the modern industrial society; it is also the result of this method that the cognitive assumptions upon which moral authority has hitherto been based have been made increasingly dubious. Thus the enormous fecundity of modern experimental procedures has been established. Nevertheless, such procedures have been withheld from the vital social problems of modern life. Unless we are to be destroyed by our technological achievements, Dewey asserts, it is necessary to apply this same experimental method to our social, or "moral," problems as well. The remedy for unrestrained exploitation of the physical sciences is not reliance on ancient nostrums, but a genuinely experimental approach to morals.

> The net conclusion of those who hold natural science to be the *fons et origo* of the undeniably serious ills of the present is the necessity of bringing science under subjection to some special institutional "authority." The alternative is a generalized reconstruction so fundamental that it has to be developed by recognition that while the evils resulting at present from the entrance of "science" into our common ways of living are undeniable they are due to the fact that no systematic efforts have as yet been made to subject the "morals" underlying old institutional customs to scientific inquiry and criticism.[34]

> Science through its physical technological consequences is now determining the relations which human beings, severally and in groups, sustain to one another. If it is incapable of developing moral techniques which will also determine these relations, the split in modern culture goes so deep that not only democracy but all civilized values are doomed. Such at least is the problem. A culture which permits science to destroy traditional values but which distrusts its power to create new ones is a culture which is destroying itself.[35]

---

[33] *Reconstruction in Philosophy*, p. xxi.

[34] *Ibid.*, pp. xxii-xxiii.

[35] *Freedom and Culture*, p. 154.

When Dewey says the morals underlying traditional customs and institutions should be subjected to scientific criticism, he simply means that these traditions must be examined to see in fact how they function to promote or hinder, enrich or deplete, the qualities of human experience. A scientific approach to morals implies, generally speaking, several aims: the attempt to test actions – personal or institutional – by their actual consequences in experience. Also, proposals for action – individual or collective – are formulated with just such tests in mind. This approach implies also that by scientific inquiry we determine the way social processes actually function and the way – physiological and social – that the individual organism interacts with its environment. Thus it may be learned how to solve specific problems and to create and maintain precious values. Such inquiries will determine the means of liberating and securing precious things which otherwise occur casually and pass away. Above all, the scientific approach to moral questions implies the possession and operation in individuals of certain intellectual habits. Discussion of these will be taken up in the concluding chapter.

Not only, however, have the possibilities of empirical method been left unexplored, but full-scale attacks on science and experimental intelligence are commonplace. Those who damn science as an instrument of evil typically do so precisely because they misunderstand it. To them, science means just physical science and its offspring: technology, industry, engines of war; while the centrality of method, with its applicability to all subject matters, goes unnoticed. To such people the "scientific" approach to morals evidently means that human desires are ruthlessly subjected to the demands of material efficiency.[36]

Of course, much of the aversion to science has been vented on Dewey himself, whose position seems invariably misunderstood or misrepresented. Pragmatism has been attacked as apologetic for American industrial capitalism, imperialism, and the ethics of opportunism and material success. This is exactly the reverse of Dewey's position. He writes,

---

[36] Some typical discussions by various authors representing both aversion to science and appreciation of its moral possibilities (together with some other materials) have been collected in *Pragmatism and American Culture,* ed. Gail Kennedy (Boston: D.C. Heath and Company, 1950).

> The essential and immanent criticism of existing industrialism and of the dead weight of science is that instruments are made into ends, that they are deflected from their intrinsic quality and thereby corrupted. The implied idealization of science and technology is not by way of acquiescence. It is by way of appreciation that the ideal values which dignify and give meaning to human life have themselves in the past been precarious in possession, arbitrary, accidental and monopolized in distribution, because of lack of means of control; by lack, in other words, of those agencies and instrumentalities with which natural science through technologies equips mankind. Not all who say *Ideals, Ideals* shall enter the kingdom of the ideal, but only those shall enter who know and who respect the roads that conduct to the kingdom.[37]

In other words, science, technology, and industry are oppressive precisely because they have *not* been subjected to criticism as moral ends and as moral means. Their overwhelming power has been utilized for private and selfish aims, while their ends have been rationalized as the working of natural law.[38]

To remedy the nightmarish conditions inflicted upon civilization by the irresponsible employment of science, what is needed is not the restriction of experimental intelligence, but its extension to areas hitherto under the sway of authorities protected by tradition, dogma, and force. When by "science" we mean essentially the experimental procedures of inquiry and verification, without limitation to any field, then the problem of science and value is neither that science is inappropriate for dealing with values nor that science is crushing values, but, on the contrary, that science has not yet been utilized in the knowledge and criticism of values and in the procedures of moral judgment. Technology and material efficiency will remain barbarous and scientific knowledge will remain irrelevant to moral concerns until experimental intelligence learns how to utilize them for the enlightenment and fulfillment of experienced human needs and aspirations.

It is impossible to underestimate the importance of Dewey's efforts to clarify the real nature of science. As indicated in Chapter II, Dewey occupied himself strenuously to exhibit the precise character of the continuity of man and nature. Given the organic

---

[37] "The Pragmatic Acquiescence," in *Pragmatism and American Culture*, p. 53.

[38] One of Dewey's fundamental objections to capitalism was that it held a virtual monopoly on scientific resources, which were, of course, used exclusively for private gain.

unity of man and nature, and given the characterization of science as practical art, then the moral responsibilities and opportunities of the scientific community are enormous. Dewey hoped that the sciences would be deliberately turned to humane subjects. In this hope he continued to be disappointed. "At the present time the widest gap in knowledge is that which exists between humanistic and nonhumanistic subjects."[39]

What has so far been said about value, art, and science indicates their continuities with one another. Even prior to undertaking the analyses of the final chapter, it is evident that on Dewey's view moral philosophy is not an autonomous discipline. Moral experience is not confined to a separate realm of some kind, but it is wholly implicated with nature. Thus any function of man's interaction with nature has a bearing on what we distinguish as the moral life. Values have no characteristics that transcend scientific treatment, and there is no special method – no distinctive method – peculiarly and exclusively applicable to problems in the moral life. Indeed, inasmuch as all facts of experience have a relevance to "morals," the moral life as subject matter is distinguishable only by focus of attention and emphasis. And, as we have seen, "science" is not an endeavor confined to only certain forms of existence. Thus, when Dewey says,

> The problem of restoring integration and cooperation between man's beliefs about the world in which he lives and his beliefs about the values and purposes that should direct his conduct is the deepest problem of modern life. It is the problem of any philosophy that is not isolated from that life.[40]

his meaning is precisely the same as when he says (in reference to a dualistic position),

> The primary function of philosophy at present is to make it clear that there is no such difference as this division assumes between science, morals, and aesthetic appreciation.[41]

---

[39] *Theory of Valuation,* p. 66. See also the entire introduction to *Reconstruction in Philosophy (op. cit.).*

[40] *The Quest for Certainty,* p. 255.

[41] *Experience and Nature,* p. 407. (Resistance to Dewey's views might be attributed not least to the very human aversion by philosophers to occupational insecurity.)

There is an important sense in which most of what I have written so far is foundational: I have attempted to indicate Dewey's basic assumptions about method, experience, and nature; to specify his thought on the character of the main continuities of man and nature; and to set forth his position concerning the status of value in nature and its connections with science. At this point, then, it is possible to reap some of the rewards of this inclusive theory of nature. Accordingly, I will turn to some of Dewey's more detailed remarks about the nature of the good life. At the conclusion of such discussion, it will then be possible to conclude this study by examining the function of intelligence in discerning, constructing, and maintaining such values.

CHAPTER VI

The Good

In this chapter I will deal with three main topics. The first, concerning the uniqueness of good, can be dealt with quite briefly. The second topic is the good of activity, and it will require more elaborate treatment. The third concern will be the nature and function of ideals, the discussion of which will also be relatively brief.

1. The Uniqueness of Good

The occurrence of any particular quality is always unique:

> Such immediate qualities as red and blue, sweet and sour, tone, the pleasant and unpleasant, depend upon an extraordinary variety and complexity of conditioning events; hence they are evanescent. They are never exactly reduplicated, because the exact combination of events of which they are termini does not precisely recur. . . . The thing of mere redness does not happen, but some thing with just this shade and tinge of red, in just this unduplicable content.[1]

Hence every good or value is likewise intrinsically unique. That is, the qualities of any particular experience are unique to that experience; they do not precisely duplicate those of any previous situation, and they will never be precisely repeated. "In quality, the good is never twice alike. It never copies itself. It is new every morning, fresh every evening. It is unique in its every presentation."[2] Or (to make explicite reference to metaphysics):

---

[1] *Experience and Nature,* pp. 115, 117.

[2] *Human Nature and Conduct,* p. 211.

> Actually, consummatory objects instead of being a graded series of numerable and unalterable species or kinds of existence ranked under still fewer genera, are infinitely numerous, variable and individualized affairs. Poets who have sung of despair in the midst of prosperity, and of hope amid darkest gloom, have been the true metaphysicians of nature.[3]

We should also be reminded that the particular goods of any situation will be a matter of human contrivance; that is, the consequences of the situation will depend on how the individual acts in the situation. Hence it is that plans of action and ends-in-view are also unique to the peculiarities of the given situation. Likewise, consummatory value is always unique, being eventual of a situation: Consummatory experience does not simply occur at large, but implies the intentional transformation of a particular problematic context.

The significance of these facts about the uniqueness of good is four-fold: First, they signify that an agent cannot determine what he should do in a situation simply by consulting some antecedently existing rule or standard. The induplicability of the situation entails that its peculiar values and possibilities cannot be seized simply by following a law of some kind. Indeed, a persistent trait of moral situations is the conflict of presumed laws or principles: Conflicts between such rules as telling the truth and doing kindness, such ideals as freedom and equality, such rights as private property and public health, are commonplaces of practical life. Reference to such notions in themselves obviously cannot resolve the conflicts.[4] Accordingly, the potentialities for consummatory experience of any given situation cannot be known a priori; the possibilities for value can only be discovered by inquiry.

Thus it is, second, that the situation can be brought to its best possible fulfillment only by the use of experimental intelligence. That is, the attempt must be made to resolve the conflicts and expand the values of each situation by consideration of its unique features, relations, and potentialities. Judgment is always prospective, not retrospective. That is, it is concerned with outcomes. (Thus also, because decision rests on foresight of conse-

---

[3] *Experience and Nature,* pp. 116-7.

[4] As we shall see in Chapter VII, so-called moral principles are not ignored. Rather, they function as aids to inquiry.

quences, there is no way to know what is the best thing to do in a situation without actually undertaking a course of conduct to see in fact whether the consequences which ensue are similar to what were anticipated. Even when consequences occur as hoped for, there can never be any certainty that some other action would not have provided even more favorable results. Nature is far too complicated to provide such assurances.)

The third implication is that ends-in-view can be evaluated only as a function of the expectations, agencies, and difficulties peculiar to the situation. Nothing can be evaluated at large – out of reference to anything else. Any action functions in relation to a variety of different events; and as the nature and composition of these events change, so will the function of the action. Hence given ends-in-view can only be assessed as functioning in specifiable relations in concrete situations.

The fourth point is that it is utterly vain (indeed, self-defeating) to attempt to establish a fixed hierarchy of values or to attempt to define the good in terms of a particular consequence. All of these facts follow from the assumption that values of all kinds are phenomena of the interactions of man and nature. They are not fixed and isolated entities. Inasmuch as the next chapter will be concerned with the functions of intelligence in the moral situation, I will at this juncture make additional remarks only about the last of these points.

The lesson of experience is evidently that what is good in one context is not good in another. Thus such so-called "lower" pleasures as wine, women, and song are in some circumstances just what the situation demands and in some others inappropriate. Conversely, the so-called "higher" or "elevated" pleasures – pleasures of our "higher" nature – yield their own much – and rightly – glorified fulfillments. But to suppose that such things should invariably preempt the occasions of feasting, celebration, exuberance, or sensuality is to fall victim to arbitrary authority or grossly misleading assumptions. In reality, the distinction between higher and lower pleasures as it is usually found *is* extremely misleading. If some such distinction is made with Dewey's criteria, we should say that in any situation that good is "highest" which most successfully integrates the powers of the particular situation and is most fecund with meanings. Any event can become "saturated" with meanings. Thus it could be that in some situations so-called higher pleasures could be vacuous, demeaning, and out of place, and "bodily" pleasures very meaningful.

It is equally obvious, however, that we can make rough generalizations about the value of actions. In most situations, friendly and honest communication is valuable, while deception is not:

> In a general way, of course, we can safely point out that certain goods are ideal in character: those of art, science, culture, interchange of knowledge and ideas, etc. But that is because past experience has shown that they are the *kind* of values which are likely to be approved upon searching reflection. Hence a *presumption* exists in their favor, but in concrete cases only a presumption.[5]

If it is impossible to establish a fixed hierarchy of goods, then it is also impossible to indicate some particular end that is *the* end, the *summum bonum:*

> Ethical theory . . . has been singularly hypnotized by the notion that its business is to discover some final end or good or some ultimate and supreme law.[6]

> To discover and define once for all the *bonum* and the *summum bonum* in a way which rationally subserves all virtues and duties, is the traditional task of morals; to deny that moral theory has any such office will seem to many equivalent to denial of the possibility of moral philosophy. Yet in other things repeated failure of achievement is regarded as evidence that we are going at the affair in a wrong way.[7]

The indefinitely plural and contextual nature of values militates against fixed ranks of value. This conclusion is highly pertinent: To bear it in mind is to start, at least, to look for the particular good of the particular situation. When we recall, moreover, the crippling limitations of fixed ends, we see the liberating and highly constructive consequences of eschewing the search for absolutes.[8]

---

[5] *Ethics,* p. 230.

[6] *Reconstruction in Philosophy,* p. 161.

[7] *Experience and Nature,* p. 431. Dewey suggests that the notion of a highest good is derivative of the metaphysics which supposes a hierarchical order of reality, descending from pure Being to non-being. (*Reconstruction in Philosophy,* p. 162.)

[8] To anticipate the next chapter a bit, it is pertinent to mention here something about ethical relativism, a concept which is to many the invitation to moral anarchy and nihilism. If Dewey can be called an ethical relativist, this is simply to say that he dismisses the use of a priori assumptions and moral absolutes, which in fact obscure and limit the endeavors to develop as much value as possible in every situation.

Dewey's conclusions indicate the futile (and wholly academic) character of trying to define the good once and for all in terms of an unvarying end or complex of ends. Such efforts are easily shown to be vain, for human experience yields an endless variety of qualitatively unique consummations. To assert, however, that the good cannot be reduced to particular consequences applicable to any and every situation is hardly to say that it cannot be defined in terms of the situation at hand. Indeed, it is precisely because the good cannot be defined once and for all that we are liberated to examine the possibilities of the particular situation and from them create consummatory experience.

Although it is important to stress the uniqueness of good, it is also possible (as mentioned a moment ago) to make generalizations about kinds of experience which tend for the most part to be good. Dewey indulges in this sort of generalization very considerably. It must be noted, however, that generalizations of this sort are never to be regarded as substitutes for inquiry in the moral situation, but as aids to inquiry; and they are never to be regarded as unexceptionable.

> The business of reflection in determining the true good cannot be done once for all, as, for instance, making out a table of values arranged in a hierarchical order of higher and lower. It needs to be done, and done over and over and over again, in terms of the conditions of concrete situations as they arise.[9]

It is signficant, moreover, that when Dewey undertakes to formulate such generalizations, he does so – not in reference to anything traditionally called an *end* – but in reference to a particular kind of *process.* Thus, almost paradoxically, he says, "Growth itself is the only moral 'end.'"[10] Or, as he concludes in the *Ethics,* cultivation of interests is the "end."[11] In *Human Nature and Conduct,* the expression "the good of activity" is equivalent to both "cultivation of interests" and "growth." This activity at its optimum is conduct as art.

2. The Good of Activity.

This subject will be considered in three parts: 1) An elabora-

---

[9] *Ethics,* p. 230.

[10] *Reconstruction in Philosophy,* p. 177.

[11] *Ethics,* p. 224ff.

tion of what Dewey means by growth, together with some specification of its values; 2) A characterization of the integrity and felt continuity of experience; 3) The values of shared experience. This third topic will also be occasion to discuss the distinction between individual and social goods.

1) A convenient way to analyze the character of growth will be to state its general nature and conditions first, and then elaborate more specifically both its meaning and the optimum requisites for its continuation. This latter discussion will include an analysis of the relation of on-going activity to its future and past.

Quite simply, the process of growth is one in which the organism enhances its ability to participate with its environment: As increasingly complex features of the environment are incorporated into modes of behavior, the organism acquires new functions in nature; and interactions become more meaningful. At the same time, it must be noted, this process of growth could not occur at all if the precarious traits of nature were not generic to all experience. More specifically, it could not occur if there were not problematic situations, in which precarious events are notably obtrusive, but in which stable events occur as well. To know that growth goes on in the context is the first step in understanding the nature of the process; for it is precisely because of the reality of problematic situations that an organism has to develop new ways of acting with its environment: It must incorporate ever-new elements into its behavior, or perish:

> Life itself consists of phases in which the organism falls out of step with the march of surrounding things and then recovers unison with it – either through effort or by some happy chance. And, in a growing life, the recovery is never mere return to a prior state, for it is enriched by the state of disparity and resistance through which it has successfully passed. If the gap between organism and environment is too wide, the creature dies. If its activity is not enhanced by the temporary alienation, it merely subsists. Life grows when a temporary falling out is a transition to a more extensive balance of energies of the organism with those of the conditions under which it lives. . . . If life continues and if in continuing it expands, there is an overcoming of factors of opposition and conflict; there is a transformation of them into differentiated aspects of a higher powered and more significant life.[12]

The development of all human powers and virtues depends of

---

[12] *Art as Experience,* p. 14.

necessity on the occurrence of the novel, precarious, contingent. The thinker, the artist, the aesthete, the lover, and the saint cannot grow unless they have the appropriate situations to grow with. Hence it is that the very process of struggle, effort, overcoming, and mastery is both necessary and desirable. It not only maintains life, but enlarges it.

Of course, it is all too frequently the case that people are engulfed in situations utterly beyond their mastery; and then their wish is to lash out blindly, or conform slavishly, or to develop ideals of withdrawal, quiescence, blissful repose. But when human powers are adquate to their challenges, the natural impulse is to engage concretely in this process called growth. "To a healthy man, inaction is the greatest of woes."[13]

This notion of growth can be given a more concrete sense by consideration of the nature of the self. The self is not a substance; it is a dynamic organization of habits, which are demands for certain kinds of activity. The self, in other words, is a set of functions *with the environment.*[14] Thus when the self "grows," it is not like a balloon swelling with air. It is, rather, that the structure of habits – functional cooperations of organism and environment – becomes more inclusive and more complex: The environment that is incorporated into behavior becomes more extensive and more meaningful and it fulfills more diverse and effectual functions in behavior; and at the same time human energies find fuller and more effective engagement with their surroundings.

Two main aspects of this process can be distinguished: the enhancement of the powers of the self and the enhancement of the meanings of experience. These two are functionally inseparable, but perhaps they can be understood most easily if analyzed separately. To deal first with the enhancement of the powers of the self: As indicated earlier, the very process of coping with ever-new problematic situations necessitates that the individual

---

[13] *Human Nature and Conduct,* pp. 118-9.

[14] Revery and imagination are derivative of overt interactions. Recall that "thought," or "mind," is a product of language, and language is social behavior. " 'Consciousness,' whether as a stream or as special sensations and images, expresses functions of habits, phenomena of their formation, operation, their interruption and reorganization." (*Human Nature and Conduct,* p. 177.)

be either buffeted and subdued by them, or strengthened and enlarged. The extreme toward which one tends depends on the extent to which one manages such situations intelligently and creatively. It depends also, of course, on the extent to which the features of the environment are cooperative, flexible, and subject to manipulation. As relatively optimum conditions are reached, the individual develops new ways of acting with the world, more various and complex modes of behavior. Thus the self literally grows in powers, habits. Existing abilities and interests are qualified in various ways; certain habits are modified, enlarged, and reinforced, while others – perhaps dysfunctional – tend to become less urgent. At the same time, new ways of acting eventually becomes sure habits.

This is a growth of power to act with characteristic features of the world: It implies a creative release of energies in on-going participation with the environment; and the latter thereby also becomes more serviceable in human action. That is, the growth of habits implies that the potentialities of the environment also become enlarged with new resources and powers. (The accomplished sportsman in the wilderness finds his surroundings more efficacious in his behavior than does his tyro companion.)

At best, then, habits and complexes of habits are forms of mastery. They are ways in which human powers and the powers of the environment are effectively engaged. Each constituent of one's affective environment poses to him at once certain provisional limitations and instrumentalities. These are possibilities to be explored, qualified, restructured, and utilized in novel and productive ways. Human powers would have no means of functioning without the environment, with its specific agencies and challenges; and the joy of the exercise and fulfillment of human powers just could not *be* without that organic relation to the environment which literally constitutes human action.

All this is in evidence as an individual acquires an art of any kind. This growth involves by its very nature that the individual is enabled to deal with greater diversity of situations and to respond constructively to novelty; and he is enabled to act with an environment which is more complex and ever more extensive in space and time and which is always disclosing new values and instrumentalities. Hence, also, his experience is more meaningful;

and his potentialities are developed and fulfilled precisely because he has learned to make nature his accomplice, rather than his antagonist.

It should be evident that the growth in forms of mastery is growth in conduct as art. In experience of this kind, there is a felt unity – a felt harmony – of man and nature. This felt unification is accomplished not by means of negating mind, or body, or desire, or the world – as various disciplines undertake. Rather, it is a dynamic integration of mind, body, and nature in a concrete situation. Principally by means of intelligence, all the functions of a complex situation work in concert. This is obviously in contrast to the usual experience, in which desires, aims, and action occur more or less in a void, or against brute and immovable obstacles; and the individual can have no sense of engagement of his thought and energies with the world. There is only random flailing about, or there is withdrawal. In neither case is there experience of objective unity and of concrete fulfillment of directed effort and action.

It might well be noted that this sort of growth by no means implies immediate gratification of every impulse that happens to occur. It is clear that the acquisition of arts requires discipline and training; and some habits are initially awkward and uncongenial. In any situation, impulses must frequently be held in check and conserved: Resistances in the environment can be neither ignored nor destroyed; and opportunities are not self-evident. The features of the situation must be intelligently examined, and specified plans of action must be conceived. The fulfillment that succeeds such preparation is more massive and meaningful than the chance satisfaction of transient desires; and it provides life-experience with a coherency and cumulativeness otherwise impossible. The further discussions of this chapter will provide considerable elaboration of this point.

There is a further important point to make about this growth in personal powers. As we have seen, it involves ever greater capacities and ways to act in and with the world. This process involves a discovery and elaboration of the possible meanings of experience. Thus it entails that one also cultivates more values in his experience. Accordingly, growth can be such as to incorporate ever wider and more various interests and sympathies, and thus a personality becomes many-sided, diversified. That is, in the process of growth a person not only enhances his powers of thinking and acting, but he also can become tolerant and appreciative of a widening and richer spectrum of values. Every new or complicated habit means that new ways of acting with the environment have acquired value; and as these habits are cultivated and expanded, their values become more firmly established, the way of acting becomes more assured and congenial.

In the present context – the discussion of the growth of personal powers – this is a consideration of some consequence; for it is such a cultivated and balanced complex of interests that makes one "reasonable": not giving way to whatever strong impulse happens to occur, not subject to enslavement by any given desire. When each desire occurs as a function of a self with many diverse and valued habits, the desire is less apt to be blind and overwhelming. It is the isolated passion – the passion occurring in an individual who is not possessed of a medley of keen and active interests – that drives a man on helplessly. In developing and exercising a rich texture of interests, an individual is saved from being a slave to a few blind impulses; and he is liberated from extreme narrowmindedness, or fanaticism:

> The conclusion is not that the emotional, passionate phase of action can be or should be eliminated in behalf of a bloodless reason. More "passions," not fewer, is the answer. To check the influence of hate there must be sympathy, while to rationalize sympathy there are needed emotions of curiosity, caution, respect for the freedom of others – . . . . "Reason" is not an antecedent force which serves as a panacea. It is a laborious achievement of habit needing to be continually worked over. A balanced arrangement of propulsive activities manifested in deliberation – namely, reason – depends upon a sensitive and proportionate emotional sensitiveness.[15]

What is called self-control or – ideally – the identity of desire and intelligence is not the work of something called the will or of a presumed reason possessed as such of motive power. It is not a cause, but a result:

> The Greek *sophrosyne*, . . . a harmonious blending of affections into a beautiful whole, was essentially an artistic idea. Self-control was its inevitable *result*, but self-control as a deliberate cause would have seemed as abhorrent to the Athenian as would "control" in a building or statue where control signified anything other

[15] *Ibid.*, pp. 195-6; 198.

> than the idea of the whole permeating all parts and bringing them into order and measured unity.[16]

> When an independent thing is made of temperance or self-control it becomes mere inhibition, a sour constraint. But as one phase of an interpenetrated whole, it is the positive harmony characteristic of integrated interest.[17]

As mentioned earlier, growth also implies an enhancement of the meanings of experience; and, again, the instrumentality of such growth is art. Thus the discussion of the enhancement of meanings will center on the concept of art. We have seen that the processes of art (in any form) involve the discovery, reconstruction, and enlargement of meanings both by discovery of novel instrumentalities and by bringing isolated events into relation. It is clear, then, that experience admits of great differences in respect to the extent to which meanings are generated and organized in it; experience may be very poor, or it may be richly funded and always growing with meanings. Dewey insists that there is no limit to the meanings which experience can absorb. The most "ethereal" meanings are precisely those which are most thoroughly infused with connections of natural events. These meanings are immanent in concrete experience. "There is no limit to the capacity of immediate sensuous experience to absorb into itself meanings and values that in and of themselves – that is in the abstract – would be designated 'ideal' and 'spiritual.'"[18]

There is nothing obscure in Dewey's assertion that "the characteristic human need is for possession and appreciation of the meaning of things, . . ."[19] It seems to be an evident fact of experience that people value things that are generously implicated in their experience with other things which they prize. It is also clear, however, that it is only by art that we are able to cultivate the meanings of experience and incorporate them into our lives:

> Our affections, when they are enlightened by understanding, are organs by which we enter into the meaning of the natural world as genuinely as by knowing, and

---

[16] *Ethics*, p. 298.

[17] *Ibid.*, p. 284. The beginning of the next chapter will elaborate the discussion of the relation between intelligence and desire. It should also be noted again that a harmony of habits is impossible when the objective social conditions are lacking which would permit the free development and release of habits.

[18] *Art as Experience*, p. 29.

[19] *Experience and Nature*, p. 362.

with greater fullness and intimacy. This deeper and richer intercourse with things can be effected only by thought and its resultant knowledge; the arts in which the potential meanings of nature are realized demand an intermediate and transitional phase of detachment and abstraction. The colder and less intimate transactions of knowing involve temporary disregard of the qualities and values to which our affections and enjoyments are attached. But knowledge is an indispensable medium of our hopes and fears, of loves and hates, if desires and preferences are to be steady, ordered, charged with meaning, secure.[20]

Growth is not the context *within* which the process of expansion of both personal powers and meanings takes place. Rather, growth *is* precisely the continuation of this process. The form at once most conducive to it and most intrinsically rewarding is what Dewey calls art. Some further aspects of this form of conduct require examination.

As long as an organism is dealing at all adequately with its environment, growth proceeds in any case in some manner. What is most important, then, is to understand the requisites for maintaining growth at its best. And at its best it is a continuous process of activity in which the focus of attention and fulfillment is always *present* conduct; and this present is enriched by drawing generously on the experience of the past and by anticipating the future in such a way that it is organic with the present. It is here that the process of growth – in this optimum sense – can become art. It is important to consider the functioning of the future and past in the present; and our understanding of the nature of growth will be clarified and enlarged by examining these functions specifically. Dewey indicates that his views are in at least one important respect like those of Epicurus,[21] for he insists that activity should be for the sake of discerning, liberating, and fulfilling the values of the present. Yet Dewey's position does not imply that we should forget the past, take no thought of the future, and remain as inert as possible in the present. Reference to the problematic situation will be an appropriate context in which to present his view.

To say that a problematic situation occurs is to say that ongoing activity has been balked. The problem might be a simple

---

[20] *The Quest for Certainty*, p. 297.

[21] *Human Nature and Conduct*, pp. 291-2.

one – like the cook running out of salt – or an extremely complex, delicate, and compelling one – like that of guaranteeing civil rights and decent conditions of life to all citizens. In any event, the problem is to get integrated, harmonious action initiated or reinstated. That is, the *present* problems must be solved, and for the sake of *present* experience. It is for this that a plan of action is devised. Thus, in the example of the cook running out of salt, the formulation of a plan of action would be a simple, but still meaningful, matter; while to rectify the problems of the poor and nonwhite requires enormous resources. In both instances, however, action is not directed towards a distant goal – a goal removed from the present. Rather, it is precisely with the present that action should be concerned: something must be done about the *existing* problematic situation. It is precisely this focus of attention which enhances the meanings and powers of present activity. In other words, it enhances the process of growth. Before proceeding in this analysis, it will be useful to indicate briefly some of the difficulties occasioned by the attempt to disregard the characteristics of the problematic situation.

As we have seen, Dewey is extremely critical of preoccupation with ends which are discontinuous with concrete circumstances. Apart from all the philosophic difficulties attending the concept of either transcendent or subjective ends, there are also crucial practical difficulties in formulating ends without reference to the experienced problematic situation. Ends discontinuous with existing means, we should recall, are the most hazardous sort of event either to predict or control. [22] And quite apart from their unpredictable and uncontrollable character, it is obvious that such ends don't do anything towards resolving the disruptions and dilemmas that actually plague on-going experience. Ends remote from the problematic situation evidently function only to convince us that on-going experience is unimportant, or is simply to be endured. Such ends reflect a desire for outright deliverance from actual problems; they are not devices with which to solve them.

> An aim not framed on the basis of a survey of those present conditions which are to be employed as means of its realization simply throws us back upon past

---

[22] See p. 185.

> habits. We then do not know what we intended to do but what we have got used to doing, or else we thrash about in a blind ineffectual way. The result is failure. Discouragement follows, assuaged perhaps by the thought that in any case the end is too ideal, too noble and remote, to be capable of realization. . . . Action fails to connect satisfactorily with surrounding conditions. Thrown back upon itself, it projects itself in an imagination of a scene which if it were present would afford satisfaction. This picture is often called an aim, more often an ideal. But in itself it is a fancy which may be only a phantasy, a dream, a castle in the air.[23]

The fact that future events are so difficult to predict and control does not, however, make the whole concept of ends vain; it simply dictates that we distinguish different kinds of ends and distinguish the functions appropriate to them. The ends which are most conducive to the process of growth and all its values are those which function to direct *present* conduct, not conduct of the future. These are ends-in-view.

It is important to see precisely what future events *can* effectively be forecast. Remember that the occasion for prediction is the occurrence of a problematic situation. The problem to be solved consists in the obstacles and conflicts of a given situation, and some action must be undertaken to remove them. Accordingly, the agent must concern himself with the active tendencies of his present situation. He has no concern with events which are not organic to it. In order to decide what plan of action would be most suitable, it is necessary to anticipate the particular consequences expected from acting in various ways with the various tendencies of the situation. In so doing, the agent is concerned with the effects such conduct would have on his present situation; and in this way he acquires the information relevant to decision. In the problematic situation, then, there is no concern to forecast other than presently operative tendencies; and there is no concern with these beyond their possible functions in present behavior. Possible ends or outcomes of any kind which have no reference to the existing predicament have no relevance to the problems of prediction and control. The purpose of forecasting eventual results is to determine neither what will happen at some later time nor what action should be taken at some such time. Rather, it is to determine what would happen right now contin-

---

[23] *Human Nature and Conduct,* pp. 233-4.

gent upon specifiable actions in the existing situation. It follows also that the end-in-view appropriate to coordinate the situation is not a future object for which the present functions as a means; it is itself a means in present activity:

> Having an end or aim is thus a characteristic of *present* activity. It is the means by which an activity becomes adapted when otherwise it would be blind and disorderly, or by which it gets meaning when otherwise it would be mechanical. In a strict sense an end-in-view is a *means* in present action; present action is not a means to a remote end.[24]

However difficult it is to determine the occurrence of ends-in-view, it is certainly true that those which are founded on the basis of the existing needs of the situation are most subject to prediction and control. "Deliberately to subordinate the present to the future is to subject the comparatively secure to the precarious, exchange resources for liabilities, surrender what is under control to what is, relatively, incapable of control."[25] When the end-in-view is settled upon, it is present activity that is released and unified. What is important is that the present be fulfilled, and that the novel and disruptive features of the situation be incorporated into the process of growth. Without dealing with on-going conflicts and disruptions, the process of growth could not occur at all.

Dewey's concern with focusing the process of growth in the present might seem to ignore preparations for future eventualities, to undertake no effort in behalf of events and institutions not yet existing. Or he might even seem to be some form of romantic, advocating glorious, but inevitably self-defeating, in-

---

[24] *Ibid.*, p. 226. Dewey is not entirely consistent in his discussion of the function of ends-in-view. In some places he indicates that it is almost wholly inconsequential whether ends-in-view are actually achieved, for their significance is exclusively in stimulating renewed activity. (See especially *Human Nature and Conduct*, p. 261.) There is some virtue in this position. However, his concepts of art and consummatory experience depend upon the notion of the achievement of the foreseen end-in-view. Consummatory experience is such precisely because it is a deliberate and intended integration of activities hitherto disorganized; it is an anticipated event which is a fulfillment of thought and effort. As we shall see in the following chapter, accuracy of prediction is crucially important in guiding conduct. The difference in the notions of ends-in-view indicated in this note do not constitute a contradiction. The former notion is simply more limited than the latter. It was formulated prior to the time when Dewey developed his explicit concept of art.

[25] *Ibid.*, p. 267.

dulgences! Dewey anticipates such presumed difficulties:

> Control of the future may be limited in extent, but it is correspondingly precious; we should jealously cherish whatever encourages and sustains effort to that end. . . . But there is a difference between future improvement as a result and as a direct aim. To make it an aim is to throw away the surest means of attaining it, namely attention to the full use of present resources in the present situation.[26]

An end-in-view is more likely of achievement than a remote end, for the former is that which will utilize the operative desires and tendencies of the existing situation. And how can it be expected that future problems can be solved and future conditions managed if those of the present remain to obstruct, and present possibilities pass unnoticed? When we are capable of coping with the problems of today, then we both minimize the difficulties that might otherwise have occurred tomorrow and prepare ourselves to deal with them when they happen. The future, when regarded in this way, is not something to be awaited, but something to be constructed by management of the present. "Until men have formed the habit of using intelligence fully as a guide to present action they will never find out how much control of future contingencies is possible."[27]

The care for the present is crucial to the process of growth; and growth means increments in effective powers of interaction. Thus it must also be recognized that the growth of certain habits in the present provides individuals with the powers to be constructive participants with nature, whatever eventualities may arise. That is, in the present we can cultivate habits which have beneficent and efficacious tendencies. "We judge present desires and habits by their tendency to produce certain consequences. It is our business to watch the course of our action so as to see what is the significance, the import of our habits and dispositions."[28] Thus we cannot control the future as such, but we can take some measure of control of the present and of the nature of the self that will be involved in whatever the future brings. As a future becomes a present, each present may thus be managed resourcefully.

---

[26] *Ibid.*, p. 266.

[27] *Ibid.*, p. 269.

[28] *Ibid.*, p. 206.

This discussion can be put in a now familiar framework: the continuity of means and ends in activity. There are no ultimate ends; and life is not a preparation. Rather, each phase of life has its characteristic possibilities and fulfillments. Moreover, insofar as on-going activity approximates to growth as art, it is intrinsically valuable and at the same time the best way to anticipate the future.

> We must know that the dependence of ends upon means is such that the only *ultimate* result is the result that is attained today, tomorrow, the next day, and day after day, in the succession of years and generations. Only thus can we be sure that we face our problems in detail one by one as they arise, with all the resources provided by collective intelligence operating in co-operative action.[29]

What has been said about the nature of growth points out the value of caring for the present and the way in which analysis of the operative tendencies of situations can be utilized to liberate and expand the meanings of the present. It will now be indicated in a general and preliminary way how the present is enriched by the past. In this matter, however, I will not go into any detail; for the subject will receive thorough attention in the following chapter in a discussion of the instrumentalities of moral reflection. The points to be made at the present juncture are obvious. It has been frequently pointed out herein that ends are also means; they are beginnings of new situations and provide the individual with increments in the powers which he brings to such situations. Hence any present is inevitably funded by the habits and meanings developed in the past. The nature of these habits and meanings is decisive. Have meanings been developed in such a way that initially precarious objects can be recognized in their continuities? Are habits such to contribute to making present problems convertible into consummations? Or is the present condemned to remain obscure and confused due to the absence of effective agencies of behavior?

For present purposes (in connection with the examination of the nature and conditions of growth) the crucial focus of attention is this: The quality of experience is always vastly enhanced when the present is a fulfillment of the past, rather than having

---

[29] *Freedom and Culture,* p. 176.

no more than a sequential relation to it. And by this is meant a *felt* fulfillment, a *felt* continuity with one's past efforts: The efforts of the past are part of the experienced meaning of the present. Thereby also the process of growth is itself enhanced, for the individual is better enabled to master and incorporate into behavior novel features of the environment, while at the same time enlarging their meaning and value.

Some summary remarks about the process of growth can now be made. It is clear that the process called growth prospers best when it takes the form of art. Intelligent and imaginative concentration on resolution of the existing problematic situation augments the forces of growth by deliberately converting agencies of conflict and frustration into effective powers. When conduct is art, the problematic situation is resolved by discerning its active tendencies and anticipating its possible outcomes, and also by drawing liberally on the past. If there is successful resolution, and consummatory experience ensues, it is clear that such experience is at the same time a fulfillment of the past and portentous of the future. And – it is always useful to be reminded – this is not properly regarded as simply a "psychological" fulfillment, for it is the conjoint operation of a person and his environment: The *situation* becomes consummatory by the organic and functional interaction of its constituents.[30]

An instance of such activity might be in the writing of a book. A writer, for example, is aware of certain problems that

---

[30] Dewey provides a rather systematic account of conduct as art in *Human Nature and Conduct,* pp. 172-277. At the time of writing that book, however, he had not yet explicitly formulated the general concept of art, which represents the perfect integrity of nature in experience. Thus Chapter Nine of *Experience and Nature,* "Experience, Nature and Art," makes explicit the implicit metaphysical assumptions of these discussions in *Human Nature and Conduct.* The relationship between the ideas in these books exemplifies the procedure in naturalistic metaphysics of examining the traits of particular forms of experience and hence undertaking to generalize the traits thus discriminated into a generic theory. And then, in turn, this "generic insight into existence" becomes the "ground-map" which serves as the basis for returning to the criticism of various specific forms of experience or analyses of experience.

The still later volume, *Art as Experience,* contains more detailed analyses of consummatory experience than any other of Dewey's writings. Indeed, *Art as Experience* might more accurately have been titled *Consummatory Experience in Nature,* for the book is precisely that: a study of consummatory experience, of which the fine arts provide only the most conspicuous example. See especially the first three chapters.

plague his discipline; or perhaps he is aware that certain problems which plague mankind need both critical examination and creative treatment. If, moreover, he is to an extent well funded with the information, methods, and assumptions which are appropriate to this set of problems; and if, finally, these problems – and even more, their constructive treatment – are very important to him (if they bear many meanings for him), then his setting to work on them is an engagement in what Dewey calls art: The writer's end-in-view (the writing of the book) unifies and releases his powers and desires; he fulfills himself in his work in that its progress is a fulfillment of the abilities and interests he has cultivated. At the same time, the novelties, difficulties, and challenges he masters in developing his project bring increments in his personal power and added meanings to his existence. As the work goes on, many considerations and problems are held in suspension; there are many expectations, rehearsals of possibilities, reassessments, reorganizations of materials. More and more experience is included and incorporated within the compass of the book; yet unity, direction, coherent growth, are maintained. There is a quickening tension; fulfillment in preliminary stages stimulates a relish for forthcoming tasks. The promise of consummation becomes more vivid and concrete; and when it occurs it is both inclusive and fulfilling, while inviting still more endeavors, stimulated and enriched by this success. The completion of the book is clearly consummatory and at the same time portentous, and as such it informs all his efforts. If the writer is working on matters which he regards as possessing great human import, then his efforts are that much more meaningful.

Although the value to mankind of the activities of most persons is rather small, it is nonetheless true that most kinds of endeavor can be converted by intelligence into art, and thus become functional in the process of growth. And more important (as we shall see later on), when activity is *shared*, its value is greatly enhanced. Thus one's efforts may not be meaningful to the human race at large, but they can be intensely meaningful in the context of shared and intimate experience.

In all such cases of growth there is a continuity of the present with the past and the future. This is not just a temporal and causal continuity, which there is in any case, but an *experienced* continuity, a *felt* continuity, in which ends-in-view arise from the appraisal of actual human predicaments and build upon the funded experience of the past. Such ends actuate, unite, and give meaning to the exertions of the past and the potentialities of the present. Hence also they endow value on the endeavors undertaken in their behalf and convert what would otherwise be mere termini into consummations. When one's continuities with man and nature are converted from merely causal connections into experienced meanings, only then do they become significant; nature and human actions thereupon acquire value otherwise unrealized. [31] Dewey's own summation of the distinctive character of this process is worth quoting at length:

> Means are at least causal conditions; but causal conditions are means only when they possess an added qualification; that, namely, of being freely used, because of perceived connection with chosen consequences. . . . Similarly, consequences, ends, are at least effects; but effects are not ends unless thought has perceived and freely chosen the conditions and processes that are their conditions. . . . The connection of means-consequences is never one of bare succession in time, such that the element that is means is past and gone when the end is instituted. An active process is strung out temporally, but there is a deposit at each stage and point entering cumulatively and constitutively into the outcome. A genuine instrumentality *for* is always an organ *of* an end. It confers continued efficacy upon the object in which it is embodied. . . .
>
> It would thus seem almost self-evident that the distinction between the instrumental and the final adopted in philosophic tradition as a solving word presents in truth a problem, a problem so deep-seated and far-reaching that it may be said to be *the* problem of experience. For all the intelligent activities of men, no matter whether expressed in science, fine arts, or social relationships, have for their task the conversion of causal bonds, relations of succession, into a connection of means-consequence, into meanings. When the task is achieved the result is art: and in art everything is common between means and ends. Whenever so-called means remain external and servile, and so-called ends are enjoyed objects whose further causative status is unperceived, ignored or denied, the situation is proof positive of limitations of art. Such a situation consists of affairs in which the problem has *not* been solved; namely that of converting physical and brute relationships into connections of meanings characteristic of the possibilities of nature.[32]

---

[31] It might be added that the values that emerge from such knowledge of nature are a main motivation and reward for indulgence in theory of nature. To learn what nature is and can do is not simply to satisfy that arid something called intellectual curiosity, and it is not only to enlighten the affairs of men. For only in the knowledge of the ways of man and nature does nature come into its full measure of value. And this, too, the philosopher seeks.

[32] *Experience and Nature,* pp. 366-70.

Most human experience is isolated, fragmentary, disordered, frustrated, without any sense of growth, aim, or connection; and it is impoverished of meanings. By contrast, when experience is art, life is cumulative, on-going, and richly informed with intrinsic values. It is so, not because authority or absolutes of some kind have presumably endowed or imposed value on what is otherwise without intrinsic worth, but because nature itself possesses traits and processes which can be guided to events which are found to be profoundly valuable in experience. The word "valuable" is simply used to mark a noteworthy distinction in nature.[33] Dewey readily becomes expansive when he writes of such experience which is luminous with meanings:

> Pleasures may come about through chance contact and stimulation; such pleasures are not to be despised in a world full of pain. But happiness and delight are a different sort of thing. They come to be through a fulfillment that reaches to the depths of our being – one that is an adjustment of our whole being with the conditions of existence. . . . The happy periods of an experience that is now complete because it absorbs into itself memories of the past and anticipations of the future, come to constitute an esthetic ideal. Only when the past ceases to trouble and anticipations of the future are not perturbing is a being wholly united with his environment and therefore fully alive. Art celebrates with peculiar intensity the moments in which the past reenforces the present and in which the future is a quickening of what now is.[34]

It has already been remarked that people frequently find themselves in circumstances too difficult to permit this activity of growth. The fact that men are overwhelmed by obstacles is

---

[33] It is ironical that Dewey should in many quarters be regarded (accursed?) as an apostle of moden nihilism. For Dewey celebrates the intrinsic values of human experience in themselves. Values of this nature require no external authority or sanction; they are valuable because human beings find them to be eminently worth realizing for their own sake. It is an odd way to assert the value of existence by insisting that it has no value apart from divine fiat.

There is a sickly character pervading much of the current literature on the human estate. The self-pity in these writings would be more excusable if the authors were deliberately reflecting the specific traits of modern life; for – to understate the matter – there is little occasion for rejoicing about the present state of affairs. But these thinkers make a dialectical leap which finds no warrant in experience and impute to Being Itself, or to human experience *sub specie aeternitatis,* traits which are neither universal nor necessary. They are victims of a morbid selective emphasis. Dewey's thesis that such reflections are the result of the lack of power to participate effectively in the world is not likely to appeal, however, to those who wallow so deliciously in *Angst* and *nausée.*

[34] *Art as Experience,* pp. 17-8.

not, however, a denial of the value of growth. Rather, it simply poses the problem for intelligence: How can life be ordered so that men may find it possible to participate in it in such a way that the environment contributes to growth rather than crushes it? Thus, whenever Dewey delineates some aspect of the good life, he inevitably turns his attention directly to considering the social reforms which are necessary to liberate the possible meanings of human endeavor. It is impossible on Dewey's assumptions to consider a moral problem which can be effectively understood or managed apart from the social context. However, I cannot enter into Dewey's specific proposals for social action. I shall instead deal with a more general problem, indicating Dewey's reflections on the fact that there is always *some* disparity between anticipated end and results achieved. Only by complete control of the environment, complete absence of conflict between persons, and complete absence of conflict of desires in the individual could this disparity be wholly negated.

The occurrence of such disparity might occasion in some the belief that their moral ideals are too pure for the world and demand that they stand aloof from the on-going course of events. Or it might give credence to the assumption that all initiative is vain and that one's duty is only to conform. Given this inevitable condition of nature, however, it is foolish to demand that the world conform to one's wishes. If one's ideal fulfillment or one's hopes for ultimate happiness are inextricably linked with somehow establishing a total and permanent harmony between self and world, then such ambitions are utterly vain. On the other hand, it is at great sacrifice of value that one attempts to disengage himself from the delights and consummations which are potential in existence.

Happily, these alternatives are not exhaustive. Rather than either identifying one's efforts with making things perfect once and for all or quitting further effort altogether, it is possible to identify one's endeavors with the continual remaking of events.

> Only by identification with remaking the objects that now obtain are we saved from complacent objectivism. Those who do not fare forth and take the risks attendant upon the formation of new objects and the growth of a new self, are subjected perforce to inevitable change of the settled and close world they have made their own. Identification of the bias and preference of selfhood with the process of intelligent remaking achieves an indestructible union of the instrumen-

> tal and final. For *this* can be satisfied no matter what the frustration of other desires and endeavors.[35]

This is a point of profound importance. It is characteristic of many people to seek wholesale acceptance of the world. Failing in this, they react with wholesale rejection, cynicism, or slavish acquiescence. These polarities entail a suffering, disappointment, and disillusion which are unnecessary. Wholesale identification is possible only if the object is change itself, growth itself (remembering that growth is a process in which the environment is a participant):

> Many a person gets morally discouraged because he has not attained the object upon which he set his resolution, but in fact his moral status is determined by his movement in that direction, not by his possession. If such a person would set his thought and desire upon the *process* of evolution instead of upon some ulterior goal, he would find a new freedom and happiness. It is the next step which lies within our power.[36]

2) The discussion of the felt integrity and continuity of experience (the second general topic of this section) is really a continuation of the analysis of growth, as the latter takes place in conduct as art. It is, indeed, to elaborate and emphasize subjects already introduced. To explain what is meant here by both "integrity" and "continuity," the main requirement is simply to make reference to the characteristics of art. A useful notion with which to begin is the unifying function of ends-in-view. These not only give meaning to activity, but they also serve, at best, to bring all the conflicting and diverse elements in the situation into a harmonious whole. As the discussions of art have shown, we may undertake actions which unify originally disruptive and conflicting features of the environment. This implies as well that initially divergent desires may all find fulfillment, in some measure, in the situation; for as the *objects* of desire are harmonized, so are the desires. Finally, recall that thought, feeling, imagination, impulse, action, and aesthetic perception are all conjoined in this process. Insofar as all this is possible, it is conditional upon the formulation of appropriate ends-in-view. Hence the formation of intelligent plans of action is critical for fully integrated

---

[35] *Experience and Nature,* p. 246.

[36] *Ethics,* pp. 340-1.

and meaningful experience; and it is precisely the unification in conduct of these distinctive functions in experience, as well as of the objects of desire, that is meant by the expression "integrity of experience."[37]

A closely related notion is that of the felt continuity in experience: Experience, to be complete and to realize its inherent values, must go through certain phases from the problematic to the consummatory, and in such a way that the instrumental and final phases comprise an undivided whole. This is a process of interaction in which objects and events in the situation are deliberately investigated in their relations and constructively utilized in the course of conduct. Thus it is that they acquire meaning; and the agent acquires a sense of the connections of his experience and nature. This sort of history – organically united in its sequences from beginning to ending, in meaningful interaction with the environment – is what is meant for experience to have felt continuity. Here again it is only necessary to recall that these are the continuities of experience as art, which need not be more fully elaborated at this point. The important matter is to remark the significance of the fact that art, in this generic sense, is not confined to studios and museums. *All* distinctive kinds of experience – sciences and arts, work, play, education, social action, love and friendship – admit of this process. It need not be limited to comparatively esoteric forms of conduct. As Dewey argues in Chapter I of *Art as Experience,* aesthetic and artistic quality are implicit in every experience; and in subsequent elaboration he points out that the only differences, as activity, between dominantly aesthetic experience, intellectual experience, and "practical" experience, when these "run their course to fulfillment," is in their materials and specific intent.[38] Whatever are men's favored kinds of activities, there is no inherent necessity in their being removed from that experience of growth in and with the world which Dewey calls art. In all such experiences, "things and events belonging to the world, physical and social, are transformed through the human context they enter, while the live creature is changed and developed through its intercourse with things previously external to it."[39]

---

[37] Chapter VII will treat the problem of the unification of desires at some length.

[38] See the discussion of science as art in Chapter V, especially pp. 214-6.

[39] *Art as Experience,* p. 246.

It is obviously desirable that experience possess both this integrity and continuity. It is an evident fact of experience, however, that persons find their activity – their life – splintered up into unrelated or conflicting desires: The satisfaction of one impulse has no meaning for the satisfaction of any other impulse; or it is satisfied at the expense of other impulses. Thought and action are not integrated; creative imagination is dormant. This life is a piecemeal, fragmentary affair; it is rarely a fully satisfying and cumulative sort of thing, but is constantly attended by frustration, conflict, and meaninglessness.

Even when one has the material resources to be always in the pursuit of individual pleasures, and even successfully so, there is a lack of that unity and continuity in experience which gives meaning to the whole, reinforces the value of every part, and imparts a sense of fulfillment and happy anticipation to every stage of experience. Experience of this latter kind is quite a different matter from the enjoyment of fugitive pleasures. There is "a difference in quality between an enduring satisfaction of the whole self and a transient satisfaction of some isolated element in the self."[40] Pleasure is the satisfaction of impulse. As the impulse is more powerful, the pleasure – if impulse is satisfied – is more intense. But pleasure becomes happiness as impulse becomes incorporated into meaningful activity. Such activity is happy in the fullest sense to the extent that it incorporates many impulses, energies, and habits – to the extent as well that it incorporates the meanings of past endeavor and carries them forward to new enlargements and fulfillments of human powers.

> The satisfaction of the whole self in any end and object is a very different *sort* of thing from the satisfaction of a single and independent appetite. It is doing no violence to ordinary speech to say that the former kind of satisfaction is denoted by the term "happiness," and the latter kind by the term "pleasure,". . .[41]

What has just been quoted suggests again that certain *kinds* of ends are conducive to the unification of experience. Somewhat will be said about this matter in connection with the discussion of shared experience. It is clear now, however, that a principal requisite to such experience is the selection of a manner of activ-

---

[40] *Ethics,* p. 212.

[41] *Ibid.*

ity which unites as many desires and values as possible. Insofar as human endeavors are of the sort that may incorporate always more and richer meanings, rather than shutting them out, the distinction between happiness and mere pleasure is manifest:

> A criterion can be given for marking off mere transient gratification from true happiness. The latter issues from objects which are enjoyable in themselves but which also reenforce and enlarge the other desires and tendencies which are sources of happiness; in a pleasure there is no such harmonizing and expanding tendency. There are powers within us whose exercise creates and strengthens objects that are enduring and stable while it excludes objects which occasion those merely transient gratifications that produce restlessness and peevishness. Harmony and readiness to expand into union with other values is a mark of happiness. Isolation and liability to conflict and interference are marks of those states which are exhausted in being pleasurable.[42]

Thus it is also clear that a crucial requirement of the moral situation is the search for and the examination of a variety of alternatives in order to determine the most unifying end-in-view. The first impulse won't do.[43]

Our usual experience, unfortunately, bears little resemblance to such unification. It is, rather, truncated and hence joyless and deprived of meanings:

> Only occasionally in the lives of many are the senses fraught with the sentiment that comes from deep realization of intrinsic meanings. We undergo sensations as mechanical stimuli or as irritated stimulations, without having a sense of the reality that is in them and behind them: in much of our experience our senses do not unite to tell a common and enlarged story.[44]

Although much of characteristically fragmented and truncated experience may be immediately a consequence of any variety of bad habits, the cause at bottom is in social institutions. Productive activities in all fields – economic, educational, intellectual – are radically divided into discrete parts, each of which is under-

---

[42] *Ibid.*, pp. 214-5. The balance of this chapter will include some additional remarks about the nature of inclusive values. Dewey is clearly referring to the sorts of activity that are both absorbing and fulfilling of many aims and that are at the same time shared with others. For example, one might find himself engrossed in a common struggle for social justice in a way that could never be provided by work on an assembly line, or by merely hedonistic pursuits.

[43] This is a point of important emphasis. It should also be obvious that no end can be evaluated without knowing what the alternative ends might be. I will return to this point in the next chapter.

[44] *Art as Experience*, p. 21.

taken by different persons; so that none may enjoy the fullness and continuity of experience. Activities are confined to very limited phases of action for any one individual; they are merely mechanical routine. Moreover, various social groups are rigidly divided; so the experience of each remains limited, gathering no nourishment from others, and becoming quickly effete:

> Compartmentalization of occupations and interests brings about separation of that mode of activity commonly called "practice" from insight, of imagination from executive doing, of significant purpose from work, of emotion from thought and doing. Each of these has, too, its own place in which it must abide. Those who write the anatomy of experience then suppose that these divisions inhere in the very constitution of human nature.[45]

Thus it is that experience is rarely art; and either transient pleasures, resignation, or otherworldliness is substituted for the good of activity.

3) The discussion of the nature and values of growth has indicated that the ideal limit of such activity is conduct as art. Shared experience is in any case a good in and of itself. But when the notion is sufficiently elaborated, it, too, is seen to receive its full measure of significance when it is integrated with the concept of art; and, conversely, growth as art also inherits its full meaning when it occurs in the context of shared experience.

Dewey says, "Shared experience is the greatest of human goods."[46] And the medium of shared experience is language, communication. Hence:

> Of all affairs, communication is the most wonderful. That all things should be able to pass from the plane of external pushing and pulling to that of revealing themselves to man, and thereby to themselves; and that the fruit of communication should be participation, sharing, is a wonder by the side of which transubstantiation pales.[47]

By "shared experience" Dewey evidently means, first, joint participation in the community of action – in the use and enjoyment of things; and, second, the sharing of the meanings of experience by communication.[48] Thus individuals are enabled to par-

---

[45] *Ibid.*, pp. 20-1.

[46] *Experience and Nature*, p. 202. This assertion could not, of course, be regarded as an unexceptionable law or generalization.

[47] *Ibid.*, p. 166.

[48] These two phases of shared experience are really inseparable, for, as we have seen in Chapter II, meanings originate and are learned in the community of action and enjoyment.

ticipate in the experience of others, for they literally share the meanings and qualities of a common world. Whatever the impediments to communication may be, they do not include – on Dewey's assumptions – some presumed inherent problem of entering into a private realm of consciousness; for the most personal and intimate meanings are derivative of the experience of the public world and are specifiable even to one's own self only with the language derivative of the community of social action. Thus as objects, events, and ideas are more or less funded with meanings, and one is in possession of more or less meanings, then also shared experience is more or less profound, intimate, and pervasive. In actuality, then, the more intimately one enters into the possible meanings of natural existence, the more one is enabled to share with another the hues, intensities, and significances of events found there; and when individuals share much experience together, events undergone in common – even apparently trivial events – become indefinitely rich in meaning. Dewey can only speak here with metaphors of the divine:

> In communication, such conjunction and contact as is characteristic of animals become endearments capable of infinite idealization; they become symbols of the very culmination of nature. That God is love is a more worthy idealization than that the divine is power. Since love at its best brings illumination and wisdom, this meaning is as worthy as that the divine is truth. Various phases of participation by one in another's joy, sorrows, sentiments and purposes, are distinguished by the scope and depth of the objects that are held in common, from a momentary caress to continued insight and loyalty.[49]

There is a third meaning to shared experience: It must be understood that it is a sincere, genuine, and intimate communication, in which there is mutual desire to understand, participate, and appreciate, and in which, as a consequence, basic interests and attitudes are affected. In Chapter II I spoke of the characteristic democratic habit of regarding others as a matter of course as coequals and approaching them with the presumption that their views are to be heard sympathetically and their values respected. In a moment of unguarded oversimplification, Dewey even says that democracy *is* shared experience.[50] Thus "shared experience"

---

[49] *Ibid.*, p. 202. Again, our modern culture is markedly deficient, for it fails to provide the conditions of shared experience. Groups are huge, impersonal, and highly structured; and the various groups of society are so rigidly compartmentalized that each shares only a limited range of experience and cannot communicate with others.

[50] Cf. *The Public and Its Problems*, pp. 148, 149.

does not describe the usual state of affairs: the impersonal and self-involved exchanges of information or the uttering of idle pleasantries that mark so much of human intercourse.

> The particular interactions that compose a human society include the give and take of participation, of a sharing that increases, that expands and deepens, the capacity and significance of the interacting factors.[51]

There can be no doubt that Dewey was thoroughly convinced that this basically democratic life must be the medium of the most profound and enduring human goods.[52] Shared experience, indeed, is not only an intrinsic good, but in one of its connotations being the very condition of language itself, it does in fact provide the very means by which men are able to convert their immediate and truncated contacts with nature into meanings; and thus events become significant and funded with values.

> Communication is uniquely instrumental and uniquely final. It is instrumental as liberating us from the otherwise overwhelming pressure of events and enabling us to live in a world of things that have meaning. It is final as sharing in the objects and arts precious to a community, a sharing whereby meanings are enhanced, deepened and solidified in the sense of communion.[53]

It was remarked in Chapter II that on Dewey's view the development of individuality was inevitably a social process: As a person interacts with numerous and varied groups and individuals, his personality develops in distinctive ways. In the present chapter the development of individuality has been further characterized as growth and art. Here it should be made clear that these are not separate processes. Growth as art is not something that describes individual conduct in isolation. On the contrary, the process of growth requires a social medium, and its values are greatly enhanced by being shared:

---

[51] *Individualism Old and New*, p. 85. Dewey adds to the remark quoted: "Conformity is a name for the absence of vital interplay; the arrest and benumbing of communication. As I have been trying to say, it is the artificial substitute used to hold men together in lack of associations that are incorporated into inner dispositions of thought and desire. . . . Our sociability is largely an effort to find substitutes for that normal consciousness of connection and union that proceeds from being a sustained and sustaining member of a social whole" (pp. 86-8).

[52] Professor Randall has characterized Dewey's position as "The Religion of Shared Experience" (in *The Philosopher of the Common Man*, pp. 106-45).

[53] *Experience and Nature*, pp. 204-5.

> The *kind* of self which is formed through action which is faithful to relations with others will be a fuller and broader self than one which is cultivated in isolation from or in opposition to the purposes and needs of others. . . . The kind of self which results from generous breadth of interest may be said alone to constitute a development and fulfillment of self, while the other way of life stunts and starves selfhood by cutting it off from the connections necessary to its growth.[54]

The good of activity and the good of shared experience are, at best, combined. One's activities will not be world-historical in import, but as immediately implicated with the good of those with whom he has intimate ties, they will have a value which is enhanced by the richness of the ties themselves. And this is no small matter. When we are aware that the good of activity occurs in the context of shared experience, we can appreciate Dewey's almost rhapsodic claims:

> That happiness which is full of content and peace is found only in enduring ties with others, which reach to such depths that they go below the surface of conscious experience to form its undisturbed foundation. No one knows how much of the frothy excitement of life, of mania for motion, of fretful discontent, of need for artificial stimulation, is the expression of frantic search for something to fill the void caused by the loosening of the bonds which hold persons together in immediate community of experience. If there is anything in human psychology to be counted upon, it may be urged that when man is satiated with restless seeking for the remote which yields no enduring satisfaction, the human spirit will return to seek calm and order within itself. This, we repeat, can be found only in the vital, steady, and deep relationships which are present only in an immediate community.[55]

> And when the emotional force, the mystic force one might say, of communication, of the miracle of shared life and shared experience is spontaneously felt, the hardness and crudeness of contemporary life will be bathed in the light that never was on land or sea.[56]

Grief, pain, and frustration are inevitable in any life, and especially when one is sensitive to the qualities of existence; but even so, one may commit his life in such a way that his experience is

---

[54] *Ethics,* p. 335. Even when growth proceeds in temporary isolation, its success is predicated on the accomplishments of social intelligence. A person developing his skills on a musical instrument could not advance far without availing himself in some way of the relevant achievements of other musicians.

[55] *The Public and Its Problems,* p. 214.

[56] *Reconstruction in Philosophy,* p. 211. See also the quotation on pp. 121-2 from *Human Nature and Conduct,* pp. 330-2, where Dewey describes the community as the principal object of religious devotion.

fundamentally informed with the values which he serves.

> Happiness is fundamental in morals only because happiness is not something to be sought for, but is something now attained, even in the midst of pain and trouble, whenever recognition of our ties with nature and with fellow-men releases and informs our action.[57]

The discussion of growth within shared experience suggests a final and highly signficant point about the good; namely, that there is no necessary dichotomy of what is good for the individual and what is good for the social group. Indeed, on Dewey's assumptions what is best for the individual are precisely those values which he can share with others. Dewey has a great deal to say in defense of this position, which runs counter to the assumptions of classical liberalism, as well as many religious and popular views, and even some presumably scientific views.

Those who assert the essential conflict of individual and social goods seem to do so on various grounds: They entertain a theory which stipulates overwhelming antisocial drives as an original endowment of human nature; they impute to all human beings the same selfish motives which have come to animate themselves; they are wedded to some form of ego psychology; or they accept as the universal and invariable traits of man in society those which they observe in particularly disrupted and trying circumstances. (Of course there are connections between these sources of theory.) None of these positions, despite their popularity, can remain intact under the pressure of rigorous experimental examination. (Indeed, they can't be reconciled with ordinary unbiased experience.)

Here I can only indicate some of Dewey's main points of attack on such positions. These positions must rely in some way on assumptions about the independent and autonomous character of human nature, whether regarded as rational egoistic will, fixed instincts, or original sin. Those theories, for example, emanating from some form of ego psychology entertained the notion of a substantial self of some kind which performed acts of willing, knowing, etc. Accordingly, all acts were presumed to be *in behalf* of this self. Dewey regarded such views as clear instances of converting an eventual function into an antecedently existing

---

[57] *Human Nature and Conduct,* p. 265.

substance; and for them he substituted his wholly functional account of human nature in nature.[58] Thus, on Dewey's view, the self is *identified* with interest (or composites of interests, habits); that is, the self *is* interest. Furthermore (and this is essential) interest is not to be understood as a private and unrelated event. Rather, interest implies interaction; interest is always interest *in* something – for the most part in objective things in the world. Strictly speaking, selfishness could not be *self*-interest, for there *is* no self underlying interest. A so-called self-centered or selfish person is one who pursues values which exclude the welfare of other persons; so the meaningful question is whether interests are exclusive or inclusive. Selfishness does not consist in *having* interests, but in the particular nature of interests.

> The fallacy consists in transforming the (truistic) fact of acting *as* a self into the fiction of acting always *for* self. Every act, truistically again, tends to a certain fulfillment or satisfaction of some habit which is an undoubted element in the structure of character. Each satisfaction is qualitatively what it is because of the disposition fulfilled in the object attained, treachery or loyalty, mercy or cruelty. But theory comes in and blankets the tremendous diversity in the quality of the satisfactions which are experienced by pointing out that they are all satisfactions. The harm done is then completed by transforming this artificial unity of result into an original love of satisfaction as the force that generates all acts alike. . . . In reality the more we concretely dwell upon the common fact of fulfillment, the more we realize the difference in kinds of selves fulfilled.[59]
>
> In short, the essence of the whole distinction between selfishness and unselfishness lies in what sort of object the self is interested.[60]

Upon examination, it is obvious that a great deal of behavior is concerned with wholly overt interests:

> Psychologically speaking, our native impulses are neither egoistic nor altruistic; that is, they are not actuated by *conscious* regard for either one's own good or that of others. They are rather direct responses to situations. . . . The scholar, artist, physician, engineer, carries on the great part of his work without consciously asking himself whether his work is going to benefit himself or some one else. He is interested in the *work* itself;. . . .[61]

---

[58] See Chapter II for the main outlines of Dewey's functional analysis of human nature in nature. What is said in the present text about some of the limitations of supposing a substantial ego could be readily applied to theories postulating any sort of entity which determines conduct in a fixed, encapsulated, and unalterable way.

[59] *Ibid.*, pp. 136-7.

[60] *Ethics*, p. 328.

[61] *Ibid.*, pp. 324, 330.

It is a clear lesson of experience, moreover, that persons are often most interested in those aims which are inclusive of entire groups. Regardless of what the scientific explanation for the phenomenon might be, it seems that individuals are not only capable of genuinely cooperative living, but in many instances actually cherish it. The older individualism has just not been sufficiently attentive to experience:

> For every existence in addition to its qualitative and intrinsic boundaries has affinities and active outreachings for connection and intimate union. It is an energy of attraction, expansion and supplementation. The ties and bonds of associated life are spontaneous uncalculated manifestations of this phase of human selfhood, as the union of hydrogen and oxygen is natural and unpremeditated. Sociability, communication are just as immediate traits of the concrete individual as is the privacy of the closet of consciousness.[62]

Hostile, hateful individuals are, of course, common (but we rarely find them bathed in happiness). There is, however, no inherent necessity in human nature for this. Theories cannot explain away the evident fact that there are individuals who are at the same time kind, benevolent, and happy.

In the present context, the import of Dewey's position is this: There is no justification for assuming a necessary antithesis of individual and social values; individuals are capable of, and exhibit in various ways, a spontaneous regard for the fulfillment of ends which are shared with others. Dewey stresses, accordingly, "the inclusive nature of social interest" (especially pp. 331-6 in the *Ethics*). By this he means that one's own good and the good of others is not a dualism, but both are included in the good of those associations in which self and others are jointly implicated. (Here it is pertinent to be reminded of the discussion just a few pages back: The process of growth thrives especially on the cultivation of those habits which bring us into harmony with others.)

If shared experience is of such consummate value, then it is clear that inclusive social interests are not a sacrifice of what is ideally best for the individual. It is a commonly held view that it would be very nice if only we could abondon ourselves to every impulse. This view is foolish. Its practice would frequently interfere with the much more precious values of shared experience; and it would also forbid the development of distinctive human

---

[62] *Experience and Nature*, pp. 243-4.

excellences, for growth and consummatory experience are only possible when impulse is converted by intelligence into effective and integrated power.[63] In sum, unrestrained gratification of impulse would prevent the realization of the most profound and enduring human goods. Hence it is that the individual's concern with inclusive social values is not the necessary, but lamentable compromise with society assumed by such as Hobbes and Freud.

> The final happiness of an individual resides in the supremacy of certain interests in the make-up of character; namely, alert, sincere, enduring interests in the objects in which all can share. It is found in such interests rather than in the accomplishment of definite external results because this kind of happiness alone is not at the mercy of circumstances. No amount of outer obstacles can destroy the happiness that comes from lively and ever-renewed interest in others and in the conditions and objects which promote their development.[64]

There is no inherent obstacle in nature to individuals' cultivating a character of this sort; and because there is no inherent necessity of sacrificing personal happiness to the general happiness, men should try to perceive their common aims, endeavoring always to develop values which are inclusive and expanding. In this connection, I will repeat a part of what was quoted on p. 258 above: "Harmony and readiness to expand into union with other values is a mark of happiness. Isolation and liability to conflict and interference are marks of those states which are exhausted in being pleasurable."[65]

3. Nature and Human Ideals

The third general subject to be considered in connection with Dewey's account of the good is that of the nature and function of ideals. They are not constituent of antecedent reality, but are eventual functions:

---

[63] Freud's assumptions that man is inherently and intensely antisocial and that an individual's real good lies in the immediate satisfaction of every impulse, indicate that he badly misunderstood the possibilities of human nature.

[64] *Ethics,* pp. 335-6.

[65] Although it is true that there is no necessary conflict between the good of the individual and the good of others, it is nevertheless a constant feature of experience that conflicts do occur and need some means of settlement. Dewey is hardly unaware of the importance of this point. Some basic issues concerning the adjudication of competing claims will be examined in the next chapter. Neither is Dewey unaware that human clash takes place on a grand and intense scale; but he has no compulsion to interpret this as evidence of original sin, religious or secular.

> Nature, if I may use the locution, is idealizable. It lends itself to operations by which it is perfected. The process is not a passive one. Rather nature gives, not always freely but in response to search, means and material by which the values we judge to have supreme quality may be embodied in existence.[66]

Men do possess, of course, remote ideals of perfection or bliss, in which – so they presume – nature has no efficacy. Such ideas are instances of fixed ends, with all their debilitating characteristics. As such, they fail to give significance to our actual existence and are to be sharply contrasted to a wholly different kind of ideal:

> The trouble with ideals of remote "perfection" is that they tend to make us negligent of the significance of the special situations in which we have to act; they are thought of as trivial in comparison with the ideal of perfection. The genuine ideal, on the contrary, is the sense that each of these special situations brings with it its own inexhaustible meaning, that its value reaches far beyond its direct local existence.[67]

The kind of ideal that provides "inexhaustible meaning" takes in many ways a familiar form: freedom, justice, truth, peace, and so on. But these ideals are not to be regarded as remote abstractions. Rather, they should be articulated specifically in reference to actual historical circumstances. They represent the best possibilities of the present as we actually find it, and they are contrived for the sake of present action. (The notion of world peace, for example, must remain an ineffectual ideal until it is characterized in terms of existing realities and instrumentalities.) When the realities of present circumstance – with all its impediments, yearnings, powers, and possibilities – are appraised, the imagination projects a vision of the best that could come from these realities:

> What I have tried to show is that the ideal itself has its roots in natural conditions; it emerges when the imagination idealizes existence by laying hold of the possibilities offered to thought and action. . . . The idealizing imagination seizes upon the most precious things found in the climacteric moments of experience and projects them. . . .
>
> The aims and ideals that move us are generated through imagination. But they are not made out of imaginary stuff. They are made out of the hard stuff of the world of physical and social experience.[68]

---

66 *The Quest for Certainty*, p. 302.

67 *Ethics*, p. 301.

68 *A Common Faith*, pp. 48-9.

Thus, of course, human ideals are subject to refinement and change, and properly so: Our knowledge of man and nature enlarges and improves; and the specific conditions and possibilities of life undergo continuous change. Thus the people of city-state Greece, medieval Europe, eighteenth-century agrarian America, and twentieth-century urban, industrial, nuclear-armed nations must of necessity envision their aims and ideals in terms of radically different social orders and methods.

Ideal ends, as Dewey conceives them, have an inclusive nature. There are two senses in which this is so: 1) These ideals should be elaborated in such a way as to be inclusive of the values of as many actual human beings as possible. 2) For any individual, they embody as many of his own values as possible. As we have just seen above, these two traits can be united. Ideals in this sense evoke what Dewey calls the religious quality of experience:

> Any activity pursued in behalf of an ideal end against obstacles and in spite of threats of personal loss because of conviction of its general and enduring value is religious in quality.[69]

And, accordingly, he speaks of "the unification of the self through allegiance to inclusive ideal ends, which imagination presents to us and to which the human will responds as worthy of controlling our desires and choices."[70] By this unification Dewey means that the ideal end is such that it incorporates – at best – all the interests and aspirations that an individual possesses. Thus his devotion to it is devotion to that which if it came into being would be a realization and unification of all one's values. Hence service to it enlists one's energies, inspires dedication, quickens and vivifies action, and enriches it with meanings.

Such ideal ends are like the ends-in-view discriminated in problematic situations. They are based on present needs and aspirations, and they give meaning to present effort. Moreover, their achievement is not an end in itself; but their evident function is to liberate human endeavor in such a way that life-experience can assume its most intrinsically valuable form: conduct as art. Such ideals as truth, freedom, social justice, democracy, in-

---

[69] *Ibid.*, p. 27.

[70] *Ibid.*, p. 33.

ternational harmony, the eradication of poverty, etc., are not absolute ends. Rather, their value lies precisely in that they constitute in a general way the *conditions* for inherently meaningful and enriched life-activity. Freedom, for example, comes to constitute an ideal because individuals find their aims and actions frustrated in so many ways. Freedom is a necessary condition for the institution or reinstatement of desired kinds of activity. Thus it is an ideal precisely because of its crucially instrumental character. The same kind of analysis is applicable to other ideals: They are not, for Dewey, states of ultimate repose and static perfection, but they are efficacious in promoting the good of activity.

Yet such ideal ends seem to differ from ends-in-view in that they do not admit of much possibility of anything like total realization. Being so grand and inclusive, action tends to their fulfillment only by the accomplishment of literally countless tasks, and the cooperation of so many individuals and forces is required for their achievement. It would be a mistake, however, to regard these ends, as such, as particular acts for accomplishment. In conduct, the end-in-view is always something attainable by action in the situation; while an ideal end indicates the general direction of a great number of individual actions and informs each of them with a wealth of meaning. This meaning provides additional continuity from situation to situation in the lives of individuals. Just because of the inclusive character of ideal ends, they inform particular situations with "inexhaustible meaning," and they have the power to unify and harmonize the endeavors of many otherwise unrelated individuals.

Finally, Dewey's formulation of the nature of inclusive ideal ends is not in conflict with his stress on commitment to the on-going remaking of events. As just indicated, the ideal end characterizes the direction in which events are to be transformed by shared effort; but actual human energies are best expended by devotion to the possibilities at hand. It would be misguided to regard individual efforts as specifically directed to the achievement of the ideal, as such. As Dewey said, it is the next step that lies within our power; and each step may have its own distinctive consummation. The ideal end unites and gives added meaning to these efforts. Such ends are obviously efficacious; they have enlisted the sympathy and devotion of many thousands of persons; and they embody so many ends of such intense value that efforts in their behalf are incalculably rich with meaning. Service to these ideals may constitute a common faith:

> The ideal ends to which we attach our faith are not shadowy and wavering. They assume concrete form in our understanding of our relations to one another and the values contained in these relations. We who now live are parts of a humanity that extends into the remote past, a humanity that has interacted with nature. The things in civilization we most prize are not of ourselves. They exist by grace of the doings and sufferings of the continuous human community in which we are a link. Ours is the responsibility of conserving, transmitting, rectifying and expanding the heritage of values we have received that those who come after us may receive it more solid and secure, more widely accessible and more generously shared than we have received it. Here are all the elements for a religious faith that shall not be confined to sect, class, or race.[71]

In the context of the present study, the most concrete example of an inclusive ideal end is Dewey's own ideal of the democratic community. Consider what the notion of democratic community means to Dewey: It incorporates a basic philosophy of man and nature, a theory of human nature, of value and value formation, of the good life; theories about individual and society, social control, social process, change, and conflict; it includes Dewey's conclusions regarding the usefulness of various institutions and all his beliefs about the nature of needed reforms. His ideal includes assumptions about the nature and function of art and science and economics and – more generally – of social intelligence in the lives of all. His notion of democracy is that of a state of affairs in which the best of human values can find their fulfillment; it is at the same time one whose reality would embody the values dear to Dewey himself. Thus it is that "democratic community" is a notion possessed of extremely abundant and concrete significance to Dewey himself. It evoked a "religious" feeling precisely because he was so keenly aware of so much that is entailed by genuine democracy, and because the circumstances entailed by democratic life were intrinsically valuable to him.

---

[71] *Ibid.*, p. 87. Dewey's remark that humanity has interacted with nature is not a lapse into truisms or irrelevancy; he intends to indicate that our continuities are not *just* with humanity.

Such an ideal cannot be the product of a moment's inspiration or a neatly packaged revelation of some kind; for it is clear that it is conceived and elaborated only with the use of very extensive knowledge and sustained efforts of intelligence. Thus, also, to appreciate the idea of a democratic community requires knowledge and intelligence. To most people the idea is abstract and vacuous and hence of little value. It acquires the sort of prodigious meaning it had for Dewey only when it becomes fully elaborated. This is a powerful ideal precisely because it has been the subject of intelligent formation and criticism. It does not acquire its strength by stimulating blind emotion.

The statement of Dewey's ideal is occasion to introduce a final consideration about ideals. Dewey repeatedly insists that the value of an ideal does not consist in its embodiment in antecedent Being; rather, it consists in the consequences its realization would bring and in the dedication, emotion, and action which its idea evokes.

> It is admitted that the objects of religion are ideal in contrast with our present state. What would be lost if it were also admitted that they have authoritative claim upon conduct just because they are ideal? The assumption that these objects of religion exist already in some realm of Being seems to add nothing to their force, while it weakens their claim over us as ideals, in so far as it bases that claim upon matters that are intellectually dubious. . . . The reality of ideal ends as ideals is vouched for by their undeniable power in action. An ideal is not an illusion because imagination is the organ through which it is apprehended. For *all* possibilities reach us through the imagination. In a definite sense the only meaning that can be assigned the term "imagination" is that things unrealized in fact come home to us and have power to stir us. The unification effected through imagination is not fanciful, for it is the reflex of the unification of practical and emotional attitudes. The unity signifies not a single Being, but the unity of loyalty and effort evoked by the fact that many ends are one in the power of their ideal, or imaginative, quality to stir and hold us.[72]

Our religious and otherwise dualistic traditions have persistently held, however, that what gives an ideal its value is the sanction, in some sense, of Being-itself, or its embodiment in Being-itself. On examination, such assumptions turn out to be outrageously misguided. To take a recent example: Paul Tillich assumes that what gives value to a person's "ultimate concern" is that it is rooted in (or grasped by) the Ground of Being, or

---

[72] *Ibid.*, pp. 41, 43.

Being-itself (God, the Absolute, the Ultimate, etc.). However secular and autonomous an ultimate concern may *seem* to be, it is ultimate only because it participates in the Ground of Being.[73] The very existence of any case of anyone being in a condition of ultimate concern for anything presupposes, Tillich insists, the "true" ultimate in which it is grounded. Such "grounding" is precisely what makes the concern ultimate. And without this true ultimate, moreover, the merely finite world is a scene of pure despair and unmitigated anxiety; its presumed value withers to nothingness; it is inherently meaningless.[74]

The "concrete content" of any genuinely ultimate concern symbolizes man's relation to the Absolute, the true Ultimate; it represents "divine-human encounters." The finite object of ultimate concern is a symbol for the infinite object of ultimate concern. Tillich is committed to the position that the "ultimate concern" for, say, democracy gets its value from the Ground of Being, *and not from the values which are realized in democratic life.* Who is the nihilist?

Moreover, if the idea of a democratic community is regarded as a symbol of ultimate concern, just what does it symbolize? According to Tillich, it symbolizes God, or man's encounter with God. Yet Tillich also says that we can have no empirical know-

---

[73] This is a sustained theme in Tillich's writings. "Scientists, artists, moralists showed clearly that they also were ultimately concerned. Their concern expressed itself even in those creations in which they wanted most radically to deny religion. A keen analysis of most philosophical, scientific and ethical systems shows how much ultimate concern is present in them, even if they are leading in the fight against what they call religion." Hence, on Tillich's analysis, "Where there is ultimate concern, God can be denied only in the name of God." (Paul Tillich, *Dynamics of Faith* [New York and Evanston: Harper & Row, n.d.], pp. 40, 45.)

[74] *Dynamics of Faith,* especially the first three chapters, provides a general statement of most of the themes raised here. *The Courage to Be* (New Haven: Yale University Press, 1952) takes as a crucial, fundamental, and wholly explicit assumption the inherent and irremediable meaninglessness of existence apart from Being-itself. And in *The Protestant Era* he says, "The human soul cannot maintain itself without the vertical line, the knowledge of an eternal meaning, however this may be expressed in mythological or theological terms . . . . If we no longer understand the words of the psalmist, that the loss of body and life and of earth and heaven cannot deprive him of the ultimate meaning of his life – or if we no longer feel what the poet means when he says that all our running, all our striving, is eternal rest in God the Lord – if all this has become strange and unreal to us, then we have lost the power of facing reality without cynicism and despair." (*The Protestant Era* [Abridged Edition], trans. James Luther Adams [Chicago: The University of Chicago Press, 1957], pp. 187-8.)

ledge of the Ground of Being.[75] Therefore, the idea of a democratic community, insofar as it is a religious symbol, symbolizes nothing that can be stated in experimentally meaningful language: It has no meaning in experience, that is, no meaning at all.

The contrast between Dewey's position and the one to which Tillich is committed is staggering. Where Dewey's ideal is so abundant in concrete and specifiable meanings, Tillich's is literally empty. The Ground of Being is a notion both vain and vacuous. And yet Tillich's ideal is supposed to provide us with true religious inspiration, while Dewey is a mere naturalist! What Dewey said of Spencer could readily be applied to Tillich:

> Merely because Spencer labeled his unknowable energy "God," this faded piece of metaphysical goods was greeted as an important and grateful concession to the reality of the spiritual realm. Were it not for the deep hold of the habit of seeking justification for ideal values in the remote and transcendent, surely this reference of them to an unknowable absolute would be despised by comparison with the demonstrations of experience that knowable energies are daily generating about us precious values.[76]

Ideals as Dewey characterizes them are invested with values which he calls religious. It is clear, however (as Dewey intended), that these are values which mark the extent to which human experience admits of enrichment by means of its own instrumentalities. This is not to signify the poverty of experience, but to observe its wonderful potentialities.

Dewey's scorn for remote and transcendent ends has been recorded in these pages in various places. Further comment on this scorn is appropriate. As he again and again points out, there are great potentialities for value – for love and delight and enduring meaning – embodied in the life around us. Friendship, arts, growth, experience of continuities with man and nature, afford profound happiness. There is great tragedy in turning from nature and experience in a wholesale way. It is simply not the case that occupation with the possibilities, fulfillments, and meanings of experience is a meager substitute for those who have lost faith

---

[75] "That which is the true ultimate transcends the realm of finite reality infinitely. Therefore, no finite reality can express it directly and properly. . . . [Myth] puts the stories of the gods into the framework of time and space although it belongs to the nature of the ultimate to be beyond time and space." (Tillich, *Dynamics of Faith*, pp. 44, 49.)

[76] *The Influence of Darwin on Philosophy*, p. 16.

in God. Rather, concern with the supernatural is precisely one of the principal human involvements to be abandoned if one is to be liberated to the life that comes only from the vital and unambiguous engagement of human energies and intelligence with the tasks, resources, and meanings of natural existence. To be wholly unconcerned with supernatural values is an emancipation. It is to have a concern with natural values, whose deficiencies are not inherent and in kind; there is no lack of this sort. Rather, the demand is for a fuller and more significant, a less precarious and less ambiguous, good. With some intimation of value of this sort, God seems remote indeed. Dewey's "theology," it is clear, is the study – in all its implications with nature – of the democratic community.

> Poetry, art, religion are precious things. They cannot be maintained by lingering in the past and futilely wishing to restore what the movement of events in science, industry and politics has destroyed. They are an out-flowering of thought and desires that unconsciously converge into a disposition of imagination as a result of thousands and thousands of daily episodes and contact. They cannot be willed into existence or coerced into being. . . . But while it is impossible to retain and recover by deliberate volition old sources of religion and art that have been discredited, it is possible to expedite the development of the vital sources of a religion and art that are yet to be. Not indeed by action directly aimed at their production, but by substituting faith in the active tendencies of the day for dread and dislike of them, and by the courage to follow whither social and scientific changes direct us. We are weak today in ideal matters because intelligence is divorced from aspiration. The bare force of circumstance compels us onwards in the daily detail of our beliefs and acts, but our deeper thoughts and desires turn backwards. When philosophy shall have co-operated with the course of events and made clear and coherent the meaning of the daily detail, science and emotion will interpenetrate, practice and imagination will embrace. Poetry and religious feeling will be the unforced flowers of life.[77]

---

[77] *Reconstruction in Philosophy,* pp. 212-3. Dewey insisted that religious feeling must be factitious and highly ambiguous so long as it seeks its traditional objects. Religious feeling must be emancipated from its inherited baggage. Remarkably, philosophical reflection on religion today tends to be very reactionary; and the so-called radical theologians, for all their foolishness, have nevertheless produced far more imaginative and useful ideas about religion than have current philosophers.

A rather interesting book on Dewey as a moral philosopher has been written by a contemporary Roman Catholic thinker: *John Dewey and Self-Realization,* by Robert J. Roth, S.J. (Englewood Cliffs, N.J.: Prentice-Hall, Inc., 1962). The volume makes a number of valuable observations and sets forth some suggestive hypotheses. I should say, however, that what Roth distinguishes as Dewey's controlling assumptions, and his understanding of Dewey's key concepts, are at variance with the analyses I have presented in this book. What is noteworthy in the present context is that the study of Dewey has enforced upon the attention of a Roman Catholic thinker that human pursuit of the good life must take nature fundamentally into account.

I will conclude by recapitulating what Dewey has undertaken: So like the Greeks, he insists on examining man in connection with the actual context of his existence. Man – in all his distinctive characteristics – must be understood as a being who is what he is and aspires to what he aspires precisely because of these connections. Nature and man are of such character that the powers of both, when they are rightly perceived, can be brought to work in concert. This is possible only *because* man is a creature of nature, Hence the good of man does not lie beyond or apart from nature, but in activity *with* nature.

Again much like Plato and Aristotle, Dewey's ideal of human nature is of an individuality which has developed and is continually developing and enlarging distinctive powers and finds intrinsic happiness in their growth and exercise. At its best, human nature in all its facets is an integrated, harmonious, concerted whole, acting with an environment both suffused with meanings and efficacious in conduct. Perhaps more emphatically than the Greeks, however, Dewey values the context of shared experience with which human nature functions and grows; and more explicitly than the Greeks, Dewey repeatedly draws attention to the fact that this integration and enlargement of experience is not a concert of human nature simply, but of man *and* nature. It is *nature* unified and fructified that is human good; and if human endeavors leave nature out of account, they must be blind, halting, ill-fated, or merely compensatory. It is clear, then, that the focal concept of Dewey's naturalistic metaphysics is that of art; and the good of man is in the cumulative transforming of nature into art in the context of shared experience.

Intelligence is above all required to achieve this ideal. Thus our final topic is provided.

CHAPTER VII

Intelligence and Value

> Fidelity to the nature to which we belong, as parts however weak, demands that we cherish our desires and ideals till we have converted them into intelligence, revised them in terms of the ways and means which nature makes possible.[1]

Dewey is widely known for his advocacy of intelligence in the moral life. Unfortunately, this knowledge rarely extends beyond a few cliches, which are usually erroneous at that. Indeed, the role of intelligence has never been examined specifically in the context of Dewey's theory of nature, where, however, its full significance can be most readily displayed. Only by an explicit awareness of the status of man and value in nature can Dewey's considerations of method in moral reasoning be adequately appreciated. Accordingly, this concluding chapter will exhibit Dewey's conclusions against the background of his fundamental assumptions about nature. There will be three main topics in this chapter: 1) intelligence and nature, 2) experimental methods of moral deliberation, and 3) ethics, science, and democracy.

1. Intelligence and Nature

My purpose here is not to provide an account of intelligence as a function of nature. My aim is in part less ambitious. Except for a few preliminary remarks, the continuity of intelligence and nature will be taken for granted; and the subsequent focus of

---

[1] *Experience and Nature,* p. 420.

attention will be the implications of that continuity for understanding and pursuing the moral life.

There seems to be a persistent desire in intellectuals of all sorts to think of human nature in terms of "levels" or "layers." That is, there is often assumed a substructure of exclusively biological instincts covered by a "veneer" of intelligence or reason, which is somehow able to function independently of biological and environmental conditions. It is usually held that such veneer is entitled to some kind of authority over the passions; or at any rate it is thought that whether or not such authority in fact exists, it would be desirable if reason *could* exert power over the instinctual forces. It is frequently held that such veneer is extremely thin and weak, unable to exercise anything but the most pitiful control, always losing in struggle with the passions for domination of conduct (perhaps, indeed, being really nothing but a veil which functions only to disguise or conceal the "true" nature of human beings).

Such familiar notions are given a great deal of credence by the obviously violent and irrational character of much of human behavior. Yet, if Dewey's basic position is correct, these views are dangerously misleading. I will summarize Dewey's position, assuming conclusions from preceding chapters and providing additional detail as appropriate.

As Dewey sees the matter, the difference between man and animals is not in a "veneer of reason." It lies in the fact that man lives in an environment vastly more complex and vastly more extended in space and time than that of any animal; and therefore the biological functions of human nature interact with the environment in ways which do not and cannot occur in mere animals.

> Experience is the result, the sign, and the reward of that interaction of organism and environment which, when it is carried to the full, is a transformation of interaction into participation and communication. . . . Full recognition, therefore, of the continuity of the organs, needs and basic impulses of the human creature with his animal forbears, implies no necessary reduction of man to the level of the brutes. On the contrary, it makes possible the drawing of a ground-plan of human experience upon which is erected the superstructure of man's marvelous and distinguishing experience. What is distinctive in man makes it possible for him . . . to carry to new and unprecedented heights that unity of sense and im-

> pulse, of brain and eye and ear, that is exemplified in animal life, saturating it with the conscious meanings derived from communication and deliberate expression.[2]

The human environment is complicated and extended because experience develops very complex meanings, and men are able to respond to events as meaningful.[3] An environment is complex and extended because events in it are meaningful. To function in such an environment is to have "mind," and to function successfully is to be intelligent.

What is called intelligence in human nature arises only because of the recurrence of precarious events in nature and hence of problematic situations. Man and nature come to function intelligently only when the on-going course of activity is impeded. "Intelligence" describes the behavior involved in attempting to solve the difficulties of the problematic situation. Thus, for present purposes, it can be said that "intelligence" describes those operations by which the meanings of the events of the environment are discovered, developed, manipulated, and tested. (Intelligence, of course, implies distinctive capacities in the organism as well as in the environment.) Clearly, these operations admit of great differences in kind and effectiveness. This effectiveness is the very measure of intelligence. It is precisely in the degree of success in resolving problematic situations that intelligence finds its test. It may be that the problem is one of being lost in the woods, or an extremely sophisticated one like inquiring into the nature of the transmission of light. Intelligence is effective when one finds his way back to camp and when one has a warranted theory of the propogation of light.

We must be reminded that intelligence is not the work of mental substance. It is, rather, the consequence of those very complex interactions from which meanings emerge and become

---

[2] *Art as Experience*, pp. 22-3. The "ground-plan" referred to in the quotation is not that ground-map of experience which refers to the traits of nature. It is simply the indication that the traits of human experience are the consequence of interaction of the biological organism and the environment. This interaction is the foundation for all human experience. The generic traits of experience are derivative of this interaction.

[3] We have seen that it is language which makes this complication and extension of the environment possible; and we have seen that language is the consequence of the effort to establish a community of social action.

manipulable. It is a biological-social emergent. Thus intelligence is not something that works independently of either the other functions of human nature or the environment. Rather, many processes conspire to produce intelligence. Literally, intelligence is function, not substance: man functions intelligently with and in nature.

It is clear that we can speak of intelligence as joint powers of man and nature. When these powers come to be systematically employed in certain ways, we can speak also of methods of intelligence. The most effective method of intelligence is one found only in many halting trials in which men compare results achieved with original aims. Men thus develop more or less effective methods of intelligence, and it is with these methods that they can deal inventively, systematically, and reliably with their environment. By developing and manipulating meanings accurately, man is able to bring remote objects of desire and interest into present imagination. Events much removed in space and time are thus immediately implicated in behavior.

In order to understand the relation between intelligence and our "passional" nature, or desire, some remarks must be made about the nature of desire. Desires, Dewey insists, have an ideational component; they are consciously implicated with an environment, real or imagined. That is, in Dewey's language, "desire" (or aversion) is always desire *for* something (or *to* something); there is some object or goal in view, and desire implies some way of acting with a situation.

> In truth, attitudes, dispositions and their kin, while capable of being distinguished and made concrete intellectual objects, are never separate existences. They are always *of, from, toward,* situations and things. . . . Except as ways of seeking, turning from, appropriating, treating things, they have no existence nor significance.[4]

Desire is distinguished from vital impulse. The latter, which is a necessary condition of desire, is exclusively biological. In *Theory*

---

[4] *Experience and Nature,* p. 238. And in the same vein, referring to emotions: "For emotion in its ordinary sense is something called out *by* objects, physical and personal; it is response *to* an objective situation. It is not something existing somewhere by itself which then employs material through which to express itself. Emotion is an indication of intimate participation, in a more or less excited way in some scene of nature or life; it is, so to speak, an attitude or disposition which is a function of objective things." (*Ibid.*, p. 390.)

of Valuation Dewey even says that desire implies not only a consciously entertained object, but a means to that object as well:

> Vital impulses are doubtless conditions *sine qua non* for the existence of desires and interests. But the latter include foreseen consequences along with ideas in the form of signs of the measures (involving expenditure of energy) required to bring the ends into existence.[5]

We need not be delayed by this conceptual imprecision: Certainly there is a difference between merely physiological functioning and a drive for some specific object. Certain physiological events must attend the desire for food, or water, or higher learning; but the desire for food, or water, or higher learning is clearly not the same thing as the mere physiological events. There is a sense in which, perhaps, no precise division between vital impulse and desire can be made, for the objects implicated in desire may be only vaguely conceived or half-consciously imagined. But the important fact to be recognized is that behavior does admit of these differences, and insofar as it involves specific goals (insofar as desire has an ideational component), it become subject to intelligent control. That is, intelligence may determine the ideational content of desire. It is important to consider the nature of this process.

The meaning of an object of desire can be enlarged and reconstituted; and as the meaning changes, so does the desire. Such results are effected both by means of inquiry and by formulation of novel hypotheses for action. By inquiry, one learns the meaning of an object. But one can also conceive of acting with an object in a variety of unexampled ways; in this manner he conceives of new meanings for the object, and these can become actual when the appropriate actions are undertaken.[6] As the meaning that an object or act has for an individual is enlarged or reconstituted, so also is the desire or aversion which the object stimulates reconstituted. Everyone has had the experience of starting gleefully on a course of conduct and subsequently

---

[5] *Theory of Valuation,* p. 18.

[6] Undertaking the proposed action is, of course, the only way of testing the validity of such hypotheses. The next section of this chapter will give these procedures somewhat closer attention.

shrinking from it when its fuller meaning became apparent. Similarly, everyone has had the experience of contriving valuable uses for otherwise indifferent objects. In both cases, formerly isolated events are seen to be implicated in a larger context. One learns to experience an event as part of a related *system* of events, both actual and potential; and thus its meaning is changed. Its meaning is that of the event as it is related to further events, or as it could be related contingent upon certain actions. In either case, the meaning is an organic whole. One now responds to the event in its new meaning; the event *as meaningful* stimulates a distinctive desire or aversion. Thus, as one investigates the implications of intended actions, his attitude towards the actions will change in some measure. One may desire to bite into an apple, but if he learns the apple is poisoned, his desire will change to aversion. If he thinks of giving the apple to a hungry child, his desire will change in still another way. In brief, the desire changes as the meaning of the apple is changed.

Consider a more complicated example: the occasion of falling into disagreement with others. Initially, one might react to such an event as a challenge to one's authority or integrity and hence become defensive or hostile. Accordingly, one might act abusively, dogmatically, etc. It is possible, however, with attentive notice to the results of such responses, to find them ultimately futile, unpleasant, self-defeating. Moreover, one may discover that different responses will bring a completely different series of consequences: He may learn to seek the sources of disagreement and the evidence relevant to its settlement; he may learn that amicable endeavor in common inquiry will bring about a much improved relationship with other parties and a greater confidence in conclusions reached. Thus the isolated event of disagreeing can come to have a meaning significantly different from its former state; and when such an event occurs, one experiences it and handles it in a way much changed from the earlier response.

In a similar manner, the meaning of *any* event can be restructured, and, accordingly, the response to that meaning will change. The desire or aversion stimulated by the meaningful event – or by thought of it – will be qualitatively different.[7]

---

[7] New knowledge will not be equally efficacious in every situation; for – as will be indicated shortly – there are a variety of determinants of meaning, and these vary in their influence.

Provided that one accepts the continuity of human nature in nature, all of this is rather elementary. As inquiry and hypotheses produce meanings, they are conditions for changing desires. Intelligence, then, can reconstitute desire by reconstituting the meaning of events. This procedure does not occur *in vacuo*, but in concrete situations. To be explicit, intelligent inquiry functions in two ways to change the meaning of a situation. First, the meanings of events may be explored simply by way of experimental inquiry: One may investigate the probable consequences of acting with the objects of desire that the situation presents. Second, intelligence can function imaginatively to contrive novel ways of acting with the situation – perhaps hitting on a plan of action which brings previously unrelated desires into harmony.

It would be inaccurate to say that intelligence, as such, directly controls human drives and affections. Rather, these drives and affections are modified by each other. It is not "reason" that causes a man to withdraw from, say, a destructive deed; but, rather, his revulsion for the expected consequences of the deed (such as, perhaps, his anticipated punishment, or his sympathy for another person). Thus reason, or intelligence, is not a veneer over the passions; but – figuratively speaking – some passions constitute a veneer over some other passions. These opposed desires may exist in a delicate balance, and a highly stimulating event may suddenly upset the balance and release dramatically different and perhaps highly excited behavior.

To speak literally, then, there is, and there can be, no struggle between desire and intelligence. The struggle is always between one desire, or complex of desires, and another. This conclusion by no means entails, however, that intelligence has no function in conduct, or is a mere slave to the passions: for intelligence – as we have seen – can reconstitute desire. Indeed, it will be evident that Dewey's general view of human nature permits an optimism about the possibilities of rational behavior which the "level" or "layer" theories of human nature seem to forbid.

The function of intelligence in guiding conduct can be readily clarified by considering first a similar but more limited function: that, namely, of vision. As one walks about a cluttered room or along difficult terrain, his vision as such does not direct his movements; but what is seen *does* determine his movements: The individual responds to what is seen in taking a specific path. Similarly, the operations called intelligence do not, as such, direct our behavior; but the objects of desire and aversion disclosed by intelligence do determine behavior. It is not a matter that such objects, if known, might or might not effect behavior; they assuredly *will* affect behavior. Hence we are moved to act in a different way when intelligence has been at work.[8]

It is a common lesson of experience that the meanings reconstituted by intelligence are sometimes slow in bringing about changed behavior. Their long-run effects, however, can be both forceful and profound. We should note that changes in behavior are not transient. Rather, these changes have at least some effect in reinforcing some habits, weakening others, and in creating new habits. Thus intelligence makes a permanent deposit of some sort on behavioral patterns every time it is used. The importance of this fact should not be underestimated. If there is any substance in the notion of growth elaborated in the preceding chapter, then genuine and enduring change in behavior is indeed a reality; and we evidently witness it in a variety of forms. Some individuals do reflect on the meaning of their actions and on possible alternatives; and in time such reflection, when it is translated into practice, brings notable effects on character. Such is what is referred to in the commonsense notion of learning from experience, or in the commonsense notion of wisdom.

This reconstitutive function of intelligence is essentially liberative:

> Analysis of desire thus reveals the falsity of theories which magnify it at the expense of intelligence. Impulse is primary and intelligence is secondary and in some sense derivative. There should be no blinking of this fact. But recognition of it as a fact exalts intelligence. For thought is not the slave of impulse to do its bidding. Impulse does not know what it is after; it cannot give orders, not even if it wants to. It rushes blindly into any opening it chances to find. Anything that expends it, satisfies it. One outlet is like another to it. It is indiscriminate. Its vagaries and excesses are the stock theme of classical moralists; and while they point the wrong moral in urging the abdication of impulse in favor of reason, their characterization of impulse is not wholly wrong. What intelligence has to do in the service of impulse is to act not as its obedient servant but as its clarifier and liberator. And this can be accomplished only by a study of the conditions and

[8] This discussion presupposes Dewey's critique of theories which hold that instinct alone determines patterns of behavior. (See Chapter II, Section 3, above.)

causes, the workings and consequences of the greatest possible variety of desires and combinations of desire. Intelligence converts desire into plans, systematic plans based on assembling facts, reporting events as they happen, keeping tab on them and analyzing them.[9]

To understand the role of intelligence in conduct, it will be instructive to analyze further this liberative function. Consider first the nature of a free act; and by this is meant conduct which unifies, releases, and fulfills desire. It is clear that activity which is free of internal conflict and liberative of desire depends in large measure on the functioning of the environment. My focus of concern here, however, is not with the nature of the social conditions which are conducive to freedom. It is, rather, with the characterization of those constituents of free conduct which are immediately dependent upon the imaginative, intellectual, and practical abilities of the agent.

The freedom of an action does not depend on whether or not one acts from desire, but on whether, and to what extent, desire is formed and stimulated by the genuine realities and possibilities of the situation. One may act on his first impulse and bring upon himself a succession of wholly unanticipated and perhaps unwanted consequences; or – by contrast – one may greatly enlarge his affective environment and respond to the meanings which potential actions in it involve. Requisite to such response is the fullest possible knowledge of the implications of one's alternative courses of conduct in the situation. Inasmuch as various actions may be possible, a crucial requisite to freedom is the imaginative construction of a course of conduct which will most effectively utilize, reorder, and unite the variables of the situation. It should also be recognized that a person with an abundance of appropriate habits of thought and action has far more opportunities for creative and effective action: The situation is more meaningful to him; he has enhanced powers of acting in it; and his desires are formed accordingly. Finally, we must note that actions which are conceived in the manner just outlined have the greatest likelihood of occurring in the way which is intended, for the action will be predicated upon the best available knowledge of the instrumentalities of the situation.

---

[9] *Human Nature and Conduct,* pp. 254-5.

An action satisfying the conditions set forth is what Dewey means by a free action. When these conditions are met, the ensuing action is not one which severs man from nature. It is simply an act which constitutes a release of the energies of the situation in a unified, rather than disrupted or limited, way. Again, this analysis leaves aside the specific problems of coercive social conditions; but it is evident that such conditions – whatever they may be – must be part of the meanings which determine any action aimed at the most inclusive possible fulfillment of desire.

On these assumptions, "choice" is that event in which hitherto conflicting desires, blocking overt action, are either reconstituted or unified in such a way that energies are once again released in on-going activity:

> To say that at last it [deliberation] ceases is to say that choice, decision, takes place.
>
> What then is choice? Simply hitting in imagination upon an object which furnishes an adequate stimulus to the recovery of overt action. Choice is made as soon as some habit, or some combination of elements of habits and impulse, finds a way open. Then energy is released. . . . This decisive direction of action constitutes choice . . . . We have to make a choice of what we *really* want, of the course of action, that is, which most fully releases activities. Choice is not the emergence of preference out of indifference. It is the emergence of a unified preference out of competing preferences.[10]

Desires already exist, but they are blocked. "Choosing" denotes that conscious behavior which is a response to some plan of action which incorporates the appropriate objects of desire.

It is clear that freedom is a function of the situation: The situation is transformed from blindness, perplexity, and conflict to knowledge, settled and unified purpose, and integration of hitherto disordered elements.

> We are free in the degree in which we act knowing what we are about. . . . Knowledge, instead of revealing a world in which preference is an illusion and does not count or make a difference, puts in our possession the instrumentality by means of which preference may be an intelligent or intentional factor in constructing a future by wary and prepared action. Knowledge of special conditions and relations is instrumental to the action which is in turn an instrument of production of situations having qualities of added significance and order. To be capable of such action is to be free.[11]

---

[10] *Ibid.*, pp. 192-3.

[11] *The Quest for Certainty*, p. 250.

I indicated a moment ago that freedom is not liberation from desire. Neither is it liberation from the world. It is, rather, a way of acting in and with the world. To put it in terms elaborated at length in Chapters III and VI: to the extent that conduct is art, conduct is free.

Within this framework one can readily make sense out of such locutions as "the harmony of desire and intelligence" or "acting wholly in accord with intelligence." Such phrases mean that by means of intelligence one has succeeded in harmonizing and unifying desires. Through imaginative consideration of the possibilities of action in a complex and extended situation, a desirable and unifying course of action is constructed. The harmony of desire and intelligence is really a harmony of desires, and this is made possible by intelligence determining the situation in such a way that it become unified, that it becomes art. This harmony, it is clear, is not simply "psychological." As we saw in the preceding chapter, this is an integration of the entire situation.

It is evident that freedom, in this sense, is not an absolute thing, but admits of great differences in degree, depending on both the conditions of the environment and the habits of the agent. It should also be clear that intelligence can indeed be a powerful instrument in human conduct: It does not struggle against desires, but is, rather, an essential condition of bringing desires out of conflict and blindness into some measure of integration. Freedom is not opposition to desire; it is the reconstitution and release of desire in a manner appropriate to the realities and potentialities of the situation. Thus it is, also, that the strength of human passions is not of necessity a fearsome thing. Rational behavior is not a consequence of extirpating desire, but depends on desires being formed by an awareness of the full implications of the situation and on the relations which these desires bear to each other.

> The separation of warm emotion and cool intelligence is the great moral tragedy. . . . The intellect is always inspired by some impulse. . . . But an actuating impulse easily hardens into isolated habit. It is unavowed and disconnected. The remedy is not lapse of thought, but its quickening and extension to contemplate the continuities of existence, and restore the connection of the isolated desire to the companionship of its fellows.[12]

---

[12] *Human Nature and Conduct,* pp. 258-9. In this connection, see also the discussion of self-control and reasonableness, above pp. 242-3.

On Dewey's view, human behavior is not governed by a rational faculty which transcends nature or commands the will, nor is it necessarily governed by mere desire. Rather, it can be a function of the *intelligent formation* of desires. And the intelligent formation of desires implies the discovery and construction of meanings of conduct with the environment. The possibilities for creative and free activity increase as the individual is possessed of more effectual habits of thought and action.

Clearly, formation of desire is inseparable from formation of value. They are different functions of the same inclusive process: As consummatory experience and ends-in-view are conceived in various specific forms for a situation, the desire for them changes conformably to the alternative meanings they acquire. Dewey's technical vocabulary is notoriously varied. He speaks now of the *formation* of meanings and values, again of their *construction, creation,* or *reconstitution.* On the basis of what has so far been said on these matters, however, anyone should find that Dewey communicates his ideas equally well by speaking of the *formation* of values and desires, or of their *construction* etc. All such terms denote the work of creative intelligence in and with the world: reconstituting the meaning of events, thereby reconstituting desire and facilitating inherently liberating and fulfilling activity.

Of course, the nature of one's actions depends significantly upon the cooperation of the environment (which usually includes other persons), and in too many situations this can be little controlled or predicted. But assuredly whatever success can be had in conduct depends – apart from blind luck – on the functioning of intelligence. Intelligence, not will, is the great instrumentality of freedom.[13]

What has been said so far should not be construed to suggest

In this matter of the relation of intelligence and desire, Dewey's position is identical to that of Aristotle, who characterized man as "desiring reason or reasoning desire" (*Nicomachean Ethics,* Bk. VI, Ch. 2). Dewey's views are also much like those of Spinoza, but Dewey had a much keener sense of the creative function of intelligence than Spinoza had or could have had.

[13] See especially *Human Nature and Conduct,* pp. 303-15. See also "philosophies of Freedom" in Horace Kallen (ed.), *Freedom in the Modern World* (New York: Coward-McCann, 1928). "Philosophies of Freedom" has been reprinted in *Philosophy and Civilization* and in Bernstein *(op. cit.).*

that the determination of meanings is exclusively an affair of intelligence. It is an affair of an entire situation with all its various features – including the fund of habits which the individual brings to it – in which intelligence might or might not be present, and in varying degrees. It is things *of the situation* that are meaningful. Social conditions especially have a crucial effect on the meanings of experience. An individual, for example, may be so situated that education has to him an unattractive meaning: a ghetto Negro may have no taste for it because the experience of it and the consequences of it are very different for him than they are for a middle-class white. More generally, recall Dewey's argument that it is the social environment (the responses of other persons) which creates the meanings of so-called moral conduct. (See above, pp. 106-8.) So it is with any form of conduct. On the other hand, the conditions of meaning might be largely physiological (rather than social) – as in the case of addictive drugs.

It is also clear that meanings are changed in a variety of ways – perhaps most frequently through a painful and limited process of trial and error, involving such things as casual joys and agonies, fears, threats, hopes, fancies, chance information, etc. It is equally clear that the habits of most people become so rigidly set – a process beginning in infancy – that such persons become incapacitated to accept new ideas. Thus the effective meaning of an object remains unchanged: One may be unable to outgrow his juvenile reactions to race, *laissez-faire* capitalism, sex, religion, politics, ghosts, and witches. Likewise, compulsive or addictive behavior may be very little modified by changed meanings. But in any case this does not mean that conduct is not a response to the meanings of experience. It means that some parts of the meaning are so affective that changes elsewhere are relatively inconsequential. (Witness the plight of the enlightened cigarette smoker.)

It has been noted that intelligence alone does not create meanings, nor can the knowledge which inquiry yields always bring an effective change in meaning. Presumably, however, certain transformations in the situation (including the habits of the agent) could produce welcome and effective changes in its meanings. Thus a way may be found to make cigarettes unattractive to the smoker; and social conditions could be instituted which would make education welcome to ghetto Negroes. Clearly, the judgments concerning what transformations in the situation and its agents would produce the most welcome and effective changes in its meanings can best be determined by the methods of experimental social intelligence. Although there are such various conditions to the constitution and change of meanings, it is still the case that intelligence is the best instrument for the remaking and control of meanings. Indeed, intelligence is indispensable precisely because the conditions of meaning are so bewilderingly complex and variable. Experimental intelligence is the most systematic and reliable way of learning the true relations and possibilities of events in nature. Upon these relations and possibilities human fate depends. For our own well being we must act in accordance with the facts and their potential meanings. We can hope to realize values in experience only by making the processes of nature our allies.[14]

Before proceeding to the next point, it will be useful to draw attention to the lessons of the foregoing discussion. It is clear that intelligence is a regulator of conduct. It functions in this way not by issuing commands to recalcitrant passions, but by disclosing and reconstituting the meaning of events and the implications of possible lines of conduct. Thus the agent responds to a complex and extended situation rather than to a fugitive and isolated stimulus. Accordingly, his desires and aversions are reconstituted, his conduct is therefore different and, presumably, far more appropriate to the realities of the situation; it approximates to art with its fund of values. Additional variables will function with intelligence to determine the meanings of the situation; but inasmuch as intelligence is the best judge of how these variables might be manipulated, it is ultimately our human intelligence on which we must rely to bring our desires and the potentialities of nature into the greatest possible accord. This is because,

[14] It may be that what psychoanalysis involves is an attempt to investigate and reconstitute the meanings of past experience in order to relieve anxieties occasioned by distorted or limited meanings. (Presumably, the reconstitution of the meanings of present experience is also facilitated by the remaking of past meanings.) In psychoanalysis, perhaps, one attempts to enlarge and reconstitute, say, the meaning of his early relationship to a parent. How far such endeavors are genuinely experimental, and how useful are the theoretical assumptions of psychoanalysis, are still further questions.

to put it simply, man and all his values are functional constituents of nature, and nature can be made partial to the support and enhancement of these values when we learn how the things of nature can and do in fact function. It is nature, again, which is ultimately regulative of conduct; and what nature "prescribes" will depend on how accurately and thoroughly nature is known to us.

To this conclusion a certain emphasis must be added. It is ultimately the conative-affective function of human nature in nature that determines choice and action. Intelligence qualifies this function by both disclosing and reconstructing the meanings of the objects of desire and aversion implied by the execution of an act. Thus the very meaning of action is changed, and the individual responds to actions in their new meanings. It must be stressed, however, that it is always the meaning of objects to the agent that stimulates action to be released or redirected in a certain way. Thus, whatever may be the conditions which produce the meanings of objects, it will be in any case these meanings which determine the course of human conduct:

> We estimate the import or significance of any present desire or impulse by forecasting what it will come or amount to if carried out; literally its consequences define its *consequence*, its meaning or import. . . . Any actual experience of reflection upon conduct will show that every foreseen result at once stirs our present affections, our likes and dislikes, our desires and aversions. There is developed a running commentary which stamps objects at once as good or evil. It is this direct sense of value, not the consciousness of general rules or ultimate goals, which finally determines the worth of the act to the agent.[15]

Two issues in the foregoing discussion must be given close attention: 1) In voluntary behavior, what determines conduct *qua* voluntary? 2) How can voluntary conduct be best directed to ends which are intrinsically most welcome and satisfying? Dewey's answers to both questions are clear: The distinctive determination of voluntary conduct is in objects of desire and aversion; that is, in *meanings*, or loosely – *values*. Second, conduct is best directed by meanings which are both accurate and sufficiently complete for the situation. That is, conduct determined by awareness of the implications of possible actions in the situation is most apt to be appropriate to the situation – to be free, con-

---

[15] *Ethics*, pp. 302-3.

summatory. To this it must be added at once that it is only by means of inquiry and by the formation of hypotheses subject to experimental test that such awareness is possible. This is the process by which meanings are discovered and developed and by which, accordingly, desires are subject to intelligent formation. The problem of the intelligent formation (construction) of meanings (or values) and the consequent reconstitution of desire is no incidental matter to Dewey. It is, rather, all important:

> If [mere] enjoyments *are* values, the judgment of value cannot regulate the form which liking takes; it cannot regulate its own conditions. Desire and purpose, and hence action, are left without guidance, although *the question of regulation of their formation is the supreme problem of practical life.*[16]

I will shortly return to these issues; but what is of most interest at the present juncture is to see that these questions bearing on the determination of human conduct are fundamental to Dewey's conception of the function of ethical theory. Against this background it can, indeed, be stated definitively what is for Dewey this function. It is to determine the intellectual assumptions and methods most appropriate for inquiry into the nature of the conditions which regulate moral conduct. This concern is not with conduct indifferently. Rather, the focus of attention is deliberate, voluntary behavior; and it is specifically concerned with conduct pertaining to experienced goods and evils. It is in such behavior where actual use of intellectual assumptions and methods is most crucial to human well being. The beliefs and methods employed in moral deliberation are principal conditions of moral behavior, for they are determinants of the meaning of proposed actions. (In the same situation, possible actions will have different meanings to the intuitionist, rationalist, dogmatist, believer in unswerving obedience to authority, the romantic, etc.) This interpretation of ethical theory is made unequivocally in *Experience and Nature*:

> The meaning of the theory advanced concerning the relationship of goods and criticism may be illustrated by ethical theory. Few I suppose would deny that in spite of the attention devoted to this subject by many minds of a high order of intention and intellectual equipment, the outcome, judged from the standpoint of scientific consensus, is rather dismaying. . . . I think that we find, amid all the

[16] *The Quest for Certainty*, p. 264. Emphasis added in last sentence.

> diversity, one common intellectual preconception which inevitably defers the possibility of attainment of scientific method. This is the assumption, implicit or overt, that moral theory is concerned with ends, values rather than with criticism of ends and values;... To discover and define once for all the *bonum* and the *summum bonum* in a way which rationally subserves all virtues and duties, is the traditional task of morals; to deny that moral theory has any such office will seem to many equivalent to denial of the possibility of moral philosophy. Yet in other things repeated failure of achievement is regarded as evidence that we are going at the affair in a wrong way....
>
> Meantime, the work which theoretical criticism might do has not been done; namely, discovery of the conditions and consequences, the existential relations, of goods which are accepted as goods not because of theory but because they are such in experience. The cause in large measure is doubtless because the prerequisite tools of physics, physiology and economics were not at hand. But now when these potential instrumentalities are more adequately prepared they will not be employed until it is recognized that the business of moral theory is not at all with consummations and goods as such, but with discovery of the conditions and consequences of their appearance, a work which is factual and analytic, not dialectic, hortatory, nor prescriptive.[17]

Whatever else may be the merits or demerits of this statement,[18] it is at least perfectly clear: Dewey is asserting that the role of the philosopher is to legislate neither principles nor values, but to determine the *conditions* of values and their consequences. This is what Dewey means by criticism of values. It includes the fundamentally important task of determining the status of value in nature. In addition, criticism of values implies at once two inseparable functions: 1) the intelligent formation of desire; 2) the enhancement of the knowledge and control of the conditions of both the attainment and enrichment of value. Let us consider these two functions of criticism a little further.

It will be useful to make a division in the subject matter which is only implicit in the quotation above. A main condition of value is the method employed in discrimination and judgment. In addition, such method implies certain further assumptions – express or implied – about such things as the nature and status of value: indeed, of man and nature and science as well. Hence an analysis of method and its presuppositions is part of that which Dewey calls criticism. But criticism also refers to the analysis of

---

[17] *Experience and Nature*, pp. 431-3.

[18] This notion of ethical theory will be defended shortly.

goods as they actually occur or might occur in experience. Criticism in this latter sense is to take events out of their isolation and examine them in their relations (actual or possible) to other events. (This process can most conveniently be termed a functional analysis of values.) To determine the various conditions and consequences of problematic goods and evils is to enlarge the meanings of these events. Thus it is to restructure the meanings which determine voluntary behavior and at the same time, precisely by such procedures, both to alter the conditions of behavior and enrich its meanings. Clearly, the former part of criticism is requisite to effective criticism in the latter sense; and both are requisite to meaningful and consummatory experience.

Criticism, then, in the inclusive sense, is the function of ethical theory; and the actual process of criticism is the intellectual activity which is necessary to enlightened conduct. The form which conduct takes is dependent upon the meanings to which we respond. Thus the all-important matter – as already remarked – consists in how these meanings are formed. Dewey makes repeated reference to the importance of determining desires by awareness of meanings formed by means of experimental inquiry and formation of hypotheses for action subject to experimental test. Summarizing his intent in *Theory of Valuation*, Dewey says,

> . . . discussion in . . . this study . . . [has] placed chief emphasis upon the importance of valid *ideas* in formation of the desires and interests which are the sources of valuation, and . . . [has] centered attention chiefly upon the possibility and the necessity of control of this ideational factor by empirically warranted matters-of-fact, . . .[19]

A main task for the balance of this chapter will be to indicate in some detail Dewey's analysis of the instrumentalities of criticism. As a prelude to such discussion, however, it will be instructive to elaborate somewhat on the very issue as to what is, or could be, the nature and function of scientific ethics. Familiarity with the history of philosophy indicates that Dewey's views – as he himself suggests – are unorthodox. Yet they are, fundamentally, I believe, the only consistent form of naturalism that can be advanced today; and – more important – his recommendations provide the soundest basis for pursuit of a good life.

---

[19] *Theory of Valuation*, p. 65.

Dewey's position can be readily appreciated by contrasting it with other views. Moral philosophers, it is well known, have been given to seeking such fancies as the highest good, the essence of good, the absolute moral law, or the assumptions and logic that produce incontrovertible prescription or obligation. Apart from all questions concerning the (dubious) desirability of such achievements, philosophers of this century have in various ways pretty much laid waste to such pretensions. Oddly enough, however, even the most toughminded, rigorous, and sophisticated contemporary philosophers have approached the subject matter of ethics by accepting precisely the same antique assumptions as to what the nature and function of ethics is. There is reliable indication, for instance, that both Ayer and Stevenson presuppose some form of legalistic model of ethical discourse. In the case of each, there is an insistence that ethics can become genuinely scientific only if it is possible to formulate empirically verifiable definitions of moral terms.[20] This is a highly revealing assumption. Both men suppose that such definitions would make possible arguments in the following form:

X is always good.
Y is a case of X.
Therefore, Y is good.

or:

We ought always to do A.
B is a case of A.
Therefore, we ought to do B.

Thus, with the appropriate definitions and the use of intersubjective empirical tests, we could demonstrate that such-and-such is good; or such-and-such ought to be done. This is obviously a

---

[20] This is clear in Chapter VI of Ayer's *Language, Truth and Logic;* the same assumption informs the entirety of Stevenson's *Ethics and Language,* as well as his many articles in ethical theory. Indeed, I believe study of recent work would show that this model of what ethical argument would have to be in order to be scientific is at least implicitly accepted by most writers. (On p. 103 of *Language, Truth and Logic,* Ayer insists that the formulation of the intersubjectively verifiable definitions of moral terms would be the first requisite of any genuinely scientifc ethics. Then, on p. 111, he provides a model of valid moral argumentation, in which a moral proposition is deduced from premises which include a defined moral term. [Of course, he denies that there can be any such premise which is empirically valid.])

legalistic model of argument, where moral authority resides in some antecedently given principle of some kind;[21] and the problem is to subsume specific events under the appropriate principle in order to prove that something is good, bad, right, obligatory, etc.[22] Ayer and Stevenson (rightly) conclude that such endeavors are impossible, and haste, therefore, to the conclusion that ethics is impossible.

In Dewey we find, by contrast, an utterly different notion of what ethics is all about. For Dewey, ethical discourse does not terminate in prescription or in "proof" that something is good; rather, it terminates in enlightened conduct, liberation. It would be silly to "prove" that shared experience or sympathy were "good" or that killing or dishonesty were "bad," for the significant questions pertaining to such things concern their function in human experience: What, for example, does sympathy do for your life? What further values does it incorporate into it, and what does it exclude? What sort of society does it presuppose? What sort does it foster? How do we bring sympathy into existence? How do we make it an enduring virtue? How can it be guided by intelligence? These are the important questions, the questions that most need answers. Human beings desire and need such information, it is of decisive value to them; and the quality of both an individual's conduct and character depends significantly upon his examining the possibilities of life in this way. Of any feature of human experience we can ask such questions – we can seek information concerning its function – its meaning – in human experience. In the case of sympathy, we can safely conclude that it has generally welcome effects and greatly enhances the quality of one's human relationships. Yet in some specific case sympathy might bring unwelcome consequences. There is no

---

[21] Of course, any explicit reference to a fixed principle also presupposes a realm of changeless perfection of some kind, which somehow serves as a standard for judging change. Neither Ayer nor Stevenson would subscribe to any notion of such a realm; they are simply unaware of the fact that they have adopted a view of "scientific" ethics which would commit them to an impossible metaphysics.

[22] According to the theory that the deductive model is the only form of moral argument appropriate to reaching decisions of practical choice, it must be the case that we cannot undertake inquiry into morally problematic situations unless we *already* possess moral truths. Inquiry, on this theory, would be for the sake of showing that certain acts satisfy the antecedently given definition.

merit whatever in trying to prove that sympathy is always desirable. We can conclude that it is a virtue well worth cultivating, but in a problematic moral situation a functional analysis of a proposed expression of sympathy could lead us to withhold it.

The point is that a scientific approach to moral conduct does not involve proofs that such-and-such is good or bad; it does not terminate in theorems. Rather, it involves an investigation of the meaning of a proposed act, and – more important – of proposed *ways* of behaving. It is clear that such an investigation can be conducted with wholly experimental procedures.

As we have seen, experience is saturated with problematic goods, or prizings. It is foolish to ask whether there are such things; so also is it foolish to ask whether people really find valuable the securing and enriching of such things. It is equally foolish to ask whether we are permitted to predicate of them any of the conventional moral terms of the English language. To say that shared experience is "good" does not add a new trait or quality to the experience. So why should there be such blind concern to seek such predication? What it is vital to know are the facts about shared experience. Thus the problem posed by the numberless provisional values of experience is not "Are they good or bad?" but "How do they function as an organic part of the life process?" Thus are desires formed, conduct enlightened and enriched.

So deeply entrenched is the idea that ethical reasoning must yield prescription that Dewey's approach might seem to be wholly irresponsible. The issue is very much worth examining. It is clearly Dewey's persuasion that the best guide to conduct is the fullest possible awareness of the meaning of one's actions. Consider an example: Suppose a man is wondering whether he should commit a robbery. One might say to him, "Stealing, Bah!" "You ought not to steal," "Stealing is bad," ". . . is wrong," etc.; or one might say, "God forbids you to steal." His intended behavior might also be called unjust or immoral. Any of these utterances, as such, might or might not result in the party forebearing from theft. On the other hand, one might also speak to the person about what the act of robbery will do to his life, in terms of both immediate and long-term consequences, and to the lives of others. One could speak as well of completely different approaches to the problem for which the robbery was a contemplated solution. Thus the individual, in this latter case, would act in response to both the values implied by his proposed behavior and by alternative modes. His purposes would be genuinely enlightened. In any of the former cases his purposes would not be enlightened; his behavior, if based on those utterances, would be, at best, nonrational. Moreover, his habits would not be the least improved; he would not be rendered more capable of autonomous, responsible behavior. He becomes, under such tutelage, a highly manipulable, slavish, human being. His acts have very little meaning even to himself.

It might also be noted that, as a matter of psychological fact, our potential robber, if he shrinks from the act in such cases, will do so because he fears the wrath or punishment that can be inflicted on him by the presumed moral authority. And, of course, consequences by way of wrath and punishment that can be expected from robbery can equally well be stated in wholly factual sentences. It is difficult to see, therefore, any kind of advantage whatsoever in mere prescription; and its disadvantages are unmistakable.

The locutions cited above – "wrong," "unjust," "immoral," etc. – might be intended and understood in a wholly descriptive sense: referring to certain consequences, or referring to the failure to satisfy empirically specifiable conditions of a certain sort. But no *more* than this could be meant; for "wrong," "unjust," and "immoral" either communicate experimentally verifiable meanings or no meaning at all. That is, anyone using these words is either making reference to an identifiable state of affairs which can be characterized in descriptive language or he is making reference to nothing. Hence these words can be meaningfully employed only to designate the descriptive meaning of various actions which the agent might undertake. As I have pointed out repeatedly, Dewey regards it as obviously preferable that these meanings be exactly and thoroughly specified. The frequent use of so-called moral words perhaps represents more than anything else the premature curtailment of inquiry.

Dewey's position in regard to the guidance of voluntary action is in many ways a repetition of one of the fundamental themes in the western liberal tradition, which has placed a great value to both individual and society on free, enlightened conduct. This is a main assumption of Dewey's moral philosophy, and he finds a basis for it in what had hitherto been lacking in philosophy: an intelligible and inclusive philosophy of nature, value, and intelligence as art. Taken together, Dewey's assumptions determine for him the function of distinctively ethical discourse.[23] It is to disclose the inherent qualities of the situation, actual and potential. The function of such disclosure is the intelligent formation of desire; and, in the long run, action determined by desires formed in this way will be inherently most satisfying.

Accordingly, Dewey is not in the least concerned with imputing some trait to experience which is in any sense additional to those which can be determined by experimental inquiry, and he makes no pretense of doing so. For Dewey, the important thing is to elucidate human experience and enlighten human conduct. The brute and crucial fact is that men *have* prizings and values; they *do* desire, seek, strive, suffer, triumph; they *do* evaluate. And it is of utmost importance that experience of this sort be enlightened. We must know how to discriminate between goods, how to unify them, enrich them, make them more enduring. We must learn what to seek and what to give up; we must know what discipline to undertake in order to incorporate the richest values into our lives. And – inasmuch as we are social beings – we must determine the sort of social order and methods which will secure, safeguard, and promote such values. We must know, then, a great deal about nature, man, society, and science; and we must develop and refine instrumentalities of inquiry and test. Thus "ethics" becomes at the same time experimental and useful. The rehearsal of these facts perhaps becomes tedious; yet they are given little or no account in contemporary ethical theory.

---

[23] For purposes of clarification, I make the following distinctions, which are not carefully attended in Dewey's own writings: *Ethical discourse* is the actual assessment of conduct and aims in the moral situation, or in an imagined situation, whether carried on by one person or several together. *Ethical theory* (as mentioned earlier) is the inquiry into the conditions of the good of human conduct, whatever they may be. They include, of course, the intellectual methods and concepts by which goods are determined. *Value theory* can be regarded as the metaphysical analysis of value. Conclusions in value theory will obviously have crucial effects on ethical theory and in turn on moral discourse proper. *Moral philosophy* is inclusive of all these things and more.

In preceding chapters I have already indicated what Dewey regarded as the most fundamental assumptions about man, nature, and science pertinent to moral philosophy. Having also indicated what Dewey regarded as the office of ethical theory, I will proceed to give some fuller indication of the intellectual instruments which Dewey's theory provides moral discourse.

I am aware that what has been said so far leaves important questions unanswered. Some of these will receive attention in the following section, such as problems surrounding the method and basis of reconciliation of competing values in society.

2. Experimental Methods of Moral Deliberation

A fruitful prelude to this subject will be to rehearse some main features of the nature of consummatory value. Seven points are pertinent: 1) Such values are continuous with gross experience, including, notably, problematic goods, but also, 2) with all those natural processes which bring it into existence and sustain it. 3) It is a discriminated event, deliberately constructed and pursued. 4) A consummatory value is not an isolated object, but a meaningful event. It is experience funded with the qualitative character of the events which action for it and with it have produced or will produce. 5) The experience is conditional upon the conversion of a situation from problematical to consummatory. That is, it is the consummatory phase of the history of a situation. It is not an event within a situation, but it is the historical unification of the situation as such. 6) Hence the particular constitution of a consummatory experience is defined in terms of the specific situation and is unique to that situation. 7) Finally, as an event in nature it is not an absolute end, but is also a condition of further events. It is perhaps again worth remarking that many things besides consummatory values are prized, esteemed, enjoyed, and sought after in various ways. Dewey insists on this; and it is precisely because of the fact that so many things are qualitatively attractive or repulsive that the entire situation anticipated to be consummatory has to be distinguished. For an event thus anticipated is that which has been rationally discriminated – amid all the temptations and fears of existence – to be worthy of effort. Moreover, as a discriminated entity (in contrast to prizings) it is subject to deliberate production and control, and it is more richly endowed with qualitative meaning.

The preceding summary suggests two general intellectual problems. The first concerns the genuinely metaphysical and philosophical problems about value: the status of value in nature. The second problem concerns the difficulties that anyone undergoes in on-going experience as he meets obstacles and dilemmas and seeks the good. These are, then, the difficulties of actual moral deliberation and endeavor; and the way in which one confronts them will be in part determined by some metaphysical and philosophical assumptions about value, however implicit, vague, or confused. Clearly, Dewey's treatment of the second set of problems is explicitly derivative of his treatment of the first set: The first set provides the assumptions necessary to make value and valuing subject matter for intelligence. That is, his analyses disclose value and valuing in their natural continuities. Thus they remove the basis for regarding value as apart from nature and science. They show that the traits of moral experience are indicative of the traits of nature; and they show as well that the latter are generic to all kinds of experience. The result is a theory of value which is organic to an inclusive theory of nature. Dewey devoted himself to showing that these consummations in experience, which he called values, are genuine and distinctive functions of nature. And he did so, primarily, so that men could see that they were subject to intelligent investigation, production, and control. They can be distinguished from prizings, tested in experience, and the conditions of their occurrence in nature can be investigated like any other natural phenomenon.

What is of particular relevance to the present stage of discussion is that consummatory experience, in its occurrence, is something that has been discriminated by inquiry and achieved by intelligently directed effort. Fulfilling thought, desire, and effort, funded with the meanings of an entire history, and quickening one's capacities for further experience, a consummatory value is enjoyed and cherished simply for its own sake. As such, then, a consummatory value – as it occurs in experience – is not occasion for doubt or inquiry. It is, rather, that for which inquiry takes place. Consummatory experience presents no problems; it is the resolution of problems. This is not to say that consummatory values cannot or should not be subject to criticism. This is not at all the case. The point is simply that the difficulties of moral deliberation and endeavor do not arise in the consummatory phase of experience, but in the problematic phase. Accordingly, Dewey brings a great deal of his thought to focus on these conditions antecedent to the occurrence of the culminating phase of a history. Thus, a chief concern is with effective procedure in actual problematic situations. Indeed, there is no way to determine values apart from the actual functioning of specific situations.

In this connection it will be useful to distinguish three different kinds of such situation. First, the occasion in which an individual (or a group) has to make a practical choice of some kind; second, the occasion in which one considers the value of a given institution, social rule, moral precept, etc.; third, the situation in which one inquires into the conditions in nature requisite to the production and sustenance of values whose worth is already well established. These situations are certainly not altogether different; it will be evident that the similarities are more fundamental than the differences. It is frequently true, moreover, that deliberation into concrete moral problems involves analyses comprehending all three of these types. By dealing with them as distinguished, however, a clearer and more systematic exposition of Dewey's position will be possible.[24] The first two situations will be dealt with in this section, the last in the concluding section. Most of the important issues pertaining to all three situations will be treated in connection with the first type; so the first discussion will be considerably longer than the succeeding ones.

It will be recalled that the type of situation in which a person or group is confronted with some problem of practical choice arises when there is no clear and unobstructed line of conduct available. In such circumstances the situation presents divergent problematic goods (or evils), each of which permits divergent courses of action. Without the intervention of intelligence, such situations remain inherently problematic and disunified. For the greatest possibilities of fulfillment, the aim is to transform an initially impeded, plural, and disunified situation into one of

---

[24] Dewey himself never explicitly made these distinctions. The confusions occasioned by some of his arguments might have been obviated if he had structured his discussions more deliberately.

restored and reunified activity by some process of reconstruction and redirection. (This process, of course, usually takes place in a social context.) The problem, then, is in determining a single course of action out of many possibilities; and its solution consists in uniting as many of one's preferences in the situation as possible. "The attained end or consequence is always an organization of activities, where organization is a co-ordination of all activities which enter as factors."[25]

In this circumstance, there are two essential requisites to successful choice:[26] 1) the functional analysis of problematic goods; 2) the contrivance of alternative possibilities for action, each of which must also be subjected to functional analysis. These two processes are phases of one continuous inquiry.

The goodness of a problematic good consists in some interaction between it and the agent; it is a good because of some way it can be acted with. Thus every problematic good (object of desire, prizing) implies some course of action, however limited. The appropriate procedure, then, is to undertake what Dewey calls a dramatic (or imaginative) rehearsal of the various possible lines of conduct which are suggested by features of the situation.

> Deliberation is actually an imaginative rehearsal of various courses of conduct. We give way, *in our mind,* to some impulse; we try, *in our mind*, some plan. Following its career through various steps, we find ourselves in imagination in the presence of the consequences that would follow, and as we then like and approve, or dislike and disapprove, these consequences, we find the original impulse or plan good or bad.[27]

> Deliberation is an experiment in finding out what the various lines of possible action are really like. It is an experiment in making various combinations of selected elements of habits and impulses, to see what the resultant action would be like if it were entered upon. But the trial is in imagination, not in overt fact. . . . In thought as well as in overt action, the objects experienced in following out a course of action attract, repel, satisfy, annoy, promote and retard. Thus deliberation proceeds.[28]

This is an investigation, in other words, into the conditions and consequences of these presumed goods: What must be under-

---

[25] *Theory of Valuation,* p. 48.

[26] These were introduced in section 1 of this chapter.

[27] *Ethics,* p. 303.

[28] *Human Nature and Conduct,* pp. 190, 192.

taken to achieve them, and what will be the further results of their achievement? These inquiries disclose that differing proposed actions will incorporate certain combinations of goods and evils into experience. Such investigation of the relations in which problematic goods potentially exist discloses, then, not cold and bloodless facts, but objects both attractive and repulsive: All of the objects presented to imagination in dramatic rehearsal are affective in some measure; and whether they are regarded as good or bad depends largely upon the specific needs and difficulties of the given situation. The result of such rehearsal is not that one is overwhelmed by an ever larger mass of unrelated goods and bads, but that possible actions become meaningful; and a course of conduct is conceived which will meet existing needs and initiate inherently satisfying activity. The original objects of the situation are enlarged and reconstituted in meaning. Desires attractive in isolation are severely qualified in relation, and activites hitherto unimportant may acquire value.

Dramatic rehearsal also suggests plans of action which were not thought of at the beginning of the situation:

> The imagining of various plans carried out furnishes an opportunity for many impulses which at first are not in evidence at all, to get under way. Many and varied direct sensings, appreciations, take place. When many tendencies are brought into play, there is clearly much greater probability that the capacity of self which is really needed and appropriate will be brought into action, and thus a truly reasonable happiness result.[29]

The play of imagination may contrive possibilities for the situation hitherto undetected, and, presumably, this process can go on until a satisfactory plan is conceived (or one is forced to act from other pressures). For each plan conceived, of course, one must also inquire fully into its function in the situation. Such deliberation is obviously creative. It reconstitutes the original meanings of the situation and it contrives novel eventuations of the situation. This creative function is precisely what Dewey has in mind when he speaks of "the construction of good" or "the formation of value"; and it is obvious that it is uniquely valuable.

It must be remembered that deliberation takes place in reference to a particular situation. Alternatives are tried out imagina-

---

[29] *Ethics*, p. 303.

tively until one of them is found suitable. This suitability is determined by the meanings of the respective alternatives. Choice occurs when some combination of these constituents entertained in imagination unifies and releases desire.[30]

This imaginative procedure provides the way of comparing competing prospects for conduct; it is the way of distinguishing the real from the apparent good. For inasmuch as the fundamental problem is the reunification of the situation in an intrinsically satisfying way, alternatives can be judged on precisely their power to accomplish just that. Apart from their expected suitability in resolving the problematic situation, the relative value of objects – in the given context – could not be determined.

> Either, then, the difference between genuine, valid, good and a counterfeit, specious good is unreal, or it is a difference consequent upon reflection, or criticism, and the significant point is that this difference is equivalent to that made by discovery of relationships, of conditions and consequences .... When the question is raised as to the "real" value of the object for belief, the appeal is to criticism, intelligence. And the court of appeal decides by the law of conditions and consquences.[31]
>
> *Immediately* nothing is better or worse than anything else; it is just what it is. Comparison is comparison of things, things in their efficacies, their promotions and hindrances. The better is that which will do more in the way of security, liberation and fecundity for other likings and values.
>
> To make a valuation, to judge appraisingly, is then to bring to conscious perception relations of productivity and resistance and thus to make value significant, intelligent and intelligible.[32]

It is clear that what is of value in the situation is always a matter of comparison. In contradistinction to, say, a natural law theory, in which one can say of an act absolutely that it is right or wrong, good or bad, Dewey perceives that evaluation is a matter of comparing the efficacy of alternatives in their expected function in the problematic situation.

Suppose in any instance a satisfactory plan of action is developed: so far, there is still only an anticipated integration of the situation; the consummatory phase of the history has not yet

---

[30] Actually, this is an incomplete account of the decisive meanings in the situation, for a further consideration of great importance is the effect conduct will have on character. This subject will receive due attention later on. Choice is ultimately a function of all these meanings of the situation.

[31] *Experience and Nature*, pp. 403, 405.

[32] *Ibid.*, p. 430.

occurred. Such a plan presumably seeks some specific object or act (the end-in-view) which will effect a welcome change in the situation. The plan can be stated as a hypothesis. The hypothesis states that certain specific consequences are conditional upon the occurrence of certain specific actions: If action X takes place, then event Y will follow. This is simply a conditional statement of means-consequences.[33] Presumably, what is predicted are certain objective results – that is, that certain events will in fact transpire. Concrete moral experience occurs in relation to real situations (or in relation to imagined realistic situations); and, as we have just seen, what must be judged are the alternative proposals to deal with the actual problems occasioned by the situation. It follows that what one needs to be able to predict is that certain actions will in fact effectively deal with the predicaments at hand and, it is hoped, convert them to art. The prediction, therefore, is *not* that such results will be liked or disliked; it is not that they will be desirable or valuable. It is, rather, that these results will in fact occur. It is predicted that certain *objects* of desire will be brought into existence and that these will harmonize the situation. The *desire* for consummatory experience and for the appropriate end-in-view are *present* facts; the actual fulfillment, however, remains potential only. Hence the conditions of fulfillment are what is at issue – not that fulfillment is desirable.

The end-in-view, whatever it may be, is desirable because of its expected efficacy in the situation. It is that which is needed to institute unified activity. In the example about the cook running out of salt, the relevant hypotheses would state the conditions necessary to resolving the problematic character of the situation: namely, that the possession of salt would reintegrate the activity, and that certain conditions are requisite to acquiring some salt.[34] Thus Dewey's statement from *The Quest for Certainty:*

---

[33] This sort of prediction is also what Dewey calls a moral judgment, or (in *Theory of Valuation)* proposition of appraisal. (Notice in the preceding quotation Dewey's reference to valuation, or judgment.) Due to the fact that critics of Dewey have been confused about *what* is predicted, and hence also about his concept of moral judgment, I will elaborate on this topic shortly.

[34] See footnote 14 in Chapter III, above, where Dewey's failure to distinguish differences in the relevant hypotheses is pointed out.

> To declare something satis*factory* is to assert that it meets specifiable conditions. It is, in effect, a judgment that the thing "will do." It involves a prediction; it contemplates a future in which the thing will continue to serve; it *will* do. It asserts a consequence the thing will actively institute; it will *do.*[35]

Of course, these predictions may have the result of altering desires, for plans of action may thereby acquire meanings which are unattractive. (The cook might discover that he has to walk five miles to get more salt.)

It is clear that such hypotheses are open to experimental test. It is simply a matter of instituting the appropriate conditions and observing their consequences. One predicts that a certain act will have certain effects; then he can perform the act and discover if his hypothesis was accurate. Dewey refers to predictions about the function of the end-in-view:

> The required appraisal of desires and ends-in-view, as means of the activities by which actual results are produced, is dependent upon observation of consequences attained when they [the consequences] are compared and contrasted with the content of ends-in-view. . . . Since desire and ends-in-view need to be appraised as means to ends (an appraisal made on the basis of warranted physical generalizations) the valuation of ends-in-view is tested by consequences that actually ensue. It is verified to the degree in which there is agreement upon results.[36]

Due to the misunderstandings which have surrounded Dewey's concept of a moral judgment,[37] it will be necessary to delay here long enough to make his position entirely clear. If this notion is misunderstood, Dewey's whole conception of scientific ethics must be misunderstood.

In connection with a different matter, I earlier quoted (p. 20)

---

[35] Pp. 260-1.

[36] *Theory of Valuation,* pp. 52-3.

[37] This has been true, for example, for both Stevenson (see especially Ch. XII of *Ethics and Language*) and White *(op. cit.)*; also of Philip Blair Rice (especially in "Types of Value Judgments," *The Journal of Philosophy,* XL [September, 1943], pp. 533-43.). R.L. Holmes *(op. cit.)* predicates his entire article on a mistaken view of Dewey's concept of judgment. It seems evident also that Hook does not have an accurate conception of Dewey's position (see above, p. 138, footnote 19).

The best treatment of Dewey's concept of moral judgment that I know of is in H.S. Thayer, *Meaning and Action: A Critical History of Pragmatism* (Indianapolis and New York: The Bobbs-Merrill Company, 1968), especially pp. 402-9. Thayer says that a value judgment implies a "policy statement"; but the latter concept is not altogether clear. (Dewey himself never uses "policy statement.") I beleive, however, that the differences between my interpretation and that of Thayer are neither great nor irreconcilable.

Dewey's statement that the denial of the subject-object dichotomy was fundamental to his philosophy, the concept of moral judgment being a specific instance of his basic view. His point was that a moral judgment is not a statement about either subjective feelings or transcendent verities, but is a fully scientific claim about nature. It is so because its subject matter is a wholly objective event in nature. These events are the occurrence of human prizings; and it is because of the distinctive character of this *subject matter* that they are called value judgments:

> And in calling my theory on this matter a special case of my *general* theory I intend to call attention to the fact that I have denied that as judgments, or in respect to method of inquiry, test, and verification, value-judgments have any peculiar or unique features. They differ from other judgments, of course, in the specific material they have to do with. But in this respect inquiries and judgment about potatoes, cats, and molecules differ from one another. The genuinely important difference resides in the fact of the much greater *importance with respect to the conduct of life-behavior* possessed by the special subject-matter of so-called value-judgments.[38]

Clearly, moral judgments are *about* prizings; they state, at least hypothetically, their conditions and consequences, their relations to other prizings, and their functions in the situation as a whole. Dewey distinguishes this sort of proposition from the mere statement that something is prized or something is enjoyed: "To say that something is enjoyed is to make a statement about a fact, something already in existence; it is not to judge the value of that fact."[39] To judge its value, we must, clearly, know its possible meanings, as well as the meanings of other possible actions in the situation.

In precisely this same vein, from the *Ethics:* "Moral deliberation differs from other forms not as a process of forming a judgment and arriving at knowledge but in the kind of value which is thought about."[40] And from *Theory of Valuation:*

---

[38] *Problems of Men,* pp. 258-9. Recall Dewey's emphasis in "Ethical Subject-Matter and Language" (see above, p. 200) that ethical and scientific statements differ only in *function.* (In the remarks just quoted he says the difference is one of *subject matter.*) These views are not inconsistent. Dewey's position, if he stated it with more care, would be that moral sentences function to direct conduct precisely because they refer to events which are attractive or repulsive in some way.

[39] *The Quest for Certainty,* p. 260.

[40] P. 302.

> Value-propositions of the distinctive sort exist whenever things are appraised as to their suitability and serviceability as means [to the solution of the problematic situation], for such propositions are not about things or events that have occurred or that already exist . . ., but are about things *to be* brought into existence.[41]

The *"tobe"*in the last sentence does *not* mean "ought to be"; it is simply Dewey's insistence that a value judgment is not about antecedent reality, but about some event to be produced by intelligent action. The reference is to the possible transformation of the situation; and the *desirability* of a consummatory transformation is not even at issue. The good of the situation is something eventual; it is created, constructed. It is not in any sense in existence in "antecedent reality." "To be" is simply a reference to the future: Something has been an effective action in *previous* situations, but is it *to be* undertaken in present circumstances? That is, will it resolve the particular difficulties of the problematic situation? Dewey is not asking whether the end-in-view *ought* to unify the elements of the situation, but whether it *will* do so. This is the question of importance, and such questions cannot be answered by reference to antecedent conditions, but by estimating conditions and consequences. Just as an immediate quality is not knowledge but is something *to be* known, so also a problematic good, as such, is neither an end-in-view nor a consummatory value, but it is something *to be* evaluated. And such evaluation is precisely to acquire knowledge of conditions and consequences in the given context. Depending on the aims and instrumentalities of the situation, the problematic good might prove something *to be* brought into existence. Using "to be" in reference to both knowing and evaluating, Dewey simply insists on our looking to future operations rather than to some form of preexisting reality in order to produce the desired result.[42] Of propositions of appraisal Dewey says,

> The problem concerns not their existence as general propositions . . . but whether they express only custom, convention, tradition, or are capable of stating rela-

---

[41] Pp. 51-2.

[42] White *(op. cit.)* always, and explicitly, reads Dewey's "to be" as "ought to be." This betrays a basic and systematic misunderstanding of what Dewey is trying to do. (Dewey himself never uses "ought to be" in the passages which White analyzes.)

> tions between things as means and other things as consequences, which relations are themselves grounded in empirically ascertained and tested existential relations such as are usually termed those of cause and effect.[43]

In *Theory of Valuation* Dewey calls such judgments normative, because they state the conditions that must be met in order to gain a specified end.[44] His own example is elementary: "'This plot of ground is worth $200 a front foot.'" It states a condition for such things as buying, assessing, taxing the land. *E.g.*, If you want to buy this land, you must pay $200 a front foot. The proposition

> states a rule for determination of an act to be performed, its reference being to the future and not to something already accomplished or done. . . . Thus the proposition may be said to lay down a norm, but "norm" must be understood simply in the sense of a condition *to be* conformed to in definite forms of future action. . . . Such rules are used as criteria or "norms" for judging the value of proposed modes of behavior.

Thus any so-called hypothetical judgment (or its equivalent) is a moral judgment, so long as it has "importance with respect to the conduct of life-behavior."

The same point can be made by reference to the terminology of *Human Nature and Conduct*, where "object of desire" is used interchangeably with "end-in-view," and where "object of desire" is defined as that which, if it were present, would release and unify activity.[45] Clearly, what is requisite is to determine what that object might be and how to attain it; and propositions conveying such information are, for Dewey, distinctively moral in both subject matter and function. By contrast, statements purporting to attribute certain presumed inherent moral properties to actions in and of themselves are simply obscure. Hence to say that something is desirable is not to invoke some autonomous norm; it is to say that it will transform the situation in specifiable

---

[43] *Theory of Valuation*, p. 21. Dewey is slightly ambiguous about the meaning of "proposition of appraisal," which he calls a "value-proposition of the distinctive sort." For at one point in *Theory of Valuation* (pp. 19-23) he seems to regard it as a verified propostion, while later (pp. 51-2) he treats it simply as a hypothesis. This ambiguity is unimportant here, however, for it has no bearing on the issue of the cognitive status and the subject matter of such claims. In either case they are empirically verifiable.

[44] This paragraph, with its quotations, is drawn from pp. 20-1 in *Theory of Valuation.*

[45] See above, Ch. III, pp.132-3., and *Human Nature and Conduct*, pp. 248-51.

ways; it is a condition of specifiable forms of action.

Any number of further arguments and quotations in this vein could be marshaled; but I take it that mere repetition is unnecessary. Thus I will make but one further citation, which is significant not only in respect to the issue of the nature of moral judgment, but also in relation to the moral functions of science. In the *Logic*, Dewey speaks in reference to social inquiry:

> The soundness of the principle that moral condemnation and approbation should be excluded from the operations of obtaining and weighing material data and from the operations by which conceptions for dealing with the data are instituted, is, however, often converted into the notion that all evaluations should be excluded. This conversion is, however, effected only through the intermediary of a thoroughly fallacious notion; the notion, namely, that the moral blames and approvals in question *are* evaluative and that they exhaust the field of evaluation. For they are *not* evaluative in any logical sense of evaluation. They are not even judgments in the logical sense of judgment. For they rest upon some preconception of *ends* that *should* or *ought* to be attained. This preconception excludes ends (consequences) from the field of inquiry and reduces inquiry at its very best to the truncated and distorted business of finding out means for realizing objectives already settled upon. Judgment which is actually judgment (that satisfies the logical conditions of judgment) institutes means-consequences (ends) in *strict conjugate relation* to each other.[46]

The pertinence of these statements to the relation of science to ethics will be indicated in the third section. In reference to the present discussion, it need only be remarked that this is a definitive statement about the nature of evaluative judgment. Such judgments make no claims of *should, ought, right, wrong,* etc.; but they state as precisely as possible relations of means-consequences, and no more.

Even without using explicit quotations about value judgments, Dewey's position could be established by reference to his fundamental assumptions – both substantive and methodological, supplemented by reference to his analyses of moral language, his discussions of desire and intelligent conduct, and his elaborate treatment of science and value. The very point of judgments (predictions) of the means-ends continuum is to provide the information requisite to the intelligent formation of desire and enlightened and meaningful conduct. Such judgments clarify and

---

[46] P. 496.

unify the initially problematic situation. They state the operations which will institute a settled and unified outcome. The entire argument of the chapter to this point is virtually summarized by the following statements from *The Quest for Certainty:*

> Thus we are led to our main proposition: *Judgments about values are judgments about the conditions and results of experienced objects; judgments about that which should regulate the formation of our desires, affections and enjoyments.* For whatever decides their formation will determine the main course of our conduct, personal and social.[47]

Notice here the explicit emphasis on formation of desires as the matter of crucial importance in conduct. This formation, again, is organic to the construction of an integrated meaning for the entire situation. Accordingly, judgments are about means and consequences of problematic goods; and it is precisely an awareness of these means and consequences that is the principal determinant of liberated and integral activity. Again, the actual value of such activity in life-experience is regarded as unimpeachably confirmed.

Clearly, a moral judgment is a statement of means-consequences, not a locution like "you ought to tell the truth" or "Shared experience is good." If "good" is used in a judgment it means "will bring such-and-such consequences into existence"; "good" means "effective for."

> "Good" from the standpoint of the more experienced person is that which serves certain ends, that which stands in certain connections with consequences.[48]

---

[47] P. 265. Many statements quoted hitherto contain similar references to values as guiding conduct and to the uses of science in the formation of values. The meaning of such remarks is, regrettably, altogether evident only in retrospect. Recall, for example, the quotation from *The Quest for Certainty,* p. 255: "The problem of restoring integration and cooperation between man's beliefs about the world in which he lives and his beliefs about the values and purposes that should direct his conduct is the deepest problem of modern life." The point is simply that for the most inclusive attainment of value, desires must be formed in response to true ideas about the world. Inasmuch as science is the method of the formation of true ideas, the continuity of science and value must be restored.

[48] *Ethics,* p. 291. A sentence like "You ought to tell the truth" reduces to a succession of statements about the conditions and consequences of telling the truth or of doing something else instead: "If you tell the truth, you can expect such-and-such outcomes to this situation, and you will experience such-and-such rewards and disappointments, you will help and hinder others in such-and-such ways, you will develop your character in such-and-such a way," etc. Thus the full meaning of "You ought to tell the truth" in a situation would amount to a rather elaborate specification of all

It should also be clear that several moral judgments may be formulated in a situation. Each of them indicates what results are contingent upon a given action. One such judgment, or combination of judgments, becomes the basis for action; that is, one plan of action is chosen on the assumption that it will unify the particular factors of the situation.

Throughout his writings, Dewey uses "estimation," "appraisal," "evaluation," "judgment" to refer to the process of determining relations of means-consequences. (Hence scientific inquiry makes repeated use of judgment.) Unless a reader has an indomitable will to believe that moral judgments *must* be either meaningless or in some sense autonomous, then there should be no difficulty with this notion. And unless one insists, by the method of tenacity, that Dewey *must* have some unrelated, absolute end-in-itself type of value in mind, he can eventually make out Dewey's position very clearly. Even a perfunctory reading of Chapter IX of the *Logic*, "Judgments of Practice: Evaluation" (especially pp.159-68) indicates unmistakably that judgments of all sorts are hypotheses stating means-ends relations. Likewise with Chapter IV of *Theory of Valuation* and "Valuation Judgments and Immediate Quality" in *Problems of Men*.[49]

I have dwelt at length on judgment both because the concept is crucial and because apparently all philosophers have great difficulty in conceiving the possibility of a moral judgment which has no distinctively ethical terms in it. It will be appropriate now to consider some possible difficulties in Dewey's treatment of deliberation. This will afford opportunity for clarification and elaboration.

Dewey's stress on both the continuity of means-ends and the

---

that is implied by truthfulness and its alternatives. Such is what any consistent naturalist means when he says something like "You ought to tell the truth." All imperatives, therefore, are more-or-less elaborated hypothetical imperatives. ("Ought" – rather than "ought not" – implies that these conditions and consequences are in general more welcome than unwelcome. The important matter in either case, however, is that these implications be specified as much as possible so that desire will be formed by the full meaning of proposed actions. The speaker's liking and disliking of the implicated values is part of the meaning of the action.)

In *Ethics*, pp. 245-56, Dewey analyzes right and obligation descriptively as characterizing specifiable kinds of reciprocal social relationships.

[49] See, for judgment in general, *Logic*, Chs. VII through IX.

forecast of consequences might seem to invite insuperable limitations to the effectiveness of deliberation: The events set in motion will ramify indefinitely, yet one could predict them neither far nor accurately. This objection has less pertinence than it initially appears to have. In the first place, it can be observed that whatever the practical limitations of deliberation happen to be, a rejection of deliberation in favor of mere guess or impulse is by no means warranted. But in more immediate relevance to the point at issue, it must be indicated that the kinds of prediction that are formulated in the problematic situation do not and need not involve a long-range forecast of specific events.[50]

There are two kinds of relevant predictions. One of them is an assessment of the effects that action in the situation will have on character. The importance of this assessment will be treated shortly in another connection. For the present, it need only be asserted that the consideration of effects on character does not involve predictions of remote events. The concern, rather, must be with the effects that conduct undertaken *right now* would have on one's habits.

The second kind of prediction pertains to the means of restructuring the situation. Here it must be remembered that deliberation takes place in a specific context for a specific purpose. The context is a problematic situation; the purpose is the institution or restoration of unified activity. Deliberation, then, seeks a solution to *present* difficulties. Accordingly, the forecast of consequences need not proceed beyond a prediction of what will resolve the problematic situation. Thus one does not have to predict events of some later time, nor does he have to know what his desires and aversions will be at some later time. What he has to do is solve his present predicament. Thus by reflection and inquiry he must try to foresee the effects a possible action will have on his situation right now.

> The "value" of different ends that suggest themselves is estimated or measured by the capacity they exhibit to guide action in making good, *satisfying,* in its literal sense, existing lacks. Here is the factor which cuts short the process of

---

[50] The following discussion utilizes and amplifies the same conclusions about the relation of future to present that were introduced earlier, in the analysis of growth (Chapter VI, Section 2).

> foreseeing and weighing ends-in-view in their function as means. Sufficient unto the day is the evil thereof and sufficient also is the *good* of that which does away with the existing evil. Sufficient because it is the means of instituting a complete situation or an integrated set of conditions.[51]

For example: American Negroes have certain desires which they want fulfilled; and they have certain impediments to their conduct which they desire to be removed. These *desires* are not predicted, and it is not doubted that they are in fact desires. The question is: In what action will the object of desire be attained? Suppose that reflection contrives a possible action. The hypothesis, or prediction, is that a certain action will produce a certain result; that is, a certain object will be produced. And, in that situation, that is as far as the forecast of consequences need go. The specific interests are, say, meaningful economic activity, relevant and quality education, fair housing opportunities, political power, social equality, etc., all of which are assumed to be efficacious in the conduct of life activity. What must be done to get these things? Various proposals can be made: voter registration, marches, demonstrations, disruptions; threats of revolution, boycotts, black capitalism, lobbying, education, forming coalitions, and so on. All of these are actions to be undertaken to fulfill existing desires. But it is not certain that they will do so, and analysis of these plans must be undertaken. In addition, such analysis may well reconstitute some desires; new hypotheses may be generated. (Blacks may come, say, to prefer socialism to black capitalism.) Finally, choices are made and plans are put to the test; that is, they are acted upon in the belief that such action will in fact resolve the problematic situation. The uncertainty in the situation is not that there are great distresses to be remedied, but that the means to relieve distress are doubtful. Clearly, what needs to be known are the means to solve existing problems; and predictions which go beyond such solutions are not simply unreliable, but irrelevant.[52]

---

[51] *Theory of Valuation,* p. 46.

[52] Of course, in many situations reliable predictions are very difficult or impossible to make. There may be too many variables or too little knowledge at the time when decision is necessary. Hence one must draw upon past experience and undertake an action whose *tendency* in apparently similar circumstances has been beneficial. This point will receive more attention later in this section.

This conclusion suggests further, and apparently more serious, questions: If predictions do not extend beyond the resolution of the situation, how is such resolution itself to be judged? Shouldn't consummatory values themselves be criticized as the condition of still further events, or are they somehow exempted from evaluation?

There is one sense in which consummatory experience, according to Dewey, is exempted from criticism. There are, however, senses in which the constituents of such experience should be examined with utmost care. These points will be taken in order.

It must first of all be pointed out that there is an important distinction between predicting *beyond* the situation and predicting the behavior of all the variables *relevant* to it. Thus deliberation by Negroes might not take into account the responses of various white blocs. But – obviously – the whites are part of the problem. It is clear that to estimate white response is not to venture beyond the situation, but to consider one of its most crucial components. Awareness of what is relevant to the situation is obviously vital to its successful transformation.

In this same connection (the freedom from criticism of consummatory values), it is suitable to recall an earlier discussion. There was in Chapter VI some consideration of the relation of present to future. One of Dewey's arguments was that the future cannot be reliably predicted, nor, in any specific sense, can it be controlled. His thesis was that the best way to look after the future is to fulfill the best possibilities of the present. This conclusion is certainly relevant to the present discussion. There are great difficulties in predicting what will be the specific events which will ensue from an anticipated consummatory experience. Thus there is a sense in which values are incapable of evaluation.

There are two ways, however, in which consummatory values are very much subject to criticism. First, in determining a course of action in the problematic situation, it is crucial, Dewey urges, to gauge the probable effects conduct will have on one's character. It is crucial, that is, to consider the habits in the process of formation.

> The choice at stake in a moral deliberation or valuation is the worth of this and that kind of character and disposition. . . . In committing oneself to a particular

course, a person gives a lasting set to his own being. Consequently, it is proper to say that in choosing this object rather than that, one is in reality choosing what kind of person or self one is going to be. Superficially, the deliberation which terminates in choice is concerned with weighing the values of particular ends. Below the surface, it is a process of discovering what sort of being a person most wants to become.[53]

In short,the thing actually at stake in any serious deliberation is not a difference of quantity, but what kind of person one is to become, what sort of self is in the making, what kind of a world is making.[54]

Here it must be emphasized that a habit is an interaction with the environment. Thus in considering the effects of action on character, one can at the same time consider what kind of relationship to his world, to other persons, he is establishing. One cannot adequately inquire into what kind of person he is becoming without at the same time inquiring into what kind of world it is which such habits encourage for himself and others. To assess what is happening to one's character is at the same time to make a judgment as to how one will tend to interact with future events. In this sense, one *can* take regard for the long-run consequences of action.

This act is only one of a multitude of acts. If we confine ourselves to the consequences of this one act we shall come out with a poor reckoning. Disposition is habitual, persistent. It shows itself therefore in many acts and in many consequences. . . . An act of gambling may be judged, for example, by its immediate overt effects, consumption of time, energy, disturbance of ordinary monetary considerations, etc. It may also be judged by its consequences upon character, setting up an enduring love of excitement, a persistent temper of speculation, and a persistent disregard of sober, steady work. To take the latter effects into account is equivalent to taking a broad view of future consequences; for these dispositions affect future companionships, vocation and avocations,the whole tenor of domestic and public life.[55]

A critic might object here that this sort of criticism of values hardly guarantees that one will not act selfishly or cruelly. Of course it doesn't. What sort of guaranteees of conduct are built into any system of criticism? But, again, thorough consideration of the implications of one's actions, in this social world, seems to

---

[53] *Ethics*, pp. 302, 317.

[54] *Human Nature and Conduct*, pp. 216-7.

[55] *Ibid.*, pp. 45, 47. And see above, Chapter VI, p. 248, pertaining to the cultivation of habits which will be efficacious in meeting unpredictable eventualities.

offer far more promise of harmonious social conduct than those methods of deliberation predicated on those "verities" which presume to transcend experience.

In effective deliberation, one should not so much ask what is good for him in an isolated situation, without regard for the effect on his habits. He should consider what *kind* of life he is making. Without such reflection, one may gain his petty advantage, and lose the conditions of a happy life. Deliberation, as Dewey recommends it, is thus a different sort of thing from mere prudentialism. Inasmuch as Dewey's philosophy requires inquiry into the full meanings of human behavior (especially as it occurs in a context where other persons funtion with equal right), it is difficult to see how any serious appraisal of his views could lead to the conclusion that they imply opportunism in conduct. So like Plato and Aristotle, Dewey emphasizes the crucial importance of questioning the kind of life-values and social relations one is creating in undertaking individual actions. A great many judgments about what one should do can be decisively affected by considerations of what *sort* of person he is becoming, about the *kind* of life he can strive to create.

The second way in which the constituents of consummatory experience can be criticized bears much resemblance to the first. This is the checking of the tendencies of acts undertaken in the situation. Although, as Dewey himself insists, it is not possible to make specific predictions of the course of events which will succeed the resolution of the existing situation, we can still make predictions about the *tendencies* of given actions. That is, one may safely assert that certain behavior will tend to have certain kinds of ramifications subsequent to the situation in which it actually takes place:

> The future outcome is not certain But neither is it certain what the present fire will do in the future. It may be unexpectedly fed or extinguished. But its *tendency* is a knowable matter, what it will do under certain circumstances. And so we know what is the tendency of malice, charity, conceit, patience.[56]

Suppose, for example, that one is trying to deceive someone in order to avoid fulfilling a promise: He might determine a way to be successful in this deception. Dewey urges, as we have seen,

---

[56] *Ibid.*, p. 206.

that the individual consider this entire *way* of dealing with other persons and approaching practical problems – consider the kind of life he is creating for himself and for others. In addition to this kind of criticism, Dewey also draws attention to the criticism of the tendencies of actions. In criticism of this sort, the individual could predict certain likely kinds of result which would not be immediately relevant to the situation, as such. The deception, for example, might later be exposed, and at once the individual would become subject to a host of difficulties. It is true, of course, that a particular event of exposure and the occurrence of particular difficulties could not be predicted in terms of specific times and places and agencies; but it is also true that these kinds of consequences are to be expected from this kind of action. Thus one might not be able to make any specific prediction that this deceit would be exposed, but he could regard it as a crucial possibility; and he could also make significant estimates about the typical results to be expected if the deceit is found out. Note that appraisals of this sort are neither to forecast specific events, nor do they necessarily imply any judgment about the formation of habits. Yet they are a valid and useful form of criticism.

In stressing the ends-means continuum, Dewey in various places urges that the way to criticize an end is to treat it also as a means – as a function of further interactions and values. This is fundamentally good advice. Yet as the preceding analyses have shown, it is a rather complex matter to apply it. Different kinds of "ends" must be discriminated, and the way in which they are to be treated as means varies accordingly. A brief summary, then, of the preceding discussion will be useful: Problematic goods (implying certain actions) should be examined in their continuities as these pertain to the problematic situation. Here specific and accurate predictions are needed. Explicit events following the consummatory phase of the situation cannot, however, be predicted with accuracy; and in this sense (and this sense alone) the consummatory end cannot be criticized as a means. On the other hand, consummatory experience (or any experience) can be criticized by considering the tendencies of the kinds of action which, within the particular situation, may or may not be effective. These tendencies do extend beyond the particular situation. Finally, and most important, the pursuits of any circumstance should be criticized as means by which one cultivates an enduring character of a certain kind.

I have been dealing with experimental methods of moral deliberation and with the kind of considerations that are crucial to its successful prosecution, as well as with some basic problems suggested by Dewey's arguments. Before dealing with situations in which social institutions and practices are problematic, it remains to introduce Dewey's thinking concerning the instrumentalities of moral reflection.

By these instrumentalities I mean the intellectual resources which aid deliberation. It is here where past moral and cognitive experience are indispensable. When one is implicated in problematic circumstances, it is seldom obvious just what might, or should, be done to restore the continuity of activity. In order to analyze the situation, what is first of all needed is a fund of experience in such matters. Indeed, it requires considerable experience simply to realize that what is first of all called for is analysis. The uses of experience are mainly four. The first two of these are immediately obvious, but nonetheless important. First, it is necessary to have the habits of consecutive, consistent, and experimental thought; and these habits are clearly not an innate possession, but are built up in experience. Second, it is necessary to have accumulated knowledge of objects of the environment. Objects are portentous; they can do a variety of things, and we can act with them in various ways and effect diverse consequences with them. Hence, in projecting possible ways of acting with the features of the environment, our funded knowledge of such features is indispensable.

The third way in which past experience is operative intellectually in the situation is in one's awareness of the meanings of his habits of conduct. Only by having judged the outcomes of our habits in previous experience will we have some intimation of where they may lead in the present. One anticipates undertaking certain actions; and especially because the outcome of the predicament is uncertain, it is of great importance to have some sense of the tendencies of behaving in certain ways:

> Always our old habits and dispositions carry us into new fields. We have to be always learning and relearning the meaning of our active tendencies. . . . Foresight which draws liberally upon the lessons of past experience reveals the tendency,

> the meaning, of present action;. . .[57]

These tendencies should be understood not only in respect to consequences in the environment, but also to their effects on character, which, of course, will be a crucial determinant of future behavior. Clearly, it is only by being attentive to the meanings of our habits in on-going activity that in any particular situation we will have that experience which is indispensable in evaluating alternatives:

> Self-deception originates in looking at an outcome in one direction only – as a satisfaction of what has gone before, ignoring the fact that what is attained is a state of habits which will continue in action and which will determine future results. Outcomes of desires are also beginnings of new acts and hence are portentous.[58]

The fourth intellectual resource could be regarded as an instance of the class of resources mentioned first, but it is so distinctively important to moral philosophy that it warrants individual treatment. I refer to that funded moral experience which involves the possession of so-called ethical principles, standards, ends. In discussing the uniqueness of good and its implications, it was indicated that there is no a priori way of deciding what to do in a given situation; recourse to antecedent principles will not determine the best course of action. To say this, however, is not to reject as worthless such things as moral principles. It is, rather, to make possible an appraisal of their genuine nature and function. Indeed, precisely because each situation is unique, inquiries into its possibilities must be guided by the fruits of previous inquiries. Thus so-called moral principles and ends are not laws which in themselves have authority over conduct; but they are *aids to inquiry* and their suitability is determined by the success of inquiry.

> *Because* situations in which deliberation is evoked are new, and therefore unique, general principles are needed. Only an uncritical vagueness will assume that the sole alternative to fixed generality is absence of continuity. . . . In denying that the meaning of any genuine case of deliberation can be exhausted by treating it as a mere case of established classification the value of classification is not denied. It is shown where its value lies, namely, in directing attention to resemblances and differences in the new case, in economizing effort in foresight.[59]

---

[57] *Ibid.*, p. 208.

[58] *Ibid.*, pp. 252-3.

[59] *Ibid.*, p. 244.

An extended analysis of Dewey's treatment of principles would disclose that his thinking about their nature and use was neither clear nor consistent, and was sometimes misleading.[60] Nevertheless, some general conclusions can safely be drawn. Principles should not be taken as directions to action, but as *suggesting* actions, which then have to be examined in their conditions and consequences. A principle might also suggest what kinds of consequences might reasonably be expected from certain kinds of action. Thus the experience accumulated in human culture can be brought to bear on particular dilemmas of which a particular individual might have little or no experience.

In an action similar to that enjoined by the principle is undertaken, it is thereby subjected to test; and if it produces the anticipated effect, its general aptness in such situations is confirmed. In this sense then, principles are hypotheses:

> Principles exist as hypotheses with which to experiment. Human history is long. There is a long record of past experimentation in conduct, and there are cumulative verifications which give many principles a well earned prestige. . . . [I]t is clear that all principles are empirical generalizations from the ways in which previous judgments of conduct have practically worked out. When this fact is apparent, these generalizations will be seen to be not fixed rules for deciding doubtful cases, but instrumentalities for their investigation, methods by which the net value of past experience is rendered available for present scrutiny of new perplexities. Then it will also follow that they are hypotheses to be tested and revised by further working.[61]

Just as hypotheses in the experimental sciences are modified through continued testing, a principle as hypothesis admits of qualification or reconstruction. Thus the funded experience of the past is neither immovable incubus nor irrelevant fancy. Rather, it permits of growth and refinement.

> . . . [T]he choice is not between throwing away rules previously developed and sticking obstinately by them. The intelligent alternative is to revise, adapt, expand and alter them. The problem is one of continuous, vital readaptation.[62]

---

[60] For example, he refers to principles as methods (in *Human Nature and Conduct,* pp. 239, 241; *Ethics,* p. 309), but assuredly a principle is not a method.

[61] *Human Nature and Conduct,* pp. 239-41. What are often called moral laws are obviously at least part of what Dewey means by principles. In general usage, a law both specifies and commands a certain act. So-called laws can be utilized as principles if they are used as hypotheses and hence as guides to inquiry, rather than as prescriptions.

[62] *Ibid.,* pp. 239-40.

A classification of ends is also useful to inquiry:

> Similar situations recur; desires and interests are carried over from one situation to another and progressively consolidated. A schedule of general ends results, the involved values being "abstract" in the sense of not being directly connected with any particular existing case but not in the sense of independence of all empirically existent cases. As with general ideas in the conduct of any natural science, these general ides are used as intellectual instrumentalities in judgment of particular cases as the latter arise; they are, in effect, tools that direct and facilitate examination of things in the concrete while they are also developed and tested by the results of their application in these cases.[63]

The sort or ends that Dewey evidently has in mind are what the Greeks called excellences or virtues; they are distinctively useful habits:

> Health, wealth, industry, temperance, amiability, courtesy, learning, esthetic capacity, initiative, courage, patience, enterprise, thoroughness and a multitude of other generalized ends are acknowledged as goods.[64],

> Virtues are ends because they are such important means. To be honest, courageous, kindly is to be in the way of producing specific natural goods or satisfactory fulfillments.[65]

The function of a classification of ends is the same as that of principles. Their general usefulness is in the summarization of human experience which can be utilized in deliberation. Dewey, indeed, uses the term "principles" in such a general way that he seems to consider ends as a class of principles. At one point he asserts that any general idea from our moral heritage can function as an aid to inquiry, and he labels all such ideas "principles":

> Out of resembling experiences general ideas develop; through language, instruction, and tradition this gathering together of experiences of value into generalized points of view is extended to take in a whole people and a race. Through intercommunication the experience of the entire human race is to some extent pooled and crystallized in general ideas. These ideas constitute *principles.*[66]

Regardless of the vagueness, Dewey's general point is clear and important: Human moral experience has been summarized in various ways, and – as in any field of inquiry – the conclusions of the past are indispensable in suggesting possibilities for action

---

[63] *Theory of Valuation,* p. 44.

[64] *Reconstruction in Philosophy,* p. 169.

[65] *Human Nature and Conduct,* p. 47.

[66] *Ethics,* p. 304.

and fulfillment. Because of the uniqueness of good and the creative possibilities of any situation, such conclusions must be taken only as advice, never as commands.

The discussion of principles and ends also constitutes an introduction to the next subject matter: the criticism of institutions, social norms, laws, etc. A great deal of moral reflection is concerned, not with individual action, but with the assessment of general rules and practices of all sorts. So-called moral principles and ends are instances. Just as problematic goods require functional analysis, so too do principles, ends, and all other institutions and practices as well. Such things can be analyzed not only as problematic for an individual, but as problematic for an entire group or society. Thus it is that economic, political, educational, religious precedures must be tested: What resources of the community are, or have been, used to bring them into existence and sustain them? What effects on the community do these things exert? What values do they promote, retard, or sacrifice? What alternative modes of action are possible, and how might they function? [67] This is not only the only effective mode of criticism, but it is at the same time, of course, the only rational way of reconstituting our evaluations of such things. Dewey provides an example, alluding to *laissez-faire* capitalism:

> Suppose, for example, that it be ascertained that a particular set of current valuations have, as their antecedent historical conditions, the interest of a small group or special class in maintaining certain exclusive privileges and advantages, and that this maintenance has the effect of limiting both the range of the desires of others and their capacity to actualize them. Is it not obvious that this knowledge of conditions and consequences would surely lead to revaluation of the desires and ends that have been assumed to be authoritative sources of valuation? Not that such revaluation would of necessity take effect immediately. But, when valuations that exist at a given time are found to lack the support they have previously been supposed to have, they exist in a context that is highly adverse to their continued maintenance. In the long run the effect is similar to a warier attitude that develops towards certain bodies of water as the result of knowledge that these bodies of water contain disease germs.[68]

---

[67] It might be noted that this criticism, no more than that already discussed, involves no long-range forecasts. What is of concern are the conditions and consequences that occur right now; and crucial among these are the social habits that are instituted.

[68] *Theory of Valuation,* pp. 59-60. Again, it should not be supposed that knowledge in and of itself is sufficient to reconstitute meanings and desires. But it is a necessary condition of any reconstitution which can release the best possibilities of human nature.

Clearly, hypotheses about the conditions and consequences of institutions and practices are open to experimental test. As in any experimental inquiry, such hypotheses need not – and should not – be either accepted or rejected in a wholesale way. Rather, they are susceptible to being refined and qualified in various ways and remain open to further inquiry. Thus inquiry becomes progressive and cumulative. Alternative modes of social action which are contrived in imagination are also to be tested experimentally. Moreover, such analyses must be renewed as the conditions with which such actions funtion undergo change. Economic and political procedures which produce desired effects in connection with one set of cultural and scientific conditions will not produce the same effects when they function with a different set of such conditions. Thus, for example, whatever merits capitalistic economic institutions might have had in eighteenth-century England have to be completely reassessed in the modern industrial state.

Criticism of the kind indicated here pertains also to matters already introduced: One should reflect on the meaning of his habits – on his ways of behaving. Our habits are the great instrumentality of freedom and conduct as art. They will determine whether we can deal with each situation as an occasion for personal growth and realization of value or for further withdrawal and acquiescence. They determine the kind of relationships with others which we typically enjoy and the characteristic values we find in experience. Clearly, this sort of analysis is vitally important to any individual: It constitutes a deliberate consideration of a way of life. Criticism of this sort is perhaps more difficult than any other; for there is a notorious difficulty simply in identifying what are in fact our habits of thought, belief, and action. It is safe to conclude that Dewey would not regard this criticism as primarily a form of introspection. It would most fruitfully be conducted in the process of communication with others (at best with a Socrates), wherein they can discern and question what is most characteristic of us. (It is perhaps not inaccurate to say that a great deal of the world's literature is, in effect, criticism of the sort discussed here. Many writers are distinguished for their astute and perceptive observations of the human scene. Their works, accordingly, help us to understand ourselves and our possibilities.)

The discussion in this section has been concerned with the resources and methods which an individual can bring to problematic situations. There is a further resource very much worthy of note; and it is, indeed, that upon which all others depend in large measure. I refer to the social intelligence embodied in institutions and efficacious in all social intercourse. The individual intelligence receives its powers from this source; and the former is vital and imaginative, or meager and dull, as the latter flourishes or is enfeebled. This matter will receive its due account and emphasis in the final section. It is appropriate now, however, to make a preliminary statement of the nature of its application to criticism of values: Moral deliberation, to be at all effective, must be carried on as a social process. When this process is cooperative and proceeds in a certain manner, it is in fact what Dewey calls democracy. (Social intelligence, however, is a more inclusive concept than democracy; and it can function morally without necessarily being democratic in the strictist sense.)

Without anticipating the particulars of the next section, it can be said that Dewey's notion of democracy is in many ways simply the logical extension of ideas already presented. (I have suggested as much in previous passages.) Whatever the usefulness of the procedures of moral deliberation detailed thus far, their effectiveness would be severely limited if they were employed simply by individuals in isolation. One cannot deliberate alone about the meaning of his social conduct, for the persons with whom he will interact will affect that conduct and its meaning in accordance with their own interests, aims, and actions. It follows that any individual must be in communication with others if he is to determine the meaning of proposed alternatives for action. This is to say, in short, that deliberation itself must be a social process; it must be part of the process of social intelligence. The fact that effective deliberation is a social process is insufficiently stressed in such works as *Experience and Nature* and *The Quest for Certainty.* On the other hand, it receives the most urgent attention in such works as *Liberalism and Social Action, Freedom and Culture,* and most especially in *The Public and Its Problems.* And Dewey regarded *Democracy and Education* as principally a work in moral philosophy. However well or ill Dewey made his point, it must be insisted that it is the keystone to his theory of the nature and function of moral deliberation; and anyone who misses this point must fail to have substantial grasp of Dewey's philosophy.[69]

The notion of democracy as the means of the formation and realization of value will be examined in due order. At present, my intention is to resume the themes of this section by dealing with a further issue concerning the criticism of values. The discussion of criticism of values provides a context for examining the problem of the actual conflict of values occurring in society. The issue could be characterized as that concerning the assumptions and methods of criticizing conflict. The fact that deliberation is conceived as a social process is especially pertinent here; and the relevance to democratic theory will also be evident.[70]

Let it be observed first that any constructive approach to the problem of conflict, as Dewey understands it, would require investigation into its causes and the means of avoiding it. In addition, the resolution of actual conflicts depends very much on the search for novel plans of action which would, if possible, be acceptable to all parties to the conflict. As Dewey envisions it, a democratic procedure is normally most effective in accomplishing such a result. I am not here going to examine just what that procedure is. Rather I will look into the *presuppositions* of his treatment of democracy and social intelligence as means of handling conflict. It must be remarked that such phrases as "accept-

---

[69] The point is conspicuously overlooked by C.L. Stevenson in "Reflections on John Dewey's Ethics" in his *Facts and Values* (New Haven and London: Yale University Press, 1963). Hence Stevenson's charge that Dewey's ethical theory is "curiously incomplete" is at least premature.

Work in contemporary ethics is given to proceeding in isolation from (among other things) social philosophy, so perhaps it doesn't occur to current philosophers to seek an understanding of Dewey's views by examining the spectrum of his works in moral philosophy.

[70] As I indicated in Chapter IV, any extended treatment of this matter has to take very seriously Dewey's philosophy of democracy. Accordingly, my comments here will be highly pertinent to Dewey's conception of the nature and function of democracy; and what is said will be an important prelude to the latter discussions of the next section. I am by no means, however, undertaking a thorough analysis of Dewey's social philosophy. Such a task would extend well beyond the scope of this book. It is true, nevertheless, that his analysis of man and value in nature provides fundamental assumptions for dealing with problems of conflict; and in this context certain of his ideas about democracy are strikingly relevant.

able to all parties" and "democratic procedure" evidently presuppose some notion of equality. That is, they imply that all persons involved in social conflict are, in some sense, to be counted equally. Equality is a fundamental ethical concept. It is assuredly central in any inquiry into the bases of settlement of social conflict. In the next few pages, therefore, I will focus on issues surrounding Dewey's ideas on this topic.

It may be noted at once that his philosophy of nature forbids the standard metaphysical justification for inequality:

> Now whatever the idea of equality means for democracy, it means, I take it, that the world is not to be construed as a fixed order of species, grades or degrees. It means that every existence deserving the name of existence has something unique and irreplaceable about it, that it does not exist to illustrate a principle, to realize a universal or to embody a kind or class.[71]

Hence, presumably, anyone claiming privilege or advantage relative to others would have to justify it by its consequences. If such consequences were simply selfish and private and hindered the good of others, the initial question recurs: What justifies private advantage over others?[72] Discussions in Chapters II and III indicated the basis for Dewey's conclusion that no one, in himself and on his own account, is inherently entitled to any right or priority of claim relative to any other individual. This argument seemed so obviously valid to Dewey that he gave it very little explicit attention, but took it rather for granted. The matters of concern to him were to determine what follows from the argument and to stress the positive values of democratic equality. He adopted, without apparent reservation, the demand for impartiality given voice by the utilitarians:

> The utilitarian theory, in addition to its insistence upon taking into consideration the widest, most general range of consequences, insists that in estimating consequences in the way of help and harm, pleasure and suffering, each one shall count as one, irrespective of distinctions of birth, sex, race, social status, economic and political position.[73]

---

[71] *Characters and Events,* II, p. 854.

[72] A capitalist might justify his private gain by justifying the economic system by means of which the gain is acquired. He is, in effect, claiming the social desirability of capitalism; and its social desirability is open to experimental inquiry. At least it is so when compared to feasible alternatives.

[73] *Ethics,* p. 262.

The idea of equality entails as well that claims advanced by an individual in his own behalf could equally well be put forward by anyone else in relevantly similar circumstances. Hence, Dewey says, an individual claim is at the same time an implicit claim about what kinds of social acts are permissible or desirable. At least this must be so if the individual is to be consistent.

> Wrong consists in faithlessness to that upon which the wrongdoer counts when he is judging and seeking for what is good to him. He betrays the principles upon which he depends; he turns to his personal advantage the very values which he refuses to acknowledge in his own conduct towards others. He contradicts, not as Kant would have it, some abstract law of reason, but the principle of reciprocity when he refuses to extend to others the goods which he seeks for himself. . . . In asserting the rightfulness of his own judgment of what is obligatory, [one] is implicitly putting forth a social claim, something therefore to be tested and confirmed by further trial by others.[74]

It follows from the notion that individual claims are implicit social claims that a principal means of testing individual claims is to communicate them to others, circulate them in the relevant social groups, and entertain alternative proposals in the same way:

> Indeed, capacity to endure publicity and communication is the test by which it is decided whether a pretended good is spurious or genuine. Moralists have always insisted upon the fact that a good is universal, objective, not just private, particular. But too often, like Plato, they have been content with a metaphysical universality or, like Kant, with a logical universality. Communication, sharing, joint participation are the only actual ways of universalizing the moral law and end. . . . Universalization means socialization, the extension of the area and range of those who share in a good.
>
> The increasing acknowledgment that goods exist and endure only through being communicated and that association is the means of conjoint sharing lies back of the modern sense of humanity and democracy.[75]

---

[74] *Ibid.*, pp. 251-2. "The justification of the moral non-conformist is that when he denies the rightfulness of a particular claim he is doing so not for the sake of private advantage, but for the sake of an object which will serve more amply and consistently the welfare of all." *(Ibid.)*

Needless to say, Dewey's usage of such terms as "wrong," "right," "obligatory" is for the sake of denoting experimentally verifiable ideas. Above, "wrong" denotes a kind of parasitical relation: One acts in a way which requires for its success precisely that other persons normally abstain from that kind of acting. Thus the deceitful may prey upon the trusting.

[75] *Reconstruction in Philosophy*, pp. 205-6. The arguments presented in the last paragraph show some resemblance to those of R.M. Hare. (See Hare's *Freedom and Reason* [New York: Oxford University Press, 1965].) There are very significant differ-

It should be noted that Dewey does not regard his idea of social universalization as conflicting with his idea of the uniqueness of good. Goods *are* unique, but they normally occur in a social context. Thus – if one accepts the notion of democratic equality – such goods must be shareable, if not actually shared:

> We insisted at the last hour upon the unique character of every intrinsic good. But the counterpart of this proposition is that the situation in which a good is consciously realized is not one of transient sensations or private appetites but one of sharing and communication – public, social.[76]

These ideas about equality, impartiality, the publicity and communication of moral claims, are presumably relevant to the basis for addressing problems of conflict. They at least indicate that the individual who would make an exception of himself must assume the burden of proof in showing what warrants the exception; and they indicate that in the absence of an argument to the contrary, all individuals have an equal claim on the values at issue. (Individuals also have, *prima facie,* equal responsibilities.) In these terms, anyone who arbitrarily regards his own claims as superior to those of others – however he may accommodate *himself* to his action – cannot expect others to be well disposed to his behavior or acquiescent in desiring to protect their own interests. If adequately enlightened, persons will be disposed to resist privileged authorities and elites. At the same time, they cannot consistently justify an attempt to transform *themselves* into a privileged elite.[77]

It is evident that Dewey's defense of equality and its implications have applicability to the clash of values. It is pertinent to

---

ences, however. Hare's position is neo-Kantian; the universalization test which he advocates is essentially formal; it does not require social communication. His universalization process does not entail the social formation and test of values. From Dewey's point of view, Hare's theory is at best a very limited tool of criticizing values. (Of course, there are further – and drastic – differences between the two. The most important of them concerns the function of moral language.) For a critique of the usefulness of Hare's theory written from a perspective highly sympathetic to that of Dewey, see David Sidorsky's "Universalizability, Rationality, and Moral Disagreement," in Kurtz (ed.), *Sidney Hook and the Contemporary World* (New York; The John Day Company, 1968), pp. 236-53.

[76] *Reconstruction in Philosophy,* p. 206.

[77] Ethical egoism, so-called, may be *logically* consistent; but anyone who advocates it as a way of life has a seriously deficient knowledge of the values which life-experience can afford.

point out, however, that his analysis presents some serious difficulties; and he had far too little to say about such difficulties and even too little explicit recognition of their existence. It is, for example, by no means a simple task to determine what are the legitimate grounds for making exceptions to the conditions of equality. But to determine such grounds is a most important task, for such exceptions are made all the time. Rather than open up all the delicate and complex issues centering in this problem, I will advance summarily one fundamental issue which, if treated in detail, would draw within its scope a great many particular controversies.

The issue is the relation between equality and justice. [78] Equality is not the same thing as justice, and it is clear that there are situations where the claims of equality and the claims of justice conflict. It may well be just, for example, that in many circumstances there be unequal distribution of wealth, reward, opportunity, position, affection, work, responsibility, and so forth. Dewey acknowledges as much.[79] Nevertheless, he gives very little attention to what, in his terms, is just, or how justice is determined, or how exactly it is related to equality. He does not take up the question of how it can be the case, on the one hand, that in the estimation of consequences each man shall count as one, and yet, on the other hand, inequalities in the distribution of wealth can be regarded as just. If wealth can be justly, yet unequally, distributed, what does it mean to say in such circumstances that each man counts as one?

Dewey says a just society is one in which the objective conditions of life are such that the general social welfare is protected and promoted. A just society is one "in which each performs his own part or function, and in which the good of the individual members is inseparable from that of the whole social body."[80]

> Is "justice" to be measured on the ground of existing social status, or on the ground of possibilities of development? Such questions suggest that social utilitarianism, when freed from its hedonistic handicap, makes justice to be a concern for the objective conditions of personal growth and achievement. . . .[81]

---

[78] The point I want to make here does not depend upon any particular definition of justice, so long as justice and equality are at least distinguished.

[79] Cf. *Ethics*, pp. 456-8.

[80] *Ibid.*, p. 458.

[81] *Ibid.*, p. 277. On p. 276 he says "the scope of justice is broad enough to cover all the conditions which make for social welfare."

Statements like this are not particularly helpful. Justice is the condition of the general social welfare; but there are many ways of construing the idea of social welfare. The notion of the *general* welfare admits of numerous possible interpretations and schemes of distribution. Few, if any, conditions satisfy the entire society; and different groups place differing values on existing laws, institutions, and practices: The common good is simply a will-o'-the-wisp. Hence in concrete cases some groups gain and others lose; and the disputing parties cannot agree on what would constitute an equitable agreement. These are facts of daily experience, and just how Dewey's notions of equality and justice could be applied to them is not clear. [82] In dealing with justice, Dewey committed the fallacy of regarding society as a unitary thing with common values. This is an especially embarrassing mistake for someone who emphasized so much the pluralistic nature of national society.

What I am pointing out here is not that Dewey's philosophy has come to a hopeless impasse. I am merely indicating that he left much to be done on these topics. My own conviction is, in fact, that constructive work on these problems must proceed in any case on naturalistic assumptions at least very similar to those of Dewey. We are not going to get far in dealing with moral problems in society by introducing presumed self-evident norms or by analyzing ordinary language. Whatever salvation man can work out for himself must come as a consequence of his determination to deal with reality such as it is and as it really could be.

Although Dewey did very little to deal with the interrelations of such ideas as equality, justice, and freedom, he nevertheless did not leave us without some useful suggestions. I believe it would be safe to infer, for example, that he was implicitly committed to the belief that equality is a more fundamental norm than justice or freedom. I take this to be true because he evidently held that it is the exception to equality that requires justification, rather than the reverse. Dewey urged, in addition, a

---

[82] In the category of unhelpful sentences, Dewey sets something of a standard with the following: "The meaning of justice in concrete cases is something to be determined by seeing what consequences will bring about human welfare in a fair and even way." (*Ethics*, p. 275.)

still more important lesson with direct relevance to problems of conflict and justice; and this lesson is predicated upon his notion of equality (as well as upon his logically more fundamental views about the nature of value). The reference is to his commitment to democracy, which is central to his moral philosophy. He unequivocally espoused social democracy, together with all the conditions which attend it, such as civil rights and liberties for all, full and free communication, and the removal of all barriers to social movement, participation and endeavor which are predicated on notions of inherently privileged status.

Given these democratic conditions, particular problems of restraint, justice, and conflict might be worked out as they arise for particular social groups. In this way, freedoms might be enlarged as much as possible and values enriched and shared on the widest scale. Democracy, as such, is not conceived to be the solution to social problems; it is social *method.* Precisely because there are no a priori laws, ends, or standards of adjudication, democracy is a necessary requisite to the reconciliation of conflicts and the uniting and enhancing of aims. Specific moral problems cannot be anticipated, and there are no fixed norms in accordance with which these problems can be settled. Thus – short of some form of authoritarian control – they can be addressed and worked out only by submitting them to the agencies of cooperative social intelligence, in which there is an initial presumption of the equality of all persons. This notion of democracy implies a clear recognition that human beings do not easily agree on substantive policies; they do not find a common good. And given also the fact that men inevitably engage in social interaction, they must determine a social method to which they can submit their differences.

Dewey's thesis of the essentially moral functions of democracy is enormously suggestive. It will receive further attention as social method in the concluding section. Nevertheless, he is not exculpated from the charge that he was neglectful in recognizing and dealing with important issues. An earnest democratic community would be limited in its capacity to deliberate if it did not have intellectual conceptions which mark genuine distinctions in the subject matter and which possess clear and unambiguous implications, coherent interrelations, and meanings sufficiently extensive to include the full range of relevant phenomena. This is not to say that the philosopher should dictate the meaning of words. It is to say that he can provide useful hypotheses and considerations for use in democratic deliberation.

Even in respect to his general thesis of the moral offices and potentialities of democracy, serious objections can be raised. First of all, it does not seem to be the case that democracy is always possible or even desirable. The so-called developing nations may be a case in point; so are armies, football teams, and hospitals. Each of these examples presents special problems and aims which cannot be analyzed here. It should be pointed out, however, that the alternative means of dealing with social conflicts and social control are not exhausted in pure participatory democracy and pure totalitariansim: Decision-making can be genuinely social and genuinely cooperative without being explicitly democratic. There are various way of utilizing a genuinely social intelligence in the interests of associated acitivity. (In addition, individuals can voluntarily give up their power to a trusted authority under limited conditions and for limited purposes.)

It should also be clear that there are grave risks involved especially when political units find it expedient to sacrifice democracy. In reference to political democracy, a second objection to Dewey's commitment might be advanced: What guarantee is there that a constituted democracy would not turn into an instrument of oppression? A majority could use formally democratic means to ravage a minority and even to destroy themselves. Yes, of course they could. There are risks in any enterprise which is human. Where is the dialectician who can propose a certain solution to all human problems? Dewey places his faith in democracy, but it is not a blind faith, and it is not primarily in the merely formal procedures, as such, of majority rule. Discussion in the next section will amplify considerably Dewey's conception of the methods and resources of democracy. For the present, I offer the reminder that formal political democracy cannot function effectively without the appropriate social habits; and I will conclude this section by summarizing Dewey's analysis of the positive values of democratic life. These are values which can come to have a widespread and compelling appeal; and, ultimately, it is only by democracy producing such concrete values for the individual that it can be fully workable in the sense Dewey envisioned.

If we focus attention on the distribution and quality of value in society, then it can be simply stated that Dewey was persuaded that the values of the democratic life provide a much richer, more meaningful experience than any other. The felt values in a democratic community are more widely and generously experienced, and they are of a different quality than those accruing to highly atomistic and/or regimented forms of associated life. It is important to see that a pervasive life-orientation is at issue: It is a matter of the kinds of meaning one finds in experience, the kinds of response he makes to every fresh problem, the kinds of aims he tries to formulate when he enters into reflection, the kinds of activity and relationships he finds precious. In the shared experience of a democratic community, Dewey holds, these take on a form which pales the experience in alternative ways of life. Genuinely democratic experience develops an individual's personality and provides him with a growth which possess their own irreplaceable fulfillments. The democratic character manifests itself as well in the amicable and cooperative attempt to resolve differences without any party either assuming or desiring that he be accorded privilege in this process on his own account.

The basic problem as Dewey sees it, is not so much to offer arguments demonstrating the superiortiy of democratic life. Rather, it consists in cultivating social intelligence and in making the conditions of democratic life a reality for actual social groups. With cultivated and freed intelligence, individuals will discern for themselves the merits of democracy; and with some genuine experience of democracy, people will know its precious values at first hand and will cherish them accordingly. Making such conditions a reality is no simple and immediate process. Undemocratic habits of thought and action and undemocratic institutions have wide currency. Change in these, if it is to be profound and enduring, must be gradual and incremental, introduced in various ways in various activities. Dewey especially stresses the developing habits of the young and the instrumentalities of education. Education is a preparation for democracy, not in *being* democratic, but essentially in developing the arts of social intelligence, free to range over all subjects.[83]

---

[83] For systematic accounts of the conditions requisite to the introduction of democracy, see Chapters III through VI of *The Public and Its Problems* and the last two chapters of *Liberalism and Social Action.* Dewey recognized that our economic structures and habits are such that they discourage and inhibit democratic control of the

Historically, it remains to be seen whether men can find mutually agreeable arrangements for settling their differences, uniting their aims, and enriching the values of their existence. There is need for a great deal of continued investigation and experiment in these matters; and it is here, according to Dewey, that moral inquiry comes to focus. To carry on with Dewey's work, such inquiry should be conceived as addressing problems in the theory and practice of cooperative social intelligence.

Intelligence in moral deliberation has been the general subject matter of this section, embracing a number of related topics. The further treatment of these themes can best be pursued in connection with an examination of the relation of science to the moral life.

3. Ethics, Science, and Democracy

Three topics will be taken up here. A brief summation will be made of the scientific standing of ethical theory and moral deliberation. Then a specific analysis of the uses of science in the moral life will be undertaken. Finally, the relation of these matters to democracy will be set forth. These subjects have occasioned considerable confusion in both students and critics of Dewey. However, in connection with the theories explicated in this study, these complex and difficult issues should be fairly manageable.

The analysis of the way in which ethics and ethical discourse can be truly experimental could be carried out in precisely the degree of detail in which Dewey analyzes experimental science. But such would be wholly unnecessary. For, in the context of the present work, the crucial point is that there are no characteristics of ethical subject matter, deliberation, or evaluation which preclude the use of scientific method or which require other than experimental procedures. The validity of this point is predicated upon Dewey's treatment of the following issues: the continuity of experience and nature, the nature of mind and thinking, the nature of experimental science, the nature of value, the function

---

uses of natural resources and national wealth. He was also aware of the great influence that economic interests wield in political affairs. He advocated an experimental form of democratic socialism. (See especially Chapter VI of *Individualism Old and New* and "The Economic Basis of the New Society," in Ratner *[op. cit.]*, pp. 416-33.)

of ethical theory and ethical discourse, and the nature of moral judgment. Clearly, moral science, like any science, is an art; and it is also clear that to Dewey it is the consummate art. It is clear, in fact, that both *Experience and Nature* and *The Quest for Certainty* were written primarily for the sake of exhibiting the foundations in nature of a wholly scientific moral philosophy; and this is also much of the point of the *Logic.* Hence there is no good reason to undertake here further treatment of Dewey's analysis of science and its characteristic procedures.

What is of pertinence, however, is to note that the validity of Dewey's theory of moral deliberation does not depend upon the detailed accuracy of his analyses of science. These latter have been subjected to responsible criticism; and it is evidently true that there are more distinctively different models of experimental investigation than Dewey suggests. It should be clear, however, that even if his theory of moral reflection does not correspond precisely to all examples of scientific inquiry, it is nevertheless true that such reflection satisfies entirely the experimental criteria of meaning and truth. And this, of course, is the crucial conclusion.[84]

Generally speaking, then, it can be asserted that moral deliberation is like any experimental inquiry: It requires thorough and accurate knowledge of the constituents of the problem; it requires imaginative contrivance of hypotheses; these hypotheses must be based on the information available, and their formation must, of course, conform to the rules of inference. Finally, they can be tested only by the initiation of specified operations.

There is, perhaps, greater room for creative discussion at this point by turning to the various uses that can be made of the sciences and their methods in forming and securing values, which is the second general topic of this section. This topic alone could easily be developed at considerable length; so the remarks here

---

[84] If one were so alert as to ask by what authority Dewey may stipulate the form that deliberation should take, the answer is readily available: Dewey recommends his views on the ground that they are most conducive to the realization of welcome and cherished ends in human experience. This position is itself verifiable. And only a person hopelessly abstracted from experience would ask "Why pursue cherished ends?" The serious questions are *How* form them? *How* choose between them? *How* pursue them?

must be of a rather summary character. The subjects to be covered are 1) the specific uses of the sciences in the moral life, and 2) the nature and value of "scientific" mentality.

1) We may begin by considering the third of the types of problematic situation referred to on p. 301, above: the inquiry into the conditions requisite to the production and sustenance of presumed values. Such inquiries are scientific in the strictest sense; that is, they can best be carried out by persons professionally trained in the various intellectual disciplines. Psychologists, economists, sociologists, political scientists, biologists, chemists, physicists, and many others can inquire into the relations of dependence between all kinds of human behavior (as well as merely physiological functioning) and natural and social processes. Men would thus be able systematically and reliably to bring prizings into relation, to investigate the conditions of both the occurrence and the satisfaction of human needs and desires, to investigate the conditions of the occurrence of values, and, indeed, to discover the determinants of all meanings in experience. Thus science becomes a potent instrument for the rational formation of desire and value, for the meeting of actual human needs, and for the attainment of an enriched life-experience.

It must be noted here that science – as a sophisticated activity carried on by trained persons – is not a substitute for reflection in moral situations. All such situations are unique; and they admit of an indefinite number of possible outcomes, depending in large part on the knowledge and desires of the persons involved. Hence inquiry and choice in each situation remain essential. It is clear, however, that decisions can be greatly enlightened by scientific knowledge, which displays the instrumentalities of nature. Hence the possibilities of any situation are much greater, and the possibilities of control of variables much greater, when appropriate scientific knowledge is at the disposal of those who must choose and act.

> Every gain in natural science makes possible new aims. That is, the discovery of how things *do* occur makes it possible to conceive of their happening at will, and gives us a start on selecting and combining the conditions, the means, to command their happening.[85]

[85] *Human Nature and Conduct*, p. 235.

This is a suitable place to give emphasis to a feature of Dewey's moral philosophy which should already be evident: His naturalism in ethics does not eliminate individual autonomy in moral choice. For Dewey's naturalism does not prescribe ends or deduce moral obligations. (Fixed ends, as we know, are hateful to Dewey's view.) It is concerned, rather, with the nature of value and the procedures of its formation and realization. All of its imperatives, as we have seen, are hypothetical. [86]

It addition to creating a plurality of possible ends, the sciences are moralized in function when they are used in the service of those ends which require no deliberation to establish their enduring desirability: matters of health and wealth, the fructification of nature, the control of the environment, the understanding of social processes and the mechanisms of human nature. [87] The latter sort of knowledge makes possible the restructuring of society in such a way to promote the growth of certain kinds of habits and inhibit the growth of others. Hypotheses in social sciences can also bring prizings into relation by showing how behavior and institutions of various sorts function within a given socioeconomic environment; and they can suggest what the nature and relations of prizings might be under alternative institutions.

It is clear that the so-called physical scientist can furnish invaluable information to the disposal of human aims and intelligence. The role of the social scientist – always a controversial issue – requires more attention. Here it must be made absolutely clear precisely how, according to Dewey, the social scientist is to fulfill these functions. He is *not* to be hired out as a technician to solve social problems. That is, he is not to serve either industry, political powers, or whomever, as a social engineer, telling his employers how to effect the changes they desire. Such a role would destroy his freedom as a scientist and limit greatly the scope of his inquiries and his critical imagination. [88] The inquirer

---

[86] See footnote 48, this chapter.

[87] It is now clear, of course, that the numerous discussions in Chapter II about the role of science in investigating man in nature have enormous moral import.

Today scientists are blamed for the destruction of the environment. The fault, however, lies with socially irresponsible technology; and it is evident that scientific knowledge is indispensable to rectify the evils of runaway technology.

[88] This argument is advanced with especial vigor in "Liberating the Social Scientist" *(op. cit.).*

should always be free (in Dewey's frequently used phrase) to follow the lead of the subject matter.

What, then, the social scientist should do is simply to provide information concerning the conditions and consequences of the various forms of social interaction and of social institutions of all kinds.[89] This would be true of social forms both actual and proposed. Thus he discloses the constituents of behavior and its meanings; he discloses the implications of social actions; and he brings what have been isolated aims into relation.

> . . . improved valuation must grow out of existing valuations, subjected to critical methods of investigation that bring them into systematic relations with one another. . . . In the field of human activities there are at present an immense number of facts of desires and purposes existing in rather complete isolation from one another. But there are no hypotheses of the same empirical order which are capable of relating them to one another so that the resulting propositions will serve as methodic controls of the formation of future desires and purposes, and, thereby, of new valuations . . . yet without such a science systematic theoretical control of valuation is impossible; . . .[90]

Thus the scientist provides the *basis* for individuals to reconstitute their desires, regulate their conduct, control their environment effectively, and jointly to determine social policy. Clearly, the social scientist is neither dictator of values nor servant of preconceived ends:

> Inquiry, indeed, is a work which devolves upon experts. But their expertness is not shown in framing and executing policies, but in discovering and making known the facts upon which the former depend.[91]

His discipline is essential to considerations of value, but it still maintains the scientific ideal of being value-free in the sense that

---

[89] Institutions most demanding such analysis are the political, the educational, the economic and – as Dewey emphasized more and more in later writings – science itself. The effects of science on existence have been overwhelming; its possibilites for both good and evil are limitless; and yet no one seems concerned to examine the institution and uses of science itself.

[90] *Theory of Valuation*, pp. 60-2.

[91] *The Public and Its Problems*, p. 208. Dewey argues that it is impossible for social science ever to formulate universal laws. Such "laws" of human nature and social behavior are, he says, impossible; for the nature and conduct of human beings will change as they enter into new interactions. Because the possibilities of these latter are limitless, so, presumably, are the forms of the former. Hence the cumulative progress of the social sciences, as sciences, lies in their developing ever more refined instruments of inquiry and analysis.

it does not, in principle, serve as a defender of any special interest. The judgments rendered by social scientists are those of means-consequences. It is precisely because he is (presumably) possessed of a technical language empty of emotive content that the social scientist provides morally important information. Thus assertions of means-consequences would not be obfuscated by existing moral biases or the emotive connotations of ordinary language.[92]

The situations in which such inquiries occur do not differ in method from the other kinds of situations examined previously; but, as we now see, they do differ in that the occasion for such inquiry is not immediately *morally* problematic. Its moral implications are clear, but the situation, as such, does not present a moral problem.

What has been said indicates that the sciences can tell us how, specifically, events in experience occur. In connection with this point, an observation might be made of one of the particular uses Dewey himself makes of science. I refer to *Human Nature and Conduct.* This book champions the functional theory of human nature in nature and also deals extensively with human values. It should be pointed out that the discussions of value in the book are not deduced from the theory. (Again: Scientific theory does not dictate ends; that is the corruption of science. Conclusions about actions to be taken are not deduced from scientific propositions; that is not only logically absurd, but mistakes the nature of value formation as well.) Rather, Dewey is concerned to show that what are acknowledged human values are derivative of man's interaction with nature. Moreover, the theory of *Human Nature and Conduct,* if correct, provides information requisite to the intelligent formation and pursuit of value: It indicates, in general, what are the vital determinants of behavior, and it indicates the kind of interactions that are most laden with value.

2) The discussion has been about the uses of science. At this point I will take up the nature and value of what Dewey calls the scientific attitude. It is abundantly clear that Dewey places fundamental reliance in the moral life on experimental social intelli-

---

[92] See above, section 2 of this chapter, p. 310, where Dewey's comments from p. 496 of the *Logic* are quoted. They pertain to the nature of judgment in social science, insisting that the very value of such judgment consists in its strictly factual nature.

gence. Intelligence, if it is to be of any enduring consequence in the conduct of men, must, of course, be a personal habit, a ready and assured disposition. To say that it is a habit means not only that the individual is acquainted with and characteristically uses experimental procedures, but that he also possesses a number of additional habits intimately related to his commitment to scientific method. These habits, too, become effective and congenial. Such habits include a rejection of dogmatism of any kind, holding propositions tentatively, welcoming further tests and evidence, receptivity to novel ideas, exercising imagination to contrive and explore alternative hypotheses, engaging in questioning and criticism of accepted beliefs of all kinds, tolerance of the views of others as hypotheses to be entertained and examined on their merits, scorn for emotive arguments and language, respect for the social character of knowledge and the communications vital to it. Speaking of the scientific attitude, Dewey says,

> Some of its obvious elements are willingness to hold belief in suspense, ability to doubt until evidence is obtained; willingness to go where evidence points instead of putting first a personally preferred conclusion; ability to hold ideas in solution and use them as hypotheses to be tested instead of as dogmas to be asserted; and (possibly the most distinctive of all) enjoyment of new fields for inquiry and of new problems.[93]

From what has been set forth in this study, it is evident that such habits are vital to intrinsically valuable conduct. They are indispensable for the discrimination, formation, and realization of value. (And the latter functions imply as well the reconstitution of desire and ways of behaving.) It will be indicated in the concluding part of this section that these habits of enlightened thought reach their greatest fruition when they are put to willing and deliberate use in the democratic community.

Dewey has illuminating analyses to make of effective intelligence. A rather complex set of habits is requisite to such disposition. (These have been discussed in one aspect, above, pp. 242-3.) Further relevant considerations about the development of the scientific attitude can be presented by introducing characteristic objections to Dewey's reliance on intelligence.

Not only are the possible uses of intelligence little understood

---

[93] *Freedom and Culture,* p. 145.

or appreciated, but many persons have been extremely skeptical about (a) the actual effect intelligence can have in changing established habits and (b) the capacities for intelligence possessed by most men. These two difficulties can best be examined together.

Some of Dewey's remarks seem quite naive. One such remark was quoted on p. 323 , above. Another example is the following: Concerning the application of science to social control, Dewey says, "What stands in the way is a lot of outworn traditions, moth-eaten slogans and catchwords, that do substitute duty for thought, as well as our entrenched predatory self-interest."[94] (Reinhold Niebuhr takes Dewey's remark to mean that conservatism is simply a product of ignorance and to suggest that Dewey has little conception of the class antagonisms in America.[95]) But such statements, when supplemented by some of Dewey's further views, are perhaps not so naive. Americans, it is true, are intoxicated by the economic institutions of *laissez-faire* capitalism. Yet this intoxication might not represent so much the ineffectuality of intelligence as its complete absence. That is, few persons are at all willing even to entertain conscientious criticism of "free enterprise." It is a holy object, which must be removed from criticism:

> Men have got used to an experimental method in physical and technical matters. They are still afraid of it in human concerns. The fear is the more efficacious because like all deep-lying fears it is covered up and disguised by all kinds of rationalizations. One of its commonest forms is a truly religious idealization of, and reverence for, established institutions; for example in our own politics, the Constitution, the Supreme Court, private property, free contract and so on. The words "sacred" and "sanctity" come readily to our lips when such things come under discussion. They testify to the religious aureole which protects the institutions. If "holy" means that which is not to be approached nor touched, save with ceremonial precautions and by specially anointed officials, then such things are holy in contemporary political life.[96]

An honest examination of social institutions and communications indicates that the possibilities of social intelligence have had precious little trial. Intelligence cannot be called a failure when it

---

[94] *Philosophy and Civilization,* p. 328.

[95] See the selection from Niebuhr's *Moral Man and Immoral Society* in Kennedy (ed.), *op. cit.,* pp. 60-1.

[96] *The Public and Its Problems,* pp. 169-70.

hasn't even been put to the trial; and all of Dewey's urgings for the use of intelligence regard the venture as an experiment, having little precedent in social practice.[97]

To find the reason for the lack of trial is to specify a fundamental contradiction in American Life. It was indicated in Chapter V that we are, on Dewey's view, trying to live with the effects of science by means of prescientific institutions. It is these institutions – structures in family, school, church, communications, neighborhood, politics, work – that determine our habits of thought. These institutions have been dominantly authoritarian. Hence critical habits of thought have not developed, and the rewards of intelligent conduct have not been widely experienced. If the reigning powers, of any sort, proclaim that America's greatness is one with the greatness of free enterprise, virtually everyone happily acquiesces in this view and refuses to consider it further.

More and more, Dewey became concerned about the compartmentalization of science, and his writings return again and again to the importance of revolutionizing the institutions that determine our uncritical habits.

> The entrenched and stubborn institutions of the past stand in the way of our thinking scientifically about human relations and social issues. Our mental habits in these respects are dominated by institutions of family, state, church and business that were formed long before men had an effective technique of inquiry and validation. It is this contradiction from which we suffer today.
>
> Disaster follows in its wake. It is impossible to overstate the mental confusion and the practical disorder which are bound to result when external and physical effects are planned and regulated, while the attitudes of mind upon which the direction of external results depends are left to the medley of chance, tradition, and dogma.[98]

In his later writings, this theme recurs more than any other, and is always a point of emphasis. Indeed, Dewey's objection to institutionalized religions was not primarily in the specific dogmas

---

[97] It is probably unusual for someone to neglect criticism of values altogether. Far more common, no doubt, is that criticism is extremely and arbitrarily limited – depending on one's prejudices and his unwillingness to undertake inquiry concerning them. If one has a stock of beliefs which he will not submit to criticism, he will undertake inquiry into a given problem simply in order to see if certain policies or actions are compatible with them. (This is yet another version of fixed ends.)

[98] *Philosophy and Civilization*, pp. 328-9.

which they propagate, but in the habits of thought which they foster:

> What is not realized . . . is that the issue does not concern this and that piecemeal *item* of belief, but centers in the question of the method by which any and every item of intellectual belief is to be arrived at and justified. . . . The fundamental question, I repeat, is not of this and that article of intellectual belief but of intellectual habit, method and criterion.[99]

The foregoing suggests that the problem of intelligent deliberation and action does not so much center on presumed innate powers of intelligence, but on *habits* of intelligence; and these are clearly social products. Dewey insists that the problem is fundamentally cultural, not individual:

> *Effective* intelligence is not an original, innate endowment. No matter what are the differences in native intelligence (allowing for the moment that intelligence can be native), the actuality of mind is dependent upon the education which social conditions effect.[100]

> I [have] . . . referred to the contempt often expressed for reliance upon intelligence as a social method, and I said this scorn is due to the identification of intelligence with native endowments of individuals. In contrast to this notion, I spoke of the power of individuals to appropriate and respond to the intelligence, the knowledge, ideas and purposes that have been integrated in the medium in which individuals live.[101]

Dewey suggests that it is absurd to speak of *native* intelligence. This is certainly so when intelligence is understood as habit – as conscious behavior with an environment. Many of the *conditions* of intelligence are, of course, physiological; and some of these make important differences. But intelligence itself is an outcome of certain complex interactions of person and environment; it is a complex mode of behavior; and it is clear that as such it is a social function.

It would be difficult to overemphasize the importance of *habits* of thought. It is altogether possible (we witness it with dismaying frequency) for distinguished intellectuals to display very inexact habits of thought in their argumentation on many subjects. It is equally possible for men of lesser gifts to become much sounder thinkers. Thus someone with a high I.Q. can be

---

[99] *A Common Faith*, pp. 32, 34.

[100] *The Public and Its Problems*, p. 209.

[101] *Liberalism and Social Action*, p. 69.

dismally irrational, while someone of lower I.Q. can be refreshingly rational.

For intelligence to be effective in social affairs, therefore, it is not necessary that each citizen be intellectually brilliant. Dewey, rather, places his faith in the habits just characterized as the scientific mentality (such as the habits of examining hypotheses on their merits and investigating as fully as possible the evidence available); and these are a consequence of social interactions. Dewey is fond of pointing out that most persons are intelligent with respect to limited subject matters; so the problem is not innate, but consists in the enlivening of these habits and their extension to problems of value formation and social action. This is evidently a matter of social practice. Dewey concludes that indictments of human intelligence are really indictments of society. Not only do existing social habits discourage intelligence, but they also prevent the distribution of the knowledge that *is* possessed about human affairs.

> The indictments that are drawn against the intelligence of individuals are in truth indictments of a social order that does not permit the average individual to have access to the rich store of the accumulated wealth of mankind in knowledge, ideas, and purposes. There does not now exist the kind of social organization that even permits the average human being to share the potentially available social intelligence.[102]

A reminder is suitable at this point: In Chapter II there was a discussion of social intelligence; and it must be remembered from that analysis that society admits of great differences in the level of intelligence which can be embodied, and hence utilized as social habit, in its institutions. Dewey said, "The level of action fixed by *embodied* intelligence is always the important thing."[103] It must also be remembered that social intelligence is not the sum of individual intelligences. It is a social process, which matures and enhances individual intelligences; and by uniting them makes their achievement far beyond the capacity of any individual intelligence. Dewey can become rhapsodic about the possibilities of social intelligence:

---

[102] *Ibid.*, pp. 52-3.

[103] *The Public and Its Problems*, p. 210.

> Given a social medium in whose institutions the available knowledge, ideas and art of humanity were incarnate, and the average individual would rise to undreamed of heights of social and political intelligence.[104]

Dewey has many proposals for changing institutions in ways which will foster the growth of intelligence. They are worked out in varying degrees of detail (mostly, of course, in connection with education). However enlightening it might be to summarize them, such would constitute too much of a digression. There are, however, some common themes running through all Dewey's discussions: As indicated previously, men have been encouraged to limit their intelligence by accepting from authorities of various sorts a division of means and ends. Thus the most important features of existence are precisely those which are exempted from criticism. (Needless to say, it is some long-established and privileged authority which declares what these "ends" are and vests them with sanctity.) A further theme is, of course, that persons should be free whenever possible to try out their intelligence. Not only this, but further, in all experiences – in work, in play, in politics, education, arts – in which intelligence is released, experience should be permitted to persist through its consummatory phase: the end should never be severed from the means. Moreover, such uses of intelligence are much invigorated when their context is a face-to-face community. Both their social origin and value are dramatically evident: Direct and vital communication is at the same time constitutive of social intelligence and one of its intrinsic rewards. Thus the use of intelligence can become a valued – a delightful – habit. It is clear that for some persons the functioning of intelligence is at once organic to richly funded consummations, intrinsically valuable in its own exercise, performed with ease and assurance. However rare a condition, it is clear that there is nothing inherently impossible about it. The value of intelligence lies in the value of all that intelligence makes possible. If men were to become aware of this value, and to share in it, devotion to intelligence might become religious: "One of the few experiments in the attachment of emotion to ends that mankind has not tried is that of devotion, so intense as to be

---

[104] *Liberalism and Social Action,* pp. 69-70.

religious, to intelligence as a force in social action."[105]

What has been said about science, intelligence, and society suggests the final subject to be examined in this section; namely, the connection of science and democracy. What I intend here is to exhibit something of the intimate relation between them as Dewey envisioned it. It has been observed in these pages that the best hope for human good seems to lie in each person's being aware of the implications of his own conduct. The inquiry into these implications is a scientific process. Recall as well that one of the most potent meanings of an individual's behavior is the way he expects this behavior to function in the experience of others. The implication of these views is very significant: Each person must be aware of the meaning of his conduct *in the context of social action.* And it is obviously impossible for an individual to reflect with any accuracy on the implications of his conduct when he does not know what aims are contemplated by others. Thus communication – between individuals, between groups – is absolutely vital to the good life for anyone. The conduct of human beings can be adjusted, their good promoted and united, *only* when their real needs and interests are communicated to each other. Except for reliance on authority, this is the only means for determining the true meaning of anticipated actions; and thus it is at the same time the only means for converting blind conflict into reconciliation. In communication, mainly in face-to-face communication, men can learn the meaning of their acts, reconstitute their desires, and adjust and unite their aims.

I am not going to give attention to the way in which a democractic society is conducive to the growth of science. Dewey has much to say on the matter of the way in which scientific methods and habits are essential to democracy; and it is this subject which I will develop. It was pointed out in Chapter II that Dewey's concern with democracy was centered more on the functioning of groups and the communications between them than on formal decision-making processes. (Indeed, as he held, the effectiveness of the latter depends upon the vitality of the former.) Hence, in the following discussion, the reference will be

---

[105] *A Common Faith,* p. 79.

to democracy as habits of social interaction.

Much of Dewey's thinking here is implied in one, seemingly innocuous, remark:

> The keynote of democracy as a way of life may be expressed, it seems to me, as the necessity for the participation of every mature human being in formation of the values that regulate the living of men together: . . .[106]

The implications of this statement can be readily drawn out. Dewey is here explicitly concerned with the *formation* of values. Let it first be noted, therefore, that Dewey does not regard democracy as a means of scrapping over preestablished values. Rather, the democratic process itself is the means for the cooperative *formation* of values. There is a great difference between contesting already fixed ends and the cooperative *creation* of ends. Values formed and pursued in the medium of democratic dialogue will presumably be more inclusive and more readily attainable than those either coveted in private selfishness or dictated by authority, dogma, or any form of absolutism. Addiction to such methods is obviously injurious to democratic value formation. The very practice of group democracy, as Dewey characterizes it, is one of the chief goods of experience. It must be recalled, moreover, that it is just such a process of value formation which constitutes the chief humanizing force in social affairs. The following was originally quoted in another context:

> To learn to be human is to develop through the give-and-take of communication an effective sense of being an individually distinctive member of a community; one who understands and appreciates its beliefs, desires, and methods, and who contributes to a further conversion of organic powers into human resources and values.[107]

The process of democratic formation of values is precisely that which has already been treated at length in these chapters. The qualification "democratic" means that the process is explicitly social and cooperative. It has three notable conditions: 1) the knowledge that is formulated in what Dewey calls propositions of appraisal; that is, in propositions which state the conditions

---

[106] Ratner (ed.), *op. cit.,* p. 400. This same statement was quoted above, Chapter II.

[107] *The Public and Its Problems,* p. 154. These statements were first quoted in Chapter II.

and consequences of acting with given prizings; 2) imaginative ideas which indicate possible reconstructions of the situation; 3) communication among individuals in order to convert blind conflict into the conditions requisite to adjusting, reconstituting, and uniting human aims. It is clear that all three conditions are necessary:

> Two [of the] things essential, then, to thorough-going social liberalism are, first, realistic study of existing conditions in their movement, and, secondly, leading ideas, in the form of policies for dealing with these conditions in the interest of development of increased individuality and liberty.[108]

> The method of democracy – inasfar as it is that of organized intelligence – is to bring . . . conflicts out into the open where their special claims can be seen and appraised, and where they can be discussed and judged in the light of more inclusive interests than are represented by . . . them separately.[109]

It must further be understood that the plans for social action thus formulated have an experimental status. That is, they are not ideologies to be superimposed on society. Rather, they are social experiments to be tried out and subjected to careful observation.

> Experimental method is not just messing around nor doing a little of this and a little of that in the hopes that things will improve. Just as in the physical sciences, it implies a coherent body of ideas, a theory, that gives direction to effort. What is implied, in contrast to every form of absolutism, is that the ideas and theory be taken as methods of action tested and continuously revised by the consequences they produce in actual social conditions. Since they are operational in nature, they modify conditions, while the first requirement, that of basing them upon realistic study of actual conditions, brings about their continuous reconstruction.[110]

In this connection, Dewey is very careful to distinguish a planning society from a planned society:

> What *claims* to be social planning is now found in Communist and Fascist countries. The *social* consequence is complete suppression of freedom of inquiry, communication and voluntary association, by means of a combination of personal violence, culminating in extirpation, and systematic partisan propaganda. The results are such that in the minds of many persons the very idea of social planning and of violation of the integrity of the individual are becoming intimately bound

---

[108] "The Future of Liberalism," *The Journal of Philosophy,* XXXII (April, 1935), p. 228.

[109] *Liberalism and Social Action,* p. 79.

[110] "The Future of Liberalism," p. 228. Dewey's reference to "messing around" is to the New Deal. His notion of plans for social reconstruction were far more radical and extensive than anything undertaken – or even entertained – in the New Deal.

together. But an immense difference divides the *planned* society from a *continuously planning* society. The former requires fixed blueprints imposed from above and therefore involving reliance upon physical and psychological force to secure conformity to them. The latter means the release of intelligence through the widest form of cooperative give-and-take. The attempt to *plan* social organization and association without the freest possible play of intelligence contradicts the very idea in *social* plann*ing*. For the latter is an operative method of activity, not a predetermined set of final "truths."[111]

He insists, moreover, that social plans should not be of a sort to determine the specific consequences of individual behavior, but to institute conditions which will encourage forms of conduct at once free and cooperative. In an experimental social method,

> Every care would be taken to surround the young with the physical and social conditions which best conduce, as far as freed knowledge extends, to release of personal potentialities. The habits thus formed would have entrusted to them the meeting of future social requirements and the development of the future state of society.[112]

> An American democracy can serve the world only as it demonstrates in the conduct of its own life the efficacy of plural, partial, and experimental methods in securing and maintaining an ever-increasing release of the powers of human nature, in service of a freedom which is co-operative and a co-operation which is voluntary.[113]

A democratic community, obviously, must be one where social experiments can be formulated and undertaken without extraordinary difficulty.

We have seen that democratic value formation is dependent upon both scientific knowledge and scientific method and upon the active participation of all those implicated in social action. This participation, to be more explicit, means that plans for social action are formulated and selected by a process of communication involving, at some level, all concerned. Ideally, the consequence would be that such plans be cooperatively formulated on the basis of all the relevant data – not on an arbitrary or limited selection. These data include all the variables known to be implicated in social process, together with whatever knowledge is possessed of their possible functions. Most significantly included are

---

[111] Ratner (ed.) *op. cit.*, pp. 431-2.

[112] *The Public and Its Problems*, pp. 200-1.

[113] *Freedom and Culture*, p. 176.

the values, both actual and potential, of all persons involved, dependent upon the forms which action might take. Finally, the test of social plans is in their consequences for all persons affected by them, not in the consequences for a limited number.

Given the fact that value formation requires knowledge and intelligence, and given also that it is an explicitly social process, it is evident that its success requires that the scientific mentality be widely shared and exercised in the community. The habits of thought so crucial to science are equally crucial for democracy; and when Dewey speaks of democratic habits he means much the same as when he speaks of scientific habits.[114] It is evident, then, that the democratic mentality, as Dewey understands it, is (a) the willing extension of scientific habits to matters of value formation and social action and (b) the conviction that all may share in these matters as equal and cooperative participants.

> Democracy is the belief that even when needs and ends or consequences are different for each individual, the habit of amicable cooperation – which may include, as in sport, rivalry and competition – is itself a priceless addition to life. To take as far as possible every conflict which arises – and they are bound to arise – out of the atmosphere and medium of force, of violence as a means of settlement, into that of discussion and of intelligence, is to treat those who disagree – even profoundly – with us as those from whom we may learn, and in so far, as friends. . . . To cooperate by giving differences a chance to show themselves because of the belief that the expression of difference is not only a right of the other persons but is a means of enriching one's own life-experience, is inherent in the democratic personal way of life.[115]

To Dewey, it was clear that thorough analysis of problems of value must lead one to a commitment to democratic social intelligence as the best medium for the formation and achievement of value. Indeed, with proper respect for the social nature of both intelligence and value and with some appreciation of the conditions of the good life, one can come to embrace social intelligence – not grudgingly, but gratefully and piously – as the principal arbiter of human disputes. It can be one of those ideals which bring "inexhaustible meaning" to human relations. In light of such an ideal, the deliberately irrational, acrimonious, and

---

[114] See especially "Science and Free Culture," in *Freedom and Culture,* which is highly pertinent to most of the issues raised in this chapter.

[115] "Creative Democracy – The Task Before Us," in *The Philosopher of the Common Man,* p. 227.

deceitful discussion that pervades so much in human relations becomes especially repugnant.

Taking a somewhat broader look at Dewey's views on intelligence and democracy, it becomes possible to understand why Dewey regarded democracy as peculiarly linked with the modern experimental temper. The reason is not only that such temper is requisite to democracy. There is also a sense in which it *implies* democracy. Some background is necessary to explicate this position: The rise of the experimental temper coincides with the demise of rationalism; and the cause for each is the same. The advances in knowledge of nature and knowledge of knowing itself bring about at once these coincident conditions. Rationalistic moral philosophy had presupposed that moral laws, obligations, rights were absolute and eternal and were independent of experience. These immutable, perfect, and systematic principles of morality were known by the unaided Reason. It was further supposed, of necessity, that there could be no conflict of laws, rights, and obligations.

The explicit implication of these rationalistic assumptions is that if men were only to use their reason and conform their will to its dictates, the earthly polity will readily assume its changeless perfection. In such circumstances, there is no problem of value *formation* or the adjustment of aims. There is no problem of facing each situation as a unique problem with a plurality of possible outcomes. Rather, Reason will disclose the natural order in which all men find a common good, in which there is a natural harmony of ends.

As the rationalistic interpretation of nature and knowing are discredited, so also are the corresponding moral and political philosophies. By contrast with such unrealities, the experimental temper must acknowledge value formation and social interaction as *problems* – and problems which admit of no permanent solution. It further acknowledges that the instrumentalities for dealing with these problems are those of experience: preeminently those of social intelligence. Finally, inasmuch as it finds the problems of value formation, social interaction and communication inseparable, it acknowledges democracy as the means by which these processes are rightly carried on and regulated. Such, at least, seems to be Dewey's line of thought. It seems difficult to resist his conclusion except on some (obscure) ground of regarding some persons inherently unfit or undeserving of participation in this process. In reference to any absolutistic moral system, Dewey says,

> It would assume the existence of final and unquestionable knowledge upon which we can fall back in order to settle automatically every moral problem. It would involve the commitment to a dogmatic theory of morals. The alternative method may be called experimental. It implies that reflective morality demands observation of particular situations, rather than fixed adherence to *a priori* principles; that free inquiry and freedom of publication and discussion must be encouraged and not merely grudgingly tolerated; that opportunity at different times and places must be given for trying different measures so that their effects may be capable of observation and of comparison with one another. It is, in short, the method of democracy, of a positive toleration which amounts to sympathetic regard for the intelligence and personality of others, even if they hold views opposed to ours, and of scientific inquiry into facts and testing of ideas.[116]

Again, social and experimental value *formation* must be the fundamental focus of concern when the notions of antecedent and independent principles and ends have been discarded, and when precariousness, conflict, tragedy, pluralism are regarded as real traits of nature.

It must be observed that this procedure of value formation constitutes anything but a complete relativism of ideas. The kind of inquiry and communication Dewey envisions constitutes the ideal limit of how a community can function to criticize ideas.[117] It is the only way to investigate the full meaning of hypotheses for social action and to determine their fitness for solving social problems.[118] The effective criticism and test of ideas must be a

---

[116] *Ethics,* pp. 364-5. See also "Philosophy and Democracy" *(op. cit.)* and "Intelligence and Morals" in *The Influence of Darwin on Philosophy.*

[117] Dewey's views are clearly like those of Mill in *Liberty.* Dewey, however, emphasized that there were two serious deficiencies in Mill's position: Mill tended to think of intelligence as an individual possession rather than as a social process, and he was insufficiently aware of the vital importance in social criticism of developing creative hypotheses to guide action. These are deficiencies which Mill shares with all the older liberals.

[118] Dewey recognizes that this process is most effective in face-to-face communites, of all sorts. He also regards such groups as the vital medium in which their members can grasp the significance of wider social issues. It is essential for national democracy that groups be represented at all levels of decision-making. "We lie, as Emerson said, in the lap of an immense intelligence. But that intelligence is dormant and its communications are broken, inarticulate and faint until it possesses the local community as its medium" *(The Public and Its Problems,* p. 219.)

social process. Social plans, in a genuine democracy, cannot be formulated apart from the participation of all concerned. For "experts" to perform the work of democracy would be a contradiction in terms. For the formation of values in a democracy, the "scientific" community and the democratic community are identical.[119]

Thus there is an important sense in which a genuinely democratic community would function as a scientific community: Scientific method constitutes the highest realization of social intelligence yet achieved. Science is the organized functioning of social intelligence; and democracy is the organized functioning of social intelligence in respect to value formation. For social intelligence to function throughout an entire community, in respect to value formation, means that that community is democratic. Dewey's idea of democracy represents the ideal functioning of social intelligence in the affairs of men; and his philosophy of democracy is, indeed, an extensively elaborated theory about the nature, formation, and realization of value.

In all likelihood, it is objected that there inevitably will be differences in what people want, regardless of the thoroughness of deliberation and communication. Of course there will be; but the issue here is not whether there will or will not be conflicts, but how they are to be treated. The point of emphasis for Dewey is precisely in the *methods* of deliberation and value formation; and when these are both social and experimental, the optimum conditions for uniting human aims are realized.

Thus it is, in Dewey's view, that the fate of democracy is one with that of the scientific attitude. It follows that the inquiry into the cultural roots of uncritical habits of thought is also the inquiry into the sources of undemocratic habits of thought: The same social habits that limit the release of intelligence also limit the growth of democracy. Prescientific habits of thought about morals are inseparable from predemocratic habits of social decision and action.

> The real trouble is that there is an intrinsic split in our habitual attitudes when we profess to depend upon discussion and persuasion in politics and then system-

---

[119] As indicated earlier, however, much of the information which serves as the *basis* to value formation can only be acquired by professional inquirers.

> atically depend upon other methods in reaching conclusions in matters of morals and religion, or in anything where we depend upon a person or group possessed of "authority." We do not have to go to theological matters to find examples. In homes and schools, the places where the essentials of character are supposed to be formed, the usual procedure is settlement of issues, intellectual and moral, by appeal to the "authority" of parent, teacher, or textbook. Dispositions formed under such conditions are so inconsistent with the democratic method that in a crisis they may be aroused to act in positively anti-democratic ways for anti-democratic ends; just as resort to coercive force and suppression of civil liberties are readily palliated in nominally democratic communities when the cry is raised that "law and order" are threatened.[120]

From this it is also clear that education for democracy is in large measure training in the arts of cooperative social intelligence. This means participation in the process of inquiry *as* social, not simply learning what such inquiry is.

However unlikely may be the prospects for genuine liberal democracy, it is an ideal to guide and unite human endeavor; and its importance can be estimated not only by considering its positive values, but by considering its alternatives as well:

> Objections that are brought against liberalism ignore the fact that the only alternatives to dependence upon intelligence are either drift and casual improvisation, or the use of coercive force stimulated by unintelligent emotion and fanatical dogmatism –. . . .[121]

> One alternative to the power of ideas is habit or custom, and when the rule of sheer habit breaks down – as it has done at the present time [1939] – all that is left is competition on the part of various bodies and interests to decide which shall come out ahead in a struggle, carried on by intimidation, coercion, bribery, and all sorts of propaganda, to shape the desires which shall predominantly control the ends of human action.[122]

Predictably, Dewey concludes:

> Social control effected through organized application of social intelligence is the sole form of social control that can and will get rid of existing evils without landing us finally in some form of coercive control from above and outside.[123]

This chapter can appropriately be concluded with some further general remarks concerning the distinctive value of intelligence. In light of a full exposition of his views, Dewey's legend-

---

[120] *Freedom and Culture,* p. 129.

[121] *Liberalism and Social Action,* p. 51.

[122] *Freedom and Culture,* p. 140.

[123] Ratner (ed.), *op. cit.,* p. 431.

ary preoccupation with method seems justified. Because values do not exist antecedently or independently in nature, but are eventual functions of unique situations; because there is not a natural harmony of such ends; and because voluntary conduct is a response to the meanings of objects of experience (which admit of indefinite variation and novelty), the perfecting of method – a social method – must take precedence over all other possible reflections about evaluation. Perfecting method is not an end in itself, of course; it has to be put to use to gain knowledge of the possibilities and implications of problematic situations, and hence for the formation and realization of value.

Traditional empiricism can provide neither an adequate theory of value nor procedure for the criticism of value. According to that philosophy of experience, goods are isolated, atomic sensations of pleasure and pain. Such a philosophy can provide no procedure for giving meaning to events or for reconstituting desires. Its authority must be "good taste" or "feeling."

On the other hand, rationalistic and transcendental theories are obviously based on a philosophy of nature that dogmatically defies any test of experience. And worse, such theories would sacrifice human good to philosophical conceits. Thus philosophers have been unable to make values intelligible:

> Any doctrine that identifies the mere fact of being liked with the value of the object liked so fails to give direction to conduct when direction is needed that it automatically calls forth the assertion that there are values eternally in Being that are the standards of all judgments and the obligatory ends of all action. Without the introduction of operational thinking, we oscillate between a theory that, in order to save the objectivity of judgments of values, isolates them from experience and nature, and a theory that, in order to save their concrete and human significance, reduces them to mere statements about our own feelings.[124]

It is pertinent to include here some brief reference to ethical relativism. I pointed out in the preceding chapter that if Dewey can be called an ethical relativist, this is simply to say that he eschews the use of both a priori assumptions and unrelated sensations, which obscure the endeavor to develop as much intrinsically valuable activity as possible in every situation.[125] One might

---

[124] *The Quest for Certainty*, p. 263.

[125] For a relatively detached treatment of the practical difficulties and evils in legalistic ethics, see *Ethics*, pp. 305-9. For one of Dewey's more impassioned attacks on absolutistic ethics, see "William James' Morals and Julien Benda's" (*Commentary*, V, [January, 1948], pp. 46-50.) This article also defends pragmatism against charges of expediency and opportunism.

object to such relativism, of course, by claiming the inherent sinfulness and stupidity of mankind and the consequent necessity of transhuman authority. Apart from the dubious validity of such premises, however, it is worthwhile to point out that the "transhuman" authority is obviously *human.* Thus the problems of discriminating the good, criticizing and forming values are removed from social intelligence and simply placed in the hands of one who might or might not be wise and benevolent, and in all likelihood little appreciative of the values inhering in the life of free self-development in society.

When science was transformed from the rationalistic to the experimental model, its conclusions lost their presumed certainty. Yet at the same time, the possibilities for growth in both knowledge and control were very greatly enhanced, and science became genuinely progressive. By the adoption of social and experimental method in moral affairs, we have nothing to lose but a specious and pernicious certainty on the one hand, or an extreme relativism and subjectivism on the other. We may gain a progressively enlightened, liberated, and richer experience. Of course, nothing of the future can be guaranteed; and much inquiry, reflection, and experiment in the philosophy of cooperative social intelligence needs to be done. In this connection, it is fitting to conclude with the final paragraph from *Experience and Nature:*

> Because intelligence is critical method applied to goods of belief, appreciation and conduct, so as to construct freer and more secure goods, turning assent and assertion into free communication of shareable meanings, turning feeling into ordered and liberal sense, turning reaction into response, it is the reasonable object of our deepest faith and loyalty, the stay and support of all reasonable hopes. To utter such a statement is not to indulge in romantic idealization. It is not to assert that intelligence will ever dominate the course of events; it is not even to imply that it will save from ruin and destruction. The issue is one of choice, and choice is always a question of alternatives. What the method of intelligence, thoughtful valuation, will accomplish, if once it be tried, is for the result of trial to determine. Since it is relative to the intersection in existence of hazard and rule, of contingency and order, faith in a wholesale and final triumph is fantastic. But some procedure has to be tried; for life itself is a sequence of trials. Carelessness and routine, Olympian aloofness, secluded contemplation are themselves choices. To claim that intelligence is a better method than its alternatives, authority, imitation, caprice and ignorance, prejudice and passion, is hardly an excessive claim. These procedures have been tried and have worked their will. The result is not such as to make it clear that the method of intelligence, the use

of science in criticizing and recreating the casual goods of nature into intentional and conclusive goods of art, the union of knowledge and values in production, is not worth trying. There may be those to whom it is treason to think of philosophy as the critical method of developing methods of criticism. But this conception of philosophy also waits to be tried, and the trial which shall approve or condemn lies in the eventual issue. The import of such knowledge as we have acquired and such experience as has been quickened by thought is to evoke and justify the trial.

Postscript

Having concluded my study, it would perhaps not be out of place to provide some brief observations about Dewey's relation to the contemporary situation in philosophy.

In these chapters I have tried to present those assumptions which are foundational to Dewey's philosophy of value. Dewey's moral philosophy is predicated upon an inclusive theory of nature, the aims of which are to render intelligible and coherent all our variegated forms of experience and to point the direction in which philosophic inquiries might fruitfully proceed. He developed his assumptions in such a way to produce the most innovative and elaborately developed philosophy of value to appear in modern history.

In the present day, however, the understanding of Dewey is remarkably superficial. Some of the members of what appear to be the most influential circles in philosophy make an occasional reference to him; but it is evident that, with very few exceptions, they write in complete ignorance of the content of his work, if not, indeed, of its very existence.[1] One such exception is C.L. Stevenson, who has urged that a concern with Dewey's ideas might well be the needed antidote to the current trivialities and irrelevance of ethical theory. Stevenson says,

---

[1] A recent book by G.J. Warnock purports to survey the substance of moral philosophy from G.E. Moore to R.M. Hare. There is not even an allusion to Dewey in this volume. This is like surveying the history of classical ethics without reference to Aristotle. (G.J. Warnock, *Contemporary Moral Philosophy* [New York: St. Martin's Press, 1967].)

> Since the second World War we have had much work on meta-ethics; but we have had, quite regrettably in my opinion, very little work by philosophers that resembles Dewey's work within ethics proper. . . . Most philosophers still like to feel that they have a special subject matter, well insulated from anything that the social scientists, and scientists in general, have to tell them. That is not healthy for philosophy; and it is all too likely to lead to an ethics that continues, as of old, to plead for its ultimates – the fact that one is totally ineffectual being decently concealed by an impressive terminology. Let us hope that Dewey's influence will help to counteract this.[2]

I agree with Stevenson's assessment of the matter; and I contend that if moral philosophy is to be consequential, and if it is to be organic to fundamental considerations about man, nature, and society, then it is to be hoped that the naturalistic tradition will regain the recognition and vigor which it earlier possessed in this country.

I don't mean to imply that naturalism of this sort has been altogether dormant. For many philosophers there has been a continuing interest in Dewey; and there is a persistent influence stemming from Ralph Barton Perry as well. Perry's influence is found in such important works as C.I. Lewis's *An Analysis of Knowledge and Valuation*[3] and Stephen C. Pepper's *The Sources of Value.*[4] These works, like those of Perry, are centrally concerned with the continuities of moral philosophy and science. Dewey's influence is quickly recognized in the ethical writings of such philosophers as Sidney Hook, Abraham Edel, Paul Kurtz and Rollo Handy.[5] Many other names could be added to this list. Indeed, the list could be extended still more if it were to include philosophers owing much to Dewey yet not primarily involved in moral philosophy. Distinguished examples are J.H. Randall, Jr. and Ernest Nagel.

I am not suggesting that the philosophers I have mentioned are slavish apostles or that they have not made their own important innovations in philosophic inquiry. Each has criticized

---

[2] *Facts and Values,* pp. 114-5. Stevenson's own understanding of Dewey's position is incomplete and hence, also, seriously flawed. I take this to be a consequence of the failure to perceive how much and in what ways so many of Dewey's writings bear directly on his moral philosophy.

[3] Chicago: The Open Court, 1946.

[4] Berkeley: The University of California Press, 1958.

[5] See the Bibliography for a selected listing of pertinent works by these writers.

Dewey in various ways and has made contributions on his own account, often notably so. It is fair to say, however, that the mode of philosophizing exhibited by all these men stands fully within that modern naturalisitc tradition so profoundly shaped by Dewey's presence. My own convictions are undisguised: Substantial progress in moral philosophy – as well as in other fields – will find its greatest stimulus and direction by studying the nature and content of this tradition and by drawing upon its abundant resources.

Bibliography

An exhaustive bibliography of Dewey's writings has been compiled by Milton Halsey Thomas: *John Dewey, A Centennial Bibliography* (Chicago: The University of Chicago Press, 1962). This volume also contains a comprehensive listing of works about Dewey, reviews of his books, and pertinent unpublished theses and dissertations.

With the exception of the authors cited in the Postscript, the following bibliography includes only those works to which explicit reference is made in the study. In each entry the publication data refer to the edition cited in the text. In the case of Dewey's works, I have added – without reference to any publisher – the year in which each book originally appeared. Where the additional data are not provided, the given publication date is for the first edition.

BOOKS

Adams, George P., and Montague, William Pepperell (eds.). *Contemporary American Philosophy,* Vol. II. New York: The Macmillan Co., 1930.

Ayer, Alfred Jules. *Language, Truth and Logic.* New York: Dover Publications, n.d.

Bernstein, Richard J. (ed.). *John Dewey on Experience, Nature and Freedom.* New York: Liberal Arts Press, 1960.

Blanshard, Brand. *Reason and Goodness.* London: George Allen and Unwin Ltd., 1961.

Conference on Methods in Philosophy. *The Philosopher of the Common Man.* New York: G.P. Putnam's Sons, 1940.

Dewey, John. *A Common Faith.* New Haven: Yale University Press, 1960. (First published in 1934.)

———. *Art as Experience.* New York: G.P. Putnam's Sons, 1958. (First published in 1934.)

———. et al. *Creative Intelligence: Essays in the Pragmatic Spirit.* New York: Henry Holt and Co., 1917.

———. *Democracy and Education.* New York: The Macmillan Co., 1916.

———. *Essays in Experimental Logic.* New York: Dover Publications, n.d. (First published in 1916.)

———, and Tufts, James H. *Ethics.* Revised Edition. New York: Henry Holt and Co., 1932. (The First Edition of this book was published in 1908.)

———. *Experience and Nature.* Chicago: The Open Court, 1925.

———. *Experience and Nature.* Second Edition, Revised. New York: Dover Publications, 1958. (First published in 1929.)

———. *Freedom and Culture.* New York: G. P. Putnam's Sons, 1963. (First Published in 1939.)

———. *Human Nature and Conduct.* New York: The Modern Library, 1930. (First published in 1922.)

———. *Individualism Old and New.* New York: G. P. Putnam's Sons, 1962. (First published in 1930.)

———, and Bentley, Arthur F. *Knowing and the Known.* Boston: Beacon Press, 1949.

———. *Liberalism and Social Action.* New York: G. P. Putnam's Sons, 1963. (First published in 1935.)

———. *Logic: The Theory of Inquiry.* New York: Holt, Rinehart and Winston, 1938.

———. *Philosophy and Civilization.* New York: G. P. Putnam's Sons, 1963. (First published in 1931.)

———. *Problems of Men.* New York: Philosophical Library, 1946.

———. *Reconstruction in Philosophy.* Enlarged Edition. Boston: Beacon Press, 1959. (Enlarged Edition first published in 1948. First Edition published in 1920.)

———. *The Influence of Darwin on Philosophy.* Bloomington: Indiana University Press, 1965. (First published in 1910.)

———. *The Public and Its Problems.* Denver: Alan Swallow, 1927.

———. *The Quest for Certainty.* New York: G.P. Putnam's Sons, 1960. (First published in 1929.)

———. *Theory of Valuation.* Chicago: University of Chicago Press, 1939.

Edel, Abraham. *Ethical Judgment.* Glencoe: The Free Press, 1955.

———. *Method in Ethical Theory.* Indianapolis and New York: The Bobbs-Merrill Company, 1963.

———. *Science and the Structure of Ethics.* Chicago: The University of Chicago Press, 1961.

Forrester, Jay W. *Urban Dynamics.* Cambridge, Massachusetts: M.I.T. Press, 1969.

Frankena, William K. *Ethics.* Englewood Cliffs, N.J.: Prentice-Hall, 1963.

Handy, Rollo. *Value Theory and the Behavioural Sciences.* Springfield, Illinois: Charles C. Thomas, 1969.

Hare, R.M. *Freedom and Reason.* New York: Oxford University Press, 1965.

Hook, Sidney. *John Dewey: His Philosophy of Education and Its Critics.* New York: Tamiment Institute, 1959.

——— (ed.). *John Dewey: Philosopher of Science and Freedom.* New York: The Dial Press, 1950.

———. *Paradoxes of Freedom.* Berkeley: The University of California Press, 1962.

———. *The Quest for Being.* New York: St. Martin's Press, 1961.

———. *Reason, Social Myths and Democracy.* New York: Harper and Row, 1965.

Kallen, Horace M. (ed.). *Freedom in the Modern World.* New York: Coward-McCann, 1928.

Kennedy, Gail (ed.). *Pragmatism and American Culture.* Boston: D.C. Heath and Co., 1950.

Kurtz, Paul. *Decision and the Condition of Man.* New York: Dell Publishing Co., 1968.

——— (ed.). *Sidney Hook and the Contemporary World.* New York: The John Day Co., 1968.

Lepley, Ray (ed.). *Value: A Cooperative Inquiry.* New York: Columbia University Press, 1949.

Lewis, C.I. *An Analysis of Knowledge and Valuation.* Chicago: The Open Court, 1946.

Mack, Robert D. *The Appeal to Immediate Experience: Philosophic Method in Bradley, Whitehead and Dewey.* New York: King's Crown Press, 1945.

Pepper, Stephen C. *The Sources of Value.* Berkeley: The University of California Press, 1958.

Perry, Ralph Barton. *General Theory of Value.* Cambridge, Massachusetts: Harvard University Press, 1954.

———. *The Thought and Character of William James,* Vol. II. Boston: Little, Brown and Company, 1935.

Randall, John Herman, Jr. *The Making of the Modern Mind,* Revised Edition. Cambridge: Houghton Mifflin, 1954.

Ratner, Joseph (ed.). *Characters and Events,* Vol. II. New York: Henry Holt and Co., 1929.

——— (ed.). *Intelligence in the Modern World.* New York: The Modern Library, 1939.

Roth, Robert J., S.J. *John Dewey and Self-Realization.* Englewood Cliffs, N.J.: Prentice-Hall, Inc., 1962.

Santayana, George. *The Life of Reason,* Vol. III: *Reason in Religion.* New York: Collier Books, 1962.

Schneider, Herbert W. *Ways of Being.* New York: Columbia University Press, 1962.

Stevenson, Charles L. *Ethics and Language.* New Haven: Yale University Press, 1962.

———. *Facts and Values.* New Haven and London: Yale University Press, 1963.

Thayer, H.S. *Meaning and Action: A Critical History of Pragmatism.* Indianapolis and New York: The Bobbs-Merrill Company, 1968.

Tillich, Paul. *Dynamics of Faith.* New York and Evanston: Harper and Row, n.d.

———. *The Courage to Be.* New Haven: Yale University Press, 1952.

———. *The Protestant Era.* Abridged Edition. Transl. by James Luther Adams. Chicago: University of Chicago Press, 1957.

Warnock, G.J. *Contemporary Moral Philosophy.* New York: St. Martin's Press, 1967.

White, Morton G. *Social Thought in America.* New York: The Viking Press, 1949.

ARTICLES

Cohen, Morris Raphael. "Some Difficulties in Dewey's Anthropocentric Naturalism," *The Philosophical Review,* XLIX, No. 2 (March 1940), pp. 196-228.

Dewey, John. "Common Sense and Science," *The Journal of Philosophy,* XLV, No. 8 (April 1948), pp. 197-208.

———. "Ethical Subject-Matter and Language," *The Journal of Philosophy,* XLII, No. 26 (December 1945), pp. 701-12.

———. "Experience and Existence: A Comment," *Philosophy and Phenomenological Research,* IX, No. 4 (June 1949), pp. 709-13.

———. "Half-Hearted Naturalism," *The Journal of Philosophy,* XXIV, No. 3 (February 1927), pp. 57-64.

———. "Liberating the Social Scientist," *Commentary,* IV (October 1947), pp. 378-85.

———. "Means and Ends: Their Interdependence, and Leon Trotsky's Essay on 'Their Morals and Ours,' " *The New International,* IV (August 1938), pp. 232-33.

———. "Nature in Experience," *The Philosophical Review,* XLIX, No. 2 (March 1940), pp. 244-58.

———. "The Ego as Cause," *The Philosophical Review,* I, No. 3 (May 1894), pp. 337-41.

———. "The Future of Liberalism," *The Journal of Philosophy,* XXXII, No. 9 (April 1935), pp. 225-30.

———. "The Reflex Arc Concept in Psychology," *The Psychological Review,* III, No. 4 (July 1896), pp. 357-70.

———. "The Subject Matter of Metaphysical Inquiry," *The Journal of Philosophy,* XII, No. 13 (June 1915), pp. 337-45.

———. "Valuation Judgments and Immediate Quality," *The Journal of Philosophy,* XL, No. 12 (June 1943), pp. 309-17.

———. "William James' Morals and Julien Benda's," *Commentary,* V (January 1948), pp. 46-50.

Foot, Philippa. "Goodness and Choice," *Proceedings of the Aristotelian Society,* Suppl. Vol. XXXV (1961).

———. "Moral Arguments," *Mind,* LXVII (1958).

———. "Moral Beliefs," *Proceedings of the Aristotelian Society,* LIX (1958).

Holmes, Robert L. "John Dewey's Moral Philosophy in Contemporary Perspective," *The Review of Metaphysics,* XX, No. 1 (September 1966), pp. 42-70.

Nagel, Ernest. "Dewey's Reconstruction of Logical Theory," in *The Philosopher of the Common Man.*

Randall, John Herman Jr. "The Religion of Shared Experience," in *The Philosopher of the Common Man.*

Rice, Philip Blair. "Types of Value Judgments," *The Journal of Philosophy,* XL, No. 20 (September 1943), pp. 533-43.

Santayana, George. "Dewey's Naturalistic Metaphysics," *The Journal of Philosophy,* XXII, No. 25 (December 1925), pp. 673-88.

Sidorsky, David. "Universalizability, Rationality, and Moral Disagreement," in *Sidney Hook and the Contemporary World.*

Sleeper, R.W. "Dewey's Metaphysical Perspective: A Note on White, Geiger, and the Problem of Obligation," *The Journal of Philosophy,* LVII (February 1960), pp. 100-15.

Trotsky, Leon. "Their Morals and Ours," *The New International,* IV (June 1938), pp. 163-73.

White, Morton. "Value and Obligation in Dewey and Lewis," *The Philosophical Review,* LVIII, No. 4 (July 1949), pp. 321-30.

Index